The Year That Changed The World
1945

By Brian Gardner

THE BIG PUSH

A Portrait of the Battle of the Somme

GERMAN EAST

The Story of the First World War in East Africa

BRIAN GARDNER

The
Year That Changed
The World
1945

COWARD-McCANN, Inc.
New York

Copyright © 1963 by Brian Gardner

FIRST AMERICAN EDITION 1964

*Library of Congress Catalog
Card Number: 64-13055*

Manufactured in the United States of America

Our pilgrimage has brought us to a sublime moment in the history of the world. From the least to the greatest, all must strive to be worthy of these supreme opportunities. There is not an hour to be wasted; there is not a day to be lost.

WINSTON S. CHURCHILL, August 16, 1945

Twice in this century the Western Powers have won a world war and lost the peace. Why? Mainly, I think, because of their continuous refusal to acknowledge political realities, without attempting to alter them; and because of their failure to comprehend the nature of the twentieth-century revolution. Despite the terrible warning of the inter-war years, the Western democracies clung, at San Francisco in 1945, to the out-dated Wilsonian principle of 'self-determination', which in practice meant secession and isolation; and covered it up with the smoke-screen of a high-sounding but impotent international superstructure. . . . There was not really much excuse for our failure in 1945. This was the moment when Britain could, and should, have taken the undisputed leadership of a united Western Europe. We were the only country which had not been defeated and occupied, our prestige was as high as it has ever been, and we could have had it on our own terms. We did nothing. The death of Roosevelt and the subsequent defeat of Churchill at the General Election left the West bereft of leadership for a critical year, and Stalin took full advantage of it. The Potsdam agreement set the seal on the Russian *fait accompli*.

Lord Boothby, in *My Yesterday, Your Tomorrow*

Since America fights for no political objective, except peace, no political directives should be given to American commanders in the field. They should be completely free to determine their strategy on military grounds alone. To pursue a political aim is to practise Imperialism. This was the doctrine applied by Marshall and his colleagues in the conduct of the war against Germany, although with an ambivalence not uncharacteristic of the American people, it was not always applied in relation to the war against Japan.

Chester Wilmot, in *The Struggle for Europe*

The Russians trust the United States more than they trust any power in the world. I believe they not only have no wish to fight with us, but are determined to take their place in world affairs in an international organization, and above all, they want to maintain friendly relations with us.

Harry Hopkins, 1945, from *The White House Papers*

Stalin's actions [in 1945] show many strange and striking contradictions which do not indicate that he had any revolutionary master-plan. They suggest, on the contrary, that he had none . . . the control of events over him was much stronger than his control over events.

Isaac Deutscher, in *Stalin: A Political Biography*

All of us want to secure peace for at least fifty years. The greatest danger is conflict among ourselves, because if we remain united the German menace is not very important.

J. V. Stalin to Winston Churchill, Yalta, 1945

The question for the future is whether the new enterprises on which such high hopes have been founded can be made, by the common effort of humanity, so to grow and prosper in the time to come that in the ultimate record of history the date 1945 shall be remembered even more vividly as the birth-time of a better world than for the vast and dramatic events on the battlefield and the crowning victory to which they led.

The Times, January 1st, 1946

CONTENTS

MAPS

1 Grand Disalliance

1 GRAND DISALLIANCE

The world was at war; once more great American and British armies rolled eastwards across the hills and plains of France towards the Rhine. For the fourth time in living memory French and Belgian farmers and townsfolk were scuttling down to cellars and shelters as the thunder and terror of war bore down on them. The clanking of tanks, the metallic whirr of armoured-cars, and the crash and fumes of explosives overwhelmed their daily lives. There was, it seemed, nothing that ordinary men could do to dissuade the politicians, the generals, the statesmen and the great leaders of the world from uprooting their existences twice in every generation. But on January 1st, 1945, after more than five years of bitter and wretched war that had seen Germany rise to a position of power that had not been equalled in Europe since the days of the Romans, it seemed that at long last peace was within reach. Just one long, desperate grasp, and those beatific days of peace, dimly remembered from the late 1930s, would return—only less anxious, more prosperous and better in every way. Even the cynical believed that this time peace would last, if not for ever, at least into the distant future. No one born before 1930, surely, it was said, would allow the same mistakes to happen again.

So strong were thoughts of the end of the war and after, which millions now permitted themselves to think of after years of denial, that Winston Churchill, Prime Minister, in a New Year message to the Primrose League, said: 'Before many months have passed the evil gang that has too long dominated this unhappy continent will be wiped out. Until that end has been achieved there can be no return to our normal habits. It would be tragic folly to prolong, by any slackening in the last phase, the agony that a megalomaniac ambition loosed upon the world.' Churchill considered that the war in Europe would be over by October 1st, 1945 (the last date officially fixed by the Cabinet Office for the likely end of the war had been December 31st, 1944). In a memorandum for the New Year, Churchill said: 'The expectation is very hard fighting all through the summer on land, a recrudescence of U-boat activity on a serious scale from February or March, and the revived challenge of the German Air Force implied in their leadership in jet-propelled aircraft.'

The year was five minutes old when Adolf Hitler, whose outrageous, half-mad ambitions had plunged the world into the state existing that day, also spoke on the situation of the war. Broadcasting to the Third Reich, but especially to his tired and anxious troops, he said that Germany was winning the war. The fact that every evidence was to the contrary did not leave him abashed. He asked the German people, dazed with saturation bombing, to trust him and his lieutenants. As he spoke, Berlin was undergoing one of the heaviest air-raids it had known, with the strongest force yet sent to the German capital dropping 4,000 lb bombs like giant eggs falling through the winter night. He concluded a rousing speech with the words: 'My belief in the future of our people is unshakeable.'

On New Year's Day the American President, Franklin D. Roosevelt, began his thirteenth year of office; the only President to have been elected for a fourth term, he had come to that office first in March 1933 in what seemed, and was, another age. It had been the same year that Hitler had first come to power in Germany. His Vice-President was a little known Senator, Harry S. Truman; but, as everyone knew, his was a comparatively unimportant post, and most people outside his own country, and even some of those in it, had never heard of him. The Deputy Prime Minister in Britain, Mr C. R. Attlee, Leader of the Labour Party, was also considered a comparatively insignificant figure in the inner Allied councils of the war. The other great leader of the world, Josif V. Stalin, did not notice the passing of the old year, apart from a curt acknowledgement of the good wishes conveyed to him on the occasion by the other two of the 'Big Three'. Like them, a man completely occupied by a mass of affairs and decisions, he preferred to conserve his time for more important matters. That other men, potentates like himself, thought such courtesies a necessary adjunct to diplomacy both bewildered and slightly amused him. Meanwhile, silent, lonely and enigmatic, he worked with his small staff in his rooms in the Kremlin. As Sir Robert Bruce Lockhart has said: 'Millions of words have been written about [Stalin], yet little is generally known of the true character of this man who launched Soviet Russia into the twentieth century and put his indelible mark on history . . . gangster, genius, bank robber, theological student, brothel-keeper, poisoner, mass-murderer and master of political strategy—the man who for thirty years ruled Russia by terror yet became a hero saint.' The world at large preferred not to think of this tough old revolutionary as in any way sinister. For some years he had been thought of by the Western World, and still was, as a gruff old ally whose forbidding exterior might even conceal a kindly heart. He was known to all, President and Prime Minister, soldier and sailor, factory worker and newspaper reporter, as 'Uncle Joe'.

The start of the year saw the Allies closing their grip around the German core in Central Europe. In Italy the advance of the army of Field-Marshal Sir Harold Alexander had come to a standstill only through a lack of supplies and men that had been diverted to the more important sector of the Western Front, but already there were signs of an impending German collapse in the area, with Italian partisans desperately and heroically attempting to salvage some honour from the débâcle of that country's recent history. In Greece, where civil war had followed the German evacuation the previous year, prompt action by British troops was restoring some stability. A Communist attempt to seize power had been met with force, and what had looked only a few weeks before a certain prize for ruthless Communist partisans was now a democratic state, as befitted the home of democracy, looking somewhat shakily to the future. Archbishop Damaskinos, Metropolitan of Athens, had been appointed Regent on December 30th, but there was still some street fighting in the capital. The British intervention in Greece had met with considerable criticism from America, but few people attached much weight to what seemed a purely isolated example of misunderstanding and suspicion of motives among friends. The Germans had retreated helter-skelter in front of irate and determined partisans in Yugoslavia, under an enterprising leader called Tito, and of a seemingly irresistible Russian advance from the East.

3

Both Rumania and Bulgaria had realized that they were on the wrong side and, having made approaches to the Allies, watched with alarm as the Red Army overran their territories. In Hungary a long and bitter battle was being waged for the city of Budapest, with the Russians encircling a German force there. In Poland the advance was temporarily halted.

In the war in the East the Axis powers, namely Japan, were also on the defensive; General Douglas MacArthur, Commander-in-Chief, South-West Pacific, had returned, in something like state, to the Philippines. In Burma, the 'forgotten' Fourteenth Army of Lieutenant-General Sir William Slim had suddenly become news. Having built up an impressive fighting force, with a tremendous *esprit de corps*, from a defeated and tired army, Slim was pushing the Japanese back through the jungle. On New Year's Day the Fourteenth Army had advanced 300 miles from the Chindwin River, which had been crossed only six weeks before, and was now eighty-five miles from Mandalay.

Across the world, in London, another well-worn battlefield was in the front line once more. To the great alarm of every expert on defence, to say nothing of countless ordinary citizens, rocket bombs were raining on the city and suburbs daily, and there was nothing much anyone could think of to stop them. The publication of the New Year's Honours List provided no comfort. The news that the Right Hon. David Lloyd George had become Earl Lloyd George came like a distant sigh from a forgotten age.

The most dramatic activity at the beginning of January 1945 was taking place at the old cockpit of Europe where Belgium, France, Luxemburg and Germany congregate.

(ii)

It was bitterly, cruelly cold in the Ardennes; colder than local inhabitants could ever remember it having been. In snow and icy wind, with temperatures below zero all day, Hitler had made the last throw of a desperate gambler. Already, during autumn and winter of 1944, the Allied advance in Europe had been slowed and halted by a brilliant, if improvised, defence; a defence that had benefited from the lack of a singleminded, concerted offensive on

4

the part of the Allies. On December 16th Hitler had struck on a front forty miles wide at the Ardennes, with the intention of crossing the Meuse and reaching Antwerp. It was a bold throw, but, from Hitler's point of view, attack was better than seeing his manpower whittled away in stationary defence. All the German generals concerned, and especially von Rundstedt, later insisted that the whole thing was Hitler's doing, even down to details of tactic and formation. Achieving some surprise (although American Intelligence had reported a German build-up at this sector), the thrust met at first with considerable success in an area where similarly concentrated German thrusts had met with success three times already in the century. The American forces holding the line reeled and fell back. The Germans, through their experiences on the Russian Front, had better techniques at this kind of winter warfare. The conflict that emerged was, according to one of its historians, 'the greatest pitched battle ever fought by the United States. . . . Unlike any other campaign in World War Two, it was conceived in its entirety by Adolf Hitler; over a million soldiers were involved.'

In the Battle of the Bulge Americans faced some of the worst and toughest fighting in the history of their nation. Fox-holes and dugouts were waterlogged and muddy when they were not frozen into hard, inhospitable wounds in the tortured earth. Snow descended continually, adding an eerie element to the battlefield. Visibility was always bad, and troops stumbling forward through snow and frozen slush would come upon road-blocks and well-disguised slit-trenches before they realized the danger. When it was not snowing, it was misty and the air nicotine-coloured with fog, smoke and fumes. Above all, it was cold.

Then, suddenly, the weather improved; still bitingly cold, the sky cleared. The German attack, which had progressed sixty miles and encircled Bastogne, around which there was desperate fighting night and day, for the first time became really vulnerable from the air. Appreciating the danger, the *Luftwaffe* attacked Allied airfields on January 1st. But the *Luftwaffe*, manned by half-trained pilots, battered in numerous fights and handicapped by a once forceful but now indolent and complacent commander, was not what it had been. However, considerable damage was done to airfields in Belgium and north-east France, and the loss of aircraft was great; but the *Luftwaffe* suffered severely, too (over 100 planes), and, as Major-General Francis de Guingand, Field-Marshal Montgomery's Chief of Staff, pointed out: 'We could afford it, whilst the enemy

5

could not afford the cost of his audacious attack.' Nevertheless, the British Chief of Air Staff got a very severe reprimand indeed from Winston Churchill about the lack of dispersion of grounded aircraft on RAF airfields in Northern Europe.

The change in weather which had permitted this unaccustomed German air activity also worked to their disadvantage. Although not as quick to take advantage of it as the Germans, the Allied air forces were soon decorating the pale blue skies in tight formations, picking out their targets on the magnificent white desert below. And their targets were two: the lines of supply and the 'neck' of the Bulge. For by the time of the good weather, and the turn of the year, the American forces were already regaining the initiative. Von Rundstedt's offensive had run out of momentum, was tottering and beginning to fall back. Its problem of supplies, practically all of which had to come down two roads through the neck, was not helped by the large number of empty trucks which had been sent up to collect loot from the captured towns and villages; these clogged up the roads and helped the Allied airmen in their simple task of blasting the vehicles massed below.

There was a good deal of confusion in the American lines at this time, the local organization of the ground forces having not yet recovered from the initial disruption. Rumours abounded; some of them were high phantasy. Everyone was on the look-out for spies with American accents, wearing American uniforms, driving American vehicles. Everyone had heard of them. No one had seen them. American commanders were well up with their men, completely contrary to the fashion in Europe in the previous war, twenty-seven years before. One of them, Major-General Matthew Ridgway, recalled the scenes of despair in the front line, and one soldier in particular: 'He was just crouched there in the ditch, cringing in utter terror. So I called my jeep driver and told him to take his carbine and march this man back to the nearest MP, and if he started to escape to shoot him without hesitation. He was an object of abject cowardice.' By this time, in a long war, the nerves of fighting men were taut, and the sensibilities of others hardened. The German generals, too, were close to the war. Field-Marshal Waelter Model, an energetic and clever tactician who commanded the northern sector of the German Front, went right up to the line to see what could be done about the waning Ardennes offensive. The desire of the generals, both of the Allies and the Germans, to get into the firing line was no doubt a subconscious effort to avoid the

6

criticisms levelled at the commanders in the previous war; it was the frequent concern of their superiors. But apart from this human foible, the standard of generalship was high. In the Second World War the generals were men of an intelligence and resourcefulness that permitted them to make the fullest use of new aspects of warfare, such as combined operations, tanks, and air support; in sharp contrast to the generals of the First World War.

The situation at the Ardennes had caused some quickening of the pulse at Allied GHQ, and in London. It would, it was realized by military and political leaders, be disastrous psychologically for the Americans to suffer a severe defeat when the war, it seemed, was so nearly won. There was a danger of a static front settling down, as in the First World War. Throughout the first week of January the situation was still serious enough, although the crisis in forming and holding a line was over. The Germans struggled to increase the area of the salient, sixty miles long and forty wide, and the Americans struggled to push it back and close in at its sides. General Dwight D. Eisenhower, Supreme Allied Commander, had sent his deputy (and main British ally), Air Chief Marshal Sir Arthur Tedder, to Moscow, via Cairo, to press for a resumption of the Russian offensive in the East to take some of the weight off the Ardennes. Tedder was held up by bad flying weather, and Churchill sent a message to Stalin politely asking if an Eastern offensive would be coming soon. 'You yourself know from your own experience how very anxious the position is when a broad front has to be defended after temporary loss of the initiative. It is General Eisenhower's great desire and need to know in outline what you plan to do.' At this time the Germans in Warsaw were mopping up the last of the resistance that had risen in that city months before at the sound of Russian artillery in the distance. Preparations were under way for the mighty Red Army to move forward once more. Churchill had decided to send another 250,000 men to the Front, and, for the first time in the war, the British Government used its special powers to compel women of the Services to go abroad. Nine fresh divisions were being got ready to be sent from the United States. Over 100,000 Negroes serving behind the lines as kitchen-hands, batmen, orderlies and at other unwarlike tasks were given the opportunity of volunteering for sterner duties with 'Negro combat units'. To strengthen the Ardennes Front still further, Eisenhower ordered the Sixth Army Group to the area, leaving Strasbourg somewhat open to the enemy. General Charles de Gaulle, heading the French

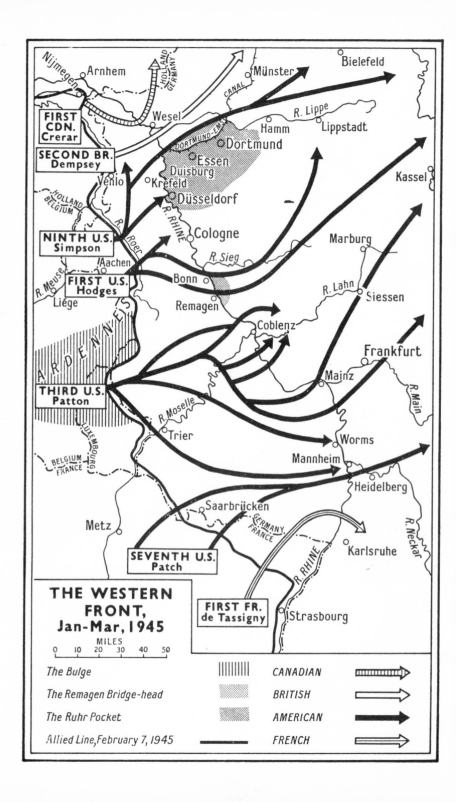

THE WESTERN FRONT, Jan-Mar, 1945

MILES
0 10 20 30 40 50

The Bulge		CANADIAN
The Remagen Bridge-head		BRITISH
The Ruhr Pocket		AMERICAN
Allied Line, February 7, 1945		FRENCH

FIRST CDN. Crerar
SECOND BR. Dempsey
NINTH U.S. Simpson
FIRST U.S. Hodges
THIRD U.S. Patton
SEVENTH U.S. Patch
FIRST FR. de Tassigny

Nijmegen · Arnhem · Münster · Bielefeld · Wesel · Hamm · Lippstadt · R. Lippe · Venlo · Dortmund · Duisburg · Essen · Krefeld · Düsseldorf · Kassel · Cologne · Marburg · Aachen · R. Sieg · Bonn · R. Lahn · Siessen · Liège · Remagen · Coblenz · Frankfurt · R. Main · Mainz · R. Moselle · Trier · Worms · Mannheim · Heidelberg · Saarbrücken · Metz · Karlsruhe · R. Neckar · Strasbourg · R. Rhine · R. Roer · R. Meuse · ARDENNES · LUXEMBOURG · BELGIUM · FRANCE · HOLLAND · GERMANY · CANAL · DORTMUND-EMS

Provisional Government in Paris, made immediate representations as soon as he heard of this plan. National prestige was involved, he pointed out. He said that Strasbourg was a place of historic importance. He told Eisenhower that any withdrawal might mean the fall of his government. Eisenhower hurriedly cancelled his order; he could not afford to have his lines of supply endangered by civil unrest. Eight German divisions actually attacked in this area on New Year's Day, but this time surprise was not achieved and the line held. De Gaulle insisted on the retaining of Strasbourg at all costs, and although some small German advance was made the city was never in serious danger. For some time de Gaulle had been depressing other Allied leaders with his insistence on putting France's concerns before those of the Allies as a whole.

Although many considered him complacent, ineffective and somewhat lazy, the amiable Eisenhower was well liked by all his subordinates, including Montgomery, but during recent months there had been deep mistrust among the British of his ability as a commander. They felt he should confine himself to the true duties of a Supreme Commander (i.e. naval, air and military) and not try to command the land forces as well. Montgomery wrote to the Chief of the Imperial General Staff, Field-Marshal Sir Alan Brooke, that he had neither seen nor spoken to Eisenhower for a month, and had, indeed, met him only four times since the end of the Normandy campaign. 'He is at Forward Headquarters at Rheims,' Montgomery wrote; 'the Directives he issues from there have no relation to the practical necessities of the battle. It is quite impossible for me to carry out my present orders. . . . Eisenhower should himself take a proper control of operations or he should appoint someone else to do this.' Alan Brooke, himself quite as critical of Eisenhower's ability as Montgomery, tried to persuade Montgomery to meet the situation, at least until 'the Command organization and strategy . . . prove themselves defective by operational results'. Like Montgomery, Alan Brooke particularly objected to Eisenhower's insistence on attacking on a broad front at as many places as possible. He replied to Montgomery: 'I have [always] agreed with you that Ike was no commander, that he had no strategic vision, was incapable of making a plan or of running operations when started. Personally I consider Bradley much better suited to carry out the tasks of land force commander than Ike; he might make plans, decide on objectives, allot forces, co-ordinate, etc.' Alan Brooke has recorded that Eisenhower's addiction to playing golf on the links at Rheims* when he was needed at For-ward Headquarters became so bad during the weeks before the Ardennes battle that a deputation of his staff, including Americans, 'went up to him to tell him that he must get down to it and RUN the war, which he said he would'. At length Alan Brooke went to Churchill about his worries, and the Prime Minister confided that he, too, was concerned about the matter. Montgomery wrote a letter to Eisenhower, couched in terms surprisingly strong for a subordinate commander, making it more than clear that he felt 'we must get away from the doctrine of attacking in so many places that nowhere are we strong. We must concentrate such strength on the main selected thrust that success will be certain.' This letter at last roused Eisenhower; he was furious. Shortly after this von Rundstedt had launched his offensive at the Ardennes. In view of the fact that Alan Brooke already believed Eisenhower's policy to be 'sheer madness . . . without any reserves anywhere', it did not come as a surprise to him and the other British commanders that the German attack met at first with considerable success.

Eisenhower's handling of the Ardennes assault, however, had been cool and masterly, in contrast to the excitement of some of his commanders. Indeed, some have considered it his greatest hour as a military commander. Against the wishes of General Omar Bradley, who commanded at the southern side of the Bulge, he actually en-couraged some of the American retreat. He said: 'By rushing out from his fixed defences the enemy may give us the chance to turn his great gamble into his worst defeat.' Refusing to be panicked, he directed operations from a champagne king's handsome château in the centre of Rheims. He watched as his line expanded and as the Germans ran into inevitable supply difficulties as soon as the weather cleared and the Allies mastered the skies once more. His calm direction, and his appreciation of the benefits deriving from the elasticity of lines, surprised those generals, mostly British, who had little opinion of either his strategy or his handling of his senior commanders. This latter facet, which was meant to be his special quality and which had been well publicized in the Press, came under a severe test during the Ardennes battle. For, after the German break-through, Eisenhower had quickly realized that Bradley's command was effectively cut in half. He gave Bradley's two northern corps to Montgomery's command—a daring and decisive stroke.

* Montgomery himself had been playing 'a few holes of golf' when the German Ardennes offensive was launched.

Eisenhower's decision, which could have led to confusion and disaster, led to total success. For Field-Marshal Bernard Law Montgomery, despite the convictions of some American staff officers not familiar with him, was not a fool. Like Eisenhower, he, too, kept his head. His gathering-in of the American divisions, co-ordinating them with his own XXX Corps, and quickly bringing them to bear on the northern flank of the German advance, was a brilliant and confident manoeuvre. Patiently he re-established his front. He visited the commanders of the US First and Ninth Armies and reported to Alan Brooke: 'Neither had seen Bradley or any of his staff since the battle began [this was not surprising, as the two American armies had been cut off from Bradley]. There were no reserves anywhere behind the Front. Morale was very low. They seemed delighted to have someone give them firm orders.'

Montgomery, however, was far too patient for Bradley and General George S. Patton, Commander of the Third US Army under Bradley. They wanted an immediate pincer movement at the neck of the Bulge. While Montgomery was in agreement with this in principle, he felt he could not put all his weight behind it until he was properly organized. During the previous year Montgomery's abrupt, clipped and somewhat supercilious manner had been steadily irritating most of the American commanders who came in contact with him. Coupled with this was the fact, annoying to them, that Montgomery seemed to be gaining all the credit from the British Press for winning the war, and even from some of the American Press too. Montgomery himself was not averse to taking any credit that came his way. This might have been all right if he had been the kind of chummy good-mixer that American military men appreciate. This, unfortunately, he was not. Ever since his wife had, tragically and unexpectedly, died many years before, Montgomery had been a cold figure who seemed to recoil from close human relationships. The fact that Montgomery, like Alexander, was a Field-Marshal, and thus senior in equivalent rank to all the American generals except Eisenhower, did not improve matters. The rift between him and Bradley came to an explosive head towards the end of the Ardennes offensive.* The break in American and British military relations, already damaged in Algeria and Normandy earlier, was to become so wide that it could only be superficially repaired for the remainder of the war.

---

* Bradley has stated that he had already threatened to resign rather than serve under Montgomery, and that Patton would have followed him.

While Patton was attacking fiercely around Bastogne, Montgomery still declined to throw in his reserves, preferring to keep some troops fresh for a later blow. The American policy, inherent especially in all Patton's military thinking, was to worry about reserves when they were needed, and in the meantime to throw everything into attack. Bradley was an excellent tactician, and a good organizer. Patton was a forceful and sometimes inspired leader, but Montgomery, as history was to show, was the only one, including Eisenhower, who had a grasp of strategy wide enough to take in the whole landscape of the war and the days that were to follow it.

The trouble really flared up at a Press conference on January 7th. At this Montgomery, in his customary fashion, spoke of the successful progress of the battle, with a number of hints that this was mainly due to him. He had, he said, taken immediate action at the start of the battle to make sure that the Germans would not get over the Meuse. When the crisis had come, he said, 'national considerations had been thrown overboard'. To the Americans this seemed as if he were saying that when the chips were really down Eisenhower had been forced to call in the best man available. Montgomery did not mean that; but he had a remarkable talent for saying things that could easily cause offence without actually intending any. Bradley and his staff (whom Bradley himself described as 'acutely sensitive') were furious. They believed that the battle was being won despite, rather than because of, Montgomery. To have a British commander in charge of American troops was bad enough. For that commander to be Montgomery was barely tolerable. But for him to claim all credit was outrageous. Bradley never forgave 'the pious, teetotalling Montgomery', as he called him in his memoirs. That Montgomery had also referred at the conference to the fact that the battle could not have been won without 'the good fighting qualities of the American soldier', and had insisted that the Germans had been halted before British divisions were even committed, went comparatively unnoticed.

Eisenhower wrote of this occasion: 'I doubt that Montgomery ever came to realize how deeply resentful some American commanders were. They believed he had belittled them—and they were not slow to voice reciprocal scorn and contempt.' Two days later Bradley issued a firm statement to the Press acknowledging Montgomery's contribution, and defending himself. On the same day, Eisenhower diplomatically awarded Bradley a Bronze Star, citing the important part he had played in the battle. Montgomery has since admitted: 'I think now that I should never have held that Press conference. So great was the feeling against me on the part of the American generals that whatever I said was bound to be wrong.'

It was unfortunate that at this time Montgomery and Churchill were trying very hard to get Eisenhower to agree that the final thrust into Germany should be undertaken under one overall command in the field, and that the thrust should take place in the north, and that the commander should be Montgomery. Although Eisenhower had not been keen on the idea previous to this point, it now became an impossibility. Bradley and Patton would not have stood for it. In retrospect it seems that Montgomery was tactless, Bradley as touchy as a *prima donna*, and Eisenhower lax in not demanding silence and discipline from his generals. That such an angry exchange could take place in public, while men were dying in some of the worst conditions of the whole war, does little credit to anyone involved. Montgomery tried unsuccessfully to smooth things over in a personal letter to Bradley, saying what an honour it had been to command American troops and how well they had done.

Meanwhile the twenty-four German divisions packed into the salient were being gradually pushed back. Realizing withdrawal was inevitable, von Rundstedt asked Hitler for permission to retire to his original lines. This was refused. The weather continued bitterly cold, and there were further snowfalls. Soldiers died of frostbite and exposure. At night men froze to death in fox-holes. Anti-freeze mixture froze in radiators. Petrol froze in vehicle tanks. Many hundreds of men lost fingers; others suffered mental breakdowns. Snow-drifts hampered the advance of American infantry, trudging through untrodden snowfields under the frosty lantern of a weak winter sun; and the frozen roads, and mines cleverly hidden in snow, brought mobility almost to zero. But during the second week in January the American push south of the Bulge had progressed five miles (at a rate of a mile a day) and now Model, too, was asking permission to withdraw. Hitler's hope that the *Wehrmacht* could repeat its success of 1940 in a powerful, irresistible thrust, had been proved hopelessly overconfident. The German attempt had failed through lack of air superiority, insufficient fuel, inexpert planning from Hitler himself, and an underestimation of the American power to recover—so different from that of the French earlier in the war. On January 8th the Fuehrer authorized a complete withdrawal. The German withdrawal, considering the conditions and the ceaseless battering from Montgomery's and Bradley's forces, was highly successful. The infantry divisions withdrew to a new position each day, the tanks forming a rearguard. Owing to the lack of fuel, many tanks and vehicles had to be abandoned. By January 16th the German army was back where it had started before Christmas, having suffered 120,000 casualties in its assault at the Ardennes. American losses, too, had been very heavy. The First and Third US Armies alone had suffered more than 75,000 casualties. Hitler was more disillusioned than ever with his generals, and turned more and more to the faithful Grand Admiral Karl Doenitz for encouragement and hope. Bewildered and angry, he told assembled generals, including von Rundstedt: 'We should not forget that even today we are defending an area . . . which is essentially larger than Germany has ever been, and that there is at our disposal an armed force which even today is unquestionably the most powerful on earth.' There were, in fact, 260 German divisions in the field, twice as many as in May 1940. These were, however, scattered about in Norway, Yugoslavia and Italy, as well as on the two main fronts. Hitler's advisers pleaded with him in vain to evacuate outlying areas. He was particularly anxious to protect the naval bases in Norway and Denmark, from which, he was assured, Doenitz's remarkable new submarines were about to launch a crippling attack on Allied shipping. Thus, of the German divisions, only seventy-six were on the Western Front; on the Eastern Front there were 133 divisions.

As the Allies reorganized their line and prepared for a final onslaught on Germany itself, Winston Churchill made an attempt to patch up the quarrel between American and British commanders. Speaking in the House of Commons, he said: 'I have seen it suggested that the terrific battle which has been proceeding since December 16th on the American front is an Anglo-American battle. In fact, however, the United States troops have done almost all the fighting, and have suffered almost all the losses. . . . According to the professional advice which I have at my disposal, what was done to meet von Rundstedt's counter-stroke was resolute, wise and militarily correct.' Even if this obvious kind of speech could have the effect intended, it was too late. American generals, as well as the already suspicious politicians, were wondering how much they could trust the British. And the British, in their turn, were wondering what kind of allies would these over-sensitive, proud Americans make after the war.

After thirteen days of misadventures with flying and weather, Tedder and his mission arrived in Moscow. Their journey had been wasted. For, on January 12th, the great Russian advance through Poland, Prussia and then on to Berlin had begun.

(iii)

If the military situation at this time was characterized by dissension and distrust among the Allied powers, the political situation was almost as chaotic. Stalin and Churchill were jockeying furiously for positions all over Europe, realizing that the coming weeks, as German power collapsed, would set the map of Europe for many years. Churchill was particularly concerned about the results of the vacuum German withdrawal was leaving in Central Europe. He was anxious to avoid a repetition of what had happened after the previous war, when an opportunity had been created for 'the Hitler monster to crawl out of its sewer on to the vacant thrones'. Roosevelt was not only far away and comparatively inexperienced in European affairs, he was also a sick man. He did not seem to appreciate the importance of the Red Army swallowing up Eastern Europe, or so it seemed in London. He believed he could negotiate eventually with Stalin. His advisers convinced him that British fears and suspicions of Russia were, if not unfounded, certainly exaggerated. This view was strengthened by what sometimes seemed to be a traditional and conventional attitude by Churchill to the Russian Government, to which he often referred in messages and memorandums as 'the Bolsheviks'.

German Intelligence knew something of these differences, especially of those between the Western powers and Russia. As the news reached Hitler, it thrilled him. Senior German officials waited for what they considered the inevitable clash between the Russians and the British. Goebbels had already written in *Das Reich* that the winter 'would see the end of the unnatural Russo-British alliance'. Hitler increasingly began to think of some kind of alliance between Germany and Britain that would halt the Russian spread into Western Europe. As the Soviet advance began again in the East, he waited daily for an approach from London. On the evening of January 27th he discussed the political situation with Reichsmarschall Hermann Goering and Colonel-General Alfred Jodl. Hitler asked whether the British could be happy about the Russian advances in the East. Jodl replied: 'Certainly not. Their plans were quite different. Only later on perhaps will the full realization of this come.' Goering added: 'They had not counted on our defending ourselves step by step and holding them off in the West like madmen while the Russians drive into Germany.' Hitler revealed at this conference that he had ordered a false report to be allowed to fall into British hands 'to the effect that the Russians are organizing 200,000 of our men led by German officers and completely infected with Communism . . . that will make them feel as if someone has stuck a needle into them'. This conference did much to raise spirits among the Fuehrer's inner circle. Happy in the belief that, despite appearances, all might not be lost and that a clever, waiting, diplomatic game might save them from catastrophe, they prepared to watch events. But the Nazi leaders understood nothing of high diplomacy, and even if they had acted on their false hopes, instead of waiting for them to develop, they would have been sorely disappointed. Although they appreciated the rift between East and West, and the dangers for Britain and America in an uncontrolled and rapid Russian advance, they knew little of the rift between the United States and Britain and the suspicions harboured by the leaders of the former towards the actions and views of the latter. Goering summed up their appraisal of the situation when, speaking of the Russian advance, he said: 'If this goes on we will get a telegram [from the West] in a few days.'

In the late autumn of the previous year Churchill and Anthony Eden, Foreign Minister, had made a hurried visit to Moscow to get some agreement from Stalin regarding Russian ambitions in Europe. Roosevelt, in the midst of an election campaign, had declined to attend the meeting. But Churchill had pointed out that the advancing Russian armies were not going to wait while the returns from Michigan, South Dakota and Oregon were counted. Much to the alarm of Roosevelt's advisers, the British had proceeded on their own. On his very first night in Moscow, Churchill, who believed the way to deal with 'Uncle Joe' was to talk straight from the shoulder when you wanted to make a deal with him, and to flatter him most of the time, had come straight to the point.* He was,

* Churchill assured Roosevelt that Harriman, US Ambassador in Moscow, would be present at all important meetings, but he was not present on this and a number of other occasions.

perhaps, glad of the opportunity to try to settle matters in Europe without interference from the Americans.

Churchill recalls that he said to Stalin at this meeting: 'Let us settle our affairs in the Balkans. Don't let us get at cross-purposes in small ways. So far as Britain and Russia are concerned, how would it do for you to have 90 per cent predominance in Rumania, for us to have 90 per cent of the say in Greece, and go fifty-fifty about Yugoslavia?' While the translator was coping with this, Churchill wrote out on a sheet of paper:

Rumania	
Russia	90 per cent
The others	10 per cent
Greece	
Great Britain	90 per cent
Russia	10 per cent
Yugoslavia	50–50 per cent
Hungary	50–50 per cent
Bulgaria	
Russia	75 per cent
The others	25 per cent

Churchill pushed this chart over to Stalin. 'There was a slight pause. Then he took his blue pencil and made a large tick on it and passed it back.' This was followed by a long silence, with the paper predominant in the middle of the table. Each thought his own thoughts. At length Churchill, apparently somewhat taken aback by the simplicity and boldness with which such matters affecting the lives of millions were, it seemed, settled, suggested that they should burn the paper. 'Might it not be thought rather cynical if it seemed we had disposed of these issues in such an off-hand manner?' he said. 'No, you keep it,' Stalin had replied. (Churchill later described these percentages as purely 'temporary' arrangements.)

Later in this visit Eden, who was well liked by Stalin, had a curious conversation with the Russian leader. Stalin had said: 'Hitler is undoubtedly a clever man, but he has one capital fault: he doesn't know when to stop.' Noticing a smile from Eden, he added: 'You are thinking that I, too, don't know when to stop.

You are profoundly mistaken, Mr Eden. I know very well when to stop, as you will see.'

It remained to be seen if Stalin was prepared to stop at the limits set down on Churchill's chart. At any rate, armed with this piece of paper, on which was Stalin's heavy tick in blue pencil, Churchill and Eden returned to London. When the State Department got to hear of it, they considered the whole scheme a cynical and sinister manoeuvre to further British ambitions in the Balkans. In Greece, where Russian armies (twenty divisions) on the Bulgarian frontier hopelessly outnumbered the small British force (10,000 men), it seemed that the scrap of paper had been observed—a fact of tremendous and gratifying importance to Churchill, for ever conscious of the Empire's vital highway through the Mediterranean. In Bulgaria, however, the British *Chargé d'affaires* had been expelled; but, on the whole, Churchill was resigned to having to forgo the 25 per cent of that country and the 10 per cent in Rumania. In Hungary the future was still uncertain. In Yugoslavia Tito had threatened to hang King Peter if he returned to his country, but Churchill still had high hopes of keeping the agreed fifty-fifty basis there, even if he had to throw King Peter overboard to get a suitable compromise. More important, Churchill's astute action in insisting upon agreement had deprived the Nazis of their trump card, whether Stalin strictly kept to the sphere of influence or not. All in all, Churchill's action, independent of the Americans, might have been thought a considerable success—if it had not been for the increasingly difficult problem of Poland, about which Stalin seemed quite unwilling to come to any kind of compromise whatever. It was this fact which disturbed Churchill more than anything else, and Roosevelt too was highly concerned at what seemed complete indifference on Stalin's part to the views of the West. Churchill, in particular, felt deeply about Poland. He could not forget that it was because of that country that Britain had originally gone to war. By the beginning of 1945 the Polish problem was uppermost in his mind. After Poland lay Germany. Rumania was one thing, but Germany was quite another. He viewed with increasing alarm the prospect of the Red Army rushing into Germany, the traditional bastion between Western and Eastern Europe.

Stalin seemed determined to set up a purely puppet government in Poland, known as the 'Lublin Government', while both Churchill and Roosevelt insisted that the exiled government in London be represented in a caretaker government before free elections were held. The Soviet Union had broken off diplomatic relations with the London Polish Government in 1943 when the Poles had asked for an inquiry by the Red Cross into the discovery at Katyn of mass graves containing the remains of 4,000 missing Polish officers. With great difficulty Churchill and Eden had been able to initiate negotiations between these two Polish authorities during their visit to Moscow in the previous autumn. These negotiations had met with failure. The London Poles had refused to admit to the Curzon Line, although Churchill himself had described it as 'reasonable and just', and their own Prime Minister, Stanislaw Micolajczyk, had been prepared to accept it under certain conditions. But Micolajczyk had resigned, and his colleagues were not prepared to make any deal with Moscow. On December 27th Stalin had written to Roosevelt: 'I have to say frankly that if the Polish Committee of National Liberation [the Lublin Government] will transform itself into a Provisional Polish Government then the Soviet Government will not have any serious ground for postponement of the question of its recognition. It is necessary to bear in mind that in the strengthening of a pro-Allied and democratic Poland the Soviet Union is interested more than any other Power, not only because the Soviet Union is bearing the main brunt of the battle for the liberation of Poland, but also because Poland is a border state with the Soviet Union and the problem of Poland is inseparable from the problem of security of the Soviet Union. To this I have to add that the successes of the Red Army in Poland in the fight against the Germans are to a great degree dependent on the presence of a peaceful and trustworthy rear in Poland.' Stalin also pointed out that the exiled government (to whom he contemptuously referred as 'a handful of Polish emigrants in London') had lost the confidence of the Polish population. This was no doubt true, as few Poles seriously wanted a return to the days of their inefficient and right-wing governments of the 1930s. Roosevelt replied that he was 'disturbed and deeply disappointed'. He went on: 'The fact is that neither the Government nor the people of the United States have as yet seen any evidence either arising from the manner of its creation or from subsequent developments to justify the conclusion that the Lublin Committee as at present constituted represents the people of Poland. I cannot ignore the fact that up to the present only a small fraction of Poland proper, west of the Curzon Line, has been liberated from German tyranny; and it is therefore an unquestioned truth that the people of Poland have had no opportunity to express themselves in regard to the Lublin Committee.' But events were moving fast. Stalin, his plans and ambitions firmly set, was unmoved by these strong words from the West. The Red Army was stronger. Already Stalin was preparing for a final invasion of Poland that would leave the entire country in his possession. On January 4th Stalin wrote to Churchill: 'I think that Poland cannot be left without a government. Accordingly, the Soviet Government has agreed to recognize the Provisional Polish Government.' This was despite a request from Roosevelt to delay the recognition for one month. Stalin had replied to Roosevelt that he was 'powerless' to do so, as he could not overrule the Presidium of the Supreme Soviet, which had already decided on this course. To this ingenious excuse, Roosevelt did not bother to reply.

Things had come to such a head that Churchill was convinced nothing more could be done without a meeting of the Big Three as soon as possible. Now that Roosevelt was seemingly thoroughly alert to the dangers in Poland, Churchill believed he might be a strong ally in a stand-fast encounter with Stalin. Clearly now was the time, for on the Polish problem at least the United States and Britain were agreed. Roosevelt also was not averse to a conference of the three leaders, although his main interest was to complete agreement on a world organization for the post-war period, in which he was passionately interested, and to ensure help from Russia in the war against Japan once Germany was defeated. (The President believed that a combined operation in the Pacific would produce harmony in the after-war years.) Stalin, also, saw the moment as an opportune one for a summit meeting. The Anglo-American forces had suffered an embarrassing reverse in the West. His new offensive in the East, which he was about to set in motion, would give him an all-powerful role in Poland. He was aware of some discord between the British and Americans.

American suspicions of Britain at this time were not only confined to the interference of British troops in Greece. There were also political crises in Belgium and Italy, following the German withdrawal. It seemed to the American Secretary of State and others close to the President that, in the words of Robert E. Sherwood, 'in the two latter countries Churchill's well-known predilection for constitutional monarchs was dictating policies which were against the people's will'. Churchill was certainly anxious to establish governments in the political vacuum in these countries as soon as possible, and in his desire to forestall Communist ambitions he no doubt seemed far too hasty to back the right-wing elements. The

American Democratic administration of this time self-consciously considered itself far left politically of the Conservative Churchill. Roosevelt, particularly, felt he was more in tune with the Socialist movements that seemed to be sweeping across Europe in 1945 than was the British leader whose past associated him with imperialism. That this was a grave miscalculation of British motives cannot be doubted; but the attitude was inherent in the contemporary American thinking. During the Atlantic Charter meeting the President had already made his position clear to Churchill. He expected Britain to renounce all its former Colonial power and set in motion a complete and widespread 'freeing' of people throughout the British Empire. Later, at the signature of the Lend-Lease agreement, he had insisted on the same thing. He told his son Elliott: 'I've tried to make it clear to Winston—and the others—that while we're their allies and in it to victory by their side, they must never get the idea that we're in it just to help them hang on to the archaic, medieval Empire ideas.' He knew that in the East especially colonialism had been entirely discredited, unable even to prevent Japanese conquest of the European possessions. He had already made it clear that the liberation of these places with the help of American arms would imply complete national freedom after the cessation of hostilities. He was less suspicious of Holland (he had a verbal agreement with Queen Wilhelmina that the Dutch East Indies would receive independence) than he was of France. But his main suspicions were reserved for Britain. He told Stettinius, his Secretary of State, that 'the British would take land anywhere in the world even if it were only rock or a sandbar'. He even considered demanding from Britain, France and Holland specific dates when independence would be granted. It had, therefore, come as a complete surprise when Churchill, the previous autumn, had offered to send a large part of the RAF and most of the British Battle Fleet to the Pacific, for Roosevelt had always assumed that Britain's only interests in that theatre were regaining Burma and Malaya. The offer only succeeded in heightening American suspicions still further. Admiral Ernest J. King, who was obsessed with anti-British feelings, at first flatly refused to have anything to do with it. However, the Americans could not be expected to know that already forces were on the move that would make a new Conservatism, with policies both domestic and foreign, different to any that had been known before. But it seems to have been Roosevelt's ambition to see Britain a compliant power after the war. He believed, moreover, that there was no fundamental national conflict of interest between the Soviets and the United States. He was by no means alone. Eisenhower said that the long, unbroken friendship between the two countries would not go for nothing, and pointed out, incorrectly, that, 'both were free from the stigma of colonial empire-building by force'. All this, however, did not affect the close personal friendliness between Roosevelt and Churchill, cemented in common interests of anti-Nazism.

That American doubts about Britain could not apply to all circumstances is shown by the strange affair of King Peter of Yugoslavia. During January Churchill, following his private fifty-fifty deal with Stalin the previous year, was attempting to get a compromise government established in Belgrade. These manoeuvres do not seem to have been widely known in Washington, although the President certainly knew of them. Recognizing the military position of Tito, which made him already virtually dictator of the country so far freed from German forces, Churchill tried to arrange for a Regency with a government headed by Tito in which the Royalist Government in London under Dr Subasic would take part. On January 11th he wrote to Stalin: 'Mr Eden and I tried our best on several occasions with King Peter. He is a spirited young man and feels that the Tito–Subasic agreement is virtual abdication. He has now put out his declaration without consultation with us and, indeed, against our advice. He thinks that if he keeps himself free of all that is going to happen in Yugoslavia in the next few years a day will dawn for him. I now suggest that we make the Tito–Subasic agreement valid and simply by-pass King Peter II.' Stalin replied: 'I accept your proposal for putting the Tito–Subasic agreement into effect. By doing so we shall stave off eventual complications.'*

This was followed by a message from Churchill to Stalin on January 14th: 'Since sending you my telegram of January 11th about Yugoslavia a new development has occurred in that Dr Subasic, basing himself on King Peter's acceptance in principle of the agreement, is trying to see whether there is any way of getting over the King's objections.' Stalin, however, was tiring of the correspondence. He had every intention of putting Tito in power anyway. He replied: 'As far as I am concerned I see no grounds for putting off execution of our decision, which I communicated to you last time.' Churchill, still playing for time, replied: 'Many thanks. At our suggestion King Peter is discussing with Dr Subasic the

---

* The Churchill–Stalin correspondence over Yugoslavia at this time is not mentioned in Churchill's history of the war.

possibility of finding a solution whereby he can accept the Tito–Subasic agreement. I think we should give them a little more time to work it out.' On the night of the 22nd there was a startling development. Churchill telegraphed to Stalin: 'King Peter, without informing us of his intention, dismissed Subasic and his government last night. We are informing Dr Subasic that the King's action does not affect His Majesty's Government's intention to see that the Tito–Subasic agreement is carried out and that we are therefore ready to transport him and his government to Belgrade. I suggest that the three great powers should now decide to put the Tito–Subasic agreement into force and that Tito should be informed that, if he will consent with Subasic and his government to carry out the agreement, the three great powers will recognize the united government formed therewith.' Stalin replied that he agreed, and once more Churchill telegraphed, repeating that it should 'be carried out whatever the King may say'. In fact, the King, this time under pressure from the State Department, restored Subasic a week later. Negotiations with Tito were opened up, and it was agreed that there should be three Regents, one to be nominated by the King. King Peter soon found the Regents did not provide him with any power in Yugoslavia. He said: 'I have been denied the right to participate in the affairs of Yugoslavia.' The young King continued to bombard Churchill with letters and messages, some of which he delivered to 10 Downing Street himself, and all of which expressed indignation at his exclusion from Yugoslav affairs. He also appealed to George VI ('Uncle Bertie'): 'Please help me to make Churchill understand my point of view.'

There was only one possible outcome to all this: a Communist dictatorship under Tito—although for Stalin, at least, the story was later to have a surprising and painful twist. Churchill's efforts to get his 50 per cent, desperate and persistent, and not helped by a proud and stubborn young King out of touch with realities, were in vain. But no one could accuse him in this instance of trying to prop up a tottering monarchy; but American suspicions remained as strong as ever. According to Sherwood: 'Liberal opinion—which was feeling particularly potent after the recent election—was becoming increasingly suspicious of Churchill's apparent determination to restore the unsavoury *status quo ante* in Europe.' The Secretary of State issued a statement in which he said: ' We have reaffirmed to both the British and the Italian Governments that we expected the Italians to work out their problems of government along democratic lines without influence from outside. This policy would apply in an even more pronounced degree with regard to government of the United Nations in their liberated territories.' This last sentence was an obvious reference to Greece and Belgium. Following this, relations between Downing Street and the White House were extremely strained. Churchill sent a very strong protest to the President, and made a long speech in the House of Commons justifying his policy, especially in Italy, where the British Government had stated its reluctance to recognize the left-wing Count Carlo Sforza. John G. Winant, the US Ambassador in London, reported that 'the Parliament [in London] is definitely to the Right of the country'.

The British Ambassador in Washington was the respected and competent Lord Halifax. Affairs had been allowed to get to such a state that neither he nor Winant was able to do much about them, especially as the President, who was worrying everyone with his tired and sickly appearance, was spending much time at Warm Springs, Georgia. One of Roosevelt's closest confidants, Harry L. Hopkins, had a unique position of trust in foreign affairs, and was sent on special assignments by the President, not always to the pleasure of the State Department. Halifax called on Hopkins and, instructed by Churchill, gave a vigorous and heated refutation of the charges that were being made in America about British foreign policy. Hopkins replied 'that public opinion about the whole Greek business in this country was very bad and that we felt the British Government had messed the whole thing up pretty thoroughly'.

The Secretary of State, Edward R. Stettinius, had succeeded Cordell Hull, who had been forced to resign due to ill health. There had been a number of candidates for the job, and Stettinius, who had been Under-Secretary, had not been the most obvious. James F. Byrnes had been the most likely choice; his high standing in the Senate would have been a great aid to Roosevelt. But he did not get on with the ubiquitous and powerful Hopkins, to whom he had once said 'keep the hell out of my business'. He was also a man likely to have views of his own, which might even from time to time differ from those of the President. Sumner Welles was another possibility, but his appointment would have been resented by Hull; so Stettinius found himself in this vital role.

President Roosevelt made his fourth inauguration speech on January 20th. He stood throughout the ceremony, his face twisted with pain as the heavy braces pressed against his body. It was a bitterly cold day. The President wore no overcoat or hat; he wore, as he usually did, a lightweight suit. One of those who was shocked by his appearance was a man who had seen comparatively little of the President in recent months: the Vice-President, Harry S. Truman. The President's voice, though less powerful than before, still had a thrilling ring of greatness about it. He said: 'We have learned to be citizens of the world, members of the human community. We have learned the simple truth, as Emerson said, that the only way to have a friend is to be one.'

They were moving words, and everyone there knew they were true. For never before in their history had the United States become so inextricably involved in the affairs of the world.

In London, Churchill kept his ceaseless pressure on all the diplomatic fronts. During January his correspondence with Stalin was well over twice that between Stalin and Roosevelt. He now tried to arrange for a meeting between himself and the President before going on to Yalta, the Crimean resort where it had been arranged the Big Three should meet. He thought it would be a good thing if they could have a talk together, although, anxious not to increase the President's suspicions any further, he insisted that it would only be to discuss such affairs as were of concern to them alone. Nevertheless, it would certainly have afforded him an opportunity of explaining his fears about Russian ambitions in Europe privately to the President. The meeting could, he pointed out, be carried on 'unostentatiously'. Roosevelt would not hear of such a suggestion. Churchill then pressed for a meeting of British and American Staff to discuss the military situation, and to try to iron out the differences now appearing between American and British military viewpoints. Roosevelt replied to this: 'I regret that in view of the time available to me for this journey it will not be possible for us to meet your suggestion and have a British–American Staff meeting at Malta before proceeding to [Yalta].' Churchill, by this time accustomed to being baulked at every move, pressed his proposal. He also pressed for a conference of the three Foreign Secretaries, Eden, Stettinius and Molotov, which he felt should take place before the Yalta conference to clear some of the ground before the Big Three actually met. Roosevelt turned this down, saying that Stettinius 'could not be spared'. Roosevelt seemed to believe that if he could get to Yalta without being distracted by Churchill, of whom he was personally fond but whom he was now finding excitable and dangerous, he could talk to Stalin alone and would stand a good chance of settling their problems. He had told Churchill long before: 'I know you will not mind my being brutally frank when I tell you that I think I can personally handle Stalin better than either your Foreign Office or my State Department.' He did, as a concession to Churchill, now agree to the meeting of the Combined Staffs at Malta.

Churchill persisted in his request for a meeting of the Foreign Ministers, this time leaving out Molotov. 'Eden has particularly asked me to suggest that Stettinius might come on forty-eight hours earlier to Malta,' he said. But Roosevelt, determined not to be ensnared into this British trap and thus offend the Russians, and bracing himself for a great effort to reach agreement with Stalin, once more replied that there was 'too much business in Washington' for Stettinius to meet Eden in anything but the briefest meeting at Malta. Hopkins was sent over to Churchill instead; his mission being more to soothe the Prime Minister than to sound out his views. He reported Churchill as being in a 'volcanic' mood. There is no record of anything useful having been achieved during Hopkins's visit, most of which appears to have been taken up with social courtesies. It is significant that, after leaving London, Hopkins went on to visit de Gaulle in Paris. No doubt Roosevelt considered the two European leaders equally troublesome, if in different ways. The State Department had been finding de Gaulle next to impossible. It was felt in Washington that the American Army had largely liberated his country, had helped him to power, and yet still the man was not satisfied. De Gaulle was deeply offended that he had not been asked to the Yalta conference. The Big Three, he thought, should be the Big Four. Hopkins found de Gaulle 'neither responsive nor conciliatory'.

In the last week in January Roosevelt boarded the USS _Quincy_ to cross the Atlantic, for what he hoped was going to be a historic and successful meeting between himself and 'Uncle Joe'. With Germany about to collapse in Europe, there would be problems in that continent, of course. They could be settled satisfactorily without panicking about Russian ambitions. Britain, after all, was not blameless. She would have to curb her ambitions in Greece. And, perhaps most important of all, the question of Russian participation in the war against Japan could be settled. Above all, he was determined to keep an open mind on all things, avoiding preconceived ideas, with no plan that had to be strictly adhered to, but with one guiding principle: that free people, no matter whether they had been freed by

British or Russians, had the right to freely elect the kind of government they wished.

Among the great many messages with which the President had
been bombarded by the Prime Minister in recent weeks were irritated ones, almost mincingly polite ones, pleading ones, and pessimistic ones such as: 'This may well be a fateful conference, coming
at a moment when the Great Allies are so divided and the shadow of
the war lengthens out before us. At the present time I think the end
of this war may well prove to be more disappointing than was the
last.'

(iv)

Meanwhile, far away in another part of the globe, the Second World
War was also reaching its climax. Although the Japanese had acquired
an immense empire, its very size was beginning to defeat them. The
Japanese Army, still strong in number, was spread out over China
and South-East Asia and in numerous Pacific and East Indian
Islands. Already its forces were retreating in Burma before the
Fourteenth Army, and were on the defensive in the Philippines
where the Americans had returned to the island of Leyte the
previous October. At the naval battle which accompanied the landings at Leyte the power of the Japanese Navy had been virtually
destroyed in a tense and confused naval battle, at which the Royal
Australian Navy had played a small but honourable part. The end of
the greedy ambitions of Japanese militarism in the East was at last in
sight. Some of the more level-headed of the Japanese leaders were
beginning to think of how best they could end the war before their
country was humiliated in the total defeat that was clearly coming.
They were overruled by the military hierarchy. At the battle of
Leyte Gulf Japanese suicide-bombers had first made their devastating appearance—an act of despair rather than a means of victory.
The High Command ordered a fight to the finish in the Philippines.

By January nearly a quarter of a million American troops were on
Leyte, and Japanese resistance was broken. There were at this time
three main schools of strategic thought about how best to defeat
Japan. The naval theory was that Japan could be defeated by means
of a blockade, especially as America now had command of most of
the Pacific and as Japan was a heavily over-populated area lacking in
internal resources. The Army theory was that Japan would have to

be gradually encircled and then itself be invaded. Many officers were certain that nothing short of physical capture and seizure of their homeland would distract the Japanese soldiers and airmen from their present hideous capitulation to the death-wish. The Air Force theory was that Japan could best be defeated by saturation bombing of her cities and industries; a few senior Air Force men knew of work in progress on a secret weapon that would support their theory and, if it were made operation-ready in time, might win the war for them against Japan. But ever since Roosevelt's great speech after Pearl Harbour American policy in the Japanese war had been one of 'unremitting pressure' on every possible front.

General Douglas MacArthur prepared now for the invasion of the largest and most important of the Philippine islands, Luzon, on which was Manila, the capital. His plan for the landing was one of the most brilliant of the war; a subtle and sophisticated series of decoys and counters, it kept the Japanese commander, General Tomoyuki Yamashita, the arrogant but by no means incapable conqueror of Singapore, in continual and, as it proved, fatal doubt. Yamashita had, however, greater forces than MacArthur had at his disposal; before the invasion had even begun he had moved his puppet government and headquarters from Manila to the hills.

There were a great number of difficulties before MacArthur could put his plan into operation; they were mostly of supply, and particularly of supplies for the engineers—vital for fighting to take place in wild country with inadequate roads and bridges. As the invasion fleet and escorts moved into position, carrier-based aircraft maintained a permanent umbrella over the Japanese airfields in an attempt to keep the enemy aircraft on the ground. This was one of several innovations of Admiral John S. McCain, a thoughtful commander who was concerned about the large-scale suicide attacks. To combat this he had cut his number of carrier dive-bombers to less than half, and more than doubled his number of fighters. Three weeks before the invasion of Luzon was scheduled to begin one of the naval forces suffered an unexpected and serious set-back. A particularly severe and concentrated typhoon blew up, undetected by the meteorologists, and caught a part of the force refuelling. At the height of the storm three destroyers—the *Hull*, the *Monaghan* and the *Spence*—capsized and all went down. Seven other ships were severely damaged and 186 planes blown overboard or destroyed. Nearly 800 men were lost. It was as if the force had been engaged in a major battle.

MacArthur's beach-head was to be at Lingayen Gulf, on the west coast of the island. It was, and this was typical of MacArthur's daring, almost arrogant plan, the very spot where the Japanese themselves had landed three years before. As the fleet steamed through the islands towards the Gulf, part of it was spotted by a Japanese look-out in a church steeple on high ground. The following day the first of the suicide-bombers arrived, hitting an oiler. Within three days a constant stream of these suicide planes was screaming down from the sky, a nerve-tingling and frightening spectacle of war at its most obstinate and depressing. A two-engined bomber dived straight into the flight-deck of the carrier *Ommaney Bay*, which had to be abandoned. The *Louisville* and HMAS *Australia* were hit, with three other warships, the following day. As the support force steamed relentlessly into Lingayen Gulf the suicide planes, or *kamikazes*, attacked for eight hours. Every few minutes a Japanese pilot was taking off, usually half-hysterical, to fly to his death. The wastage in planes was high, as the vast majority never reached a target. They had, however, obviously been trained in the manoeuvre, as their deception was excellent, making skilful use of land masses, metal tape to confuse radar readings, and low-level flying. McCain's frantic efforts to keep them on the ground were failing. During these eight hectic hours, while the sky was diseased with puffs of smoke and planes darting in every direction, the cruisers *Louisville* and *Australia* again both received direct hits; the battleships *New Mexico* and *California*, the cruiser *Columbia*, three destroyers, a destroyer-transport, a seaplane-tender and a minesweeper also suffered direct hits; the minesweeper, hit twice, capsized with its back broken. Later in the day the *Australia* was hit yet again, but somehow managed to keep going. Her captain refused the US Admiral Jesse Oldendorf's offer to relieve her of further duties.

The assault took place on January 9th. More ships were hit by the fanatical *kamikazes*, including the *Columbia* for the second time and the battleship *Mississippi*. During the landings the *Australia* sustained her fifth hit from suicide bombers. In the whole operation the Japanese suicide planes damaged forty-five Allied vessels, sinking four; 738 men were killed, and nearly 1,400 wounded. Congratulating the naval forces on their part in the landings, Admiral William F. Halsey said: 'I am so proud of you that no words can express my feelings . . . superlatively well done!'

The landings received little opposition. Once MacArthur's intention had been obvious, it was too late for Yamashita to do anything effective to stop it, apart from attempting to destroy the American fleet by destroying his own air force. Yamashita's tactics were to ignore the beach-heads but to make a stand in the hills.

The first landing was at 9.30 a.m., and by 9.40 all advance echelons were on the beach. By late afternoon four divisions were assembling; by sunset American troops had penetrated three miles inland. During the following days MacArthur pushed his men on south-east, straight towards Manila. By January 15th the Agno River had been successfully crossed. There were stories of starving Allied prisoners in the capital, and MacArthur was in a hurry. He was also, it would seem, in his element. A great deal of his life had been associated with the Philippines. There, more than anywhere else, he was already a legendary figure. To many of the Filipinos he was a kind of superman. His father before him had won a great victory on the same scene. He knew the terrain well; every wrinkle of its topography. He must, in days of peace, have considered and practised many times the way to invade Luzon and take Manila. No one was in a better position to undertake the task he had been given; it was almost his right. The landings had been a brilliant success. As he himself said of his plan: 'It worked like a charm.' He was everywhere; working himself to near-sickness. His appetite went; he seemed to some to be nervy and over-tense. Some even dared to suggest, but not in his presence, that he spent more time right up at the front than a general who wished to get a clear picture of the battle should.

When Major-General Kenney called at headquarters to report, he noticed that MacArthur was not eating. The Commander-in-Chief said he was so tired he could not eat. Kenney had to leave early the next morning and, not wanting to disturb MacArthur, he told the orderly officer to apologize for him. Said the officer: 'General MacArthur left for the front two hours ago, sir.'

Douglas MacArthur had a tremendous reputation, of which he was extremely conscious and inordinately proud. Yamashita was proving stubborn; and not only stubborn, but clever too. The American force had to pass over a series of ridges. These not only provided fine cover for artillery, they were also heavily fortified with tunnels and caves, which were by then well supplied and prepared. At some places tanks had been half-buried in the ground and were being used as pill-boxes in support of infantry. It was quite clear that the line which MacArthur had drawn on his map was going to be a difficult one to follow. The Japanese were going to fight hard and well. Three American columns pushed on with a front of thirty miles, but Manila, to say nothing of Tokyo, was still a long way off.

(v)

In London and south-east England the final terror of the war made the winter a strange mixture of excitement at the prospect of victory and of fear of a dreaded new German weapon: the V.2 rocket bomb. On the home front there had been a slight moving away from the rigid austerity of wartime regulations. The previous summer had been a brilliant one; large crowds had watched cricket at Lord's, disturbed only now and again by the ominous purring of 'flying bombs' (V.1s). Bread was whiter. Cheering and singing repatriated prisoners of war were arriving at London and Liverpool docks in beflagged boats to the noisy welcome of wailing ships' hooters. Barrage balloons, which had made the skies ugly for so long, were disappearing. Fire-guard duties were being relaxed. Articles in the newspapers were beginning to be about such matters as what attention a car needs after being laid up for five years, and how to renew tennis-courts.

In the early weeks of the winter the occasional plane-launched flying bomb had still come rumbling across the Channel and the North Sea, blindly speeding over the fields of Kent, clearly seen by people on the ground, who were able to do nothing to stop it, and on towards London, where suddenly the rumbling had stopped, to be followed by an even louder silence while everyone for miles cowered in fear under the nearest shelter they could find, with up to a minute to wonder whether their time had come at last. Only London, of all the cities of the war, had this particularly nerve-racking kind of attack on a large scale. The next most-favoured targets were the liberated cities of Antwerp and Liège. Only Londoners and Belgians who were there know how, after a long war, it had seemed the final insult to nerves and sensitivities already tautened to full stretch. Even more calculated to cause psychological strain were the V.2s. For these descended from the sky with no warning whatever. They could blow a man and his home into infinity, or blast him to nothing at his place of work, in the street, or as he sat in the cinema. The only certain thing was that it would come before he could do anything to help himself. The effect of this worked in two ways. In the first place it meant that there was, in effect, a permanent warning. Death could come at any time. On the other hand, one could be only a few miles away from a V.2 and know little or nothing about it, there having been no air-raid siren. All this made for a particular and weird atmosphere in London during the first quarter of 1945. The capital had already, as far as fatal casualties were concerned, taken the heaviest load of anywhere in the Commonwealth. By February 1945 one in five of all British deaths during the war had been Londoners. The war death rate among Londoners at this time was one in 130, compared to one in 165 for the whole of England, one in 175 for New Zealand, and one in 775 for the United States.

Germany had been working on rocket bombs for at least fifteen years before the war, much of the research being directed by a Colonel Dornberger. In 1937 a rocket organization had been set up at Peenemünde on the Baltic coast. It seems that there had been some indecision as to whether to concentrate on the flying bombs, favoured by the *Luftwaffe*, or on the V.2, favoured by the army, and this had held up development. In 1940 Hitler had reduced the claims of the V.2 to a low level of priority, thus delaying its production and operation by several months. Only a few months before, in October 1939, a rocket had climbed five miles with perfect stability (the success of this was largely due to a brilliant young scientist, Werner von Braun). In Britain at this time no official research had been made into long-range rocket projectiles. Some comparatively small rockets were produced in 1940 for anti-aircraft purposes, but had practically no success (they were later to be of inestimable value when fired from aircraft at tanks, vehicles and shipping). The first British rocket battery was not formed until November 1940. The commanding officer was Major Duncan Sandys, who spent most of the war engaged in rocket investigations. One of his tasks was to discover whether Britain, or the Germans at Peenemünde, could send up a rocket with a warhead of quite exceptional power (i.e. atomic). In 1944 Sandys had said: 'In the future the possession of superiority in long-distance rocket artillery may count for as much as superiority in naval or air power. There are signs that the Americans have already embarked upon an ambitious programme of development, and it is possible that the Russians are not far behind as they are much impressed by this new technique.' But by 1945 no effective method had been devised to stop 'the drizzle of rockets' (in the phrase of the official historian) on London. Weighing twelve and a half tons, with a one-ton warhead, the V.2 had a range of 207 miles.

The average monthly production during the winter was 618; about 1,300 fell on England, causing 9,277 casualties, nearly a third of them fatal. Rockets were also aimed at Antwerp and Brussels. It seemed that Hitler's men had, indeed, produced a trump card.*

Intelligence discovered that the rockets came from Holland; from the race course at The Hague, the neighbourhood of Wassenaar, the pine woods and sand dunes close to Leiden, and from Walcheren Island. These areas were heavily bombed, but with no effect apart from the destruction of much Dutch property. Until land forces could overrun the area there was clearly to be no respite for the Londoners. Some alarm was caused in the United States when Admiral Ingram, commanding the US Atlantic Fleet, said: 'Robot bomb raids against New York and the east coast are possible and probable within the next thirty or sixty days.'

In London during the winter rockets fell on the doctors' quarters of a hospital, and on a blind people's home. One fell on a cinema during a performance, another at lunch-time on a crowded suburban store, Woolworth's at New Cross. In the latter case the building and the pavement outside were crowded with women and children. This rocket killed 160 people and seriously injured as many more. Another rocket fell outside the LCC Infectious Diseases Hospital at Blackheath, demolished a hotel, blew a passing bus into small bits, and shattered the hospital. Sixty-eight people were killed by a rocket which fell on a domestic street in Islington: Mackenzie Road. A rocket fell into the middle of Farringdon Market, when the stalls were crowded with shoppers, and killed 110 and injured 123 people. Another destroyed two blocks of flats in Stepney, which had seen so much of the Blitz four years before, reduced them both to rubble and killed 134 occupants. Another disaster occurred at Dalston Public Library, where many women with shopping-bags who had called in to change a book had been peacefully examining the shelves one second and were blown into eternity the next. One of the problems, as always, was rescuing people trapped under heaps of débris. On one occasion five people were trapped for two hours while rescue workers, aided by police and firemen, tried to extricate them. Fire broke out, setting surface wreckage ablaze. While firefighters attempted to keep the flames from spreading downwards, the rescue workers continued digging feverishly. The entombed people were rescued. After another rocket which fell on a terrace of

* The Japanese had perfected a V.1 type rocket, launched from a bomber in flight and piloted by a suicide pilot; about fifty were launched against US positions in the Pacific.

small houses during the night, an anti-aircraft searchlight unit was rushed to the scene while rescuers worked furiously to bring out people still alive. A tunnel nearly five yards long had to be drilled through smashed débris and masonry. The tunnel collapsed, trapping three firemen. When these were eventually extricated they were found to be seriously injured and were taken to hospital. Volunteers took their place and the tunnel was completed again. During the morning two brothers, one aged eight and one five, were rescued on this site. There were hundreds of other episodes, resulting from the rocket bombs, where hurried improvisation and the rescuing skill that ordinary London people had learnt in recent years saved numerous families from death by suffocation in ruins.

Lord Beaverbrook, the Lord Privy Seal, writing to his friend Harry Hopkins, well illustrated the prevailing tension: 'The rockets come to us in London at the rate of six a day. Last Saturday morning we suffered a disaster when one fell in a suburban district, causing the heaviest single bomb incident of the war. I do not know how much injury we shall have to sustain before the winter is over. The slogan of "London Can Take It" will prevail. But there may be quite a lot to take. The Prime Minister is fully alive to the situation. He knows very well how much the public can stand before they begin to grumble, and knows, too, how to suppress the grumbles when they come. His method is to set up in the people's minds a feeling of kinship with the men at the battle-front. Anyway, the rocket is to be preferred to the flying-bomb with its two warnings —first the siren and then the noise of the approaching engine. The experience was strange indeed. For while there was noise there was safety. Only when the engine cut off and silence fell did you stand in need of prayer.'

(vi)

The long and strangely sinister quiet on the Eastern Front, which had lasted from August 1944, was rudely shattered on the early morning of January 12th, when the first of a series of brilliantly synchronized and tremendously powerful Soviet attacks was launched. The halt on this front was due, as Stalin had told Churchill, to atrocious weather. But this would not have applied the previous autumn. At that time the reason had been stated to be severe difficulties of supply. But if this was so, it is strange that these difficulties

34

did not also affect the Hungarian front, where the lines of communication were very much longer. There is no doubt that the Russians suffered a defeat to the east of Warsaw (two armoured divisions were said to be lost), but not a defeat strong enough to halt a whole Soviet army for nearly half a year. Whatever the Russian reasons, which have never been fully explained, it is certain that the Polish resistance led by the gallant if rash Bor-Komorowsky was successfully crushed by the Germans during this five-month delay. The Poles have always been the first to suspect the Russians of the very worst motives.

Owing to the heavy fighting on the Danube, especially at Budapest, and the attempt to build up a powerful defence of East Prussia, the centre of the German line in the east was relatively weak. The reserves were few, defences thin. The German divisions here contained a great number of newly raised young troops of little fighting value. The assault they had to face on the 12th was preceded by an enormous artillery bombardment, and German resistance crumbled during the day. Some units were isolated and remained fighting in strong positions, others fled before the irresistible force of the mighty Red Army that had been preparing for this day for so long. The Russian tanks of Marshal Konev's army roared across Poland towards Cracow and Silesia. Two days later another Russian army, under Marshal Zhukov, launched a second blow at the German line, to the north of Konev's forces, between Lodz and Warsaw. Here, too, German resistance, although desperate and sometimes courageous, collapsed before the Russian pressure. The Red Army's superiority was at least threefold. North of Warsaw Marshal Rokossovsky's forces crashed through the German forces attempting to secure East Prussia. Zhukov's armour had soon reached far west of Warsaw, and began turning round to attack the city from that side. This led to the evacuation of the ruined Polish capital by the Germans, and it was occupied by the Russians on January 17th. In an Order of the Day by Stalin, however, the Russian Generalissimo made much of the forcing of a passage across the Vistula in a frontal attack. The announcement of the taking of the city had first been made by Radio Lublin, the propaganda-broadcasting system of the Polish Provisional Government. As news of the city's condition began to drift slowly through the news channels, the world could only pause in amazement at the thoroughness of war's devastation. This great European city had enjoyed a population of 1,289,000 on January 1st, 1939. It had surrendered on September 27th, 1939, after a

THE EASTERN FRONT,
January-April, 1945.

MILES

100   50   0   100

German Front, January 11th, 1945.
Pre -War German Frontier, 1939.
German-Held Territory, April 6th. 1945.

COURLAND

Riga

BALTIC SEA

Memel

Rostock
Wismar
Stettin

Königsberg
Pillau
Danzig

EAST
PRUSSIA

CHERNIAKOVSKY

BERLIN
Frankfurt

Torgau

Leipzig

Poznan

R. Vistula Warsaw

Lodz

ROKOSSOVSKY

ZHUKOV

P O L A N D

Breslau

Dresden

CZECHO

Prague

R. Oder

Cracow

Lvov

KONEV

PETROV

S L O V A K I A

R. Danube

Vienna

Berchtesgaden

Budapest

MALINOVSKY

AUSTRIA

H U N G A R Y

TOLBUKHIN

I T A L Y

Zagreb

Trieste

R. Danube

ADRIATIC
SEA

Y U G O S L A V I A

heroic resistance of twenty days. For five years and four months it had been ruled by Hitler's lieutenants. It had suffered aerial and land bombardment so intense that hardly a building in the whole city remained undamaged. Latterly it had been ravished by a bitter and bloody revolt. Its population in January 1945 was approximately 25,000.

The greatest Soviet offensive of the war was now under way. One hundred and eighty divisions were rolling across the plains of central Poland. Within a week the Russian armour, leaving behind many pockets of German resistance in a huge area that bubbled with desperate fighting like some boiling cauldron, had advanced 100 miles. Hitler insisted on a policy of unyielding defence; there was to be no tactical withdrawal. This meant some of the most fanatical, if hopeless, fighting of the whole war by German troops, as the Russians were known to take few prisoners. Casualties were appalling. In twelve days there were 200,000 German dead. Pockets of resistance continued to fight to the death at Courland, Danzig and in east Prussia. The ten divisions of the 6th Panzer Army were transferred from the west, but it was like throwing a leaf against a tornado. There was no question of a large-scale movement of troops from west to east, always the classic German move since Bismarck, as the railways, bombed and short of fuel, were only able to move one-third of the traffic they had carried six months earlier. As for the great autobahn, which stretched from the Rhine nearly to the Oder, there was little petrol with which to make use of it. It had always been Hitler's belief that in a drastic emergency these interior lines of communication would save him.

By the end of January most of Poland, gasping and almost as dead as a nation can be, was freed from Nazi rule. Konev had advanced 225 miles along the road from Warsaw to Berlin. By January 27th Zhukov had crossed the German frontier and was less than 100 miles from Berlin. On the same day Hitler threw his last card, the *Volkssturm*, or Home Guard, against the first of the Soviet assault. Youths and old men marched side by side, wondering, singing and afraid.

Cracow, the ancient capital, and Lodz and Danzig, where the war had begun on September 1st, 1939, all fell.* Poznan was surrounded. Breslau was being attacked from several directions and

* The people of Gdansk (Danzig) are fully conscious of the city's history, and every year mark the anniversary of the war's start with quiet but moving ceremony; there is no area in Europe where anti-Germanism (by no means excluding East Germany) is so strong.

seemed destined for a siege. There was now only one barrier left at which the German forces could possibly stand, and at which the German Chief of Staff in the east, General Heinz Guderian, could perhaps gain enough time to launch a counter-stroke—the Oder River. After that there were only fifty miles to Berlin. Stalin, on his way to the conference at Yalta, assembled his generals (who apparently had a poor opinion of his generalship) at Minsk. He explained to them the dangers of their present position. A sudden and unexpected defeat of the Red Army at this juncture could have a catastrophic psychological effect on the Russian troops who were so near to victory. He warned them that the Red Army, no longer fighting on its own territory, could not expect to have the same resistance to any set-back as previously. It was, he explained, most important to him politically that the Red Army should now proceed to Berlin without further delay. He then dispatched his commanders, suitably aware of their responsibilities, back to their respective fronts—and made his way to the Crimea.

(vii)

On January 29th Churchill flew out of London on the Skymaster that had been given to him by the Chief of the US Air Staff, General H. H. Arnold. His daughter Sarah flew with him, as nearly always, to attend to his personal needs and provide loving companionship during the stress of the coming conference. Most of the Prime Minister's staff, and the officials, flew in two other planes. During the journey Churchill developed a high temperature. He arrived at Malta's famous Luqa airfield, which for years had been the target of countless German and Italian bombers, in the chill early morning of the following day. There he learnt that one of the other two aircraft had crashed near the island of Pantellaria; there were only five survivors. It could well have been the Prime Minister's plane that had crashed. 'Such', said Churchill, 'are the strange ways of fate.' On the morning of February 2nd he watched from the deck of a British warship as the USS *Quincy* steamed into Valletta harbour, under a glorious sunny sky. As the American ship got closer and slid slowly towards its berth, Churchill was able to discern the unmistakable figure of the President sitting on the bridge. The two men raised their arms in mutual salute. Suddenly an escort of Spitfires roared overhead, guns thudded out a salute, a band at the harbour struck up 'The Star-Spangled Banner'. It was a most impressive scene. The great American President had crossed the ocean once more to exert his country's will on the shaping of the world.

At six o'clock that evening the two leaders reviewed the report that had been prepared for them by the Combined Chiefs of Staff during the previous three days. This meeting had been, perhaps, the most bitter between Allied commanders of the entire war. There had been an almost total lack of understanding and sympathy on both sides. Dissension had arisen over Eisenhower's plan for the final defeat of Germany in the west. In outline this consisted of assaulting the Germans west of the Rhine and then establishing bridge-heads. He then planned two deep and simultaneous thrusts into Germany: one, under Montgomery, across the northern edge of the Ruhr, which would be by-passed, and then on across the north German plain towards Hamburg and the Baltic; the other, south of the Rhur, between Frankfurt and Stuttgart, was to head towards Kassel and then the heart of Germany. The British were totally against this plan. They wanted all the effort to be made by the northern thrust under Montgomery, which seemed to be the most important. There even seemed some hope of reaching Berlin and achieving a knock-out blow by this route, they argued, whereas the southern thrust could achieve nothing except a useless punch into the flabby belly of Germany. They were most anxious to secure all ports on the North Sea before the Russians. Although they confined their arguments to the purely military aspect, political motives were clearly behind their thinking. The Americans viewed these British objections with extreme scepticism. It seemed to them only too obvious what the British were up to: a trick to get all the glory at the end of the war for the Twenty-First Army Group, its British and Canadian troops, and particularly for its commander, Field-Marshal Bernard Montgomery. They saw 'Monty's' work in the whole affair. (Churchill has denied this, stating that it was a combined British view.)

Eisenhower was not present at the conference. He was represented by his Chief of Staff, Lieutenant-General Walter Bedell Smith, who defended his chief's intentions with some vehemence and, apparently, not a little volubility. The arguments reached a high pitch. General George C. Marshall, US Chief of Staff in Washington, said that if the British plan were accepted he would recommend to Eisenhower that he ought to ask to be relieved of his command. The British gave in, but only after it had been agreed that of the two thrusts the northern one was to be the most powerful, receiving a predominance in divisions and supply.

The document which the two Western leaders now studied contained little that revealed this violent and bitter controversy; a controversy that had been settled but which was not to be forgotten. Churchill still viewed the American plan 'with some concern', but the matter was hardly discussed with the President.

Roosevelt took the opportunity of getting Britain to agree to withdrawing two divisions from Greece, a victory which, with his persistent suspicions of British intentions in that country, must have particularly pleased him. The President was also anxious to withdraw troops from the Italian theatre to North-West Europe, but Churchill stressed that 'it was very important to follow up any German surrender in Italy and . . . that we ought to occupy as much of Austria as possible as it was undesirable that more of Western Europe than necessary should be occupied by the Russians'. It was agreed, however, that three divisions were to be sent from Italy to the Western Front.

A few hours later a large party dined together on the *Quincy*, and the talks between Stettinius and Eden that had taken place were informally discussed. Everything seemed very much in order. There had been 'agreement' over the military plan in the West. There had been 'wide agreement' on political issues between the two Foreign Secretaries. If this agreement had been reached by the British giving way to the Americans at every point, it was only to be expected. Britain might have been the senior partner in the association as far as length of service in the Second World War was concerned, but America was senior in every other matter, especially in the might of her munitions and manpower. Besides, the British considered it absolutely essential that the two Western allies should present a united front when meeting Stalin.

The President must have been glad to get the brief Malta meeting over—he had always considered it of little account. Indeed, he still had fears that it could be positively dangerous; it was essential to his plan of campaign that he and Stalin should deal freely together without the latter having any suspicions of the two Western powers 'ganging-up' against him. Moreover, Roosevelt was anxious to return to Washington as soon as possible. He was feeling none too well. Several people in Malta, including Admiral E. J. King, were shocked at the President's sickly appearance, particularly worrying after a calm and relaxing sea voyage. Roosevelt had not bothered to study the pre-conference briefs prepared for him by the State Department on the voyage, and had enjoyed something of a holiday. James F. Byrnes wrote: 'Later, when I saw some of these splendid studies, I greatly regretted they had not been considered on board ship. I am sure the failure to study them was due to the President's illness. And I am sure that only President Roosevelt, with his intimate knowledge of the problems, could have handled the situation so well with so little preparation.' Byrnes was disconcerted to observe the President sitting with his mouth hanging open during the cinema shows.

That same night, of February 2nd, saw more activity than the little Luqa airfield had ever known before. At ten-minute intervals the transport planes took off, carrying the 700 persons of the British and American delegations through a dark night to the conference at Yalta, 1,400 miles away, where the world's three greatest leaders were meeting expressly to discuss the shape of the world during the coming peace. As his plane trundled through the night, Churchill went to bed. For him the meeting at Malta had not been satisfactory. His hope of strengthening the Anglo-American alliance, through the mutual concern of the two countries over the Polish question, had met with a strange and disappointing frustration. Perhaps there had not been enough time. Perhaps the President did not wish at this juncture to have his eyes opened any more than they were already. There was still a little time to save the situation—but precious little. In any event, Churchill was almost resigned to the fact that Eastern Europe was lost. Only Poland and Germany remained. The President had only been at Malta a few hours; Churchill had hardly had more than a few minutes with him alone. All in all, the Prime Minister was in a disheartened mood as he dropped off to sleep. Roosevelt, in his plane, rested as best he could, his mind wrestling, as it always did, with physical pain, his thoughts on the enigmatic 'Uncle Joe' with whom he had come so far to reason. In the cockpit of the plane the navigator studied the latest weather report for the airport of Saki, near Yalta, in the Crimea. It indicated poor conditions: snow and extreme cold.

2 Exultant Discord

2 EXULTANT DISCORD

The planes started to land at Saki airport late the next morning. Churchill's was one of the first to get there, and he stood waiting for a while in the bitter cold for the President to arrive. As Roosevelt was lifted from his plane, Churchill noted that he looked 'frail and ill'. They inspected a guard of honour, and then were led into a marquee for drinks with Molotov, who had come to welcome the two Western leaders. There followed a long drive, about eighty miles, from Saki to Yalta.* Churchill, never a man to forget such matters, had cabled Stalin to tell him that his party would have lunched on the plane. In fact, they had kept sandwiches for the car, and as soon as they left the airport Churchill began to eat. He was therefore surprised when his car pulled in at a house beside the road, where he found Molotov awaiting him with a magnificent meal. 'He was in the best of humours and offered us all the delicacies of the Russian table. We did our best to conceal the fact that we had already blunted our appetites.' The President's party 'had apparently slipped past unawares'. The journey continued. Here and there Russian soldiers, some of them women, lined the road, and in the streets of villages through which the cavalcade hurtled, curious country folk peered at the famous British imperialist as he passed. Suddenly the road descended from the mountains and, far below, could be seen the glistening Black Sea. The climate dramatically changed. It was cool, sunny and mild.

The three national delegations were centred on three large,

---

* Churchill recalls that this took 'nearly eight hours'. It is more probable that it *seemed* that long.

ornate palaces. The Soviets were at Yusupov Palace. Here Stalin* had assembled his machinery for running the war, and here also was the Permanent Committee of the Politburo to follow the negotiations on the spot. The committee consisted of Beria, Molotov, Malenkov, Bulganin, Voroshilov and Mikoyan. Stalin's son Basil acted as secretary to the committee. (Several people brought members of their families along to the conference in one role or another; apart from Sarah Churchill Oliver, Roosevelt and Harriman both had daughters with them, and Harry Hopkins's son was present.) The committee was to become more than a nuisance to Stalin in the following days. He was already having trouble with Molotov, who suspected him of having become far too close personally with Roosevelt at Tehran. Molotov saw it as his duty to protect Stalin from the wiles of this charming but dangerous American statesman. All Stalin's decisions at the conference had to be referred to the committee, which, although it could not challenge Stalin's authority, could act as a brake on him. Stalin also had with him his three chiefs of staff, with whom he conferred every day at midnight precisely or after the business of the conference was done. A direct telephone linked him with the headquarters of Konev, Zhukov and Rokossovsky.

All the Russian delegates, Stalin included, were used occasionally to living rough. The Western delegates were not. The lack of comfort at Yalta brought astonishment, mirth and embarrassment to nearly all of them. Stalin, especially, was bemused by the tales he heard of their fussy ways. He had thought they had come to Yalta to work; but if it was a holiday they wanted, then he could provide that too. He ordered those responsible to see that nothing was spared for the comfort of the foreign visitors.

President Roosevelt was at the Livadia Palace, close to Stalin's, but even more magnificent in appearance. It had been a summer home of the Czars. Admiral King was assigned the Czarina's boudoir, and was endlessly teased about this throughout the conference by diplomats and high-ranking servicemen. The Russians had spent three weeks renovating the palace, but, noted Byrnes, 'some of the conveniences we fortunate Americans are accustomed to were missing'. Sherwood described the accommodation as 'unexceptionable for those on the Very Important Person level'. Sixteen US Army colonels had to share one bedroom. Hopkins was

---

* Sherwood says that Stalin did not arrive till the day after the Western delegations. In fact, he was there at least two days before them (he cabled Churchill from Yalta on February 1st).

44

sick. He spent all the time in his bedroom, only coming downstairs to the Grand Ballroom of the Livadia Palace (where, in deference to Roosevelt's disability, all the official conferences were held) for the big meetings.

Yalta had, in fact, only been vacated by the Germans ten months before. When the Russians had returned to the Crimea they had found it almost a waste land, blackened and burned by the enemy. They had done their best to restore the resort to something like its former glory by detaching some thousands of soldiers to repair the roads, fill in bomb craters and redecorate and refurnish the three leading palaces (among other things, thousands of panes of glass had to be replaced). The best hotel staff in Moscow (which may not have been saying a great deal) were brought down to the Black Sea for the occasion. Moscow's hotels were practically denuded of carpets for the occasion. All this, it seems, was not enough.

It was very noticeable to everyone at Yalta that the palace assigned to the British was easily the most shabby of the three. Not only that, their palace, the Vorontzov Palace, was five miles out of town,* while the other two huddled almost side by side. Nothing could have indicated more bluntly whom the Russians considered the more important guests. Roosevelt must have reflected that he could hardly have planned it better himself. There was, however, some aptness in the choice, for the Vorontzov Palace had been built by an Englishman for a Russian Ambassador to the Court of St James. Those of the British delegation who could not fit into the palace stayed at two small rest-houses about a mile away, five or six sleeping to a room. Churchill and his delegation were warned that the area had not been completely cleared of mines, except for the immediate grounds of the house. Churchill, with characteristic sweep of eye, took in the scene: 'Behind the villa, half Gothic and half Moorish in style, rose the mountains, covered in snow, culminating in the highest peak in the Crimea. Before us lay the dark expanse of the Black Sea, severe, but still agreeable and warm even at this time of the year. Carved white lions guarded the entrance to the house, and beyond the courtyard lay a fine park with sub-tropical plants and cypresses. In the dining-room I recognized the two paintings hanging each side of the fireplace as copies of family portraits of the Herberts at Wilton.' Yalta harbour was still full of mines and sunken vessels, so the British and American warships, which were the sole reliable links of the Western delegations with

* According to Churchill; twelve miles according to Sherwood. *See* Notes.

their home countries, had to anchor off Sebastopol, about forty miles away.

At the Vorontzov Palace as many as twenty high-ranking officers shared one bathroom, hilariously reminding many of them of their schooldays. Sir Charles Portal, Chief of the Air Staff, objected to the bathroom door being locked when beyond lay the lavatory. As delegates wandered round the palace, viewing with dismay its long, draughty corridors and sparse furnishings, more inconveniences were discovered. Portal, admiring a large glass tank with plants in it, casually remarked that it contained no fish. Two days later a consignment of goldfish arrived. At cocktail time someone noticed that there was no lemon peel in the drinks. Next day a whole lemon tree was placed in the hall. Anthony Eden was surprised to find that the windows of his room did not open. Instead of a proper desk for him to work at, the only thing that could be found was a small French table with unequal legs. Most important of all, a bed for the Prime Minister had only just arrived. Churchill liked to sleep in a large bed. Before his arrival the advance staff discovered that the one supplied to him was extremely narrow. It was suggested to the Russians, that, as Roosevelt and Stettinius both had double beds, could not Stettinius and Churchill do a swap—so that at least the two heads of state had large beds each. This could not be done. Instead, a special train was sent to Moscow to return with a large double bed for the Prime Minister.

General Sir Leslie Hollis has recalled that at the rest-houses, also, as many as twenty would be queueing each morning to use the wash-house. Everyone lived in barrack-room conditions. While those who had served a long war in more humble positions might have reflected that all this did the 'brass-hats' and politicians no harm, it was at any rate enough to make everyone anxious to conclude the conference as soon as possible.

The first move was made by Stalin at three o'clock on Sunday afternoon, February 4th. He called on Winston Churchill at the Vorontzov Palace, and the two leaders discussed the progress of the war. Stalin was in an optimistic mood. He said that already the Red Army had bridge-heads over the Oder; that Germany was short of coal and bread; that her transport was badly damaged. The *Volkssturm* were untrained, badly led and ill-equipped. He considered the Ardennes offensive a stupid adventure that had been done for prestige. The best German generals were no longer on the scene, with the possible exception of Guderian. He felt that Germany was no longer a power of much consequence. Churchill then took him to his map-room, which had been mounted and prepared exactly as it was in London. He called on Field-Marshal Sir Harold Alexander to explain the situation in Italy, the only front in Europe in which the British were predominant. Stalin then made a comment no doubt calculated to further dampen Churchill's powder, which was already wet enough. As there was nothing much happening in Italy, he asked, why did Churchill not redirect some British divisions from that front, transfer them to Yugoslavia and Hungary and direct them on Vienna? He must have known that something like this was what Churchill had for long wanted, only prevented from doing so by American recalcitrance.

'The Red Army,' Churchill now answered, 'may not give us time to complete the operation.'

The meeting had been cordial and easy. It was noticed that Stalin had chosen to call on Churchill first, which, as Britain was the senior partner in the war, was strictly correct.

At four o'clock 'Uncle Joe' called on Roosevelt. Here the meeting was more jovial. A joke was made about whether the Russians would get to Berlin before the Americans to Manila. There was a resumé of the military situation on Russian and American fronts, but with far less formality than the one in the Vorontzov Palace. Roosevelt asked how Stalin had got on with de Gaulle, who had recently visited Moscow. 'The most obstinate man I have met in my life,' said the Generalissimo. Roosevelt explained that there had been some disagreement between himself and Churchill over policy towards France, and in other matters. On this note the two leaders left Roosevelt's private study, where the talk had taken place, and repaired to the ballroom a few minutes before 5 p.m. for the first formal session of the conference.

(ii)

No sooner had the delegates seated themselves round the table and a hush fallen on the assembly than Marshal Stalin suggested that President Roosevelt should preside over the meetings. This the President was delighted to accept. The stage was now set—with Stalin in one corner and Churchill in the other. Roosevelt was to be the referee, and both corners believed he was, if anything, slightly biased in each of their favours.

This first discussion dealt almost entirely with military matters. The atmosphere was cordial and friendly. The Russian Chief of Staff, General Antonov, read a paper giving a long and detailed exposition of the situation on the Eastern Front, and General George C. Marshall reviewed the situation in the West. Churchill then suggested that the Russian offensive could be helped by an Anglo-American expedition across the Adriatic, which would delve into the Balkans and join up with the Russian left flank, an idea similar to that suggested by Stalin just over an hour before. His proposal was now met with disinterest, not only by Roosevelt but by Stalin as well, and was not mentioned again. It was decided that the demand for a German unconditional surrender should be persisted in; a move that had its opponents in both Western delegations.

After this meeting Roosevelt was host at dinner at the Livadia Palace. The President's personal Filipino mess-men served the strictly Russian food. Once again the atmosphere was cordial, no doubt helped by the vodka and five different wines. The only sour note of the day seems to have been struck when Charles E. Bohlen, the President's special adviser on Russian affairs from the State Department, had a brief exchange with Andrei Vyshinsky. During this dinner Churchill pointed out that he was the only one of the three leaders present who could be removed from office at any moment by the votes of his people, and yet he was constantly being described as a reactionary. Stalin replied that evidently the Prime Minister of Great Britain was worried about the result of the forthcoming election. Churchill said that, on the contrary, he did not fear the election.

After the meal Roosevelt and Stettinius were alone for a few minutes with Stalin and the Russian interpreter. Stalin said: 'You are mistaken in believing that I am a dictator like Hitler.' He said that he had difficulties with Molotov, whom he found 'difficult to bring to reason'. He was also worried about the situation in the Ukraine, where any negotiations about the Polish eastern frontier would be closely watched.

At breakfast the following morning, Monday, February 5th, Roosevelt received his White House mail by courier. The mail had been dispatched from Washington five days before. This meant that the President was now at the limit of the distance he could travel from Washington under the ten-day limitation on his power to act on Congressional bills. It was now known to the President and his party that Manila had been reached by MacArthur's force on Luzon.

The next meeting began at 3.45 p.m. that day, after a very heavy lunch at which Molotov was host, and during which Harriman had proudly announced 'the fall' of Manila;* so many mock-formal toasts had been drunk that the atmosphere was again one of smiling benevolence all round.

The discussion opened on the question of the future of Germany. It was already agreed by all three leaders that Germany should be dismembered: Roosevelt was inclined to think it should be split into five parts; Stalin had agreed. Churchill wanted only two states— Prussia and Austro-Bavaria, with the Ruhr under international control. Churchill now pointed out that there was so much to study in this matter, including historic, ethnographical and economic factors, that they could not possibly reach a decision there and then. Roosevelt suggested the question should be examined by the Foreign Secretaries. This was agreed, and there the matter was left.

A long exchange then developed between Churchill and Stalin on whether France should be allotted a zone of occupation in Germany, and whether she should have a representative on the Allied Control Council. Stalin was clearly not impressed with French claims. He thought that Yugoslavia and Poland were more entitled to consideration than France. He said he did not mind France being given a zone, so long as the British and Americans supplied the area out of their own zones. He certainly would not be prepared to give the French any of the Russian zone. As for a representative on the Control Council, he was very much against it. He said he could not forget that it was France that had opened the gates to Nazi Germany. He complained that de Gaulle was unrealistic; that France had done little fighting in the war. If France was given a place on the Control Council, then what would other countries who had done more fighting than France say? He pointed out that France had, at that moment, only eight divisions, while even the Lublin Government had ten—a typical and revealing statement. Soon, he said, France would be demanding a place at the Big Three conferences.

Churchill replied that there was no question of France being allowed to join the Big Three. It was an exclusive club, the entrance fee of which was five million soldiers at the very least. Such a

---

* In a series of brilliant surprise movements, MacArthur had penetrated the Japanese lines at a number of points, but the Japanese had made a strong stand at the city itself. Corregidor had to be captured by a parachute assault; the city was then open to attack from the sea, and landings took place. The outskirts were reached on February 4th. A month of bitter street fighting followed, during which the city was reduced to a shambles. Harriman's announcement was therefore premature, to say the least.

demand on the part of de Gaulle could not be tolerated. But he felt that France should have a place on the Council, as Britain alone, in the event of the withdrawal of the United States, could not defend Western Europe (against precisely whom it was not made clear). The President had already said that although the United States was prepared to take all reasonable steps to keep the peace after the war, the maintenance of a large army in Europe, 3,000 miles from home, was a step that his country would not be prepared to take. Roosevelt was inclined to sympathize with Stalin. He had a personal distaste for de Gaulle, and he referred to the occasion when de Gaulle had compared himself to him with Joan of Arc. Hopkins and Harriman, however, urged him to support the British view on this matter at least, and he eventually persuaded the reluctant Stalin to agree to both Churchill's proposals regarding France. This had been a difficult discussion, and a victory for Churchill.*

No sooner had this problem been put aside than Churchill and the Russians were at loggerheads again, this time on the question of German reparations after the war. It was soon obvious that of the several matters concerning Germany, this was the one that interested Stalin most.

I. M. Maisky, who had been Russian Ambassador in London for eleven years, and was now Molotov's deputy, outlined in English the Russian proposal. As soon as the war was over, he said, Germany should be denuded of its wealth. Factories, land, machinery, machine tools, rolling stock, investments abroad, aircraft factories and all military enterprises should be withdrawn. He explained that by withdrawn he meant actually physically carried away. Not only this, but every year for ten years payments in kind should be made by Germany. A system of priorities should be arranged so that those countries who had suffered most under the Germans should receive most reparations. The total worth of the reparations should be twenty billion dollars; of this, Russia should receive half. Germany should be allowed to retain 20 per cent of her industry, which would be enough to keep the country going.

Churchill and members of both British and American delegations had listened to this speech, so indicative of naïve Communist economic thinking, with growing depression. Churchill responded immediately. He reminded the conference of the experience after

---

* Strangely, Churchill deals with this in less than six lines. It would seem that de Gaulle has not entirely appreciated British efforts on his behalf at Yalta and Potsdam.

the First World War; an experience which he described as 'very disappointing'. He pointed out that Britain, too, had suffered greatly. Her foreign investments, which had provided so much of Britain's strength in the past, had been decimated in order to pay for the war. But in his opinion it would be impossible to extract from Germany total reparations sufficient to complete the figure that Maisky suggested should be paid to Russia alone. Besides, what would happen if Germany were reduced to utter starvation through these measures —as seemed very likely? If the intention was to bring eighty million people to the brink of starvation, were the great powers then to sit back and say 'it serves you right'? He pointed out that if you have a horse you must provide it with hay if you want it to pull the wagon— whereupon Maisky butted in: 'But the horse must not kick'. With laboured patience, Churchill tried another example. If you have a motor-car, he said, it is necessary to give it a certain amount of petrol to make it go.

Roosevelt then said that after the First War the United States had been obliged to pay out millions of dollars to Germany, and this certainly could not be allowed to happen again. But he said he supported the Soviet Union's proposal that a reparations committee should be set up. Stalin, who had been listening to the translation of all this with considerable care, then entered the discussion. He said that the trouble after the First War had been that the reparations were demanded in money; this time they should be demanded in kind. He said that 'the Reparations Commission should take in its initial studies, as a basis for discussion, the suggestion of the Soviet Government that the total sum of reparations should be twenty billion dollars and that half of it should go to the Soviet Union'.* It was agreed by all three that the Russian proposal should be examined by such a committee in Moscow, and that Stalin's words should be incorporated in the protocol to be issued after the conference (the protocol, signed by Churchill and Roosevelt, contained the statement that the committee was to consider 'the use of labour' as a means of reparation).

The President opened the discussion on the World Instrument for Peace on February 6th. He said that in the United States public opinion on this matter was decisive, and public opinion would be very much in favour of a world organization along the lines of

* It has been suggested that Stalin's insistence on this matter was due to his fear of large-scale discontent in Russia after the severities of war; when peace had arrived without much lessening of the ardours of the Soviet régime. The thought of vast wealth coming from Germany might act as a sop to the Russian people.

those suggested by the United States at the conference at Dumbarton Oaks in the autumn of the previous year. This conference had reached broad agreement on most points except the vital matter of voting rights in the Security Council. Prior to the Yalta meeting, however, Roosevelt had made a new suggestion to Churchill and Stalin. This was that unless the Big Four, i.e. Russia, America, Britain and China, were unanimous, no important actions could be carried out by the Security Council. If any one of the four disagreed, therefore, that one could render the Council powerless to act. In this way the 'exclusive club', which had won the war for the rest of the world, could protect their own interests. Roosevelt, addressing the Yalta conference, reminded them of their pledge at Tehran: 'We recognize fully that supreme responsibility resting upon us and all the United Nations to make a peace that will command the goodwill of the overwhelming mass of the peoples of the world and banish the scourge and terror of war for many generations.' Stettinius then presented the American plan in detail. There followed another long and argumentative exchange between Stalin and Churchill.

The Prime Minister began this extraordinary affair with, for him, a rather confused speech. He said he saw no dangers in Britain associating herself with the proposal of the United States, but on the other hand he was anxious that the three great powers should not appear to have the power to rule the world after the war. He thought it would be a good thing that Egypt, for instance, could raise a question in the world organization about the Suez Canal. He thought it would be wrong if states that felt they had a grievance against one of the powers that had the right of veto could not air their grievances. Britain would not fear such airing of grievances because, by means of the veto, she would be able to kill any action suggested by the world organization. He stressed that it would be wrong for the three great powers to rule the rest of the world without even allowing other countries to state their case against them. (Churchill omits this speech from his account of the conference.) The Prime Minister was followed by Stalin, who caused a surprise by saying that he had not yet had time to study the American proposal (it had been sent to him by diplomatic pouch a month before). From what he had heard of Mr Churchill's views, however, he had some doubts about the proposal. The Prime Minister seemed to think that China, if it raised the question of Hong Kong, would be content only with expressing its opinion. Similarly, he suspected that Egypt would not have much pleasure in simply expressing the opinion that the canal should be given to Egypt. She might expect a decision on the matter. He continued in this vein for some time, not allowing Churchill, who was anxiously trying to interrupt him, to speak. When Churchill was at last able to answer he said that what had really worried him was the future, after the present leaders had gone. The world could feel safe under its present leaders, but in ten years' time they might disappear. A new generation would come that had not known the horrors of the war, and the experiences that they had all lived through together. What he wanted was to secure the peace for at least fifty years, and to build up obstacles to prevent the future generations quarrelling among themselves.* Stalin replied that the real danger to the future was conflict among the Big Three present at Yalta. The danger from Germany would not be great. He feared that disputes about Hong Kong or Suez would break the unity of the three great powers. Churchill replied that normal diplomatic channels would continue as before, in no way affected by the Security Council, and would no doubt be able to deal with such problems. He said he felt certain that Marshal Stalin would not make an attack on the British Empire—verbally, of course—without discussing the matter privately with Britain first. Stalin agreed that this was so. He promised to study the plan and to discuss it further the next day. There followed a long and somewhat superficial argument about what countries, especially South American, should be admitted to the United Nations. The President seemed to enjoy this, and as soon as he had finished with the respective cases of Ecuador and Peru, Uruguay and Paraguay, the Marshal kept him going by asking: 'What about the Argentine?' This took up some time.

The discussion then turned to Poland.

The President began by admitting that he took a distant view of the Polish question. There were five or six million Poles in the United States, and most of them agreed to the Curzon Line,† realizing they would have to give up eastern Poland to Russia, but they would like some German territory in return. Stalin interrupted to say that most of the American-Poles never voted anyway. He had gone into the matter thoroughly. Taken aback by this, Roosevelt said he thought the Russians ought to modify the Curzon

* According to the shorthand notes taken at the time by James F. Byrnes this was said by Churchill; but Churchill (p. 309–10) credits the same remarks to Stalin. See Notes.

† The line put forward by Curzon and Clemenceau after the First World War, which would bring Poland's eastern frontier about 150 miles to the west.

Line so as to give the oil-bearing regions around Lvov to Poland. He thought that the question of a government for Poland was more important than the question of her boundaries. Churchill then said he agreed about the Curzon Line, and pointed out that both he and Eden had been constantly attacked for this in England. But he had always thought that because of Russia's tremendous efforts in liberating Poland her claim was founded on right rather than might. It would, however, be a magnanimous gesture that would be widely applauded if she granted the Lvov region to a much weaker power. But he, too, thought the governmental issue was far more important. He wanted the Poles to be able to live freely, and to live their own lives in their own way. It was for this very object that Britain had gone to war against Germany. Everyone knew what a terrible risk had been involved, for Britain was ill-armed at that time. It had been a risk that had nearly cost Britain its life as a nation. The question was a matter of honour. He asked for a compromise government pending free elections; one that could be temporarily recognized by all.

This was Churchill's most impassioned speech at the conference. After a short adjournment, Stalin spoke. He was clearly in an excited state. He rose to his feet and spoke beside the table (it was the only occasion during the Yalta conference that he did this). For Russia, he said, the Polish question was not so much a matter of honour as of security. Throughout history Poland had been a corridor through which Russia had been attacked. It was a matter of life and death for the Soviet Union, which thought very differently about the matter than had the Czarist government. The Czars had always wanted to suppress and assimilate Poland. The Soviet attitude, on the other hand, was to secure a strong, independent and free Poland. As for the present question of a temporary government the situation was very difficult, as the exiled government in London had described the Lublin Government as a collection of bandits and criminals. This was not calculated to help matters. Now the Lublin Government was replying in similar coin. The agents of the exiled government had killed 212 Russian soldiers. It was vital for the Red Army to have a safe rear area.

The evening was closing in, but Stalin continued along this line. At length Roosevelt suggested they should adjourn till the following day, but Churchill would not comply. Thoroughly roused himself, he pointed out, as he had so often in recent months, that the Lublin Government was not based on the expressed will of the Polish people.

He continued with this and other arguments he had used on many occasions until the President, pointing out that Poland had already been a source of trouble for over 500 years, insisted on bringing the meeting to a close.

Churchill, always meticulous in such matters, sent off a long report to Attlee, Deputy Prime Minister, which he did not finish till after 2 a.m. He concluded it by writing: 'In spite of our gloomy warning and forebodings [the conference] has turned out very well so far. It is a sheltered strip of austere Riviera, with winding Corniche roads. The villas and palaces, more or less undamaged, are of an extinct imperialism and nobility. In these we squat on furniture carried with extraordinary effort from Moscow. The plumbing and road-making has been done without regard to cost in a few days by our hosts, whose prodigality exceeds all belief. All the chiefs of staff have taken a holiday today to look at the battlefield of Balaclava. This is not being stressed in our conversations with our Russian friends.'

The conference resumed the next day, February 7th. Roosevelt suggested that two members of the Polish London Government and two of the Lublin Government should be sent for immediately and asked to agree on a provisional government in the presence of the conference. Stalin said there might not be time to arrange this. Molotov then stated that his government were prepared to accept the Curzon Line, a western boundary for Poland along the rivers Oder and Neisse, and that the Lublin Government should have a number of exiles added to it; the two Western ambassadors could discuss the exact composition with himself. Roosevelt and Churchill both considered this was evident of some progress, although the latter expressed doubts about the western frontier and the large-scale movement of population that would result.

To make matters seem even brighter, Molotov then announced that the Soviet Union was prepared to accept the veto proposal of the United States in the world organization. The only problem to be settled was how many seats were to be allotted to Russia, for the Soviet Union consisted of a number of republics. He thought that two or possibly three such republics should be admitted as original members, namely the Ukraine, White Russia and Lithuania. This was a great relief to all the Western delegates, as there had been a fear that the Russians would persist in asking for representation for all the republics. Roosevelt went into a long and woolly speech about small nations and large nations, the object apparently being to confuse the issue and to gain time to give himself what he always sought, freedom of action later. Hopkins scribbled him a note, and passed it to him, suggesting that the President should deal with the subject as quickly as possible, as 'the Russians have given in so much at this conference'. Churchill spoke out strongly in favour of the Russian proposal; he had the Dominions, and especially India, to think of. It was decided to refer the matter to the Foreign Secretaries the following day.

At the meeting of the Foreign Secretaries it was agreed that two Russian republics be admitted, and that only nations which had declared war on Germany by March 1st, or had signed the United Nations' Declaration by the last day of the Yalta conference, should be invited to attend at the first full meeting of all the United Nations which was to be held at San Francisco in April. (Stalin said he thought he could get the signatures of White Russia and the Ukraine in time.) Roosevelt said there might well be 'howls of protest' in Congress, but he would agree to support the Russian request if it were made at San Francisco. Both Churchill and Stalin agreed to support the United States having two more votes, if such a move proved necessary to soothe public opinion in America. (Roosevelt later dropped all idea of this.) There the matter was left.

As for Poland, nearly all Molotov's suggestions of the previous day were accepted by Roosevelt and Churchill, with reservations in the case of the western frontier of Poland reaching as far as the Neisse (although there was no objection to the Oder). Roosevelt asked how soon could free elections be held. 'Within a month,' replied Stalin, without hesitation. This seemed to decide Churchill; he agreed that the question of enlarging the Lublin Government should be examined by the Foreign Secretaries.*

That evening Stalin held a dinner party at the Yusupov Palace. There were a great number of toasts (one account says forty-five; another thirty-eight) in which the three leaders all spoke of each other in the most flattering terms, and also much mutual congratulation by the lesser figures. Churchill said: 'I earnestly hope that the Marshal may be spared to the people of the Soviet Union and to help us all to move forward to a less unhappy time than that through which we have recently come. I walk through this world with greater courage and hope when I find myself in a relation of friendship and intimacy with this great man.' It was, at these meetings, always the Russian custom to outdo the other countries in

* The one-party elections were not held till January 1947.

hospitality and the quantity of food and drink, especially the latter. They seemed to take a mischievious delight in this. That night the wine and vodka flowed well. Stalin replied to Churchill, describing him as 'the most courageous of all Prime Ministers in the world'. Churchill rose again: 'My hope is in the illustrious President of the United States and in Marshal Stalin, in whom we shall find the champions of peace, who after smiting the foe will lead us to carry on the task against poverty, confusion, chaos and oppression. I propose the toast to the broad sunlight of victorious peace.' Stalin replied to this in terms that astonished everyone. 'I had never believed he could be so expansive,' said Churchill.

Stalin said: 'I am talking as an old man—that is why I am talking so much. But I want to drink to our alliance, that it should not lose its character of intimacy, of its free expression of views. I know that some circles will regard this remark as naïve.* In an alliance the allies should not deceive each other. Perhaps that is naïve? Experienced diplomats may say: Why should I not deceive my ally? But I, as a naïve man, think it best not to deceive my ally even if he is a fool. Possibly our alliance is so firm just because we do not deceive each other; or is it because it is not so easy to deceive each other? I propose a toast to the firmness of our three-power alliance. May it be strong and stable. May we be as frank as possible.'† There were some more similar words. At the time most observers felt that the Russian dictator had been a little overcome by the numerous toasts and the rather emotional atmosphere. The toast has often been considered a prime example of Stalin's supposed tongue-in-cheek brand of super-cynicism. As more is learnt about the Kremlin scene at that time, however, it looks now as if this speech, unique in its terms of unequivocable friendship, was directed at the airy, but no doubt real, powers that existed behind Stalin.

The following morning the Foreign Secretaries met to discuss the Polish Government question, as agreed the previous day, but they were unable to reach agreement. The conference proper re-assembled at four that afternoon (February 9th). Molotov then made what seemed a further concession. He agreed that new members of the Lublin Government should not only include exiles living abroad, but also 'democratic leaders' from Poland itself. This

* Molotov?

† 'Throughout this phase of the war Stalin, on the one hand, advocated . . . the world condominium of the Big Three, resenting any suggestion that tended to weaken it, and on the other, he at every step betrayed his fear and suspicion of Russia's would-be partners.'—I. Deutscher. *Stalin: A Political Biography.*

THE STRUGGLE FOR POLAND, 1914-45

MILES
0   100   200   300   400

------- Oder-Neisse Line

••••••••••••• Curzon Line

━━━━━ Russian Frontier, December 1945

—·—·—·— International Frontiers, Pre-War, 1939

░░░░░ Areas annexed by Poland, 1945, considered
at the Potsdam conference

++++++++++ Russia's Western Frontier, 1914

seemed a considerable advance to both Western leaders, and Roosevelt said that the whole difference was now only a matter of words. As the Russians had agreed to hold elections in Poland shortly, both he and Churchill were reluctant to demand anything further, although Churchill raised the question of observers at the election.

On February 10th Roosevelt had a private discussion with Stalin, to which Churchill was not invited. They had already met in secret two days earlier for a short time. The only people present were the two leaders, the Russian interpreter, Averell Harriman and Charles E. Bohlen. It was agreed by Stalin that Russia would enter the war against Japan within four months of the surrender of Germany. A number of American advisers, including Admiral William D. Leahy, Chief of Staff to the President, had told Roosevelt that they did not believe Russian intervention in the Japanese war was necessary; they were not heeded by the President. In return Russia would be granted a number of territories in the Far East. These included the southern half of Sakhalin Island, Port Dairen, Port Arthur, a 50 per cent interest in the East Chinese and Manchurian railroads, the Kurile Islands, and a predominant influence over Outer Mongolia. Most of these territories affected not Japan so much as China, and China was an ally of the Western powers. Roosevelt undertook to secure Chiang Kai-shek's compliance in due course, although it was agreed that these decisions about Chinese territory should be kept from the Chinese for the time being. (He also told Stalin confidentially that he thought Hong Kong should be returned to the Chinese, or internationalized.) Stalin asked whether it would be necessary to send American troops to Korea, and when Roosevelt replied in the negative he expressed approval. All observers agree that Roosevelt was tiring rapidly by this time in the conference. Not the least surprising aspect of this strange agreement was that it committed the President (something which he always tried to avoid anyway) to accepting spheres of influence and territorial changes, both of which struck at his own philosophy. Stalin later called on Churchill, and the Prime Minister agreed to the conditions of Russian entry in the war against Japan, although, as he later made clear, 'neither I nor Eden took any part in making them'. Eden, in fact, tried to dissuade him from agreeing.*

Later that day the conference reassembled, and agreement was reached about Poland. A New Provisional Government, 'more

---

* Chiang, when told months later, was horrified at the US 'betrayal' (Wedemeyer). The two ports were returned to the Chinese in 1955, but Sakhalin and the Kuriles are in the USSR.

59

broadly based', was to be established. It would include the members of the Lublin Government and others (although no mention was made in the declaration about members of the London Polish Government). The exact composition was to be discussed by Molotov and the two Western ambassadors in Moscow with a number of Polish leaders. The new government was to hold 'free and unfettered elections as soon as possible on the basis of universal suffrage and secret ballot . . . all democratic and anti-Nazi parties shall have the right to take part and to put forward candidates'. Poland's eastern frontier was to be basically the Curzon Line, and the western frontier was to be moved to the west—its final delimitation remaining in abeyance.

Churchill was not entirely dissatisfied. The Russians had, it appeared, made a concession about the provisional government, even if the basis of it was still to be the Lublin one. If they kept to their word about the elections all might be well. His incessant fighting and pleading on behalf of the Poles had, it seemed, brought some reward.

That night it was Churchill's turn to be host at dinner. More rounds of flattering toasts were proposed and drunk. Stalin was especially generous in his terms towards the President, who looked pale and tired. Roosevelt, in his turn, moved Stalin almost to tears by saying: 'You see, Winston, there is something here that you are not capable of understanding. You have in your veins the blood of tens of generations of people accustomed to conquering. . . . We are here at Yalta to build up a new world which will know neither injustice nor violence, a world of justice and equity.' Churchill endeavoured to explain to Stalin the forthcoming General Election in Britain, which was bound to follow Hitler's defeat. The Russian leader dismissed the thought that Churchill would not continue in his eminent position. Churchill explained that there were two parties in Britain, and that he belonged to only one of them. 'One party is much better,' replied the Marshal. The evening 'passed away agreeably'. When Stalin left the Vorontzov Palace, the British delegation assembled in the hall and Churchill called for three cheers. They were boisterously given.

Next day the final declaration was signed at lunch by the three leaders in the Czar's former billiard-room at the Livadia Palace. Roosevelt's mood at this time was described as one of 'extreme exultation'. He was confident that the conference had been a real success. Hopkins later said: 'We really believed in our hearts that this was the dawn of the new day we had all been praying for and talking about for so many years.' Leahy wrote of a 'feeling of great hope, almost exultation'. Before leaving Yalta, Churchill and his daughter went off to see the battlefield of Balaclava (having got a brigadier of the Intelligence staff 'to look up all the details of the action and prepare himself to show us round'). The great statesman and historian gazed on the valley down which the Light Brigade had thundered many years before. He flew from Saki airfield on February 14th.

He intended to make a quick visit to Athens on the way home, and made sure his plane detoured over the island of Skyros, where Rupert Brooke, whom he had known in 1914, was buried. In Athens he drove through the streets in an open car, and in the evening addressed a crowd of 50,000 in Constitution Square. Suitably impressed with the grandeur of the setting, in bright evening sunlight, he made an impassioned speech, appealing for Anglo-Greek friendship. In the early hours of the following day he left for Egypt.

(iii)

Throughout the conference Roosevelt had remained ostentatiously apart from the Prime Minister, remembering the advice of Oumansky, a Soviet Ambassador to Washington, who had often warned him of the innate suspiciousness of the Russians. The conference had been five days old before he had lunched privately with Churchill, although having met Stalin alone before that. He had told Stettinius to avoid any private meeting with Eden. Convinced that Britain was now a second-rate power, in terms of armies, wealth and munitions, he sought to prove that he could be trusted by the Russians by being quick to reveal, and even magnify, every difference between Churchill and himself, particularly on colonialism. Churchill was therefore dismayed when, on the last night of the conference, Roosevelt had told him that he was going to visit Egypt on the way home. He had already summoned King Ibn Saud of Saudi Arabia, King Farouk of Egypt, and Emperor Haile Selassie of Ethiopia to meet him, on three successive days, aboard the *Quincy* on the Great Bitter Lake. It was the first Churchill had heard about this. He was, according to Hopkins, 'flabbergasted'. He attempted to find out what were the President's intentions, but no one had any very clear idea. It seemed, however, that Roosevelt believed he could make some decisive contribution to Middle East affairs in this short visit. As he might never be in the area again, he was not going to miss the opportunity. Churchill, worried about British interests in the area, told the President next day that he, too, intended to go to Egypt.

The meetings duly took place. Roosevelt was especially impressed with Ibn Saud, with whom he tried to discuss the Palestine question. The 'discussion' soon turned into a monologue by Ibn Saud. At a Press conference the President said that he had learned more about Palestine in five minutes from Ibn Saud than he had previously learnt in his whole life. But according to Hopkins, who was depressed by Roosevelt's apparent naïvety, 'the only thing he learnt, which all people well acquainted with the Palestine cause know, is that the Arabs don't want any more Jews in Palestine'.

By no means aware that the President's intentions were not in the least sinister, Churchill saw Ibn Saud two days later. A grand reception was arranged for the potentate at the Hotel du Lac at Fayoum oasis—'from which we had temporarily removed all the residents'. Churchill had been warned that neither alcohol nor tobacco was allowed in Ibn Saud's presence. He was not long in raising the matter and told the interpreter 'that if it was the religion of His Majesty to deprive himself of smoking and alcohol I must point out that my rule of life prescribed as an absolutely sacred rite smoking cigars and also the drinking of alcohol before, after and, if need be, during all meals and in the intervals between them'. The King accepted the position. Not only that, but he lavished the whole British party with priceless gifts, including jewelled swords with diamond-studded hilts. Churchill's daughter Sarah received an enormous portmanteau. Beneath a profusion of Arab robes and vessels of rare perfume she discovered some cardboard boxes; one of them contained a diamond with the valuation tag of £1,200 still attached. Eden also received a diamond. It occurred to Churchill that his own present in return, a case of perfumes, was rather outclassed, so he promised the King that he was to receive 'the finest motor car in the world'. This was duly sent out from Britain, Churchill having reported the whole affair to the Cabinet, and was almost paid for by the presents the party had received (which, with admirable self-denial, they turned over to the Treasury).

After meeting Farouk and the President of Syria, Churchill went north to say farewell to Roosevelt. At Alexandria he went aboard the *Quincy* for lunch, after which the two noble heads of state parted to go their various ways. Roosevelt steamed with the cruiser to Algiers, where he was expecting to meet de Gaulle. The Frenchman, however, had changed his mind, and a message was received from Paris saying that it was no longer convenient for him to go to Algiers —he was upset, it seemed, because the Yalta declaration had paid little attention to him and to France. This renewed example of de Gaulle's pride infuriated the President. He was further irritated by Hopkins's illness, which necessitated his being left at Algiers; for Hopkins was to have helped him prepare the speech which he was to deliver to Congress on his return. The two men parted on bad terms —Hopkins was never to see his chief again. However, the President's mood soon changed when he began to receive the flood of cables that poured in from the United States congratulating him on the Yalta communiqués which had just been published. 'It will offer a great hope to the world', said Herbert Hoover, speaking of the conference. William L. Shirer said it was a 'landmark in human history'. Alben W. Berkeley cabled: 'Accept my sincere felicitations upon the historic Joint Statement issued today. I read it to the Senate immediately upon release, and it made a profound impression. I regard it as one of the most important steps ever taken to promote peace and happiness in the world.'

Churchill reached Lyneham aerodrome, in Wiltshire, on February 19th. He was driven up to London in thick fog. The great meeting of the Big Three, which had promised little but had, so it was said, achieved much, was at an end.

(iv)

The Yalta communiqué was issued in the three capitals on February 14th. Soon everyone throughout the world was discussing it. They have discussed it ever since, mostly in terms of abuse of the Western participants or (like Robert E. Sherwood) as devoted admirers. But the Yalta conference was not an affair of simple black or white, and the men who attended it were neither gods nor superhumans above the multitude of extraneous pressures and insidious suspicions. Some things have been easy to see in the light of later history. Roosevelt's wish for 'freedom to act', which merely meant putting off decisions, was not a strong counter to Russian manoeuvres. The constant references of Churchill and Roosevelt to the feelings of their public at home did not impress the Russians. The joyful acceptance of promises that could be interpreted in two, at least, ways was premature to say the least; what the Communist interpretation of democratic elections in Poland was to be should have been clear to anyone with a cursory knowledge of Communist practice and theory. The inability, or the unwillingness, of the Western delegates to quite appreciate the full implications of occupation by the Red Army did not strengthen them in their arguments. The failure to understand that the only possible way the Red Army could be prevailed upon to withdraw from Eastern Europe was by offering some alternative in exchange, left the two Western leaders appealing to fairness, honour and the rules of 'an exclusive club'. Above all, the lack of bargaining strength that a totally united and cohesive Anglo-American front would have presented to Stalin lost any small chance there might have been of enforcing a tolerable after-war situation. On the other hand, it has been pointed out by Leahy: 'Stalin had shown a conciliatory attitude on the United Nations, on giving France a voice in the Control Council of Germany. . . . In fact, on almost every political problem, after a forceful statement of their views, the Russians had made sufficient concessions for an agreement to be reached, on paper at least. It is true that the ink was hardly dry on the Yalta Protocol before serious difficulties in interpretation arose.' How much Roosevelt's close advisers and admirers were responsible for his belief that he could deal with the Russians alone is still not clear. It is of interest to remember that one of those employed on the American Advisory Committee on Post-War Foreign Affairs was Alger Hiss. He boasted at his trial: 'It would be an accurate and not immodest statement to say that I helped to formulate the Yalta agreement.' In any event, the great issues were seldom touched on at Yalta. The decisions taken were few. A high percentage of the words spoken consisted of meaningless mutual admiration. Much of the rest consisted of side-tracking and waffle by both Roosevelt and Stalin. Stalin was quite happy to lead the talk round to whether the Argentine should be included among the United Nations. This, and a great deal else, could have been much better discussed by the Foreign Ministers at a less exceptional time. But if Yalta looks like muddled appeasement now, at the time it seemed to be preventing a clash between the Russian hordes advancing into Western Europe and the British and American armies conscious of their responsibilities to the liberated peoples. Lord Ismay has said: 'Perhaps we were all deceived by the spirit of exuberant *bonhomie* which had prevailed throughout the conference; or perhaps we preferred not to look unpleasant facts in the face.'

Some things have not been so easy to discover. To what extent Stalin was restricted by others could only then have been known to very few, and thus it is likely that the full facts will remain unrecorded and lost to history. But that he had lost some power since the conference at Tehran seems certain. It is similarly unrewarding to speculate how different things would have been if he had been free—there *is* evidence that he felt some personal warmth towards both Churchill and Roosevelt, and even sympathy for their predicaments, perhaps partly due to his own position of extreme loneliness. Certainly his heartening and continued attitude on Greece gave Churchill much hope at the time.

Since Yalta one controversy has remained above all others: can democratic, elected leaders usefully bargain and negotiate with a dictator? It seems that Stalin may well have wished to come to an accommodation with the Western powers, and almost certainly wished to preserve the alliance; but he expected the Anglo-Americans to show their goodwill by recognizing authoritarian régimes in Eastern Europe, while he showed his by providing a face-saver for the Western leaders through admitting a few non-Communists to unimportant posts and holding (one party) elections.

In February 1945 nearly everyone thought the conference a success. The future of Poland had been settled; it seemed possible that country was to be free. The Russians had made a notable concession with regard to the Lublin Government. A World Organization had been agreed to. It had been agreed that reparations from Germany should be studied; the Atlantic Charter had been reaffirmed in respect of liberated nations. . . .

The *Christian Science Monitor* said: 'The Crimea conference stands out from previous such conferences because of its mood of decision . . . it was plainly dominated by a desire, willingness and determination to reach solid decisions.' The New York *Herald Tribune* said the conference had been 'proof of Allied unity, strength and power of decision'. *Time* magazine said: 'All doubts about the Big Three's ability to co-operate in peace as well as in war seem now to have been swept away.' In London the reaction was a little more guarded. The *Daily Telegraph* described 'decisions of far-reaching importance to the future of the world'.

But not quite everyone felt relieved. In Britain there were still doubts about Poland. General Anders, commanding the Polish troops in Italy, said: 'We do not recognize and shall never recognize unilateral decisions.' But on the whole these worries and doubts were held by only a handful of people, whose protest was hardly heard above the many expressions of congratulation accorded the Prime Minister. The latter made his statement to the House of Commons on February 27th. He said: 'Most solemn declarations have been made by Marshal Stalin and the Soviet Union that the sovereign independence of Poland is to be maintained, and this decision is now joined in by both Britain and the United States. The impression I brought back from the Crimea, and from all my other contacts, is that Marshal Stalin and the Soviet leaders wish to live in honourable friendship and equality with the Western democracies. I feel also that their word is their bond. I know of no government which stands to its obligations, even in its own despite, more solidly than the Russian Soviet Government.* It is quite evident that these matters touch the whole future of the world. Sombre indeed would be the fortunes of mankind if some awful schism arose between the Western democracies and the Russian Soviet Union.' He asked the House for unanimous approval for the measures he had taken at Yalta. But a number of Members spoke in opposition. One of them was the Member of Parliament for South Lanark, Lord Dunglass, later better known as Lord Home. Dunglass had recently made a prolonged study of Communism. He pointed out that the agreements about Poland had been carried out without the consent of the Polish people, for whom Britain had gone to war. The agreement was based on an act of power. Russia's relations with Poland were the first test-case of the post-war period; a test between a great military power and her weaker neighbours. As international supervision of the forthcoming elections had not been secured, there was, he said, a certainty of the Russians exploiting the situation. Twenty-four members voted with Dunglass against the Government, and eleven members of the Government abstained. In addition, Mr H. G. Strauss, Parliamentary Secretary to the Ministry of Town and Country Planning, resigned.

Roosevelt made his speech to Congress on March 2nd. He delivered it sitting down, referring for the first time publicly to the weight of the metal braces on his legs. His mood was hardly less exultant than it had been immediately after the conference had finished. He said: 'It has been a long journey. I hope you will all

* i.e. in Greece.

agree that it has been a fruitful one. . . . The Crimea conference spells the end of the system of unilateral action, exclusive alliances and spheres of influence, and balances of power and all the other expedients which have been tried for centuries and have always failed. . . . I am sure that there will be a more stable political Europe than ever before. . . .'

3 Unremitting Battle

3 UNREMITTING BATTLE

The Anglo-American offensive, delayed because of the Battle of the Bulge at the Ardennes, began near the end of the Yalta conference, on February 8th. It opened after the most concentrated artillery bombardment of the war in the West, in which 1,034 guns put down more than half a million shells in five and a half hours on a seven-mile front. As had been agreed, General Eisenhower planned three operations: the destruction of the enemy west of the River Rhine, the establishment of bridge-heads across the river, and then the two thrusts into Germany north and south of the Ruhr. Even before the meeting at Malta the British had been worried about this plan, considering that Eisenhower did not have enough forces at his disposal to merit two assaults. Neither was General Bradley, who was to command the southern attack, happy about it, as he felt that his Twelfth Army Group, entirely American, should have the predominant role, rather than Montgomery's British, Canadian and American Twenty-First Army Group. (Montgomery could count on thirty-five divisions, Bradley twenty-five.) The move to the Rhine would have to be on a 'broad front' rather than the thrusts which were to come later, as Eisenhower did not have enough reserves available to permit the two assaults to take place while large pockets of German forces remained west of the river. It was not, however, expected that either of these armies would have much trouble in reaching the Rhine, which was obviously a fine natural barrier for the Germans to retreat behind. But from the moment the British and

Canadians attacked it was clear that this was not to be the case. The Allied staff officers had forgotten that not only was the Rhine a natural barrier, it was also a means of transporting coal from the Ruhr to the various industrial centres near the great river, and therefore of vital importance to the German economy. Hitler had no intention of giving up the western bank. The area that had to be fought over included the redoubtable Siegfried Line. Its defences included well-laid minefields, an intricate network of tank obstacles and ditches, and concrete fortifications connected, as Eisenhower pointed out, by 'a superlative communications system'. According to General Patton, however, 'the amazing thing about all these defences is that they produced no results'. One division alone of Patton's early on knocked out 120 pill-boxes in forty-eight hours. Abandoning their static defences, the Germans were fighting hard; and they were in considerable strength. To make matters worse, there was heavy rain and much flooding. Lieutenant-General B. G. Horrocks's XXX Corps became bogged down in water and mud, and tanks and transport were soon hopelessly jammed on the only main road. Confusion won the day. The Ninth US Army was delayed by the flooding of the River Roer, the Germans having broken the dams, and the British and Canadians were left to try to push on alone, in the Reichswald forest, for a fortnight. On February 23rd the Ninth Army started to move forward, and met surprisingly little opposition. By March it had reached the Rhine at several points. One of the American armoured columns penetrated ten miles through the disintegrating German lines, its tanks disguised to look German. Soon the Canadians were at Wesel, and the Americans looking across the broad river to Duisburg and Dusseldorf. Everywhere the bridges were down.

Several attempts by local commanders to rush the river met with total failure.

Meanwhile Bradley's Army Group, too, had been pushing von Rundstedt's force back on the river. The famous Third Army of General Patton, which had the longest way to go, covered fifty-six miles in three days. Bradley's northernmost army, the First, also made good progress. Leading its advance was the Ninth US Armoured Division. It encountered little opposition and hurtled on through quiet villages bedecked in drooping white flags. As the advanced troops reached the ridge overlooking the Rhine, they were astonished to look down and see the railway bridge at the town of Remagen stretching away across the river to the east bank and the heart of central Germany beyond—still intact. A prisoner told them that it was due to be blown up at 4 p.m. The charges had already been set. The time was then 3.15 p.m. Ten minutes before the hour the Americans reached the bridge, and a number dashed across. The first Allied soldier across the Rhine was Sergeant Alexander Drabik, thirty-four years old, a butcher from Holland, Ohio. He said: 'We ran down the middle of the bridge, shouting as we went. I didn't stop because I knew that if we kept moving they couldn't hit me. We took cover in some bomb craters. Then we just sat and waited for the others to come. That's the way it was.' Engineers hacked at everything in sight that might have been a demolition cable. Infantry raced on across the bridge. At four, two charges went off; the structure shuddered, but remained intact. Reinforcements rumbled over as fast as they could go. Within hours a bridge-head had been established across the Rhine. The Americans' speed of advance had surprised the Germans, and their *élan* had been rewarded by one of those unexpected strokes of luck that occur from time to time in war, to confound the best-laid plans of even the most brilliant tacticians.

After six weeks of rather unco-ordinated and hectic fighting—sometimes fierce, sometimes with little opposition—the Allies had reached Hitler's last great barrier in the west. Killed and wounded in the First Canadian Army had been very severe: 16,000. The US Ninth Army had suffered 7,300 killed and wounded. Across the murky, swift waters, over which they were now able to gaze, lay the prize of victory that would lead them once more to their homes far away. Churchill visited S.H.A.E.F., and, being taken on a car tour, was the first British statesman to set foot in Germany since Neville Chamberlain had made his journey to Munich six and a half years before.

For the first time the American and British troops were seeing the homeland of the enemy. As they had rolled towards the Rhine they observed the countryside and villages with particular interest; for this was where 'Jerry' lived. It was the first time they had come into contact with large numbers of German civilians, and were able to see the way they lived and dressed and behaved. Alan Moorehead, a correspondent who went forward with the troops, noticed that the countryside, at least, was a surprisingly clean and friendly-looking place. 'The first thing that struck you in the lush green countryside was the cattle, so numerous, so well fed. The farms were rich, wonderfully well-equipped and managed. The farming people and their foreign workers were well dressed, and they looked strong and healthy. One could turn into any house at random and find a cellar lined with glass jars of preserved vegetables and fruits. It was nothing unusual to come on many sides of bacon, and larders of fresh meat and dairy butter.' Within a few days of living with the Germans it became clear that they expected to be ill-treated. When a car got stuck in mud, willing German civilians would appear from everywhere to help push it out. The requisitioning of houses and small hotels was simple; the families went off to live in the cellars before they were even asked. They cleaned rooms, washed clothes, did the cooking for the troops as if they knew it was only their duty as a defeated people. Moorehead found most to be 'mortally and utterly afraid'.

Then the Americans entered Cologne. This was different; whole streets had been obliterated by the numerous air-raids. The place was hardly recognizable. There were 25,000 survivors still in the city, mostly living in cellars. Christopher Buckley, *Daily Telegraph* war correspondent, wrote: 'Walking along many of the streets is largely a matter of guess work. The houses have been brought so low and the rubble is piled so high that one really does not know when one is walking in the street and when one is going across the ruins of buildings. The remarkable thing is that life goes on . . . the inhabitants have adapted themselves to an almost wholly troglodyte existence.' Only the cathedral spires still soared, majestically and miraculously, over the devastation, to the sky above.

(ii)

Meanwhile, on the Eastern Front, the Red Army was still pushing relentlessly towards Berlin. By February German resistance had hardened, and a line had been formed at the Oder. Left behind in Poland, however, were large pockets of German troops that could no longer play an effective role in the defence of the Reich. Nearly a quarter of a million men were cut off in East Prussia. Another pocket was left behind on the coast at Courland, being steadily pushed back towards the sea. These areas beside the Baltic were not only packed with military, they were also the refuge of hundreds of thousands of East Prussian and Polish refugees fleeing from the Red Army, which they feared was little better than a horde of terrible and uncivilized barbarians. Neutrals arriving in Zürich for their own safety described the long columns, thirty-five to forty miles long, advancing on foot, winding serpent-like across the country. An eye-witness said: 'These people arrive at the villages at night with no energy left. The route is dotted with the dead bodies of those who were unable to continue, or who fell victims to disease. Men who tried to push handcarts with a few belongings hastily gathered together were often obliged to desist and to leave their only remaining property on the roadside. Weary, unkempt, often bootless and in rags, they drag their way through snow and mud.'

By the first week in February Zhukov's tank vanguards were only forty miles from Berlin, at the most westerly point of the Oder. General Guderian, having suffered a 300-mile retreat in three weeks, ordered a stand east of Berlin. Every man and youth from the city itself who was not already in uniform was taken out to the line. The pitiful and wretched *Volkssturm*, an unreliable mixture of fanatical boys and disillusioned elderly men, were hardly trained or equipped; many of them were without uniform, with only an arm-band to identify them as soldiers. Anti-tank ditches thirty feet wide were dug, concrete and steel pill-boxes hastily constructed, and an intricate system of trenches and wire lined the river's forested banks. Against this Zhukov's breathless offensive came to a slow halt, although the advance continued further south. There the Silesian coal-field was soon in Russian hands. This was a catastrophic blow to the German High Command because, since the decline of the Ruhr due to Allied bombing, these coal-mines had been developed into Germany's main source of supply, accounting for 60 per cent of total production in 1944. In February 1945 German coal production was less than a third of the previous March; steel was down to a sixth.

Against all expectations, the besieged city of Breslau was somehow holding out; the result of occasional parachute supply drops, stub-born house-to-house fighting and a brilliant defensive commander. In February more infantry and armoured divisions were sent from the west to attempt to stop the irrepressible Russian flood. There were no reserves to fall back on. Budapest fell on February 12th, after a siege of seven weeks during which 49,000 Germans were killed; the biggest loss in one operation since Stalingrad. Now the Red Army was striking across Czechoslovakia and Hungary towards Vienna.

In Berlin itself the atmosphere was wholly Wagnerian, with fires smouldering everywhere, constant air-raids—both real and false alarms—and feverish efforts being made to throw up fortifications in the eastern outskirts of the city. Trenches were dug at cross-roads and in the *Tiergarten*. Women, and even children, laboured on these works. There was no coal and very little food. Thousands of refugees camped out as best they could. A report from the German Overseas News Agency described the scene: 'Tank columns are driving over slushy roads to the east. Troop and supply columns dominate the picture in the centre of the city. Policemen with steel helmets and guns are posted at outer positions. A system of trenches is being dug around Berlin. After their day's work, Berliners who have not yet been sent to the front are being trained in the use of anti-tank weapons and machine-guns. More and more Berliners are being thrown into the surrounds of the city in *Volkssturm* battalions.' In his weekly article in *Das Reich*, Joseph Goebbels wrote: 'It will be a decision of life and death. One would think that the people of Europe, who fear, hate and despise Bolshevism, would hasten to aid the German nation. But no—the German people today stand almost completely deserted.'

On the morning of February 3rd nearly a thousand American B.29s (Flying Fortresses) raided the capital with incendiaries and high explosive.* A Swedish reporter in the city described it as 'incomparably the biggest trial Berlin has faced in the whole war'. Deserters and foreign slave workers were beginning to appear, scavanging and terrorizing in the streets. With Germany nearing collapse, there was no sign of any letting up in the policy of saturation bombing of the German cities. Between February 13th and 16th there was one of the vastest series of raids of the war. One of the principal targets was Dresden, only seventy miles from Konev's tanks. The assault on that city took place on the night of February 13th, and was conducted by 770 aircraft of the RAF and 310 of the US Eighth Air Force; 135,000 people died. A war correspondent of the German News Agency reported: 'In the inner town not a single block of buildings, not a single detached building, remains intact or even capable of reconstruction. The town area is devoid of human life. A great city has been wiped from the map of Europe. There were 1,000,000 people in Dresden at the time, including 600,000 bombed-out evacuees, and refugees from the east. The raging fires which spread in the narrow streets killed a great many from sheer lack of oxygen. The siren system had long ceased to function as more waves of bombers spread further destruction.' This raid brought to

* Only twenty-four planes were reported missing.

74

a head the controversy about 'terror bombing' that had been simmering between Sir Arthur Harris, commanding Bomber Command, and the Prime Minister. Since December 1940, when it had originally been adopted as a retaliatory measure, saturation bombing had taken up the greater part of Bomber Command's effort. This offensive had been supported by the Cabinet; but now that German resistance was clearly doomed the Prime Minister began to be distinctly uneasy about such tactics. He doubted the wisdom of more 'bombing of German cities simply for the sake of increasing the terror. . . . The destruction of Dresden remains a serious query against the conduct of Allied bombing.'* Churchill was strongly supported by Eden. The matter was complicated by an Associated Press report, which received wide publicity and was quoted in the House of Commons, declaring that raids 'on residential areas' were part of 'deliberate terror bombing of German population centres as a ruthless expedient to hastening Hitler's doom'. This report was suppressed, after its release, in Britain. In America, where a great deal of emphasis in the past had been carefully placed on the selective and precise nature of American bombing, it caused serious embarrassment. In Britain, too, there had been repeated Government declarations—in answer, for instance, to the Archbishop of Canterbury—that the RAF was bombing only military or industrial targets. (After the war it was officially admitted—indeed it became self-evident—that Bomber Command had been aiming most of its bombs at the centres of residential areas.) Despite political pressure it was April 4th, 1945, when German resistance was practically over, before the Air Staff agreed that nothing further was to be gained from such bombing; but during the previous week the RAF had dropped 67,365 tons of bombs on Germany—something of a record. The last big American raid, on Berlin, was on April 10th.

As his empire and dreams blazed and crashed to earth all about him, the instigator and architect of the terror that had spread across the world, causing indescribable suffering, misery and death to many millions of people who had never seen him or been nearer to him than thousands of miles, had scurried below ground in Berlin like a rat frightened by the disturbance it has made in the yard above. In his bunker, surrounded by his staff and sycophants, Adolf Hitler, the Fuehrer, planned and pontificated, ranted and accused. He had arrived at the bunker on January 16th (having called on the way for

---

* In the air attack on Dresden more people were killed than at Hiroshima or Nagasaki.

75

afternoon tea with Frau Goebbels and the children—bringing his own tea in a thermos flask), straight from his headquarters at Rastenburg, where he had been directing the Ardennes offensive. After the collapse of this attempt to change his destiny, Hitler took less active control of the direction of the war. Convinced that all his generals were useless, he sat in his bunker in the heart of the destroyed city and waited. He waited for he hardly knew what; for the collapse of the Allied coalition (especially after receiving from Kesselring a captured document giving the lay-out of the occupation zones, from which he divined the likelihood of inter-Allied squabbles); for the lucky stroke that the astrologers assured him would yet save all; or—and he was privately prepared to admit it—for his total eclipse. Closest to him was Martin Bormann, who by now had successfully dealt with nearly all his rivals, and was in effect internal ruler of the collapsing Reich. Himmler, whom the outside world considered to be almost omnipotent in Germany, was in fact out of favour (since the attempt on the Fuehrer's life the previous year; as chief of police it had reflected on him).* He was now in command of an SS Army Group on the Eastern Front vainly trying to contain the Russians. Goering, who was nominally Hitler's successor, was entirely discredited due to the failure of the *Luftwaffe* to protect Germany and to his somewhat sensational and ridiculous private life. Goebbels spent most of his time in the bunker trying to spur the German people to a final bloodbath sacrifice in the name of National Socialism, but he, too, had lost influence.

From January 16th Hitler never left the bunker, apart from an occasional brisk walk in the compound above. He rose every day at noon, received a string of officials and officers calling, even at that late date, often merely to receive his favour. This string of interviews was interrupted for irregular meals and sessions with secretaries and doctors. Every bite he ate had to be tasted by his personal chef. Some time during the day he would find time to pore over his plans for the reconstruction of Linz, to which he intended to retire. He lost his thoughts in elaborate designs for a new opera house and art gallery for that town. He would also find time to see his two favourites, Eva Braun, the loyal, dull, simple woman whom he had secretly been close to for twelve years, and his Alsatian dog Blondi. Braun spent the time polishing her finger-nails and changing her

---

* Since the attempt on Hitler's life, British and American newspapers had indulged in the foolish but popular journalistic game of suggesting that Hitler was dead, using rumour and comparisons of photographs, etc., to make their point. Some even said he had been imprisoned by Himmler.

clothes almost hourly. At 2 a.m. there would be a supper party, at which the Fuehrer would tell his attentive audience his philosophy and his thoughts on the war.

Those who were summoned to the bunker were amazed at Hitler's appearance. His face had thinned to a startling extent, and was a greyish colour. His body was stooped; his voice weak; his eyes dull. His hands were seen to shake. The theory that his undoubted debility at this time was due to after-effects of the bomb explosion which had so nearly killed him has been discounted.* It is more likely that it was a direct result of his unhealthy life, with little exercise or fresh air, and of the attentions of his well-meaning but incompetent physician, Professor Theodore Morell. This ex-ship's doctor was a quack of the most absurd and dangerous sort. He claimed that, after years of research, he had discovered penicillin, but that the secret had been stolen by the British Secret Service. He had first met Hitler when attending the Fuehrer's photographer for venereal disease, on which he considered himself an expert. Since those days he had become obsessed with the techniques of injection, and was now injecting various drugs into the rapidly sickening Hitler every day.

What Hitler, unable to adjust himself to purely defensive thinking, liked to hear most from those who came to him at the bunker were the three things that he believed might still turn the war in his favour; the jet fighters, the rockets, and the electro-submarines. The former were having difficulty in getting off the ground due to Allied attacks on airfields, the second were being threatened by Montgomery's forces in the west, and it was the last which appealed to Hitler most. One person who was being seen much more of in the bunker was Grand Admiral Karl Doenitz, who had been commander-in-chief of the German Navy since January 1943. Hitler was in touch with him nearly every day. Doenitz, shrewd, calculating and competent, had become the only high-ranking officer whom Hitler still trusted. The Navy's performance, in contrast to that of the Army, had been good (in the last four months of the war in Europe Britain lost more tonnage through enemy action than in the previous five months). Although by no means an out-and-out Nazi, Doenitz was certainly more in favour of the Party than most of the generals were; he had become, moreover, completely overwhelmed by Hitler's personal magnetism. Strangely, Hitler seemed to respect the Admiral's lack of sycophancy—the two men could disagree

* by H. R. Trevor-Roper.

77

without any mad ravings from Hitler. The new U-boats that Doenitz had been developing were certainly dramatically advanced on the older type. They could stay under water for days on end, reaching the Atlantic without surfacing. They could travel submerged at fifteen knots. There was no doubt that, once in service, they could bring the initiative on the seas back to Germany. Hitler was delighted; even when Doenitz had to inform him that owing to training difficulties the submarines were going to be months late, his interest remained as keen as ever. To bring the crews to a proper degree of competence would take up to six months. For this reason Doenitz told Hitler that it was imperative that the Baltic be kept open as a training and testing ground for these revolutionary weapons. Hitler agreed. This was one of the reasons why he insisted on large forces remaining in Norway and Denmark when the generals were begging for men for the Eastern Front, and why he ordered the troops in East Prussia, around Danzig and Courland, to fight to the last man.

It was a grotesque miscalculation. For the submarines, however successful, could no longer have any strategic significance in the war. Like the V.2s and the jet fighters, they were too late.*

While Hitler talked and talked, Bormann, at his command, wrote down and preserved what seemed his more important utterances. Some of them were wild rambles, some were merely to show off his incomplete knowledge of European history. He spoke of why he had attacked Russia (to take the initiative before the Russians made the inevitable attack on Germany, although he was, he said, fully aware of the dangers of waging war on two fronts); on the Italians ('the greatest service Italy could have rendered to us would have been to remain aloof from this conflict'); on Roosevelt (a 'madman' in the power of Jews); on Churchill ('an old man, capable, and only just capable at that, of carrying out the orders of Roosevelt'); of Russia ('their philosophy allows them to avoid taking risks and to wait—a year, a generation, a century, if necessary—until the time is ripe for the implementation of their plans. Time means nothing to them'); on Stalin (his 'empire is, in all its essentials, only the spiritual successor to the empire of Peter the Great'); on Germany ('post-war Germany's . . . preoccupation should be to preserve indissoluble the union of all the German races'). On February 4th he said that Britain could, if she had wanted, have put an end to the war at the

---

* One hundred and twenty of the new submarines were ready for service by May 1945; only two were sent on operations, and they saw no action.

beginning of 1941. 'Peace then would have allowed us to prevent the Americans from meddling in European affairs. Under the guidance of the Reich, Europe would speedily have become unified . . . Germany could then have thrown herself heart and soul into her essential task, the ambition of my life and the *raison d'être* of National Socialism—the destruction of Bolshevism . . . we ourselves were disposed to compromise. . . . We can with safety make one prophecy: Germany will emerge from this war stronger than ever before, and Britain more enfeebled than ever.' Some of his talk was indicative of his wishful mood. On February 6th he expounded on one of his favourite subjects: 'If Churchill were suddenly to disappear, everything could change in a flash. . . . We can still snatch victory in the final sprint.' On February 7th: 'What we want is a Monroe Doctrine in Europe. Europe for the Europeans.' He talked increasingly of European Union. The last entry Bormann made in his lovingly kept book was for April 2nd. Hitler said: 'With the defeat of the Reich and pending the emergence of the Asiatic, the African, and perhaps the South American nationalisms, there will remain in the world only two great powers capable of confronting each other—the United States and Soviet Russia. The laws of both history and geography will compel these two powers to a trial of strength, either military or in the fields of economics and ideology. These same laws make it inevitable that both powers should become enemies of Europe. And it is equally certain that both these powers will sooner or later find it desirable to seek the support of the sole surviving great nation in Europe, the German people. . . .'

(iii)

The Japanese, too, were facing their cataclysm. That they would lose their war was now inevitable, but the Japanese leaders, in stubborn mood, intended that their country should go down fighting, in an orgy of courage, death and self-pity.

While MacArthur was still fighting in Luzon, plans had been made to carry the war still nearer to Japan itself. It had been stated at a meeting at San Francisco the previous year that it was essential that the two islands of Iwo Jima and Okinawa, which lay in the path of American long-range bombers, should be occupied before an air offensive could be launched against the main Japanese island of

Honshu. The spokesman for this plan was Admiral Chester W. Nimitz, Commander-in-Chief Central Pacific (distinct from MacArthur's South-West Pacific Command). It had been accepted by the Chiefs of Staff, but not without opposition. It was eventually decided that the two islands were to be taken in February and April respectively.

If Iwo Jima had strategic importance, it certainly held no other interest for mankind whatever. A volcanic rock, it had only emerged from the sea less than fifty years before. Shaped like a pork chop on its side, it was four and a half miles long and two and a half wide. The volcanic crater of Mount Suribachi, 550 feet above sea level, was the extreme southern tip. There was practically no vegetation on the island, which was greyish in colour; the terrain was of volcanic ash and soft rock only recently formed from volcanic mud. The features below the crater were jumbled and rugged. Throughout the island, jets of steam and sulphur rose from fissures in the rock.

The landing force was to consist entirely of Marines, the Third, Fourth and Fifth Marine Divisions, the largest self-contained Marine force ever to go to war.

Since March 1944 the Japanese had realized that Iwo Jima would be an obvious objective for the Americans. Of all the islands in the vicinity it was the only one suitable as an air base. They themselves had already constructed two landing-strips and were now engaged in building a third. Fully expecting an assault, they increased the garrison from 1,500 men to 21,000. The whole island was turned into a fortress of tremendous strength, every defensive position being dug into the rock. Casements were strengthened with four to six feet of concrete, a system of tunnels connected the various positions and cave-like shelters, and anti-aircraft guns were placed in pits so that only direct hits could knock them out. In six months the island became a labyrinthine catacomb-fort put under the command of Lieutenant-General Tadamichi Kuribayaski, a most determined commander whose arrangements for static defence were of the highest class. Emplacements were so constructed that each beach came under several lines of enfilade fire.

Just after daybreak on February 19th there opened one of the heaviest bombardments of the Second World War. Seven battleships, seven cruisers and ten destroyers rained shells on to the tiny island, which had already been under fire during the two preceding days. So close was the manoeuvring for this massive force to get into range for their small target that three of the ships were involved in a collision. At 8.05 a.m. carrier-based planes joined in. The whole island became covered in a cloud of smoke, dust and risen ash. It seemed impossible that anything could stay alive under such a massive battering; it almost seemed that the rock itself ought to be submerged back into the sea from whence it had so recently come. The US *Official Naval History* says: 'The operation looked like a pushover. Optimists predicted that the island would be secured in four days.'

The assault began at 8.30, hitting the beach at 9 a.m., and was completed in twenty-three minutes. By 9.44 tanks were arriving at the beach. As the launches raced in towards the beaches, their long thin wakes streaming behind them in the early morning sunlight, it seemed that everything was going according to plan.

In fact, the Marines had walked into a nightmare. The beach selected had been the easiest of approach and was therefore the most heavily defended. The volcanic ash and cinder made quick movement difficult, and men who came running out of the launches found themselves reduced to a slow walk within a few steps. Tanks became bogged down on the beach, and both men and machines found it impossible to scale the terraces behind the beaches, which rose as high as fifteen feet. A ceaseless and withering fire seemed to be aimed at everyone from all directions. By 11.30 one battalion had gained 600 yards, but many others were still pinned down on the beaches, which had become the scene of bloody and awful chaos. Not only were men and machines all tightly packed together in a small space, but the landing craft continuing to arrive behind them were disintegrating under the battering they were receiving from mortars, and the beach was already so littered with wrecked craft that it was difficult to find a place to land. By nightfall about 30,000 troops had been landed on Iwo Jima; of these, nearly 2,500 were already casualties. The beach-head was so crowded that there was hardly room to move, let alone find somewhere to take cover.

The story of the taking of the island is one of relentless and bitter fighting, as valiant and terrible as any in the history of war. Bit by bit, day by day, the bedraggled and nerve-shattered Marines struggled northwards and inwards up the island, which, steaming and hissing and so willingly embracing death, seemed to many of them like a real hell on earth. Fighting became desperate and savage, with quarter seldom asked and never given; the taking of prisoners was practically unknown. Robert Sherrod, war correspondent, described the beach on the second day: 'Whether the dead were Japs or Americans, they had died with the greatest possible violence. Nowhere in the Pacific War had I seen such badly mangled bodies. Many were cut squarely in half. Legs and arms lay fifty feet away from any body. In one spot on the sand, far from the nearest cluster of dead, I saw a string of guts fifteen feet long. The smell of burning flesh was heavy. . . .'

The truth was that the Japanese had sat out the bombardment in their deep caves in comfort, and had not emerged until the assault took place and the barrage had ceased—a simple technique employed by the Germans in the First World War. The tremendous and expensive American bombardment had hardly inflicted one Japanese casualty. In the end, it was only the flame-throwing teams, infantry with grenades and engineers with demolition charges that secured the ground. Long-range artillery, except in the rare and necessarily somewhat flukish event of a direct hit, was as useless as the infantrymen's rifles. The advance of troops on Iwo Jima has been described as 'like throwing human flesh against reinforced concrete'.

On February 23rd a forty-man detachment of the Twenty-Eighth Marines, commanded by Lieutenant H. G. Schreier, scaled the side of Mount Suribachi, which had become isolated from the main Japanese force. As they scrambled over the rim of the crater, they were met by heavy fire from the opposite rim, and it was some time before they could claim the height unchallenged. One of the Marines picked up a length of iron piping that had been discarded or blown up and attached to it a small American flag which he had brought up in his pocket. It did not look very impressive, and, as the peak could be seen from nearly all points on the island, a larger flag—eight foot long—was brought up, and Joe Rosenthal, Associated Press photographer, also made the climb. Seventeen minutes after the first flag had been raised he took the great photograph of grimy and battleworn Marines holding up the Stars and Stripes; a picture that was shortly to become one of the most famous of the war.

Iwo Jima was declared 'secured' on March 16th. But there were still pockets of isolated Japanese holding out till March 26th, on which day the announcement was made 'operation completed'. On March 21st Kuribayaski had informed, by wireless, the Japanese commander of the neighbouring island of Chichi Jima: 'We have not eaten or drunk for five days. But our fighting spirit is still high. We are going to fight bravely to the last.' On March 24th he had

sent his last message: 'All officers and men of Chichi Jima, good-bye.'
Those of the remaining Japanese who could not be taken without
more loss of American life were sealed up in their caves and left
to their fate. Total identified Japanese dead were 20,703, but this
clearly left a great many unaccounted for.* Only 216 were taken
prisoner. The American casualties actually exceeded the Japanese,
totalling 26,000. It was, said Lieutenant-General Holland Smith,
'the most savage and the most costly battle in the history of the
Marine Corps'.

There was soon much doubt as to whether the fighting had not
been too costly altogether. It was learnt that a ten-day bombardment had been asked for, but a three-day bombardment was all
that had been supplied by the Navy. Not surprisingly, this caused a
great deal of bitter comment. An attack on both the Navy, for
strategy, and the Marine Corps, for tactics, was made in the Hearst
and McCormick press. It was suggested that Marine commanders
were inclined to demand tough fighting from their Corps merely
for the sake of the fighting itself, and for the glory of the Marines.
It was said that Iwo Jima was far too obvious a target, and that its
capture was not worth the effort involved. It was pointed out that
well before the capture of the island had been completed over 200
bombers had been able to bomb Tokyo (but by that time the Japanese
airfields in Iwo Jima were out of action). No doubt the matter will
remain a controversy. About the only certain thing seems to be that
perhaps the US Marines were the only unit in the world that could
have eventually succeeded in such a badly planned and overconfident scheme.

(iv)

Now that Hitler's much-vaunted Siegfried Line, west of the Rhine,
had been overrun, preparations were complete for the crossing of
the river. Germany was clearly done for, but there was no thought
of making a peace. The Allied agreement to demand unconditional
surrender made it certain that the German state was to be annihilated and that there was to be chaos in Central Europe, for
Hitler had no intention of making any move towards a surrender.

* Spasmodic fighting, as more small groups of Japanese were discovered, continued
well into May.

Montgomery's preparations for the crossing (his was to be, it will be recalled, the major thrust) were nothing if not thorough. He was assuming that the far bank would be strongly defended. More than 250,000 tons of stores, ammunition and bridging equipment had been dumped near the west bank of the Rhine. While all these preparations were being made, Montgomery refused to be rushed, although he was well aware that a desperate situation was developing in Holland, where famine seemed likely, and also that every day he delayed meant more lives lost in London. Like most successful commanders, he never fought a battle unless he could be absolutely sure of winning it. In common with all of the British commanders, he had been deeply depressed by what he had seen of the Allied generals in the First World War, and had never forgotten the lessons he had learnt from observing their failure and the needless waste of life that they had caused.* His first plan was to let General M. C. Dempsey's Second (British) Army make the initial crossing, with Simpson's Ninth US Army playing no part. Dempsey, a most efficient commander, was a sound choice. He was described by Moorehead as 'a lean and nervous figure, a manipulator of facts, not so much a popular leader as a remarkable co-ordinator and a planner. There was a certain greyhound quality about him.' But, strangely, after all the trouble of recent months, Montgomery still had not learnt his lesson. The Americans were flabbergasted. To them, of course, it seemed that he was callously getting his revenge, and was this time determined to steal all the glory for the British. Once again, however, they misjudged the Field-Marshal, who, in fact, was far too good a commander ever to take national considerations into account—as a commander of allies, this was precisely his trouble. The plan was greeted with a storm of bitter protest, and he modified it, with the two armies now having responsibilities on the narrow front. But he insisted on his plan for a 'tidy' assault rather than the improvised and lightning stroke that the Americans preferred. As always, he was influenced by the thought of heavy casualties.

Meanwhile Patton's Third Army was dashing on, and taking part in fighting as hard as any since the Ardennes, and harder than most other forces had undergone in the 'run up to the river'. He was spurred on by messages from Bradley warning him that if he did not secure a bridge-head, as General C. H. Hodges' First Army had done at Remagen, Eisenhower might take away some of his divisions

---

* q.v. his *Memoirs* p. 35.

to give to Montgomery—an unthinkable suggestion. In point of fact, because of the trouble over the Ninth Army, Eisenhower was already dubious about giving any more US troops to Montgomery, despite the promises made at Malta. He feared the reaction from Marshall, Bradley and American public opinion. On the night of March 22nd six battalions of Patton's Fifth Infantry Division slipped across the Rhine in pursuit of the fleeing German Seventh Army. The following day, his bridge-head well established, Patton telephoned Bradley with the ridiculous statement: 'I want the world to know Third Army made it before Monty starts across.' Patton had been reprimanded before this about the colourful language in which he composed his official reports, and the dispatch he sent to the War Department on this occasion was written in studiously correct and formal language; below it was the famous postscript: 'I peed in the Rhine today.' Patton had brought home the point, and this time no one could or wished to deny it, that himself, Hodges and Bradley, if not expert strategists, were exceedingly good tacticians—brilliantly good against a half-beaten foe.

On the same night as Patton's crossing, Montgomery, his preparations completed, opened his assault with a massive and typical bombardment from over 2,000 guns on a front of twenty-five miles. A very heavy bombing programme had already taken place behind the German lines in order to disrupt communications and supply lines. A brigade of Commandos got across the river almost unnoticed to take Wesel, while two British and two American divisions made the crossing of 400–500 yards on either side of the town with little difficulty. By daylight there were thus three firm bridge-heads in Montgomery's sector, all of which were pressing into the interior. The amount of opposition can be gauged from the fact that the Ninth Army lost forty-one men killed in the first day. On the 24th Montgomery followed up the crossing by a massive parachute and glider assault of two airborne divisions, involving more than 5,000 planes, gliders and protective aircraft. These were dropped not far in front of the advancing troops, in careful determination to avoid another Arnhem. There was little opposition, as by now the *Luftwaffe* was practically non-existent, but there were a large number of parachutes which 'candled', a sickening spectacle for the troops on the ground, and many of the gliders were wrecked or caught fire (the petrol in the jeeps inside being ignited) on landing. In fact, there were probably as many casualties from these causes as there were from German opposition. For Montgomery had completely overestimated the strength of the enemy. His tremendously powerful operation was faced by only three parachute and three weak infantry divisions, with two battered armoured divisions in reserve. The German forces in the west, now under command of Field-Marshal Albrecht Kesselring, who had replaced von Rundstedt after the American seizure of Remagen, had now been fatally depleted to strengthen the line at the Oder. In the first few days the most urgent problem of Montgomery's staff was to establish communications in the area, which had been 'over-bombed', particularly in the demolished town of Wesel. A dozen bridges were quickly thrown over the Rhine, and on the fifth day of the crossing the bridge-head was thirty-five miles wide and as many miles in depth. The German line snapped on that night, and the northern plains were open to Montgomery. His progress would have been quicker if it had not been for the difficulty in passing through the towns which recently had been so heavily bombed. Within a week he had twenty divisions and 1,500 tanks across the river.

The Rhine crossing had been observed by a distinguished visitor. Winston Churchill had come over especially for the occasion, and by all accounts, including his own, enjoyed himself immensely. On arrival he had been taken to Montgomery's famous caravan, and after dinner the British commander had gone over his plan in the map-wagon which always accompanied him. Churchill, as a student of military history, was not greatly worried about the Rhine as a barrier. 'Everything I had seen or studied in war, or read, made me doubt that a river could be a good barrier of defence against superior force . . . a river running parallel to the line of advance is a much more dangerous feature than one which lies squarely athwart it.' He therefore went to bed in hopeful mood. Unknown to him, Eisenhower was not far away, watching the barrage from a clock tower—on his own except for his driver. The following morning Churchill looked down on the river, where troops were still crossing in boats and on rafts, from a near-by hill. 'I should have liked to have deployed my men in red coats on the plain down there and ordered them to charge,' he said. 'But now my armies are too vast.' After watching the parachute drop, he was taken on a long motor tour. He was amused by two signs he passed on the roadside. The first read 'This was the Siegried Line'; the second, a hundred yards further on, was a post bearing a clothes line and the words 'This is the washing'—a reference to the song 'We're Going to Hang Out the Washing on the Siegfried Line', so sadly premature, which had been sung on the old Western Front in the first weeks of 1940. After a visit to Eisenhower for lunch, the Supreme Commander had taken him to a specially prepared, sandbagged house from which he could see the opposite bank of the river. There Eisenhower left him, content no doubt that this proximity to the battle would satisfy the Prime Minister. No sooner had Eisenhower gone than Churchill, accompanied by Montgomery, persuaded some Americans to boat him across to the other side. During the afternoon he came within a hundred yards of shell-fire, a fact which apparently made his day. Brooke recalled in his diary: ' . . . General Simpson, on whose front we were, coming up to Winston and saying: "Prime Minister, there are snipers in front of you; they are shelling both sides of the bridge and now they have started shelling the road behind you. I cannot accept the responsibility for your being here, and must ask you to come away." The look on Winston's face was just like that of a small boy being called away from his sand-castles on the beach by his nurse!' The junior officers around, to whom, in their recent past, war had meant more than a noisy game to be enjoyed by ebullient spectators, may well have wondered if the British Field-Marshal and the famous Prime Minister did not have better ways of spending an entire day.

A week after the crossing, Montgomery gave orders for Dempsey and Simpson to drive on towards the Elbe, with the Canadians, now also across the river, advancing north to seal off the Germans in Holland. Simpson's Ninth US Army was to connect with the First US Army, now coming up from south of the Ruhr, having burst out of the Remagen bridge-head. Hodges' Army was advancing with extraordinary speed as it skirted the Ruhr, as was Patton's Third Army, which was in Frankfurt by March 29th. Further south still both the Seventh US Army and the First French Army were over the Rhine and heading east and south-east respectively. All these crossings and movements had been achieved with only very small losses indeed, a fact that Eisenhower was rightly quick to point out—although the lack of German opposition and the disintegration of their forces by the end of March was not fully brought out in official dispatches. As Major-General J. F. C. Fuller has written: 'Within a week of crossing the Rhine the German forces were in complete disintegration. All organization on the Western Front had collapsed; yet the fighting went on so that unconditional surrender might receive its belly-full.' All these thrusts were now probing deep into Germany, but it seemed that it must only be a matter of weeks before the mightiest of all, that under Montgomery, burst across the Westphalian plain and then on irresistably to Berlin.

But this was not to be. Eisenhower had already decided that Bradley, after all, was to get the additional American divisions originally intended for the north. This decision brought to a head the row in the Anglo-American military alliance which had been crackling away all year.

The main difference between the two schools was, as has been seen, a strategic one; the British believing in one strong thrust and in lack of dissipation; the Americans believing in a broader front in which all thrusts should be strong, a policy with which the British disagreed not only on strategical grounds, but on logistical ones as well. Irritants to this main dissension were the suspicion that the British were up to at least one trick to steal the main glory of victory for themselves, and the personal dislike in which all the Americans (except Eisenhower, who disliked no one) held Montgomery. It was the strategic difference which had now come to the boil. A secondary point of the British view was that by concentrating on one advance only there was a chance that Berlin could be reached, if not before the Russians, at least at the same time. This was seen to have certain political advantages. Eisenhower, however, was disinterested in any such considerations. He saw his task as beating the Germans. He looked forward to the surrender of the German armies opposing him, but he looked no further than that.

In reply to a query from Churchill, the Supreme Commander wrote: 'As soon as the US Ninth and First Armies join hands and enemy encircled in Ruhr area is incapable of further offensive action, I propose driving eastwards to join hands with the Russians or to attain general line of Elbe. This will be my main thrust, and until it is quite clear that concentration of all our effort on it alone will not be necessary I am prepared to direct all my forces to ensuring its success. It lies in Bradley's zone. . . .' Thus Bradley had won after all. There was a feeling of acute frustration in London and at Montgomery's headquarters. At about the same time it had been learnt that Eisenhower, without any authority from Washington, had communicated this plan to Stalin, without consulting the Combined Chiefs of Staff. When the British heard of this they believed they had got hold of something which would help them to bend Eisenhower more to their will. Eisenhower made a rather unconvincing excuse for his surprising action (his direct contact with

Stalin and the Russians seems to have dated from Tedder's visit to Moscow in January, at the end of the Ardennes campaign). The British chiefs of staff complained at length, as always on purely military considerations, about Eisenhower's new strategy, and his direct approach to Moscow. As was to be expected, they received a reply from their opposite numbers in Washington supporting the Supreme Commander to the hilt; it said, in fairly icy tones, that the matter was best left to the Supreme Commander in the field. The US chiefs of staff said that the battle for Germany had now reached the stage where Eisenhower alone could judge what measures ought to be taken. As for communication with Stalin, they agreed that he should first show them any such messages in future.

There was at this time still considerable veiled criticism of Eisenhower in the British Press, where he was frequently described, somewhat disparagingly, as the 'Chairman of the Board' rather than as a real Commander-in-Chief. Although the public knew little of the controversy now raging, rumours abounded among the pressmen. The trouble with Eisenhower, as some people saw it, was that he not only obviously did not enjoy war, he also did not appear to enjoy high command—both, until that time, considered to be essential qualifications for any great military commander. He was personally popular with the Press, but not at all approachable. On February 24th he had given only his first Press conference since November. Matters were not helped by the extraordinary circumvention of syntax and phrase which he seemed to find necessary to express himself on even the most straightforward matters. Some saw his glaucous statements as a desire not to commit himself on anything, revealing a basic lack of confidence. When in Paris, he sometimes stayed at a small hotel in semi-secrecy. However, as the war progressed successfully, he became noticeably more relaxed, as did his staff, who were often to be seen at the bar of the Scribe Hotel entertaining journalists, Congressmen and other visitors. One of the British visitors was Leslie Hore-Belisha, who had been Minister of War at the beginning of hostilities and had been invited to Europe (apparently at the Army's expense) by de Guingand in order 'to see the end'.

At the end of March Churchill intervened on behalf of his rebuffed chiefs of staff. In a letter to Eisenhower he wrote: 'If the enemy's resistance should weaken, as you evidently expect, and which may well be fulfilled, why should we not cross the Elbe and advance as far eastward as possible? This has an important political bearing, as the Russian armies of the south seem certain to enter Vienna and overrun Austria. If we deliberately leave Berlin to them, even if it should be in our grasp, the double event may strengthen their conviction, already apparent, that they have done everything.' The last sentence indicates how unwilling the Prime Minister was to put his real fears bluntly to the Americans, although, as he claims, by this time his policy was based on the tenets that 'Soviet Russia had become a mortal danger to the free world' and 'that a new front must immediately be created against her onward sweep' and 'that this front in Europe should be as far east as possible'. Although he went on in this letter to Eisenhower to point out the advantages of taking Berlin, Churchill nowhere mentioned that it would be in any way fatally disadvantageous for the Russians to take it instead. This may have been because Eisenhower was well known to shy-off from political considerations. Churchill also wrote to Roosevelt, in carefully politic tones ('I venture to put to you a few considerations upon the merits of the changes in our original plans now desired by General Eisenhower'). Ralph Ingersoll pointed out in this connection: 'Mr Churchill apparently said everything but the truth, which was that the military situation had nothing to do with it.' Although he did not know it, Churchill's letter was dealt with, not by Roosevelt, but by Marshall, for the President's health was causing great concern to those in his innermost circle.

Eisenhower replied to Churchill at length (and almost totally incomprehensibly). He seemed to say that he had not changed his plan at all; that he had always thought the main thrust should be in the north, but that he thought the centre one should be strong too. This was, to say the least, a disingenuous answer. He made his position more clear, later, in his *Supreme Commander's Report*: 'Berlin, I was now certain, no longer represented a military objective of major importance. The function of our forces must be to crush the German armies rather than dissipate our strength in the occupation of empty and ruined cities.' He also believed that an entanglement with the Russians, who were only forty miles from Berlin, was to be avoided, and that there was a strong possibility that the Germans would concentrate on the Tyrol and South Germany, forming a powerful redoubt. If this was so, clearly it was better to strengthen Bradley, who could be directed to the danger area in question, rather than Montgomery, who could not. Churchill himself had wondered about the possibility of the Germans retreating to such a fortress, but British Intelligence thought it unlikely.

Two of Eisenhower's harshest critics have been Ingersoll and J. F. C. Fuller. The former blames Bradley more than the Supreme Commander, as he claims Bradley 'was completely the boss'. He says that to the American chiefs of staff war 'was a game played for cheers from the grandstand—a game in which people get hurt and a grim game which is taken seriously—but still a game'. Fuller has written: 'The Americans were such military amateurs that they failed to realize that war is a political instrument, and that the defeat of the enemy is but a means to a political end. Looking upon war as a game, they imagined that once it was won both sides would disperse and, like Candide, go home and cultivate their gardens.'

Churchill now wrote a little more strongly to Eisenhower, almost coming to the point: 'I deem it highly important that we shake hands with the Russians as far to the east as possible.' The Supreme Commander, however, with Marshall, Bradley and the whole American executive and military machine behind him, did not feel he had to give way.

Meanwhile, Eisenhower's military moves had met with total success. Patton's army was ploughing deep into the southern Germany of small, bell-ringing towns, which smelt of incense, wood fires, beer and fatty sausages. There was little opposition. Further north it had been a sound and well-conceived plan to encircle the Ruhr rather than get held up in months of delaying street fighting. The movement of the armies, being free, had been quick. Whereas Montgomery had been right about his desire for a powerful narrow front in 1944, Eisenhower, from a purely military point of view, was right on this occasion. His connected strokes across the Rhine had been a masterly series of operations, conceived with a broad sweep of eye, and in their ruthless execution they had prevented any possible stand by Kesselring. The irony is that the strategy of the British chiefs of staff, no longer applicable militarily at this stage of the war, would have been—perhaps not a little accidentally— the correct strategy from a political point of view. The tragedy is that Eisenhower's, which was so militarily copybook, was undoubtedly the wrong one from a Western point of view in the larger world of international politics.

Churchill reserves his strongest criticism for the Americans in this affair. 'In Washington especially longer and wider views should have prevailed. It is true that American thought is at least disinterested in matters which seem to relate to territorial acquisitions, but when wolves are about the shepherd must guard his flock, even if

THE COLLAPSE OF GERMANY, APRIL 1945

MILES
0   100   200

German Territory, April 27, 1945

Neutral Countries

he does not himself care for mutton. At this time the points of issue did not seem to the United States chiefs of staff to be of capital importance. Nevertheless, as will not now be disputed, they played a dominating part in the destiny of Europe, and may well have denied us all the lasting peace for which we had fought so long and hard.'

This may indeed be so, but some Westerners might wish that the Prime Minister had made his point louder and clearer at the time; for he alone had the vision and clarity to see the future by reading current trends. But he clearly saw his primary duty as preserving the tattered shreds of the Anglo-American alliance; and who, even with the benefit of afterthought, can blame him?

(v)

By now the Allied armies were meeting only spasmodic opposition. Some of it was bitter, conducted by fanatical groups of soldiers who were prepared to fight to the last. But it was piecemeal and unable to stop the various thrusts from the west, which seemed to the British and American public like great and hard-fought victories in the field. There was a brief gleam of hope in the German High Command when their first jet fighter, the Me.262, appeared in the skies. These brilliant planes could outstrip even the Allied jets, and caused a little consternation among some RAF pilots still flying Spitfires. But, like the submarines and the 'flying bombs' and the rockets, they were too late.

The *Volkssturm*, Hitler's last reserve in the west as in the east, was just fading away. The Commanding Officer of the 41st *Volkssturm* Battalion described what happened when, in March, his unit was sent into battle: 'We were ordered to go into the line in civilian clothes. I told the local Party Leader that I could not accept the responsibility of leading men into battle without uniforms. Just before commitment the unit was given 180 Danish rifles, but there was no ammunition. We also had four machine-guns and 100 anti-tank bazookas. None of the men had received any training in firing a machine-gun, and they were all afraid of handling the anti-tank weapon. . . . What can a *Volkssturm* man do with a rifle without ammunition?' The Reich's very last defenders were now in action. The best fighters among them were young boys of fourteen and fifteen, who fought without skill but to the death. Although they made no difference to the course of the war, groups of them at bridges, or entrenched at cross-roads, caused minor hold-ups. They seldom allowed themselves to be taken prisoner. Thus had the Fuehrer, with the aid of Goebbels, gained a kind of loyalty from Germans too young even to have been much influenced by the Hitler Youth. The girls did not lag behind the boys. Patton's Eightieth US Division encountered and shot at least one girl sniper. A number of stratagems were adopted in an attempt to keep the *Wehrmacht* fighting. Awards were lavished upon all units; Iron Crosses of all classes being handed out by the dozen. Goebbels made a desperate attempt to heighten his campaign of terror about the Communists. The German people were told of the horrors that would befall them if they allowed the Russians to enter the homeland. Children would be taken from their parents by force, women would be 'raped by beasts in human guise', families would be torn asunder for deportation. The death sentence was laid down for an ever-increasing number of offences: for neglecting to blow up a bridge on time, for being a deserter, for being related to a deserter, and, finally, for failing to hold a town. But it was of no avail.

Kesselring, who had a great reputation for last-ditch stands since his brilliantly conducted defence in Italy, was unable to stem the Allied tide. Hitler had ordered that the Ruhr must be held; even if surrounded, it should be held as a fortress. On April 1st the Ninth and First US Armies met at Lippstadt and the Ruhr was, indeed, isolated; an enormous gap had been torn out of Kesselring's tottering line. He was unable to do any more. One of his commanders, General G. Blumentritt, said: 'Nevertheless, orders from the Supreme Command were still couched in the most rigorous terms enjoining us to "hold" and "fight" under threats of court martial. But I no longer insisted on these orders being carried out. It was a nerve-racking time we experienced—while we secretly allowed things to go their own way. By April 1st I had decided to direct things in such a way that the army could be withdrawn in a more or less orderly manner and without suffering any great casualties.'

The whole of Model's Army Group was cut off in the Ruhr. Hitler ordered a scorched-earth policy, destroying even what remained of the industrial plant in the area and turning the Ruhr pocket into a 'desert'. But Model had already received a plea from Albert Speer, Minister of Armaments and War Production, to ignore this order, with which, indeed, he had no intention of complying. Conditions inside the Ruhr worsened rapidly; quicker than anyone had expected. With Allied planes still keeping up their bombardment, communications broke down. (Allied tactical bombing raids continued until the very last days, until, as Churchill says, 'it became difficult to bomb ahead of our troops without risk to the Russians'. Churchill wrote in a memo: 'If we come into control of an entirely ruined land, there will be a great shortage of accommodation. . . . We must see to it that our attacks do not do more harm to ourselves than they do to the enemy's immediate war effort.') Although there were both ammunition and food for civilians and military in the pocket, it became impossible to distribute it. Above all, the troops had no wish to fight on. Model released his oldest and youngest soldiers. The remainder started giving themselves up rapidly. On April 18th, after eighteen days of siege, 325,000 troops, representing two armies with all supporting services, including thirty generals, gave themselves up. One person was found to be not among them. Field-Marshal Walter Model had shot himself in a wood near Duisberg. He had told his senior Intelligence officer that he feared he would be handed over to the Russians, who had accused him of being a war criminal.

(vi)

The Japanese in defeat were an altogether tougher proposition than the Germans. Many of their troops were prepared to fight to the death, even in hopeless situations, and would not surrender. This made it necessary for the British and Americans in Asia and the Pacific to fight hard to *win* the war, although the Japanese had already lost it.

The battle for Burma had reached a crucial stage. Admiral Lord Louis Mountbatten, Supreme Commander South-East Asia, had decided on an all-out offensive against the main Japanese force west of Mandalay. This had to be accomplished as quickly as possible, as General Marshall had indicated that American air support would soon be withdrawn, partly to aid the campaign of General Chiang Kai-shek in China. Mountbatten's was still the 'Cinderella' theatre of the war; he had six divisions to put against the Japanese nine. Bridge-heads had already been seized on the Irrawaddy north of Mandalay, and these were able to be held despite fierce counter-attacks. Bridge-heads were now also taken south of the city, and about fifty miles south again. From these latter bridge-heads two columns broke out eastwards and eventually met near the important Japanese centre of Meiktila. Fifty per cent of the Japanese strength in Burma was thus cut off. It had been a daring and brilliant flank attack by General Slim, commanding the Fourteenth Army. A British correspondent went with the southern column and reported: 'Mules would have been a handicap in this dry area, so the force was completely motorized, with a spearhead of tanks and armoured vehicles. It carried five days' supplies, which were supplemented by a few air drops before Meiktila was reached, including more than 100,000 gallons of petrol. The column had to be kept compact when settling down after the day's schedule had been completed. Everything was concentrated into one great box with its perimeter heavily manned. On the broken roads dust lay a foot thick, like a great pile of cocoa. Dazed Burmese, pathetically huddled on the outskirts of their burnt-out villages, stared at the lumbering tanks and at the apparently endless procession of trucks behind them, and wondered what new terrors of war had come among them.' The two converging columns sandwiched a Japanese force attempting to escape between the gap. There was a massacre in a scrub-covered valley, in which one Indian battalion alone accounted for 113 enemy killed. Of the 1,500 garrison at Meiktila, 1,000 were killed. The loss of this important centre, at which there were eight airfields, proved fatal to the Japanese. Three years before, General Slim had fought a stubborn rearguard action through the same town. The Japanese Commander-in-Chief later described this attack as 'the master-stroke of Allied strategy'.

Further north, the fighting at Mandalay was particularly bitter even for this hard-fought campaign. Captain Frank Owen described the scene in a BBC broadcast: 'You are sitting in a forest. The nearest city to you is 500 miles away. If you're unlucky you're squatting in a foxhole under Japanese mortar fire, waiting to assault a Japanese machine-gun nest, and it is probably raining. This is the Burma Front. A quarter of a million British soldiers live there, fight there, march, patrol and stick it out. Some have been on duty there for three years, guarding the gates to India. Now they are deep into Burma, driving the enemy down the road to Mandalay, down the long, long road to Singapore, where 60,000 of our comrades, prisoners of war in the hands of the Japanese, are waiting for us to come and set them free. . . . It is the largest single army in the world. For besides the British there are Indians [and others]—

altogether 600,000 troops are fighting in the Fourteenth Army and all must eat. So every twenty-four hours 2,000 tons of food go rattling up a single-track mountain railway and along that military road. War in the jungle is really the art of keeping that road open; if you don't you may die. And secondly, it is the art of cutting the road behind the enemy; then he will die. And the jungle. . . . It is a place of treachery and, for those who don't know it, of terror. In this murky, shadowy war, if a soldier is brave few even of his comrades see it. If he quits, perhaps nobody will see it. All then depends on the soldier himself, on his loyalty to his comrades, to his regiment, to the Army. All depends on what each man feels in his own heart.' As the British broke out of their bridge-heads and fought their way into Mandalay, they met suicide-opposition all the way. The garrison defended two strongpoints, Mandalay Hill and Fort Dufferin, to the end. General Slim has written: 'Mandalay Hill is a great rock rising abruptly from the plain to nearly 800 feet and dominating the whole north-eastern quarter of the city. Its steep sides are covered with temples and pagodas, now honey-combed for machine-guns, well supplied and heavily garrisoned. Throughout the day and night of March 9th the fiercest hand-to-hand fighting went on, as a Gurkha battalion stormed up the slopes and bombed and tommy-gunned their way into the concrete buildings. Next day two companies of a British battalion joined them, and the bitter fighting went on. The Japanese stood to the end, until the last defenders, holding out in cellars, were destroyed by petrol rolled down in drums and ignited by tracer bullets. It was not until March 11th that the hill was completely in our hands. When, shortly afterwards, I visited it, the blackened marks of fire and the sight and stench of carnage were only too obvious, while distant bumps and bangs and the nearer rattle of machine-guns showed that the clearing of the city was still going on.' Fort Dufferin was even more difficult to conquer. Its massive walls, impenetrable to artillery, withstood everything the Fourteenth Army could hurl at it. It was not finally taken until March 20th, whe a 2,000 lb bomb breached its tough old walls.

By the end of March the enemy were falling back through the mountains to the east, and down the road to Rangoon. If the conquest of Burma was to be completed, Mountbatten had to act quickly. He could permit his battle-worn, but tremendously proud troops no rest. Chiang Kai-shek had decided to withdraw the support he had been supplying on Slim's left flank in order to attempt to free the rice-producing areas of China from the Japanese. He also demanded the US air squadrons that had been supporting his divisions in the area. This could hardly have happened at a more inopportune moment for the 'Cinderella Campaign', which had fought so long with so little, and was now in sight of victory. If the transport planes, especially, were withdrawn, Slim's men would have been forced through lack of supplies to trudge back again until they could be supplied from the road and railhead. The recent campaign would have been a complete waste of life. Churchill himself urged Marshall to leave the planes where they were, and it was eventually agreed they should remain with Mountbatten until June 1st or until Rangoon was reached. Slim, however, was almost immune to lack of support from every quarter. Typically, he wrote: 'There seemed to be nothing that I, or apparently anyone else, could do about it, except to remember our motto—God helps those who help themselves—and to get on with the war without the Chinese. So with little hope of help on either of my flanks I continued the main battle.' The Fourteenth Army pushed south in three main columns towards Rangoon.

Mountbatten decided to speed up the campaign by launching an amphibious and airborne assault on the city, as Slim approached it. A battalion of Ghurka paratroopers was dropped on the approaches to the town around Rangoon River. The following day a division was safely landed, in heavy seas and a deluge of rain, south of the city. During the previous day a pilot flying over Rangoon had seen written on the roof of the gaol, in huge letters: 'Japs gone. Exdigitate.' Another RAF pilot now flew his Mosquito aircraft low over the city. Seeing no signs of the enemy, he landed on an airstrip eight miles to the north. The airstrip turned out to be damaged, and he crashed his aircraft. Undismayed, he set out on the eight-mile walk and entered the city, the only man to take a capital city single-handed during the war. The Japanese had, in fact, withdrawn some days before. He visited the British prisoners in the gaol, who had been waiting for this day for three years and more, commandeered a sampan, and sailed down the river to meet the division advancing up-stream.

Rangoon was freed. But a fierce battle developed to the north of the capital.

The Japanese had now lost two capitals from their crumbling empire. At the other, Manila, General MacArthur was already well installed. The remaining Japanese defenders in the area had been sealed up in the deep caves to which they had taken, and left to their fate. Unlike Mountbatten, MacArthur made the most of his position as returning saviour of the country which he knew and loved so well. The Commonwealth Government of the Philippines had been restored, although much of the country was still in enemy hands. MacArthur spoke to the Assembly in Malacanan Palace, where his father before him had lived as Governor-General, and where he himself had once become Field-Marshal in the Philippine Army. He said: 'More than three years have elapsed since I withdrew our forces from this beautiful city that, open and undefended, its churches, monuments and cultural centres might be spared the violence of military ravage. The enemy would not have it so . . . but my country has kept its faith.'

After Manila Bay had been cleared, the fighting went on. MacArthur was hampered in his task of freeing the remainder of the archipelago by the fact that the 100 transport ships which had brought him to Lingayen Gulf, and had supplied him ever since, had been ordered to Vladivostok to carry munitions and supplies for the Russians. He protested bitterly that his entire campaign might be seriously jeopardized, but to no avail. He blamed the decision on Hopkins's influence on Roosevelt. To secure Luzon, MacArthur launched a three-pronged attack on the Japanese, who had retreated to the most hilly and inaccessible parts of the island. Making considerable use of bulldozers, he got tanks and artillery to positions that confounded the Japanese, under no mean command themselves. The fighting was everywhere hard. The Japanese defenders fought with fanatical ferocity. MacArthur said: 'The campaign was one of the most savage and bitterly fought in American history. No terrain has ever presented greater logistical difficulties and none has ever provided an adversary with more naturally impregnable strongholds.'

One of the few campaigns which was even more bitterly fought was the conquest of Okinawa. About half-way between Formosa and Japan, Okinawa, about sixty miles long and five miles wide, was in a highly strategic position; more so even than Iwo Jima, of which it was the twin operation. Some critics have said since (and some said at the time) that it would have been wiser to have concentrated everything on taking Formosa rather than Luzon and the two fortress islands. In any event, Japanese preparations at Okinawa were quite as thorough as they had been at Iwo Jima. Awaiting the American invasion were some 100,000 Japanese troops in a clever system of pill-boxes, caves, trenches, blockhouses and tunnels, with an extremely strong defence-citadel as a final retreat. They were well stocked with food and ammunition to last a long siege. The defenders had orders not to waste ammunition at the landings, as these could not indefinitely be stopped, but to prepare for a long-drawn-out battle of attrition. After a huge process of 'softening-up' by aerial and naval bombardment, the Tenth US Army went ashore on April 1st, at the very beach where the Japanese commander had been expecting them. The element of surprise seemed to have utterly escaped from all operations in the Central Pacific theatre. The landing parties were met by only scattered small-arms fire. By the end of the day 50,000 soldiers and Marines were ashore. In three weeks they had captured nearly all of the northern sector of the island. Only the citadel remained—on the southernmost tip of Okinawa. Repeated attacks on this were bloodily repulsed. Great difficulty was found in maintaining the naval and supply link with the island. Suicide *kamikaze* planes, with incessant and mad sorties, had already caused much damage. Nearly every day they came screaming down from the skies, the red suns on their wings easily visible to the taut and horrified crews below, the young pilots shouting 'Babe Ruth, go to hell' (which they had been told was the supreme insult) as they lowered their planes, in the noses of which were packed more than 250 lb of TNT, into their last dives. Now a new danger was apparent. For many of the *kamikazes* were flying in with bombs attached below the fuselage. The flagship, *Indianapolis*, was hit and had to retire. A destroyer was so mangled by another crashing plane that it had to be sunk. On April 6th, in a mass suicide that horrified and appalled those who saw it, 355 pilots walked to their planes on airfields in Japan and set off for the American fleet near Okinawa. Many of them were intercepted, but about 200 reached the fleet. Anti-aircraft fire became so intense in the hectic desire to hit the advancing planes before they themselves hit the ships that thirty-eight American casualties were caused by the hail of falling shell fragments. Six vessels were sunk and twenty-two damaged. Two of the ships that had gone down were the destroyers *Bush* and *Calhoun*, an outlying radar patrol. They met, alone, the first fury of the death-seeking pilots as they swarmed past them, and the crews of each refused to abandon their burning, battered and sinking ships till the last minute, in an incredible display of mass courage, as notable as the display of mass suicide all about them was revolting. In conjunction with the *kamikazes*, a fleet had also put out from Japan, including the last remaining Imperial battleship. This force, too, was intent on self-destruction. The force was powered by the last suitable fuel oil left in Japan; there was just enough for a one-way journey to Okinawa. The intention was to beach the ships on the island and to pour shell-fire into the American ground forces until there was no more ammunition left. Fortunately the force was sighted and destroyed before it reached the island. During this very testing week, the US Navy acquitted itself with exemplary calmness. At the end it remained, despite all odds against a maddened and ruthless foe, almost entirely afloat. A British fleet, newly arrived from Sydney under Admiral Sir Bernard Rawlings, had also taken an active part in all these affairs. Its four carriers proved particularly valuable as their armoured flight-decks gave them added protection against the *kamikazes*, as compared to the wooden flight-decks of the American carriers.

But the citadel fortress of Okinawa remained to be taken; and it was obvious that before this obscure and tiny outpost of the Japanese Empire could be secured many thousands of Americans would have to die.

(vii)

On the very evening that Churchill spoke to the House of Commons so hopefully about the results of the Yalta conference, a violation of the spirit of agreements made there was, unknown to him, being made. All the Allies were committed to bringing about free elections in the countries that they freed from Nazi rule. In Rumania, where King Michael was struggling to maintain the position of his all-party government which had expelled the Germans from the country in 1944, the Russians were showing a contemptuous disregard for that commitment. Vyshinsky appeared unexpectedly in Bucharest, stormed into the King's office, banged his fist on the table, demanded the dismissal of the government and, looking at his watch, said that the King had just two hours five minutes to obey. He then stalked out, slamming the door behind him (so hard that, according to the American political representative, the plaster round the door-frame was badly cracked). With Soviet tanks and troops taking up positions in the streets and vital points of the capital, he could afford such behaviour. A few days later a Russian-nominated government took office. A Communist minority had thus seized power by the ruthless use of force. Although Churchill was deeply disturbed—suspecting that it might prove a pattern of things to come—he decided against a strong protest. In the first place, he felt handicapped by the agreement he had made with Stalin about Russian influence in Rumania and the Balkans; and, in the second, he was fully conscious of the fact that the same agreement provided for British influence in Greece, which Stalin seemed to be observing, and which the Prime Minister deemed to be of vital importance to the interests of the Empire. As Churchill says, writing of the Greek agreement: 'Stalin had kept very strictly to this understanding during the six weeks' fighting against the Communists and ELAS in the city of Athens, in spite of the fact that all this was most disagreeable to him and those around him.' It was, of course, just this kind of attitude of the Prime Minister's which made Roosevelt, who hated all idea of spheres of influence, so suspicious of him. It was left to the United States to take the initiative over Rumania. Averell Harriman made an effort in Moscow to intervene on behalf of the Rumanians, but met with a blunt rejection from Molotov.

Only a few days after his address on returning from Yalta, the President, too, like Churchill, was suffering from disappointment. Once more the trouble was Poland. At first Churchill again took the lead in the West on the Polish question. It had become clear that the Russians had no intention of carrying out the agreements about broadening the basis of the Lublin Government. None of the 'Free Poles' suggested by London were allowed to enter the discussions in Moscow. Molotov steadfastly refused to allow observers into liberated Poland. There was no sign of the promised free elections. As each day passed, the Lublin Government was becoming a *fait accompli*. Churchill has written: 'Time was on the side of the Russians and their Polish adherents, who were fastening their grip upon the country by all kinds of severe measures which they did not wish outside observers to see. Every day's delay was a gain to these hard forces.' Churchill appealed to the President for concerted pressure on Stalin before it was too late. He believed that only a direct and tough approach to 'Uncle Joe' could achieve results.

Roosevelt, however, was against the direct approach on this occasion, and Churchill had some difficulty in convincing him as to the seriousness of the situation. The Prime Minister was deeply aware, as he frequently pointed out to both Stalin and Roosevelt, that he had to report to Parliament on Poland (but not Rumania).

According to Churchill, Roosevelt was at this time so ill that he was not able to attend to these matters himself. Churchill says: 'I was no longer being fully heard by him. The President's devoted aides were anxious to keep their knowledge of his condition within the narrowest circle, and various hands drafted in combination the answers which were given in his name.' Other evidence,* however, suggests that Roosevelt, while being weak enough, and writing few of the messages of these weeks himself, was not as out of touch as Churchill believed. At any event, Churchill deferred, with much reluctance, to the President's wish not to approach Stalin.

Roosevelt was busily occupied with problems at home that had arisen as an aftermath to Yalta. News of the voting procedure in the proposed Security Council of the World Organization had not yet been released. The President, expecting a storm, had been anxious to delay this revelation until a favourable moment. The veto procedure was announced by Stettinius on March 5th. The fact that the United States would support Russia's request for three votes was 'leaked', either accidentally or deliberately, to the *Herald Tribune*, which printed the story on March 29th. These two revelations received much adverse Press criticism and public comment. The news came as a shock, especially as the State Department had been carefully conducting an educational campaign emphasizing that one of the main points about the United Nations' Organization was to be that small countries would get exactly the same rights as big ones. To make matters worse, Stalin had now indicated that he would not be sending Molotov to the San Francisco conference. As Eden and Stettinius were going, this was taken not only as an indication of what the Russians expected from the United Nations, but also as a personal rebuff to the President, whose high hopes for the organization were well known.

In the midst of all this, a personal telegram from Churchill to Roosevelt arrived in Washington stating that a dangerous divergence in views on the Polish question was developing between Britain and the United States. The long and cold answer that Churchill received three days later clearly came as a shock to the Prime Minister. It was written in a tone quite different from any that the President had used before. It contained none of the flourishes that Roosevelt liked to use, even when irritated. It seems certain that it was written by the State Department. That Roosevelt signed it at all shows how strained relations had become between the two leaders during the year. In

* *When F.D.R. Died*, page 20.

fact, the message said little except that the United States recognized no divergences of opinion, that the President could not agree that there was a breakdown of the Yalta agreement, and that Churchill's suggestions were not helpful. It indicated the latent anti-British feeling in the State Department; and the conviction that Britain was a second-class power, and that the United States could better deal with the Russians without the nagging encumbrance of Churchill. The Prime Minister was not, however, an easy man to rebuff, and he kept up his barrage of communications to the President, begging for some action on Poland. At length, at the end of the month, Roosevelt agreed to approach Stalin about the broken agreements of Yalta. Both the Western leaders sent off long letters to Stalin, detailing their complaints about the Lublin Government and the non-admittance of observers into Poland.

Stalin replied a week later. The whole dispute had arisen, he said, because of the inability of the British and American ambassadors in Moscow to negotiate properly. They had led the Polish affair into a blind alley. No new members could be admitted to the Lublin Government unless they were friendly to the Soviet Government.

At this time, the first week in April, Roosevelt had at last been stirred to strong words against Stalin—not on anything to do with the Polish question, but on a matter of personal pique. This resulted from the fact that the Germans on the Italian front had been making hesitant peace moves. The commander of the SS in Italy had appeared in Zürich and contacted Allen Dulles, the head of US Intelligence in Switzerland. He was told that negotiations could only take place on the basis of unconditional surrender. Although the SS chief did not appear to accept at that time the notion of such a surrender, it was decided that the British and American Chiefs of Staff in Italy, Generals T. Airey and L. Lemnitzer, should go to Switzerland to meet the SS commander. This they did—in disguise. Dulles was well known among those involved in the heady world of espionage as being well cocooned in intrigue and the mystiques of spying; so much so, some believed, that he was not always able to see as clearly as he might.

Stalin had been informed by his own Intelligence of these over-tures from the Germans on the Italian front, and he soon became thoroughly alarmed. The visits of the two Chiefs of Staff in disguise convinced him that the Western allies were about to prepare a separate peace with Germany. Molotov handed a strong and insulting note to the British Ambassador, Sir Archibald Clark Kerr, and a harsh exchange developed between Roosevelt and Stalin. Roosevelt, horrified that 'Uncle Joe' was as good as accusing him of being a liar and a cheat, was angered. Stalin however was not concerned with anyone's honour. Buried in the heart of one of his messages to the President was his major interest in the matter. 'I understand that there are certain advantages for the Anglo-American troops as a result of these separate negotiations in Berne or some other place, since the Anglo-American troops get the possibility to advance into the heart of Germany almost without resistance on the part of the Germans, but why was it necessary to conceal this from the Russians, and why were your allies, the Russians, not notified?' Roosevelt's reply was in similarly straightforward terms, and, in hotly denying the charge, it bore some evidence of the President's own anger. He pointed out that no real negotiations had taken place, only a certain amount of preliminary probing, and thus it had not been possible to notify Moscow of any negotiations. After an equally outraged message from the Prime Minister, Stalin seems to have realized that his fears were unfounded. He was surprised by the reception that his charges had received. He wrote to Churchill: 'My messages are personal and strictly confidential. This makes it possible to speak one's mind clearly and frankly. This is the advantage of confidential communications. If however you are going to regard every frank statement of mine as offensive it will make this kind of communication very difficult.'

The matter of the non-existent separate peace treaty having been settled to the satisfaction of all, there remained only the Polish dispute. Roosevelt was hopeful that it might similarly be cleared up. He wrote to Churchill on April 12th: 'I would minimize the general Soviet problem as much as possible. . . .' It was his final advice.

4 Inconclusive Victory

4 INCONCLUSIVE VICTORY

President Roosevelt was at the home of his cousins in Warm Springs, Georgia. He had gone there for a few days' rest, and on the morning of April 12th, the courier plane not having arrived with mail and papers from Washington, due to bad weather, he lay late in bed with only the Atlanta *Constitution* to read. He read there that the Ninth US Army was only fifty-seven miles from Berlin, and that 150 Flying Fortresses had made a visit to Tokyo in a two-hour daylight raid. He read for a while the thriller by John Dickson Carr that had been engaging his attention the previous night, complained of a pain in his head, got up, and went to the living-room to pose for a portrait painter, Madame Shoumatoff. He then signed a number of papers (the plane having arrived) handed to him by William D. Hassett, Secretary to the President, including the note to Churchill. To the devoted staff, the portrait painter seemed to be worrying the President unnecessarily with measurements and frequent requests to turn his head this way and that. Hassett considered it 'hounding of a sick man'. She arranged a heavy blue cape on his shoulders and carefully arranged its folds. The room grew quiet. The President seemed to be lost in his papers. He placed a cigarette in his holder, lit it, and smoked reflectively. Suddenly he pressed the palm of his left hand behind his neck, closed his eyes and said, very softly: 'I have a terrific headache.' His head nodded on to his left shoulder, his arms slipped down, and his body sagged in the chair. It was 1.15 p.m.

It seems that the President remained there for twenty minutes or more—his two lady cousins, who had been in the room at the time, quietly sitting on the couch—before Roosevelt's doctor, Commander H. G. Bruenn, arrived at the house. Roosevelt was then carried into his bedroom, where he was laid on the bed and his clothes torn from him. A call was put through to the Navy Surgeon-General in Washington, nearly an hour after the President's collapse, and the symptoms of a cerebral stroke were reported. The Surgeon-General, Admiral Ross McIntire, called a distinguished Atlanta physician, Dr James E. Paullin, and told him to get to Warm Springs immediately. A Secret Service car was sent to patrol the main highway to facilitate Paullin's progress, but the doctor had taken to small side-roads through the Georgia hills. He arrived at Warm Springs after about an hour of fast driving. He later wrote in his report to McIntire: 'The President was *in extremis* when I reached him. He was in a cold sweat, ashy grey, and breathing with difficulty. Numerous ronchi in his chest. He was propped up in bed. His pupils were dilated, and his hands slightly cyanosed. Commander Bruenn started artificial respiration. On examination the President's pulse was barely perceptible. His heart-sounds could be heard, but about three and a half minutes after my arrival they disappeared completely. I gave him an intercardiac dose of adrenalin in the hope that we might stimulate his heart to action.' By 3.35 all evidence of life had passed away.

One of the greatest figures in the history of the United States had disappeared; an American era was over. Roosevelt had become one of the truly great men of the half-century. He had fought and won hard battles against strong opposition in the domestic field; had restored the respect of Americans for the politician who held executive posts; and had showed that he fully understood America's responsibility as a world power.

It was several hours before the world at large became aware of its loss. Mrs Roosevelt was contacted while making a speech in Washington, and brought back to the White House. It had been decided by the President's personal staff that no one should be told of the news until the President's wife had first been informed. On being told, she shortly suggested that the Vice-President should be brought to the White House.

The Vice-President was in a room in the Senate, about to drink a glass of bourbon with tap water, when he received the message to go over to the White House at once. The Senate was perhaps the only place where the Vice-President was likely to be immediately recognized for the purpose of handing him a message, or, indeed, for any purpose at all. Harry S. Truman had been chosen as Vice-President as a compromise between the more colourful and ambitious Henry A. Wallace and James F. Byrnes, between whom the Democratic Party could not agree. It seems that the main reason for Truman in particular being chosen was his almost universal popularity in the Senate, where he was widely respected, and the fact that such a choice did not tread on anyone's toes.* Roosevelt was determined that his vision for the post-war world should not become clogged in the Senate. Truman was a poor speaker (in that he could never think of anything to say except making his point and then sitting down), but he had popularity and respect, although no one found it easy to say exactly why, unless it was for his intelligent and firm chairmanship of a well-known investigating committee. Two days after he had become Vice-President, Roosevelt had gone off to Yalta (the President had, in fact, been in Washington for less than a month of the eighty-two-day-old term). Apart from Cabinet meetings, Truman had met Roosevelt only twice since his appointment as Vice-President.

On the afternoon of April 12th Truman had found little enough to do. The main duty of the Vice-President is to act as Chairman in the Senate. On that day he had indicated to one Senator that if he wished to cast his vote he had best be present in person in order to cast it—an old Senate rule which had long been ignored; his suggestion was practically revolutionary, but it was quite clear that he meant it. He had then sat on at his dais while the Senator from Wisconsin talked interminably; he leant over and asked the clerk below for a sheet of paper, had written a letter to his mother back home in Missouri, and, after a recess had been called for, had called at the room of the Speaker of the House of Representatives, Sam Rayburn, for a bourbon and a chat.

On arrival at the White House, the Vice-President was ushered to Mrs Roosevelt's second-floor study. Roosevelt's widow said: 'Harry, the President is dead.' Truman was shocked, and remained speechless for some moments. The last news he had heard of the President's health was that it was satisfactory. He has recalled: 'I had been afraid for many weeks that something might happen to this

---

* This is the reason usually given; it may underrate the fact that Roosevelt, who was well aware of his own ill-health, was a shrewd judge of a man.

great leader, but now that the worst had happened I was unprepared for it.' After a brief expression of sympathy, there was a long silence, broken by a knock on the study door. Edward R. Stettinius, Secretary of State, walked in. His appearance shocked Truman out of his reflective trance; for the Secretary of State, a man widely known for his urbane suavity, was weeping.

The Presidential Press Secretary, Steve Early, was also in the study. Truman briskly asked him to arrange a Cabinet meeting as soon as possible. He then went down to the first floor, along a deserted, covered terrace to the west wing, and into the oval office of the President of the United States.

The Cabinet quickly assembled in the Cabinet Room and stood muttering in small groups about the news, which was now rapidly spreading. Truman, meanwhile, had picked up a telephone and spoken to his wife and daughter at their five-room apartment on the second floor of 4701 Connecticut Avenue. He asked them to come over to see him sworn in. Soon all the necessary officials and Cabinet members were gathered, together with a large group of Press photographers who, the news of Roosevelt's death having been given to the three main news agencies, had rushed to the scene and now seemed to be taking control of the proceedings. While the Chief Justice of the Supreme Court, Harlan F. Stone, waited nervously to fulfil the highest function of his office, Bill Simmons, the President's receptionist, searched from office to office, rummaging through desks and shelves, for a copy of the Bible. He eventually found one in the absent Hassett's office—a cheap Nelson edition, used for checking the accuracy of quotations. He took it to the crowded Cabinet Room and showed it to Truman, explaining that it was all he could find. Mr Truman said it would be perfectly satisfactory.

The Chief Justice began to intone to the squat little man in a lounge suit, with beady eyes behind trim spectacles, and a straight mouth clamped tightly shut over a well-proportioned and determined-looking jaw: 'I, Harry Shippe Truman . . .'

Truman solemnly repeated: 'I, Harry S. Truman . . .' (He later explained that the 'S' did not stand for Shippe, his grandfather's name—it stood for nothing at all.) The short ceremony was quickly over. There was a certain amount of pandemonium. The photographers insisted on a second performance. It was 7.09 p.m., two hours, thirty-four minutes since Roosevelt had died.

As everyone calmed down, people began leaving the room, each shaking hands with the new President, until only the Cabinet were left. The members of the Cabinet seated themselves in their accustomed places, Truman taking the President's chair; only the second man to sit in it for twelve years. He was about to speak when a secretary burst into the room and said that the Press were asking whether the San Francisco conference of the United Nations would still take place. The members of the Cabinet all turned and carefully watched the new President who replied, according to those who were there, without any hesitation whatever, that the conference would most certainly be held as planned; it was of supreme importance to the future of the world. His first Presidential decision having been made clearly and impressively, Truman then told the Cabinet that he wished them all to remain in their present posts, but, although he intended to follow the general line of Roosevelt's policy, he also intended to be President in his own right, and he indicated that there would shortly be some Cabinet changes. The Cabinet then rose and silently filed out of the room.

One man remained—the Secretary of War, Henry Stimson. In what Truman thought were strangely urgent tones, he told the new President that the latter ought to be made aware at the earliest convenient moment of an extremely secret project known to hardly anyone even in the Government or Cabinet. It was, Truman gathered, something to do with a new explosive or bomb of exceptional destructive power. Stimson having left, Truman followed and returned to the car which had been waiting for him since bringing the Vice-President, the holder of the job often referred to as 'a political graveyard', to the White House after an unexpected summons.

The President found his wife and daughter Margaret with some neighbours. His neighbour's wife made him a ham-and-turkey sandwich and a glass of milk. Having eaten this, Truman telephoned his mother, telling her that she would be unlikely to be hearing from him for some time, and then went straight to bed.

While the President relaxed peacefully at home, the communication media of the world were flashing across the globe the most sensational news for many years. Radio programmes throughout the United States were interrupted with brief and explosive announcements of Roosevelt's death. In New York the news spread like some massive instantaneous plague from person to person. Shocked office workers stood around in lobbies; restaurants, bars and theatre foyers were crowded while total strangers, in half-disbelief, stood discussing the loss as though of a mutual relative. Commuters who heard the news in the subway came pouring out again on to the streets. Mounted police in Times Square fought to keep the crowds on the pavements.

Churchill heard the news, from a Press agency, in the early hours of the following morning. 'I felt as if I had been struck a physical blow,' he later wrote. He personally telephoned the news to Buckingham Palace. The BBC telephoned the famous American servicemen's canteen in London's West End, the Rainbow Club, warning them that an important announcement was to be broadcast shortly. In Germany, Eisenhower had been having a conference with Generals Bradley and Patton at the latter's trailer. After Eisenhower and Bradley had left to spend the night at a small house nearby, Patton switched on his radio to check his watch with the midnight news bulletin on the BBC. Hearing the announcement, he ran to the house and informed Bradley and Eisenhower; the three soldiers talked of Roosevelt late into the night. Within an hour of the news being received in Moscow, Molotov called at the American Embassy, apparently genuinely moved.

In Germany, Goebbels was the first of the senior figures to hear of the news. He telephoned Hitler and, with immense excitement, exclaimed: 'My Fuehrer, I congratulate you. Roosevelt is dead.' He informed Hitler that according to the stars the second half of April would be a turning point in Nazi fortunes, and that this piece of happy news was certainly the start of such a process. A number of other senior German leaders were also confident that Roosevelt's death might well lead to some dramatic improvement in their country's position. Hitler himself, however, was not roused from his moody depression.

Short-wave radio had flashed the news to Tokyo, where the broadcasting system made a special announcement. It was followed by a few minutes of sombre music 'in honour of the passing of this great man'. Before long the Japanese Premier had himself arrived at the studio, and he went on the air. To the astonishment of the US monitoring service, he said: 'I can easily understand the great loss his passing means to the American people, and my profound sympathy goes to them.' Could it mean that Japan was about to attempt to 'soften up' American resistance before suing for peace? Some people thought so, but not the American troops fighting desperately against suicide brigades in Okinawa—they considered it just one more example of what was widely considered in the Pacific theatre to be the national hysteria of the Japanese. (Two of the late

President's sons were, as it happened, serving with the fleet near Okinawa.)

The following morning the new President was up at 6.30 a.m. Waiting beside his car, when he emerged from the apartment block, were a number of reporters. The President knew one of them, and greeted him thus: 'Hey, Tony, if you're going down to the White House you may as well hop in with me.' For press-men attuned to a President who had always moved with distant, if graceful, grandeur, it was an extraordinary scene. It had, indeed, been a tremendously dramatic moment a few seconds earlier to see the President of the United States actually trotting down a flight of steps, walking briskly to his car and getting into it unaided. The few people who stood in Connecticut Avenue that morning were among the first to dimly realize that the previous day had not only marked the end of a great career, it had also marked the beginning of a change in the whole tone of American government.

On arrival shortly after 9 a.m., Truman found that the machinery of the White House, which had worked so smoothly round Roosevelt's special needs and long-established habits, had almost completely collapsed. As the morning progressed he improvised as best he could, dealing with caller after caller behind Roosevelt's desk, which he had already divested of the more obvious symbols of F. D. R., while confusion reigned in the anterooms around him. Stettinius was the first to be admitted to see the new President; he was asked to prepare in brief outline a statement of American foreign relations. He was followed by Stimson, Secretary of the Navy James Forrestal, Presidential Chief of Staff Admiral William D. Leahy, and the Chiefs of Staff of the Army and Navy, Marshall and King. From these visits Truman, who had previously known very little indeed about how the war was waged, gathered that the defeat of Germany could be expected in six months, and that Japan would probably be conquered about a year after that. That, at any rate, was the opinion of the experts. After an informal lunch with some old friends in Congress, Truman met the Press. 'Boys, if newspapermen ever pray,' he said, 'pray for me now. . . . I've got the most terribly responsible job a man ever had.' Afterwards he met James F. Byrnes, who had resigned from the Roosevelt administration, in which he had been Director of War Mobilization, only five days earlier. Truman, already aware through his experience of a few hours that international affairs were in a critical state, and that his knowledge of them was totally inadequate, seems to have decided that all other business would have to wait while he got himself briefed on these matters. He asked Byrnes to tell him everything he could remember of the Yalta conference, and later was given a resumé of the Polish question by Stettinius and Charles Bohlen. Truman returned home in the evening laden with papers which had been prepared by most of the departments to bring him up to date in their affairs.

In London, Churchill had made a short announcement in the House of Commons, which had adjourned in respect. In Moscow, Harriman had called on Stalin. The Marshal was visibly moved and spoke of Roosevelt in glowing terms as of a respected and close personal friend. But his grief was probably not entirely unselfish, for with the death of Roosevelt he had lost one of his best cards in his uncomfortable relationship with the Politburo. He knew that so long as Roosevelt had been in power there had been no question of the United States taking the lead in an anti-Soviet bloc. He said that in his opinion the late President had been the welding force in the alliance, and asked if there was anything he could do to ensure that the solidarity between the Allies was maintained. With creditable promptitude, Harriman replied that indeed there was: the sending of Molotov to the San Francisco conference. Molotov, who was present, immediately protested that such an idea was impossible. Stalin, however, overruled him, and said that Molotov would go. The delighted Harriman rushed off to radio Stettinius, who immediately informed Truman.*

The world's newspapers had met the situation as best they could. Everywhere there had been fervent eulogies to Roosevelt. The normally restrained *New York Times* said: 'Men will thank God, a hundred years from now, that Franklin D. Roosevelt was in the White House. . . .' As the hours went by, however, it was becoming more and more obvious to editors as well as others that there was a new man in the White House. By April 14th the initial shock of Roosevelt's death had worn off, and there was a furious quest for information—any information—about Harry S. Truman. As the *New York Times* resoundingly put it: 'In one of the great moments of history there steps into the office of the Presidency of the United States, and into a position of world-wide influence and authority

* Official Russian policy has been to look back on the Roosevelt era with nostalgia. As recently as 1962 Khruschev said (in an exclusive interview with the *Daily Express*): 'The best thing would be for co-operation pervaded with the spirit which prevailed in our relations at the time of the great President Franklin Roosevelt. This is the avenue for Soviet–American relations.'

such as no other living American has ever held, a man who is less well known to the people of this country than many other public figures, and almost totally unknown abroad.' London newspapers were offering exceptional prices for a thousand words on the new President. Associated Press reported from Paris that a few days before not one Frenchman in ten had even heard of Truman. As editorials and articles groped about, it sometimes seemed that the writers were valiantly attempting to hide the fear that the man was a nonentity. Although such a frightening thought was not openly voiced in the newspapers, it was widely mentioned in private. There were, however, two reports which gave to the careful reader a completely contrary view of the little man who had stepped into the big man's shoes. The first to appear was by Roy Roberts, managing editor of the *Kansas City Star*. He had known Truman, and followed his career, for many years. His article was widely syndicated. He recalled that only twenty years before, Truman, then a man of forty, was looking at the rear of a horse as he ploughed a furrow in a Missouri field. Later he had sold haberdashery, and failed at it. He had been, apparently, a failure in life. 'The sheer fact that he is this average man, understands the average man and his quality, is probably Truman's greatest asset.' Rogers pointed out that Truman's friendships and associations dated from the First World War, when he had fought in France. But was he really as 'average' as he appeared? To some extent, perhaps; but a slightly different view appeared in the London *Observer* a day or two later. In the main article, Dorothy Thompson wrote: 'The new President ended his short career as Vice-President of the United States Senate admirably, and even dramatically, especially in view of the fact that he had not the slightest idea that he was ending it. . . . And he began his administration by the simple statement that the San Francisco conference would go on. That was also a decision taken immediately and without timidity. President Truman did not express himself as overwhelmed. He rose to an immediate crisis. . . . The Truman "Report" I remember as courageous, meticulous and fair.'

Meanwhile the object of all this attention and conjecture had begun another day of hurried education at the White House. Senior government officials and Cabinet members who continually called on him, glad of the chance to study this man whom they had neglected to observe closely before and hardly knew, were surprised to find themselves curtly dealt with and then dismissed. Henry Morgenthau,

Secretary of the Treasury, was disconcerted when his interview was quickly cut short by a request for a written report on the state of the nation's finances. Truman had summoned Byrnes and Henry Wallace to the White House, and they duly appeared in the oval office. There was no urgent reason for his seeing these two men, and they talked idly for a few minutes before Truman announced that it was time for him to go to Union Station to meet Roosevelt's funeral train from Warm Springs. These were the two men who had been, as all the world knew, rivals for the Vice-Presidency only a few weeks before. With all his other worries and new responsibilities, Truman had nevertheless initiated this brilliant move. The three men went down to the station together, and from there the cortège moved slowly through the streets, past silent and weeping crowds, to the White House. Arrangements for a funeral had been hastily made by the White House Social Bureau, after a search through the files for the records of the funeral of Warren Harding, the last President to have died in office. (Roosevelt had prepared a most detailed programme for his own funeral as far back as 1937, asking, among other things, that a gun-carriage and not a hearse should be used throughout, and that 'there be no lying in state anywhere'; it was found in his bedroom three days after the burial.) As the coffin was carried into the White House, and a Navy band played the National Anthem on the lawn, and men, women and officials stood around openly weeping, Truman rushed back to the President's office, for the world had not stopped going round, and it was still at war. He had sent for Harry Hopkins, who had flown straight from hospital, and F. D. R.'s old adviser and confidant now talked for two hours, giving a background picture to the events leading up to Yalta, and describing in detail the characters of those involved ('Stalin is a forthright, rough, tough Russian . . . but he can be talked to frankly'). During the afternoon two messages came from Churchill; the first calling for a joint statement to celebrate the fast-approaching junction of Soviet and Anglo-American forces in Germany. Truman dealt with this by asking Churchill to submit a draft. The second was a reply to a suggestion of Roosevelt's that pilotless bombers, guided by remote control, should be launched from England on industrial targets in Germany. Churchill now begged that this should not be carried out; the state of the war no longer demanded such drastic methods, which might even yet result in heavy retaliation against the South of England, which had already, especially London, suffered severely (he pointed out that 30,000 civilians had been killed in raids on

London). Truman agreed to postpone the plan for pilotless bombers.

At four o'clock Truman walked from his office to the East Room, where 200 guests were assembled for the funeral of Franklin Delano Roosevelt. The guests included Eden and Gromyko, the Philippine President Osmena, Thomas E. Dewey and Harold Stassen (Roosevelt's Republican rivals), and Mrs Woodrow Wilson. Eighty years earlier to the day Abraham Lincoln had been shot dead, and had lain in state in the same room. Throughout the United States a two minutes' silence was observed. Telephone services were cut off, in newspaper offices teletype machines tapped out SILENCE, trains in New York's subway ground to a halt, production halted in factories. While many millions that evening genuinely mourned a man who had become a legend in his own lifetime, the lights burned bright on the second floor of 4701 Connecticut Avenue—the new President was still at work.

On Tuesday, April 17th, Churchill made one of his most famous speeches in the House of Commons; a generous and heartfelt tribute to the late President, who, as he pointed out, was 'the greatest champion of freedom who has ever brought help and comfort from the New World to the Old'. During this time he became aware that the new President was a man still trying to find his feet in a world on which he had never trod before. 'It seemed to me extraordinary, especially during the last few months, that Roosevelt had not made his deputy and potential successor thoroughly acquainted with the whole story, and brought him into the decisions that were being taken. This proved of grave disadvantage to our affairs. There is no comparison between reading about events afterwards and living through them from hour to hour. How could Mr Truman know and weigh the issues at stake at this climax of the war? In these early months his position was one of extreme difficulty, and did not enable him to bring his outstanding qualities fully into action.' The British Ambassador in Washington, Lord Halifax, sent Churchill some good news on the subject of the new President: 'It may be of interest that Truman's hobby is history of military strategy, of which he is reported to have read widely.' Nothing could have been calculated to please Churchill more. After a meeting with Truman, Eden reported: 'My impression from the interview is that the President is honest and friendly. He is conscious of but not overwhelmed by his new responsibilities.' On the whole, this view of Eden's reflected the general opinion that was gaining currency in Washington.

(ii)

It is difficult to see why the American military experts expected the war in Europe to last another six months, for at the time of Roosevelt's death organized German resistance in the west had practically ceased. With mopping-up still taking place in the Ruhr, Eisenhower was pushing on towards the Elbe with astonishing speed. The encirclement of the Ruhr had deprived Kesselring of his centre, and his movements were now confined to concentrating his two flanks, one being rolled back on to the northern ports, and the other (with which he remained in person) falling back on the southern mountains. Most of the Nazi administration, loot, hostages and important personages had already begun drifting into the fastnesses of the southern sector, including a nuclear reactor and a group of nuclear physicists who were evacuated to a cave in the Bavarian Alps. Already a rail bridge had been constructed by the Allies across the Rhine at Wesel, and supplies were pouring into Germany for the advancing armies. Only the fierce resistance of the German force outside Berlin, holding back the Russian advance, was preventing a junction of Russian and Anglo-American forces; when that happened German resistance would be cut in two. The Americans were already deep into the zone which had been allocated for Russian occupation, but there had been no agreement at Yalta about the Allied armies restricting themselves to any particular areas in pursuit of the common enemy, and certainly nothing had been said about the occupation of Berlin (it having been taken for granted, at that time, that the Russians would reach the capital first). As has been seen, Eisenhower was not, in any event, interested in the capture of Berlin. In his report he said: 'Military factors when the enemy was on the brink of final defeat were more important in my eyes than the political considerations involved in an Allied capture of the capital.' He was now more than ever convinced that the Nazis intended a final stand in the Bavarian hills and mountains, and especially at a super-fortress of almost impregnable passes, which would be difficult and costly to overrun, around Berchtesgaden. Bradley wrote afterwards: 'Not until after the campaign ended were we to learn that this Redoubt existed largely in the imaginations of a few fanatic Nazis. It grew into so exaggerated a scheme that I am astonished that we could have believed it as innocently as we did.' It was with this fear very much in mind that Eisenhower decided to give all the support he could in the south, at the expense of Montgomery in the north. He was also influenced by Bradley's recent performance, a series of brilliant tactical strokes against a crumbling enemy. He told his naval aide, in an obvious reference to Montgomery: 'Bradley has never held back and never has paused to regroup when he saw an opportunity to advance.' This was perfectly true. For Montgomery's whole tactical thinking, and especially his fear of careless planning and the resulting heavy casualties, was conditioned, unlike Bradley's, by his experiences in the First World War. Bradley, militarily speaking, was the better man for the hour, and Eisenhower sensed this. With all this in mind, Eisenhower ordered a halt at the Elbe. He had no wish to get entangled around Berlin. All this was a bitter disappointment to Montgomery, who had lost the Ninth US Army to Bradley, but he now realized, as he has said, that 'it was useless for me to pursue the matter further'. (Montgomery insists that Berlin, Vienna and Prague could all have been 'grabbed before the Russians'.) After an advance of fifty-seven miles in the day, the armoured vanguard of the Ninth US Army reached the Elbe, near Magdeburg, on April 11th. Bradley's forces were fifty-three miles from Berlin, not much further than the Russians, who had been held up not long before by an inconvenient thaw of the Oder. There is no doubt that they could have crossed the Elbe with little opposition and taken the city from the rear. Eisenhower promptly sent a message to Stalin, informing him of his intention of stopping at the Elbe, and ordered Patton, already at the Czech frontier, not to probe towards Prague (which, according to Bradley, could have been taken within twenty-four hours), but to concentrate on the so-called National Redoubt. Thus half-way through April American forces were more than 100 miles inside the Russian Zone of Germany before the Russians had themselves hardly entered it, and were in an excellent position for driving on to Prague. At this time Stalin became extremely apprehensive about the success of his intentions in Central Europe, and his own advance from the Oder was conducted with the utmost secrecy so far as the West was concerned, and brief Soviet statements gave little away.

Meanwhile Montgomery, urged on by Churchill, was racing for Lübeck to cut off the Danish peninsula from the Russians. Churchill was suspicious of Russian intentions in this area, as in all others. With Denmark in their hands, the Russians would have control of the Baltic. Montgomery's armoured divisions operated in great depth on narrow thrust-lines, by-passing areas of enemy resistance. On the far left flank the First Canadian Army was meanwhile striking deep into the Netherlands with three targets: the capturing of the V-bomb sites, the liberation of the Dutch people (many of whom were by this time dying from starvation) and the destruction of the German forces under the local commissar Artur von Seyss-Inquart. The latter, indulging in blackmail of grand enormity, threatened to break a dyke for every kilometre the Canadians advanced. He indicated that he was quite prepared to smash the great dyke across the Zuider Zee, thus putting much of Holland under water. The Canadians halted; but Seyss-Inquart, after representations from Bedell Smith, agreed to supplies being allowed in to the starving Dutch. The Canadians, however, had already reached the North Sea, and the last V.2 had fallen on England. Throughout their advance the Canadians had come upon railway sidings jammed with V-bomb-laden trucks.

By the third week in April Allied troops were well ensconced in Western Germany. Already tentative efforts were being made to bring some order to the anarchy they found there. Military Government officers went around delivering proclamations (one had actually crossed the Rhine with the assaulting troops) which demanded: the abolition of all Nazi organizations and law courts; the destruction of Nazi emblems; lists of inmates to be posted on the doors of all houses. It was stated that marks were to be held at the rate of forty to the pound sterling. According to Alan Moorehead: 'Looting was widespread and heavy. German cars by the hundred were dragged out of garages and hiding-places under the straw in the barns, painted khaki and driven away. Cameras and watches and revolvers were taken automatically from prisoners, and frequently from civilians. In nearly every town the shops were broached, the distilleries emptied. Even pictures were stripped from their frames.' Within weeks, when men returned on leave, Britain seemed to be flooded with German cameras.

It was at this time that the prisoner-of-war camps were relieved. Men who had waited with mounting excitement, almost unable to believe that the rumours they had heard were true, burst into freedom like a sudden joyous eruption from a volcano. In most cases, so fast was the Allied advance, the gates were actually opened for them by the forward troops themselves. Their release could not have been more dramatically ordered; it happened exactly as they had dreamed. At one of the biggest camps, Fallingbostel, the British troops found their comrades drawn up in the compound inside, before the Union Jack; gaiters, belts and badges immaculately turned out. The relieving troops watched as the prisoners-of-war came, as one man, to the salute. Among those released in the last days of the war were Captain Earl Haig, Lieutenant Lord Lascelles (cousin of the Queen), Captain the Master of Elphinstone (nephew of the Queen), Lieutenant John Winant (son of the US Ambassador to Britain), Jean Borotra, in somewhat adventurous circumstances, and French leaders like Daladier, Reynaud, Gamelin and Weygand. (And from the concentration camps staggered many eminent Jewish scientists, writers and academics who had long since been forgotten by the world.) But all was not to be joy and gladness; men who had, it seemed, 'missed the war', who had been taken prisoner at Dunkirk or in the desert years before, were naturally bitter and apart; not all their hearty relievers were quick to appreciate this. It was, perhaps, a classic remark made by a released prisoner-of-war that first brought home to the invading troops, and the public at home, what five years 'out of life' had meant. It was a true remark that, within days, was to be reported around the world: 'So that's what a jeep looks like.'

The greatest administrative problem of the American and British military authorities, apart from the huge number of German surrenders growing every day, was the mass of foreign slave-labour that was found in West Germany, mostly wandering around, living off the land, and in sleazy camps. French, Dutch, Belgian, Czech, Poles and, especially, in their green overalls with S.U. painted in white on the backs, Russians. It was soon clear that there were many millions of these; no one knew exactly how many. Millions wished to return home; hundreds of thousands did not. All were uprooted from families. All were suspicious of authority, even when it was kindly and for their own benefit. They were a hopeless, introspective legion, cut off by experience and outlook from the conquerors who had come to free them, and with whom, for the time being, they had lost all meaningful communication. A phrase was coined for these wretched people: Displaced Persons.

But now an event was to occur which was to shock the world in a way that it had never been shocked before; that was to send an involuntary shudder of disgust and grief through every country.

On April 13th, 1945, Patton's Third US Army reached an apparently insignificant spot, called Buchenwald. What the American troops saw there is well enough known today. At the time there was a shock which touched the roots of humanity; for in all recorded history, even in the times of the barbarians, there had never been anything like Buchenwald. There had been rumours of the concentration camps for many years; on several occasions, even in the 'thirties, there had been evidence of them, particularly of Dachau. Many people had put down such stories to Allied propaganda. Others had accepted that there were such camps. But no one had even been able to conceive in their minds anything quite like what was now to be unveiled before their reluctant gaze.

Camp after camp, in quick succession, fell into Allied hands. For the dehumanized objects that were found in them, alive only as any organism is alive, it was mostly far too late. They continued to die like flies. At first the horrified troops who burst into the camps in almost all cases went berserk. The few German guards still present were beaten and shot out of hand. Those Germans who survived the first few days were put to work to dig communal graves; they were forcibly joined at a number of camps by civilians, including women and children, who lived in the vicinity. After a few days the Press and selected visitors were allowed in.

The first camp to fall into British hands was Belsen, the Germans having asked the British to take it over for fear that the typhus there, if left uncontrolled, would spread throughout the Reich. (Hitler had ordered that the camp should be evacuated and the inmates compelled to march 190 miles to a less vulnerable spot; as the inmates would have found difficulty in marching 190 yards, he was persuaded to cancel this order.) Although few British people had been in Belsen, and although it was in fact one of the smallest and, if possible, a camp slightly less appalling than some of the others (there were, for instance, no gas chambers), it was, because it was associated with the initial shock, to become a part of the British conscience. In Britain the word Belsen became more than the name for a concentration camp. For the first time there was a word in the language for the unmentionable. Reporters who were shown round the camp begged to be excused after the first few minutes, but were forced to continue. What they saw was what was seen at all other camps: an entire new species of the human animal, that was soon to become familiar through pictures released over the world: a small, childlike, skintight, hairless, sexless, pearly coloured being which made occasional high-pitched squeaks and smelt of its own excrement and urine—in which it lay. The reporters were, after the inspection, taken to see the German guards locked up in cells. They had been 'interrogated' that morning and were covered in blood; a number were unable to get off the floor. A camp 'doctor' begged to be killed before undergoing further 'interrogation'. His request was turned down.

A British Parliamentary delegation visited Buchenwald, at the insistence of General Eisenhower. Their report stated that 'such camps as this mark the lowest point of degradation to which humanity has yet descended'. The Government fully supported their backing of General Eisenhower's action in forcing Germans living in the vicinity of the camps to visit them. Two sentences of the long and horrible Parliamentary report riveted the attention of the world: 'They were informed that Frau Koch, the wife of the German Commandant, had collected articles made of human skin. They obtained, among other pieces of hide which Sir Bernard Spilsbury identified as human skin, one clearly forming part of a lamp-shade.' Why this, among all the many horrors, should have surfaced above the others is a mystery, but surface it did. There was no degree of horror. It was all total horror; experiments on human beings in changes of air pressure (resulting in haemorrhages of the brain); experimental injection of every conceivable disease; experiments in immersion in iced water (resulting in death or insanity); surgical 'experiments' conducted without anaesthetic; all were the ultimate in refined inhumanity. Skin-collecting was widespread at all the camps, not just Buchenwald. A survivor, who had worked in the hospital at Dachau, testified at the Nuremberg trial: 'It was common practice to remove the skin from dead prisoners. It was chemically treated and placed in the sun to dry. After that it was cut into various sizes for use as saddles, riding breeches, gloves, house slippers and ladies' handbags. Tattooed skin was particularly valued by SS men. This skin would have to be from healthy prisoners and free from defects . . . we would receive twenty or thirty bodies of young people. They would have been shot in the neck or struck on the head so that the skin would be uninjured. Also we frequently got requests for the skulls or skeletons of prisoners. In those cases we boiled the skull or the body. Then the soft parts were removed and the bones were bleached and dried and reassembled. In the case of skulls it was important to have a good set of teeth. So it was dangerous to have a good skin or good teeth. . . .' The first American troops to reach Dachau ranged through the camp spraying bullets from machine-guns and pistols at the guards; released prisoners exacted terrible vengeance on their tormentors. But Buchenwald was the camp to which the American military authorities took most of their selected visitors. After one such visit Colonel Charles Codman wrote: 'The shelves were still well filled. Some of them were living human beings, but the majority were almost indistinguishable from the corpses we saw in the death cart. On one shelf barer than the rest, three shadowy figures huddled together for warmth. Cold comfort for the outside two, since the middle one had been dead for several hours. Under the old régime he would eventually have been stripped and thrown out on to the flagstones to await the next tour of the wagon. Further on, an emaciated spectre of a man . . . was crawling up on to the next shelf. It was only three feet from the floor but he could not make it.' One of the first correspondents to visit the camp was the American broadcaster Edward Murrow. Several almost naked skeletons came up to him, and, touching him hesitantly, told him that they knew him. He remembered them, but could not recognize them; one was the ex-Mayor of Prague. 'They were in rags . . . death had already marked many of them. I looked out over that mass of men to the green fields beyond where well-fed Germans were ploughing.'

How much did the German people know of the concentration camps? It was said that the smoke from the incinerators, with the unmistakable stench of burning flesh and bone, had been both visible and well known to the nostrils for miles around. It was said that for this reason there had been petitions by local residents to the authorities to have the camps removed. But this was a question that was not satisfactorily answered; and it most certainly never will be.

What required no answer was that in the concentration camps an utter and total contempt had been displayed by humans for the lives of fellow humans; that there had been a massive and well-organized orgy of the most depraved sadism and inhumanity. The reaction in America, Britain, in Europe, and in other countries, was quite clear. After the initial shock, there was no anger; only shame.

(iii)

While in Germany the Allied advance revealed the nightmarish secrets of the Nazis, as if rolling back some carpet which had been hiding a vermin-covered floor, in Italy, too, the advance of the British, American and Polish armies was bringing Italian Fascism to its last moments; but in this case there was more bathos than gigantic horror.

The campaign was coming to a brilliant close. Alexander, Supreme Commander in the Mediterranean, and General Mark Clark, Commander of the Fifteenth Army Group, had delayed all thought of an offensive till the spring; previous experience of winter campaigning in Italy left them with no other choice. But the Allied air forces, outnumbering the enemy by thirty to one, had kept up a ceaseless attack on the passes connecting northern Italy with Austria and Germany. Some passes were blocked in this way for weeks at a time; supplies, especially of fuel, were thus rapidly diminishing among the German forces. German morale, however, was comparatively high, units were up to strength, and, as nearly always in the entire Italian campaign, they outnumbered the Allied divisions; but they were fatally hampered by their lack of fuel and the rigid defensive position south of the River Po on which Hitler insisted. They would have done far better, as all the German commanders realized, to have retired to the Tyrol. But Hitler had told Kesselring's successor: 'The Fuehrer expects . . . [you] to defend every inch of the North Italian areas entrusted to your command.' But under modern conditions the holding of such static lines is impossible. The Allied forces struck on April 9th. There were two main thrusts, by the Eighth and Fifth Armies, which made up one of the most polyglot forces of the war, including British, New Zealand, Indian, American, Polish, Brazilian and Italian troops. According to Attlee, there were twenty-two nations under Alexander's command. A superbly commanded campaign, in which land, air and naval (supporting both flanks) forces concerted with notable success, followed. The enemy, by no means already beaten as they were in Germany, were forced to steadily withdraw. In fourteen days the Po was reached and crossed. The Fifth US Army headed north-west towards Milan, Turin and Genoa, and the Eighth north-west towards Trieste. Although the Allied forces in Italy were only expected to contain the Germans and to keep as many enemy divisions in that theatre as possible, they had of their own accord broken free from their secondary role and won an important victory. Italian partisans, who for many weeks had been conducting guerrilla war in the back areas, now rose with confidence and gained control of several cities and towns, including Venice. The negotiations that had begun in Switzerland some time before were hurriedly reopened by German emissaries, after moves by the Cardinal Archbishop of Milan. In a message to Alexander, Churchill said: 'This great final battle in Italy will long stand out in history as one of the most famous episodes in the Second World War.' Alas, this was not to be so; the advance from the Rhine was to steal the glory.

In Milan, Mussolini's puppet government kept up a pretence of authority until mid-April; but by then extensive partisan activity throughout northern Italy had made the Duce's position impossible. (As late as March he had visited Hitler and returned much encouraged at the news of the V.2s and the super-submarines.) On April 25th, with Allied forces rapidly approaching the city, he held a meeting of what could still be found of his Cabinet. Graziani, his Minister of War, reported on the complete collapse of the front at the Po. But Mussolini still believed he would be able to salvage something from the wreckage of his empire; he harboured the illusion that he could make a deal with the leaders of the extreme left, who controlled the partisans. A meeting was arranged at the Palace of the Cardinal. The Cardinal, comparing the disconsolate Duce with Napoleon, argued that the world would appreciate it as a gesture if he capitulated now. It seemed that Mussolini was about to do so when he suddenly broke up the meeting and stormed out. He was dazed by the news that the German forces in Italy were already preparing to surrender, a fact which had previously been kept from him. In fact, as no doubt he realized, it no longer mattered a scrap to the world whether he capitulated or not; events were entirely beyond his control, and would now take their ordained course. On arrival at the Prefecture, which he had turned into the seat of his so-called government, he ordered an immediate departure for Como. He gave no reason for this particular destination; and, indeed, there was none. As usual, his familiar abruptness hid his indecision. A column of ten cars was assembled, and together with some truck-loads of German troops who had been assigned to him as a personal guard, the Duce and the few Ministers and officials who were still with him set off at 8 p.m. on April 25th. His last act before leaving was to release all party members and troops from their oath of allegiance. He wanted no fighting in Milan. On his arrival at Como he refused to give any orders, and made it plain that he had abandoned all authority.

Thus ended the political career of a remarkable and ambitious man, equipped with an extraordinary power of dramatizing himself and his policies; a bombastic self-adulator whose performance would have received scant recognition among any people but the opera-loving Italians; a ruthless and violent conniver who nevertheless did not descend to gas-ovens and mass-slaughter. Had he died or retired in the early 'thirties he would possibly have gone down in history as the spiritual descendant of the medieval despots of the city states; a dictator who had brought a few worthwhile achievements to his country. But dictators seldom retire. Now, with no coherent plan and surrounded only by those minions who sought personal safety through keeping in his company, he was, too fast for him to fully appreciate it, changing from a head of state (of sorts) to a hunted outcast. After a day at Como he set off once more, having agreed to attempt to cross the Swiss frontier. Despair and confusion were all that he found at the border; a scouting party which had been sent ahead discovering that the Italian border guards had joined the partisans. The cavalcade was driving around the border area, without any clear plan, when it was stopped by a strong partisan patrol at a place called, ironically enough, Musso. After a long wait, during which the commander of the German guard and the partisan leader conferred, it was agreed that the German soldiers would be allowed through but not the mysterious Italian civilians. Mussolini hurriedly donned a German greatcoat and helmet and, a sten-gun between his knees, he pretended to be asleep in one of the trucks. But even in the thin and haggard condition to which he had been reduced in recent months there was no adequate disguise, in Italy, for the Duce. He was docilely taken prisoner, only complaining when someone picked up his leather brief-case: 'Be careful, that case contains documents of great historical importance.' He spent the evening, during which it rained incessantly, being taken from one party of guerrillas to another; no one wanting to take the responsibility of doing anything with the once-mighty Duce himself. His faithful mistress, Claretta Petacci, who had always adored him, had also been taken prisoner in the same convoy, and, at her request, she was taken to him. The two spent the night, under guard, at a peasant's house in a remote village. Up till this time they had been considerately treated, and kept in disguise (Mussolini in an old workman's cap), in case they should be recognized by more ardent partisans who might execute them before orders as to what to do with them could come from Milan. Those orders arrived during the night. Early in the morning three women kneeling by the village pump, washing clothes, saw a small party with a smartly dressed woman in tears and a man with a look of utter despair on his features under his shabby cap get into a black car, which roared out of the village.

Benito Mussolini and Claretta Petacci were taken up a steep hill, bundled out of the car, and stood up against a wall beside a gatepost. From where they stood they could have had a brief glimpse of the waters of Lake Como glistening far below in the early morning sunlight. No one saw the execution except the three partisans present;* it is not clear whether the death of Petacci was intended or not. A maid at a house opposite heard the shooting (it took six shots to kill Mussolini), and peeped through a hedge shortly afterwards. She saw the bodies, which lay there in the rain, which was now falling, before being thrown into a lorry containing the dead ministers and officials who had been caught with Mussolini but separated from him after capture. Before it left for Milan, a partisan climbed into the truck and took from Petacci's neck a gold pendant on which was inscribed: 'Clara, I am you—you are me, Ben: 24.4.32–24.4.41.'

The truck was unloaded in a garage on the Piazzale Loreto, Milan. As the news spread, a crowd assembled at the garage and demanded to be shown the bodies, whereupon a tall man in shirt-sleeves lifted them up one by one as the crowd shouted their names. After this had gone on for some time, the tall man wearied of his task, and someone had the idea of stringing the corpses up by meat-hooks from the roof. This was done; Mussolini being the first to be strung up, head downwards. When he appeared, the crowd, which had now grown to an enormous size, let out a prolonged burst of hissing, jeering and catcalls. Those near enough spat. They were the same people who had, for so many years, cheered, fawned upon and grovelled before the same man. The faithful Petacci's body was next to be displayed, followed by the remainder. The bodies were already rigid, and the arms stuck out in various attitudes. A slight wind swept them to and fro as in some ghoulish dance; a photographer snapped them, and yet another famous picture of the Second World War was taken.

Winston Churchill was, like many others, 'profoundly shocked'. He wrote to Alexander: 'The man who murdered Mussolini made a confession, published in the *Daily Express*, gloating over the treacherous and cowardly method of his action. In particular he said he shot Mussolini's mistress. Was she on the list of war criminals? Had he any authority from anybody to shoot this woman? It seems to me the cleansing hand of British military power should make inquiries on these points.' But inquiries were inconclusive and passive. The act had been done, and the world was spared another Nuremberg.

* And only one of them has given a full version of what happened.

Two German delegates reached Alexander's headquarters on April 29th. They signed an unconditional surrender (in the presence of Russian observers), and on May 2nd nearly a million German troops surrendered. The war in Italy had ended in the way that everyone, including Hitler, knew it had to. In an order of the day, Field-Marshal Alexander, aloof, shy, widely respected but immensely reserved, wrote perhaps the only really relaxed words of his public life: 'After nearly two years of hard and continuous fighting which started in Sicily in the summer of 1943, you stand today as victors in the Italian campaign. You have won a victory which has ended in the complete and utter rout of the German armed forces in the Mediterranean. Today the remnants of the once-proud army have laid down their arms to you—close on a million men with all their arms, equipment and impedimenta. You may well be proud of this great victorious campaign. . . . No praise is high enough for you, sailors, soldiers, airmen, and workers of the united forces in Italy, for your magnificent triumph. My gratitude to you and my admiration is unbounded and only equalled by the pride which is mine of being your Commander-in-Chief.'

Adolf Hitler, in his testament carefully recorded by Bormann, contrived to get the final and most apt word on the Italian war, during which he had scattered his armies from Tobruk to the Po in the service of the Duce, whom he had once so admired. 'It is quite obvious that our Italian alliance has been of more service to our enemies than to ourselves. Italian intervention has conferred benefits which are modest in the extreme in comparison with the numerous difficulties to which it has given rise. If, in spite of our efforts, we fail to win this war, the Italian alliance will have contributed to our defeat. To ensure her abstention, no sacrifices, no presents on our part, would have been too great.'

(iv)

On the same day that Mussolini had attempted to discard his responsibilities by leaving Milan, two events of far greater importance had occurred in Germany; Berlin was encircled, if somewhat tenuously, by the Russian armies which had been steadily pushing back the German defence from the Oder, and, at 1.30 p.m., the forward patrols of Konev's 58th Guards Division linked up on the Elbe with the van of the 273rd Regiment of the First US Army at Torgau, on the Elbe.

The defences that had been prepared on the outskirts of Berlin now took the full brunt of the Russian onslaught as much of the remaining *Wehrmacht* on the north-eastern front, about 250,000 strong, withdrew behind them to make a last stand in defence of the city. Little information about this great Russian advance was given at the time (the same applies, to a lesser extent, to the advance into Austria and the fall of Vienna on April 13th, the bitter siege of Breslau, which lasted eighty-two days, and other fighting on the Eastern Front in the last stages of the war), but there is no doubt that the full weight of two whole Soviet armies, Konev's and Zhukov's, were hurled at Berlin. Hitler's much-heralded and pathetic *Volkssturm*, ill armed and wretched, had mostly faded away. As in the west, the Hitler Youth had done better. Such a bombardment was now poured on to the city that the whole area became hidden in a cloud of dust and smoke; many soldiers, and some of the civilians lurking in cellars, were suffocated by the stifling air. Detachments of defenders were rushed from one threatened spot to another, stumbling over the ruined city, already blasted to rubble by British and American bombers, in a haze of blinding grit and powdered plaster. All the while the Red Army, advancing in stages of 100 yards or so, inexorably closed in like a circular vice. The remaining German forces now began concentrating in the centre of the city, having fortified the demolished buildings. Russian artillery was brought up, with great difficulty, into the few uncluttered open spaces in order to blast, from the shortest range, this final stronghold into eternity. Tunnels and sewers were used by the German defenders to good effect; for linking their own positions, for appearing behind the Soviet lines, and as ammunition and supply depots. Fearful hand-to-hand fighting took place below ground in engagements that must have savoured of Danté's *Inferno*. None of the senior commanders dared to open negotiations with the Russians in order to bring this brutal and senseless fighting to an end; as much through fear of the Fuehrer as of the Russians. Roughly in the centre of the German position was the plain entrance of solid concrete to Hitler's bunker. Here, fifty feet beneath the Chancellery and its garden, in his enormous study with walls of blood-red marble, the Fuehrer sat pondering on his horoscope and the plans for the opera house at Linz, with only the distant thudding from far above to remind him of the cataclysm that he had himself caused. In the last hours before the encirclement, and (from Tempel-hof and down the banks of the Havel) even after it, many of his senior aides had departed, either to the concentration in the north or, with most of the Ministries, to Berchtesgaden, in the south, where an emergency 'capital' had been prepared and from where some still hoped to prolong the stand in an Alpine Redoubt. Hitler himself refused to leave for the latter, stubbornly preferring to remain in the capital and to personally conduct its defence. Only five days before the encirclement he had, on his fifty-sixth birthday, held his last grand conference, at which Himmler, Goering, Goebbels, Axmann (leader of the Hitler Youth), Doenitz, Keitel, Speer, Jodl and Bormann had all been present; most of them en-treated him to leave the city, and all, apart from Goebbels, Axmann and Bormann, immediately did so themselves. Two days later, at a military conference, he had perhaps the greatest fit of anger ever in his stormy life, accusing everyone present of total incompetence and disloyalty, and it was apparently on this occasion that he decided not to join in the hasty and undignified escape to north and south. His decision to remain meant some confusion as to leadership of the Reich. He had already made arrangements that if a geographical split should occur, Doenitz should take command in the north if that area were separated, and Kesselring if it were the south. It had not occurred to anyone till too late that Berlin might be cut off from both. Goering, however, as soon as he learned of Hitler's decision to remain, had asked whether he, as titular deputy, did not now take overall command. The Fuehrer, infuriated and con-fused, replied by dismissing him. Hitler even now clung to his hope of a clash between Soviet and Anglo-American interests in Germany, resulting in a clash between their forces, which would in some devious way save him from total disaster; failing that, there was, he hoped, always the possibility of a relief reaching the city in the form of the German Ninth Army (which to all practical purposes no longer existed). But as the hours ticked remorselessly by and the thudding from above grew more insistent, he became drained of everything except despair. Goering, who had been attempting to run the scattered remnants of the *Luftwaffe* from a lunatic asylum near Munich, before evacuating to Berchtesgaden, had been har-bouring similar delusions, and tried to negotiate with the Americans on the basis that the German forces would join with them in warding off the Russians from Central Europe.

On the night of April 26th shells began to fall on the Chancellery building itself. It started to crack and chunks of it fell to the ground, sending explosive shudders through the bunker below. At midday on April 29th the usual situation conference was held, and at it Hitler was told that the Russians had advanced in Grunewald and at the Anhalter railway station. Of the Ninth Army there was no news. There was another conference at four, and yet another at ten at night. At the last, together with various officers, were Goebbels, Bormann and General Weidling, Commandant of the city. The latter reported that a Russian group was at that moment advancing down the Wilhelmstrasse and had almost reached the Air Ministry.

A senior staff officer, Colonel Nicolaus von Below, was given the Fuehrer's final message to the Chiefs of Staff at the northern 'capital', Fuerstenberg, in which he poured recrimination on them for not relieving the city and gave his command that the fight should be continued on other fronts to the last man. Von Below accordingly emerged from the bunker at midnight and reached the Havel, from where he was escorted by guides of the Hitler Youth.* By April 28th Spandau and Potsdam had been prised from the defenders' tenuous and slipping grasp. By the morning of the 29th Zhukov's advance tanks were slowly rumbling three abreast over the débris that had once been the Unter Den Linden. There was panic and desperation. Deserters were shot on the spot by fanatical SS men, who began to go berserk. SS men delved into the underground stations and picked out people at random from among those sheltering there and shot them for no reason whatever. Walloon SS and White Russian detachments who had been recruited by the SS years before, and even French SS, fought in the streets beside the *Wehrmacht* and Hitler Youth. Drunken orgies took place at night. Bread and water was doled out in ever-decreasing portions; military doctors with makeshift surgeries in the cellars ran out of anaesthetics; bodies were left lying in the streets. Meanwhile, in the shattered Ministries, those civil servants who had not been evacuated to the south continued with their work as best they could. While Russian tanks clattered past the Party Headquarters, the Fuehrer's faithful were actually working out paper-clip requirements for the third quarter of 1945.

Now Hitler's rule and the days of Nazism were nearly at an end. In the west fighting had practically ceased except in small pockets

---

* Von Below failed to deliver his message, and was next heard of in January 1946 when he was discovered reading law at Bonn University.

where fanatical youths and children fought fiercely on; in the east the line had disintegrated everywhere. Only on the coast of East Prussia, in Czechoslavakia and at Breslau was the defence as determined as at Berlin. In East Prussia the army which had been cut off many weeks before had now been pushed back to the coast, together with hundreds of thousands of refugees. What remained of the German fleet had been assembled to conduct a vast Dunkirk operation. An extraordinarily dramatic evacuation, that is still little known in the west, ensued. Seemingly endless lines of fugitives streamed down the roads to Königsberg and Pillau. Earlier in the year the International Red Cross had discovered that several thousands of these refugees had literally been frozen to death in the exceptionally severe winter. Civilians, animals, troops, cars and trucks could be seen from the range-finder of the *Admiral Scheer*, in long treks, approaching across the countryside. Russian artillery followed and fired into the columns and towns at close range. The German Navy, close to the coast in order to cover the evacuation in merchant and naval vessels, were bombed by Russian raiders, and many of them were sent to the bottom.* Hundreds of craft came from Norway, Denmark and Germany to rescue the soldiers now withdrawing to the quays of the two ports and other smaller harbours. The Navy was ordered to evacuate 250,000 military and 25,000 civilians in the last few days of April, having already organized the evacuation of 1,500,000 from East Prussia, Latvia and Danzig. Russian fighters and bombers roared over the ports and craft, casting their shadows on those who looked up, and hurtling down death. Piers were constructed and ships packed so that every inch was crammed with standing refugees. In one day alone 43,000 were taken away. Somebody remembered, in all the confusion, to stow aboard one ship the coffins of Field-Marshal von Hindenburg and his wife Gertrud, which had been rescued by a pioneer detachment a few hours before the Russians had reached the Tannenberg Memorial, and which had been brought by lorry to Königsberg. Thus the old soldier who had witnessed Germany's ambitions collapse to nothing in 1918 was now rudely plucked from his rest to participate in the demented collapse of yet another Reich in yet another world war.† When the Russians reached Königsberg the ships were rushed

* The *Admiral Scheer* was hit and sunk in Kiel dockyard while undergoing repairs; the dock was filled with rubble after the war, and every day people now walk over the famous warship unawares.

† The coffins were discovered by the Americans in August 1946 and were buried beside Frederick I and Frederick II at Marburg.

by the flocks of terrified peasants and townspeople, while the German troops retreated, still firing, on to the vessels; but only two harbour tugs did not get away. An extraordinary armada made its way across the Baltic to Germany and Denmark: minesweepers, speed-boats, fishing-boats, cabin cruisers, ferries, river-boats, even a floating crane—to say nothing of the destroyers and warships. There were 'detachments of troops; children picked up in some street or other in East Prussia and brought along; old bodies with six weeks' foot-slogging behind them; young mothers who had endured their worst hours on the icy roads, and now carried their new-born babies with them—all with fears and privations plainly written on their faces'. Their tribulations were not over, for Russian submarines and planes sent several ships down (and continued to do so up to six hours after the end of the war); in one sinking 400 were drowned.

If the evacuation from East Prussia of 2,022,600 people was one of the most remarkable in history, it was no repetition of Dunkirk. For when the shivering, hungry refugees arrived once more behind the German lines, they were not in a land which could any longer overcome its defeats and arise, phoenix-like, to victory. They were in a land where there was nothing but the stench of defeat.

Himmler, who had been the main liaison officer between the bunker and the north, had already tried to make peace overtures to the West through Count Folke Bernadotte, head of the International Red Cross in Germany. But Bernadotte had felt unable to act as an intermediary without some better indication that Himmler was in fact acting on behalf of Germany and not just on behalf of himself. He suggested that Himmler should launch a *putsch* (and the latter did once hint at ways of 'liquidating' the Fuehrer). Bernadotte, however, kept in touch with Himmler through Walter Schellenberg, Head of Intelligence, a lawyer still in his thirties who was making some attempt to salvage Germany's honour and to combat the bestialities of the Gestapo. Bernadotte's main interest was in getting Norwegians and Danes released from the concentration camps, a task with which he had some success in conjunction with Felix Kersten, Himmler's doctor, until Hitler discovered what was going on. (The Swiss ex-President, Musy, had already succeeded in getting a similar concession out of Himmler, only to have it cancelled by Hitler.) Bernadotte's missions were extremely dangerous. He took two chauffeurs, one of whom travelled outside the car and banged on the roof whenever aircraft were sighted, whereupon the car halted and everyone jumped into a ditch. He was actually in Berlin on Hitler's birthday, seeking an interview with Himmler. He met him again at the Swedish legation at Lübeck, where their conference partly took place in a cellar to flickering candlelight while Allied bombs fell all around. Himmler, like Goering in the south, sought an agreement whereby the line in the east could be maintained through a capitulation in the west. Bernadotte doubted whether the Allies could deal with a man of Himmler's terrible reputation. Himmler himself, who was sensitive to the foreign Press, had to admit: 'As for me—well, of course, I am regarded as the cruellest and most sadistic man alive.' Himmler now met the Swede again. He explained that Hitler's end was near, that the High Command had abandoned Berlin to its fate, and that he wished to convey to Eisenhower an offer of capitulation. He seems still to have believed, as did Doenitz, that Germany could continue after the war with some sort of semi-Nazi government, descended from Hitler's, in which he no doubt would have a part to play. Bernadotte was doubtful if Britain and America would recognize his authority, or would agree to a separate capitulation. In that case, Himmler said, he would take a battalion and die fighting the Bolsheviks. Bernadotte also met Ribbentrop, the Foreign Minister and Himmler's personal enemy, who shouted at him for about an hour to no particular purpose, saying that Bolshevism threatened Europe, India and China, and something would have to be done immediately. Himmler's efforts met with failure for the reasons that Bernadotte had expected. The news reached the world's public via a *Reuter*'s news-agency message; a message which Churchill later seemed to deny. Himmler's Anglo-American approach caused the predictable embarrassment between the West and Moscow, which resulted in the first telephone conversation between Churchill and the new President. Churchill, who seemed to accept that Himmler was now the German head of state, was in an excited and somewhat incoherent mood (the talk was recorded). The call lasted about a half-hour, during which time Truman managed to squeeze in a few short sentences. Himmler, far from leading a battalion into battle, now hung around in Doenitz's headquarters, such prestige as he had ever had among his colleagues having suffered a fatal blow.

In the bunker itself Hitler prepared for the end.

On the afternoon of April 29th he had his dog Blondi poisoned. During the evening he said good-bye to all the staff in the bunker, shaking hands with each in turn. He appeared to be in distant mood, perhaps drugged. The following morning there was the usual conference on the state of the defence of Berlin. After lunch Hitler and Eva Braun emerged from the Fuehrer's room into the central corridor-room of the bunker. They had been married during the night of 28th–29th at a short ceremony witnessed by Goebbels and Bormann. The final testament had been written: 'My wife and I choose to die in order to escape the shame of overthrow or capitulation. It is our wish that our bodies be burnt immediately in the place where I have performed the greater part of my daily work during the course of my twelve years' service to my people.'* Another farewell took place. Frau Goebbels, who had learnt that her six children were shortly to be poisoned by their father, was, however, unable to be present. These children, scampering about in the passageways, had been the one ray of brightness in the oppressive bunker. They referred to Hitler, who was fond of them, as their 'Uncle Fuehrer'. Frau Goebbels remained all day in her own room, and was only seen once again. Hitler shook hands all round once again, and then the couple returned to their room. (The fact that Hitler said little or nothing at both farewells, and appeared dazed or drugged, gave some credence to the theory that it was in fact a 'double' who had been especially kept for such an event, and that the real Hitler may thus have escaped after all; a report in *The Times* of June 20th, 1945, gave the statement of one of the first Russian officers on the scene, who declared that some charred remains which had been discovered were of an obvious double of Hitler.†) There was a silence of a few minutes. A single shot was heard. After a pause those waiting outside entered the private suite. They found Adolf Hitler, soaked in blood, lying on the sofa. Eva Braun was on the same sofa; dead with poison. Thus died‡ the man who only three years before had wielded a power greater and more extensive than any man's since Caesar; a man whose personal empire stretched throughout most of Europe and even beyond; a man who surely had a more evil influence on the course of the history of mankind than any other single human; and who died like a cornered rat in a world it had set ablaze.

* He also said that his personal possessions, 'in so far as they are worth anything', should go to the state ('if the Party no longer exists'). His considerable royalties now seem to go to his family.

† At Potsdam Stalin impressed American diplomats with his conviction that Hitler was still alive.

‡ According to Trevor-Roper's superb and definitive account, which must be accepted, if not as a proven fact, at least as the nearest thing to a factual account that the world is ever likely to get in the matter.

Hitler's body was wrapped in a blanket, concealing the shattered face, and was taken up to the Chancellery garden; Braun's, carried by Bormann, followed. In accordance with Hitler's instructions, the two bodies were placed side by side a few feet from the entrance, and petrol was poured over them. A Russian artillery barrage was in progress, and with splinters and débris falling in the vicinity the mourners withdrew to the entrance of the bunker, from where a lighted rag was tossed on to the bodies. The two corpses were immediately enveloped in leaping flames, and the small group stood to attention and gave the Nazi salute. They then scurried below once more.

Bormann sent off two radio telegrams to Doenitz hinting that the Grand Admiral was now the Fuehrer; but he was not quite able to bring himself to admit Hitler's death. That evening he and Goebbels decided to make a peace move towards the Russians, in the hope that a safe passage to Doenitz's headquarters could be arranged for those in the bunker, and an officer was accordingly sent off to Zhukov's headquarters under the white flag. He returned about noon the following day with the answer that there were to be no safe passages or privileges, only unconditional surrender. That being so, only an attempt to make a mass escape remained. This Bormann now hastily organized.

Goebbels, who had taken his decision long before, had no intention of joining any escape. Suspecting that Bormann was up to some intrigue, he sent off a message to Doenitz informing him bluntly of Hitler's death, and then arranged for himself and his wife to be shot by an SS orderly, after having first carefully poisoned all his children. The imitative funeral-pyre for which he had wished was not efficiently conducted, and the two bodies were left smouldering in the garden while the remainder busied themselves with frantic plans of escape.

At 11 p.m. a party of officials, soldiers and women gathered in the bunker (some had come from the shelters near by). Having been briefed as to the route to be taken, they left at intervals in small groups, while the flames were still flickering around the bodies of Goebbels and his wife. By the time they reached the Friedrichstrasse Station they were already in an unrecognizable maze of ruins, with blazing buildings lighting up the night sky and shells falling and exploding all around. The groups became scattered and broke up as individuals tried to continue alone. Some followed the railway line, dodging Russian patrols, others, including Bormann and Axmann, went eastwards down the Invalidenstrasse. Most were killed or captured by the Russians. At least one reached the American lines. And a number, including Axmann, escaped altogether. (Axmann eventually reached a group of the Hitler Youth in a secret hide-out in the Bavarian Alps, where he remained for six months.) Bormann was last seen beside a blazing tank on the Weidendamm Bridge. He may have got away.

The Red Flag had already been hoisted over the ruins of the Reichstag. The battle reached its climax in the Tiergarten district and on the banks of the Spree, the surface of which was whipped into an angry storm by the hail of lead. At 3 p.m. on May 2nd Weidling and his staff surrendered to the Russians. Six hours later the battle for Berlin was officially over and 70,000 of the surviving German troops in the city had been taken prisoner. But some large groups of the *Wehrmacht* refused to give in and vainly attempted to break out, fighting on for at least three more days.

(v)

The news of Hitler's death was announced to the German people by Doenitz, on Radio Hamburg, at 10.37 p.m. on May 1st. The announcer warned that a grave and important announcement was shortly to be made, and after an interval during which Bruckner's Seventh Symphony was played, Doenitz spoke. 'Our Fuehrer, Adolf Hitler, has fallen. The German people bow in deepest mourning and veneration. He recognized beforehand the terrible danger of Bolshevism and devoted his life to fighting it . . . his battle against the Bolshevist flood benefited not only Europe but the entire world. The Fuehrer has appointed me his successor. Fully conscious of the responsibility, I take over the leadership of the German people at this fateful hour. It is my first task to save the German people from the Bolshevists, and it is only to achieve this that the fight continues. As long as the British and Americans hamper us from reaching this end we shall fight and defend ourselves against them as well. The British and Americans do not fight for the interests of their own people, but for the spreading of Bolshevism.' The news of Hitler's death was greeted with considerable joy in most countries of the world. In Portugal, however, two days' mourning were ordered, and all flags hung at half-mast. In Eire, the Premier, Mr de Valera, called on the German Ambassador to express his condolences. The Swiss and Swedes were quick to point out that they had no intention of following his example. Not everyone was prepared to take Doenitz's word for it that Hitler was dead, and rumours abounded. The *Daily Express* speculated that Hitler, Goebbels and Himmler were, in fact, on their way to Japan in a U-boat.

The new Fuehrer had followed in his speech the line of all the leading Nazis since Goebbels and Hitler, many weeks before, had seen a clash between East and West as the only possible escape for Nazi Germany. As could have been predicted, this proud and straightforward naval officer, who had been completely under the spell of Hitler and the Nazi political movement, acted, at first, as a single and unquestioning disciple; and that, no doubt, is why Hitler had chosen him as his successor instead of the more complicated Himmler. Doenitz, in his memoirs, attempted to give a different interpretation to his actions, but his pronouncements at the time speak for themselves. Speaking to the *Wehrmacht*, the same evening, he said: 'The oath pledged by you to the Fuehrer now applies for each one of you to me. German soldiers! Do your duty! The life of our nation is at stake!' Although he wrote later that 'the only thing that now mattered was to prevent a reign of chaos, which would inevitably lead to further bloodshed', he acted for the first two days of his hopeless rule as if he intended to carry on till the last round had been fired. All down the Western Front, or what was left of it, German battalion and brigade groups were surrendering at confusing speed. At the news of Hitler's death, divisional commanders joined them. The army commanders begged Doenitz, at the northern headquarters, which had now retreated to the village of Ploen, half-way between Lübeck and Kiel, for permission to capitulate at once to avoid further chaos, but they were refused and informed that the Fuehrer himself was planning a surrender bit by bit, in order to keep the fight going as long as possible. For Doenitz realized that the best policy for himself and the remaining Nazi leaders was to keep the war going in order to give him time to find room for diplomatic manoeuvre between East and West. His advisers assured him that such manoeuvring was still possible. Even if this were so, which it was not, such efforts were doomed since the political intitiative had passed to the northern sector, which could not hold out for more than a few hours, instead of the Alpine sector, which, if it had been organized with determination, could have lasted some weeks.

On May 2nd, after the failure of a feeble German counter-attack, the advanced troops of the British Sixth (Airborne) Division reached the Baltic coast at Wismar. Within hours the Eleventh Armoured Division carried their famous sign, the fighting bull, into Lübeck. Organized resistance had ceased. A British tank officer wrote: 'Through this carnival of chaos the *Wehrmacht* in enormous numbers, bewildered and glum, either sat by the roadside waiting for orders or walked vaguely down the road. At one point the advance was brought to a standstill by a general marching his entire division in to surrender. Soon the fields around Moelln began to fill with vast herds of field-grey, like cattle, silent, tired and beaten. Panthers, all brand new, were abandoned by the crews at crossroads; gunners manning their 88s watched the tanks go by with their hands in their pockets. The SS was pretending to be something else, and trying to slip away without any idea where to go.'

Doenitz was now cut off in the narrow strip of Schleswig-Holstein, pressed up against the Danish border. He withdrew his 'capital' to Flensburg, the furthest town still on German soil from the British lines. Churchill was delighted that the Danish peninsula, for which he had greatly feared, was now safely isolated from the Russian advance. In a telegram to Eden, at San Francisco for the world organization conference, he said: 'In the north, Eisenhower threw in an American corps with dexterity to help Montgomery in his advance on Lübeck. He got there with twelve hours to spare.' British troops now began to fill up the whole area south of Hamburg to Hanover. Almost the entire western bank of the Elbe between Hamburg and Torgau was manned by Anglo-American forces. But on the far side, where the Russian advance was much slower than that of the Western allies, there were two large pockets of German troops; one south of Rostock and one west of Berlin. Practically every human being in these two areas now attempted to cross the Elbe, so effective had been the final propaganda of that perverse genius Goebbels. The Germans, troops and civilians, were hampered in getting across by the mass of their own slave labour, who were equally terrified of the advancing Russian armies. A British reporter watched as ant-like humans fled across the river: 'Russian mortar shells burst in the midst of German soldiers and civilians waiting to cross the Tangermunde Bridge to the American side of the Elbe. Scores of women and children were killed or wounded. German soldiers pushed old women out of the boats in which they were trying to cross the river. German officers, stripped naked, paddled a rubber boat loaded with soldiers and three women, with their baggage and bicycles. A girl drowned in midstream, screaming for help. Soldiers swam the river in their vests, climbed up the west bank and were sent straight to the prisoners' cages. German troops panicked and rushed in waves towards the river as Russian tanks burst out from the woods. In the past five days 50,000 Germans have walked into our lines across a catwalk they built along the blown bridge which lies awash in the Elbe. Today, about noon, Russian tanks arrived only a thousand yards from the river bank.' Another British reporter, Stanley Baron of the *News Chronicle*, in his dispatch from Konev's headquarters, vividly described the hectic Russian advance so clearly lagging behind the Anglo-Americans who had been patiently waiting on the Elbe. 'Tens of thousands of Russian troops have been pouring in to fill up the vacuums between the Soviet and US First Army lines. . . . The Russian infantry moves on whatever it can gather on the way, and it gathers everything on wheels with only one consideration— that the wheels are still capable of turning. Traps and incredibly old landaus, horse and ox-drawn farm carts, civilian motor cars, motor-cycles, sidecars, saddle horses—any and all of these may travel among marching men in any given column. "We are not proud," a Red Army major told me. "There is one golden rule—keep going."'

All that remained of the Reich, apart from the two areas east of the Elbe, were the tiny pocket in Schleswig-Holstein; Breslau, where the defenders, besieged since February, were still holding out; Denmark and Norway; a portion of Holland where Seyss-Inquart still remained by means of his blackmail; the Channel Islands and a few French ports; a large pocket around Zagreb in Yugoslavia; the whole of Western Czechoslavakia and some of Austria; and a small portion of Bavaria south of Munich, in which was the southern 'capital' of Berchtesgaden, from where Goering, who had broken free from a brief period of house arrest by the SS, attempted to contact the Americans, apparently with some confidence (he managed to get a message through to Doenitz informing him that he hoped soon to be taken to see Eisenhower, where he and the American would discuss matters 'as one Marshal to another'). Communications had broken between most of these areas, and Doenitz was unaware of the full situation. The atmosphere at Flensburg was tense, to say the least. Doenitz had informed Himmler, who vehemently denied his separate efforts to surrender through Bernadotte, that he would not require him in his government. Himmler, as head of the SS, which amounted to his private army, had taken it for granted that he would be a man of power after Hitler's death, if not indeed Hitler's successor. When Doenitz handed him the message from the bunker naming the Grand Admiral as the new Fuehrer, 'an expression of astonishment, indeed of consternation, spread over his face. He went very pale. Finally he stood up and bowed. "Allow me," he said, "to become the second man in your State." I told him that it was out of the question.' The tenseness of this meeting can be judged by the fact that Doenitz had placed a pistol, with the safety-catch off, beneath some papers on his desk. Ribbentrop arrived in Doenitz's office soon afterwards and demanded to be appointed Foreign Minister, to which he said he had 'a legal right'. He suggested that he was the right man for the task, as the British knew him and had always got on with him. Goebbels' final message from the bunker had instructed Doenitz that his Foreign Minister was to be Seyss-Inquart. A worse choice than this universally detested man as Foreign Minister at this juncture of Germany's affairs could scarcely be imagined. Doenitz decided to ignore this instruction and, ignoring Ribbentrop too, he appointed Count Schwerin von Krosigk, who had been a Rhodes scholar. The absurdity of this intrigue and ambition for non-existent power in the corridors of the sixteenth-century castle at Flensburg was not apparent at the time, for many of the actors believed that they still might be able to play a part during an Allied occupation. Doenitz realized that there was no hope of his government surviving if it contained names as loathsome to the Allies as Himmler and Seyss-Inquart. The irony was that it was Himmler who wanted to end the war immediately, and Doenitz, supported by Keitel and Jodl, who was thinking of ways of continuing hostilities, especially as regards to the strategically well-placed Norway.*

On May 3rd the local German forces had surrendered Hamburg, ignoring demands from Doenitz's staff to delay giving up the city. To the amazement of the British at the surrender, one of the German officers who had come out to hand over the city was sporting a Brasenose College, Oxford, scarf, to which it turned out he was perfectly entitled. At Hamburg the Allies gained control of Doenitz's last big radio transmitter. At lunch-time that day Radio Hamburg had been in a state of obvious emotional distress. An announcer said: 'It is doubtful whether we shall broadcast news any more. We therefore say good-bye to you all. Long live Germany.' He was followed at

---

* Doenitz's Adjutant, Ludde-Neurath, and others, have denied this; but, in the early days at least, the evidence seems incontrovertible.

1.15 by a woman who said: 'I wish Hamburgers whatever one can wish at this hour. . . .' She could be heard weeping. Then came the national anthem, *Deutschland Uber Alles*, followed by passages from Beethoven's Fifth Symphony. British troops began rolling into the city, which, although one of the most devastated of the war, had managed to maintain a more ordered existence than some of the cities of the Ruhr. Alan Moorehead reported: 'When the first soldiers got in they found the trains running, the shops open, tens of thousands of people in the streets—people who as yet do not know the full magnitude of the disaster that has hit them and the appalling chaos of the German Army around them. The city was plastered with notices telling the people to get indoors and stay there, and by the time the main British columns entered, the city appeared deserted.' Although Doenitz's government managed to make some announcements by means of a radio station in Holland ('The Voice of the Reich'), one at Flensburg and one at Wilhelmshaven, the taking over of Radio Hamburg by the British had the effect of convincing the German people that the end had arrived. When they tuned in at nine that night they were astounded to hear the deep tones of Big Ben giving the time signal; the same booming strokes that had become a symbol of freedom among resistance workers and secret wireless-listeners throughout Europe. Nothing could have been more dramatic; nothing more convincing of Germany's defeat.

On the same day a delegation from Keitel arrived at Montgomery's headquarters on Lüneburg Heath, for Doenitz had now decided to cut off this useless portion of his dying estate, like a cancerous limb, as a kind of offering to gain a few more days to argue and nervously ponder with his advisers in Flensburg Castle. The delegation, which arrived in a Mercedes flying a white flag, was headed by Admiral von Friedeburg, whom Doenitz had appointed to replace himself as Naval Commander-in-Chief; there were three other officers.* Montgomery had prepared a tent and a Union Jack on a flag-pole for the occasion. He was in his most intimidating mood, and kept the delegation waiting outside for some time. When he appeared, the four Germans saluted under the flag. Montgomery then uttered his well-known phrase: 'Who are these men?' Von Friedeburg asked to surrender to Montgomery the three armies south of Rostock which faced the Russians. This Montgomery refused to accept, and when von Friedeburg followed this up by describing at length the plight of

* One of them, Rear-Admiral Wagner, became a senior official in the West German Ministry of Defence. Friedeburg and one of the other two later committed suicide.

German civilians in that and other areas, Montgomery remained unmoved. 'I said the Germans should have thought of all these things before they began the war, and particularly before they attacked the Russians in June 1941.' Montgomery did offer to accept the surrender of all German forces facing, or in support of those facing, his command, i.e. in Holland, Schleswig-Holstein and Denmark. Von Friedeburg was unable to agree to this. Montgomery then took the German delegation to his map-room so that they could see how hopeless their position was (a move of the utmost confidence from a commander to his enemies), and the German quartet showed plainly by their expressions that it was worse than even they had expected. The Field-Marshal cannily sent them off to have lunch, to talk things over among themselves, with only one British officer present. During lunch von Friedeburg wept. Afterwards Montgomery, speaking very toughly, demanded an immediate surrender on his front or he would order the battle to recommence. At this von Friedeburg returned for further instructions to Doenitz. He convinced the new Fuehrer that Montgomery would accept no conditions, and he was told to return, accept the ultimatum and then fly on to Eisenhower at Rheims and to try to organize another separate surrender of the German forces facing American troops in the southern sector. On Lüneberg Heath, on a windy, overcast day, the wretched German delegation was once more paraded beneath the fluttering Union Jack. Montgomery had already prepared a surrender document (typed on a sheet of foolscap), and he and the Germans filed into the tent, where they sat at a trestle table covered with an army blanket, on which were an ink-pot and a scratchy Service pen. The Germans were extremely nervous, and one of them pulled out a cigarette; Montgomery, who did not smoke, looked at him coldly, and he put the cigarette away. Montgomery then asked them to sign the document immediately, and they did so; although, being in English, they could not understand it. There was considerable criticism in American quarters of this separate surrender, but this has never worried Montgomery, for he had every right to accept a battlefield surrender whenever it was offered him in order to save useless loss of life and property; just such a surrender had, indeed, been the object of his endeavours for some years.*

* In 1962 the author visited the spot where the surrender to Montgomery took place. It was discovered, after half a day's searching, in a wood-clearing off a main road outside the village of Wendisch-Evern, near the East German border. There was no notice or sign to identify this historic place, and no memorial of any sort; only some overgrown trenches and a mound of stones.

This surrender, signed on May 4th, brought to an end the Anglo-German war that had begun on September 3rd, 1939, and which had lasted for exactly five years and eight months; through the doubt and unpreparedness of the early days; the trance-like weeks of the Phoney War; the disasters of Norway and France; the escape at Dunkirk; through two years of perilous danger from invasion by air and sea; through the Blitz; and through the battles of the Atlantic, the Desert, the Mediterranean and Western Europe. It had been a long time, and that it was now over British troops and civilians found it difficult at first to fully appreciate. A war correspondent, Christopher Buckley of the *Daily Telegraph*, wrote in his dispatch that night: 'The familiar procession of transport vehicles passes up the roads as units take up fresh positions; possibly their final positions of the war. But the tanks and guns that move up the roads in steady rhythm will fire no more shots. The ambulances which drove forward this morning will, blessedly, be empty again when they return. One feels as though the mighty engine of war, so steadily developed during these past six years, is running and will continue to run on its own impetus. One feels that even when the cease-fire has sounded battery commanders will still, from habit, prospect good sighting for their guns, the sappers will automatically continue to test the roads for mines. . . . For though a war is ending, it is always difficult to believe that tomorrow will be radically different from today.' That night Very lights and mortar signals lit up the sky above the British lines in North-East Europe. A victory salvo of twenty-one rounds was fired by twenty-four AA guns on Lüneberg Heath. The following morning another war correspondent reported from the British line: 'When I arrived, on the stroke of eight this morning, at a forward platoon of the Dorsets, of the 43rd (West Country) Division, they were mostly having a lie-in. Those who were awake talked of only one thing: What is your age-group number? And when do you get that bowler hat?'

At an RAF station the mood was sombre, and comrades lost and gone for ever were remembered. 'That evening, in the mess, was like some extraordinary vigil over a corpse. The pilots were slumped in their chairs—no one spoke a word, or sang, or anything. . . . It was all over. No more would I see my flight of Tempests line up behind [me], clumsy looking on their long legs, offering the yawning hole of their radiators to the wind from their propellers, with the trustful faces of their pilots leaning out of the cockpits, waiting for my signal. The Big Show was over. The public had been satisfied.

The programme had been rather heavy, the actors not too bad.' Thus wrote a Frenchman serving with the RAF. The Chief of the Imperial General Staff, Sir Alan Brooke, wrote in his diary: 'So this is at last the end of the war! It is hard to realize. I can't feel thrilled; my sensation is one of infinite mental weariness.'

(vi)

The surrender of the forces facing the American and Russian armies remained, but after this mass capitulation of over 1,500,000 troops, which consisted of the whole northern sector, the end had clearly arrived. Already German leaders were falling into Allied hands. In one day twenty generals walked into the Allied lines. Von Rundstedt had been taken prisoner in a hospital near Munich. Marshal Petain and Pierre Laval had been arrested on passing into France from Switzerland. A rather bewildered Crown Prince Wilhelm, sixty-three years old, 'Little Willie' of the First World War, had been plucked off the street and taken into captivity by the First French Army. A few companies of the *Wehrmacht* began a revolt in Munich as the Seventh US Army raced for the city. In Britain, America and France, arrangements were being made for victory celebrations. The end of the war was at hand.

Von Friedeburg had proceeded as planned to Rheims. Here, however, he found that Eisenhower would not even listen to a surrender on a separate front. Eisenhower's attitude was that if von Friedeburg came from Doenitz, then he had the power to offer total unconditional surrender, and this was what the Supreme Commander demanded. By now the German attempts to cast a wedge between Anglo-American interests and Russian had, in face of continued failure, been replaced by a sulky clinging to what they considered was a righteous cause—an attempt to convince the Americans of the dangers to the Western World of the Russian advance. They clung to this final strand of self-justification to the end. Doenitz wrote in his memoirs: 'The fact is that Eisenhower's final operational moves showed that he had no proper appreciation of the new turn of events in world affairs. Once the Americans had crossed the Rhine at Remagen their *strategic* aim, the conquest of Germany, had been accomplished. It should at once have been replaced by the *political* aim of occupying as much German territory as possible with British and American forces before the Russians marched in.' General Jodl was now sent to Rheims to reinforce von Friedeburg, who was rapidly wilting under the continual humiliation. After much argument, Eisenhower still refused to accept a separate surrender. He stated that his alternative to total unconditional surrender would be to close his lines to all surrendering Germans. Eisenhower, annoyed at Montgomery (he had demanded the Lüneberg Heath surrender document, but Montgomery had no intention of parting with such a souvenir and sent a copy instead), was in unyielding mood, and his faultless determination at this stage put an end to the plans of Doenitz's advisers. It appears that Bedell Smith leant some support to the German request for a day's grace, and this was granted. The instrument for surrender was thus signed by Jodl with an American gold fountain pen at Rheims at 2.41 a.m. on May 7th, 1945, to take effect at midnight the following day. Eisenhower was not present. After the signing, Jodl, who seemed to have fortified himself with a few drinks, rose from the table and delivered a plea for the German people. Bedell Smith looked him straight in the eye and made no comment whatever. When Jodl eventually petered out, the meeting broke up in complete silence. Jodl and von Friedeburg were allowed to return to Flensburg, and they took with them a copy of the American Forces newspaper, the *Stars and Stripes*, which contained pictures of Buchenwald. Doenitz claims that they were all horrified by these terrible indications of the perversity of Nazi rule. Right up to the signing, Doenitz had been broadcasting that he intended to continue fighting the Russians 'to save as many Germans as possible from the Bolshevik terror'. But, impressed at the way Jodl had wilted under American pressure, he had given up hope of gaining time or concessions. He refused to consider the idea of continuing the fight in Norway, urged on him by staff officers, and a cease-fire was announced for all fronts at midnight on May 8th–9th. The last communiqué of the German armed forces stated: 'A heroic fight that has lasted for nearly six years thus comes to an end. It has brought us resounding victories but also heavy defeats. Ultimately the German armed forces have succumbed to overwhelming superior strength.' Doenitz and his colleagues sat waiting for they knew not what in their handsome castle. In an area still unoccupied by Allied troops, Doenitz reminded himself that 'we were living in sovereign territory'. In a remarkable broadcast, von Krosigk, who was to some extent a moderating influence on Doenitz and expedited the capitulation, said: 'We must now shoulder and loyally carry out our obligations. But we must not despair, either, or fall into dumb apathy. We must light and guide our path through the dark future. Then we may hope that our freedom will be restored to us without which no nation can lead a bearable and dignified existence. We wish to devote the future of our nation to the return of the innermost and best forces of German nature which have given to the world imperishable works and values. We view with pride the heroic struggle of our people, and we shall combine with our pride the will to contribute, as a member of Western culture, honest peaceful labour—a contribution which expresses the best traditions of our nation. May God not forsake us in our distress and bless us in our heavy task.' This speech, almost contrite in places, was the first really diplomatic statement to have been made since the formation of the Flensburg government; the first, indeed, from Germany for many years. But few people were interested in what von Krosigk said, or what was said by anyone in an utterly discredited nation. The thirteen years of the Third Reich were at an end, and most people were ready to take a long vacation from anything to do with Germany.

In many of the capitals of the Western World the people, overjoyed at the end of the terror and bloodshed that Germany had brought, were gaily pouring into the streets.

(vii)

Since the news of the surrender to Montgomery, people had been waiting, with diminishing patience, to celebrate the end of the German war. In New York, particularly, the tension was great. The Associated Press had come out with unofficial news of the Rheims signing a day early* (it had made a similar announcement two weeks previously, acting on inaccurate 'confidential' information, which had caused a premature outburst of rejoicing and a hasty telephone call from Truman to Eisenhower). On May 7th the office buildings of New York disgorged their hundreds of thousands into the streets, there was much uncontrolled excitement, and the traditional cloudburst of ticker-tape. Some time during the afternoon New York

* The reporter in question, Edward Kennedy, who appears to have misunderstood the embargo on the news until the next day, suffered professional abuse and was discredited by his colleagues and employers.

became aware that it was acting on its own; the celebrations eased. Throughout the rest of the United States it had been a quiet, normal working day. That night Churchill, in a frenzy of excitement and indecision, telephoned Washington and told Leahy that the announcement of the signing would have to be made immediately; the news having been leaked by AP, he could no longer contain the public, who were gathering in the streets. 'What is the use of me and of the President looking to be the only two people in the world who don't know what is going on?' he asked. Newspapers in America, Britain and France revealed the following morning, May 8th, that the end of the war would be announced at 3 p.m. that afternoon, London time (8.15 a.m. Washington time). The same news was not announced in Moscow until more than eight hours afterwards.

In a simple statement, Harry Truman, whose sixty-first birthday it was, made a moving reference to Roosevelt, who had not lived to see the victorious result of so much of his effort. But the main keynote of his speech, and of the mood of the whole nation, was: 'When the last Japanese division has surrendered unconditionally, then only will our fighting job be done.' In New York, Washington, Los Angeles, Chicago and in most cities the population went to work as usual. War plants worked through the day.

In Paris there were scenes of communal joy in the crowded boulevards; but not comparable to those at the Liberation. The French Army paraded through the centre of the city, led by the Republican Guards, on horseback and in their traditional colourful uniforms. In Moscow, where a statement was somewhat reluctantly issued (Stalin was not convinced that fighting would actually stop on the Eastern Front—and his doubt was well founded), a crowd, mostly of students, heard a brief announcement over the public address system in Red Square. Moscow Radio said: 'This is the victory of all freedom-living nations, but first and foremost it is our victory. It was on our own soil that our great people and its Red Army, led by Marshal Stalin, broke the back of the Fascist beast. We have suffered indescribable hardships. The Allied advance in the west facilitated the Red Army's task, but our troops were still faced by the main German forces. A great historic task has been accomplished.' But there was little rejoicing. Radio Tokyo was equally adamant in its views on the occasion: 'The end of the war in Europe has created a serious situation for Japan. It is obvious that the British–US enemy will concentrate their forces for an intensified attack on Japan, but . . . with unshakeable faith in the righteousness of her cause, Japan is determined to overcome all obstacles until final victory.' In most capitals of the United Nations and of neutral nations there were scenes of celebration at the end of the war, although there were few in which a holiday was given or in which business and industrial activity did not continue. In Germany itself it was a day that began and ended with few people even aware that it had passed. The military were busy with attempts to inject some order into chaos, the civilian population stunned into silence. Alan Moorehead was driving down the autobahn, 'the long, white ribbons of road stretching for mile after mile between green banks of trees. And there, just for a moment, one had a glimpse of peace. A fleet of British bombers went over carrying our wounded and released prisoners homeward. Suddenly one realized: There is nothing for them to bomb any longer. In all Europe no single target.' In Rome there were not many scenes of great excitement; a few Italian flags appeared in isolated windows, but the poverty, squalor and disillusion of the time was not conducive to celebration. During the evening the military authorities declared a curfew.

In the recently liberated cities and capitals it was a different matter. There were wild scenes in Oslo and Copenhagen, where German soldiers, ill-at-ease and bewildered, were still wandering around. In Oslo no Allied troops had arrived, and German patrols actually guarded some buildings to prevent damage in the rejoicing over their own defeat. In Brussels the gaiety was tempered by a serious political and constitutional crisis. In Holland, into which Canadian troops were advancing, it was a day of unbounded emotion and relief. The population had been saved from famine by supplies dropped by parachute from Allied planes, and they were clearly overcome with gratitude for that and for the release from the goose-stepping conqueror. A British correspondent with the Canadians wrote: 'We are on the road to Amsterdam, and it is a road of laughter and tears. The laughter is that of a people wild with excitement and the tears spring from an emotion that is too great to bear. We drove into Utrecht this morning with a reconnaissance squadron of the Fortieth Division to meet a welcome that was a deluge. Only by going into hiding and locking myself up can this message be written. At the approaches to the town the deluge began. . . . Here were great crowds of people so massed that the armoured cars had to halt. Our halting was a signal, and in a moment we were overwhelmed. We were embraced and thumped and handshaken. Women and even men, with tears streaming down their cheeks, said over and over:

"We have waited five years for you. Five years we have waited and now you are here." So we rolled slowly into Utrecht, where the flags could be measured only by the acre. Without measure was the joy of these people. . . .' Only those who had lived without freedom under Nazi rule knew what the sight of the Canadians meant; five years is a long period of human life.

But there was no outburst of rejoicing more ardent and more deeply felt than that which occurred in London. Many who saw both consider VE Day to have surpassed even the extraordinary mass emotion of Armistice Day, 1918. There had been a special relationship between Londoners during the war, as they were frequently being told, and this had continued up till the very end because of the 'flying bombs' and rockets, which the provincial cities had for the most part escaped. Now, as a kind of last act of some vast congress, they joined together once more, not as millions of strangers living together in a sprawling metropolis, but as friends who had suffered together in emergency first-aid centres, who had seen each other's most private belongings rudely blasted into the street, who had slept beside each other in the 'Tube'.

Already during the waiting days since May 4th there had been a good deal of abandon in the streets and public places. Flags had appeared (including, perhaps for the first and last time, an enormous Red Flag from the building in Fleet Street of the *Daily Telegraph*). Arrangements for VE Day, which was so obviously and so happily coming, had been made; floodlighting was hastily put in place, fireworks mysteriously appeared in the shops, bonfires were prepared, licensing hours extended to midnight, the ban on street-lighting (which had been reimposed for economy) temporarily lifted, civic processions and celebrations organized, and street parties (especially in the poorer districts of the large cities) arranged. May 8th was announced a public holiday; and the following day as well. The British people, who had been in the German war from the start, intended to have a real 'do'. No matter how many pronouncements were made about the continuing war against Japan, few people could forget that Britain only a few years before was itself near to total defeat; no one felt like disciplining themselves unduly at this great moment in the country's history. *The Times* printed one of the longest leading articles in its history, taking up three columns. It finished: 'Finally, on a day that will stand as a solemn date in history, it is not possible to celebrate so great a deliverance without the sense that a larger design has been fulfilled than is comprehended in the calculations of strategy. Now that the danger is passed, it may be acknowledged that there was a time when, had the enemy's mastery of the art of war matched the immense superiority of his material power, no human valour or effort could have thwarted his deadly purpose. In the last resort, that which has sustained resistance when all seemed lost, not only in England but in all the enslaved lands, is the faith that in the order of the Universe the just cause, provided that the last measure of devotion and sacrifice is offered to it, will not be allowed to fail. It is right to affirm today that that faith stands justified.' The length of *The Times*' editorial was not the only surprise in the newspapers that morning. Nearly all proudly displayed on their front pages, under large headings, the day's weather forecast, a service that had been stopped, for security reasons, five years before. It was: 'Weather will continue warm and thundery, with bright intervals in most districts. Further outlook: little change.'

The day started on a note of confusion. Thousands of people reported as usual to their places of work, not having seen the early morning papers and unaware of the national holiday. They found factories, offices and shops closed; crowds rapidly assembled in central London during the morning. By the time Churchill made a broadcast a large crowd had assembled outside Buckingham Palace (above which flew the vast full-size Royal Standard for the first time since the Coronation in 1937), the Houses of Parliament, and in Trafalgar Square. His broadcast, which was also heard in America, was relayed by loudspeakers. A straightforward (strangely so for him) announcement of the act of unconditional surrender by the enemy was followed by a dramatic ending: 'We may allow ourselves a brief period of rejoicing; but let us not forget for a moment the toil and efforts that lie ahead. Japan, with all her treachery and greed, remains unsubdued. . . . We must now devote all our strength and resources to the completion of our task, both at home and abroad. Advance, Britannia. God save the King.' The Prime Minister then went immediately to the House of Commons; some difficulty was encountered in getting his open car through a tightly packed crowd in Parliament Square. Churchill, enjoying the public mood, stood up as the car slowly pressed forward and, smoking a giant-sized cigar, made his V-sign, like a blessing, far above the wildly cheering crowd. On arrival at the Commons (which was sitting, as it had done since its own chamber was bombed, in the Lords), all the members sprang to their feet immediately he appeared from behind the Speaker's Chair. It was some time before order was resumed sufficiently for him to be heard. He repeated his broadcast speech, finishing with a few words of personal gratitude to the House, which he said had been proved 'the strongest foundation for waging war that has ever been seen in the whole of our long history'. Then, following the precedent set by Lloyd George, Prime Minister at the end of the First World War, he led the Members out through the crowd to a Service of Thanksgiving at St Margaret's Church, Westminster. At this service the twenty-one Members of Parliament who had given their lives in the war were recalled, each being mentioned by name.

Churchill's broadcast, relayed in the main squares of all the great cities, had initiated everywhere riotous scenes which continued well into the following day. In Manchester an illuminated tramcar toured the city all night, clanging through the crowds. In Liverpool sirens of ships and liners on the Mersey provided a background to the singing by 20,000 people of 'Land of Hope and Glory' outside the Town Hall. In Glasgow ships played their searchlights over the murky Clyde while thousands danced in the streets, beneath fairy lights, to the playing of pipes. In Belfast the streets were smothered in flags and emblems; in some districts even the lamp-posts were painted red, white and blue. In Nottingham bells of all the churches rang victory peals throughout the day. In Folkestone the 'all-clear' was sounded on the city's air-raid sirens immediately after Churchill's speech.

By the time the King made his broadcast a vast crowd in London estimated at 100,000 had assembled in the area between the Palace and the Strand, and Piccadilly and Westminster. A silence fell across it as the familiar tones of Big Ben rang out nine o'clock. Then the King's voice, its sincere and hesitant tones so well known to his people, drifted across Green Park and over the heads of the multitude. His message, less triumphant than Churchill's had been, dwelt on the losses the country had sustained. He said: 'We shall have failed, and the blood of our dearest will have flown in vain, if the victory which they died to win does not lead to a lasting peace, founded on justice and established on good will. To that, then, let us turn our thoughts on this day of just triumph and proud sorrow; and then take up our work again, resolved as a people to do nothing unworthy of those who died for us and to make the world such a place as they would have desired for their children and for ours.' It was perhaps the best speech of his reign. By now the huge crowd was incessantly chanting for the Royal Family to appear on the balcony of Buckingham Palace, and the King, sometimes with members of his family, sometimes with members of the Government, appeared until late into the night. The same demand, for Churchill, was made time and again in Whitehall. By now the Prime Minister had changed into his famous blue 'siren-suit', and was assembled with his Cabinet colleagues, Service chiefs and others at the Ministry of Health. Soon after 5 p.m. he appeared on the balcony, and after a tremendous roar that was heard the other side of the Thames, he spoke into a microphone, his words thundering down Whitehall. There had been nothing quite like it before in British history. Speaking slowly and with great emphasis, he said: 'This is your victory! It is the victory of the cause of freedom in every land. In all our long history we have never seen a greater day than this.' The ovation he was accorded cannot have been given to any other British public figure this century. He appeared again, in answer to continuous chanting of his name, several times during the evening.

A reporter, Macdonald Hastings of *Picture Post*, roamed among the dancing, singing, laughing crowds. 'Just outside the inner ring of London the streets on VE Day were quite empty. Inside it all London was sardined together in a solid mass that spread, so far as I could calculate in the thick of it, over a square mile. Among the crowds, hopelessly bogged down, were the remains of the London traffic. The drivers just sat at their wheels and grinned, or did their best to prevent the crowds from smothering their vehicles completely (I saw the roof of one car collapse under the weight of six guards-men). It was impossible to walk freely. All you could hope to do was to move with the natural rhythm of the crowd. . . . All this VE Day I've been saying to myself: This is it. This is what we've all been waiting for. No more bombs. No more nights in the air-raid shelter. No more sudden death out of the sky. No more black-out. This is peace in Europe. Peace. . . . But you can't efface six years by waving a flag and putting your head in a paper hat. Peace is something you need time to get used to, like a new house. On the night of VE Day it still looked wrong, somehow, to see naked lights blazing through the windows. And, when the rockets hissed and banged overhead, when the skyline was picked out by the glow of victory bonfires, I, for one, had to make a conscious effort to remind myself that everything now is different; the fires and explosions in the night can be friendly. Thinking peace again is going to be as difficult as it was to think war, far away in September 1939. Remember?'

(viii)

During the next few days it was indeed difficult for many people to realize that Europe was at last at peace. Confusing reports came from Yugoslavia, where Marshal Tito appeared to be mopping-up not only the Germans but also the rival, anti-Communist group of partisans. There were indignant complaints in the British and American Press of the ill treatment of repatriated British and American prisoners returning home from Poland via Russia; a number of British women were raped by Russian soldiers in Odessa. Counter-charges from Moscow claimed that Russian refugees were being held in three camps in Britain under close American guard, and that Soviet citizens had been transported to the United States against their will. (These latter were half-truths; the State Department admitted that 4,300 German prisoners of war, who turned out to be Russians, had been taken to the US.) There were disturbing reports from Trieste. In Prague the German Commander-in-Chief refused to acknowledge the unconditional surrender, and furious street fighting broke out between resistance fighters and the *Wehrmacht*. General Patton was reported to be only fifteen miles away, but was held back by Eisenhower, despite Churchill's objections ('I am hoping that your plan does not inhibit you to advance to Prague if you have the troops'), while a Russian army encircled the city. Churchill had already approached Truman on this subject: 'There can be little doubt that the liberation of Prague and as much as possible of the territory of Western Czechoslovakia by your forces might make the whole difference to the post-war situation in Czechoslovakia, and might well influence that in near-by countries. On the other hand, if the Western allies play no significant part in Czechoslovakian liberation, that country will go the way of Yugoslavia.' Truman, somewhat curtly, replied that the Supreme Commander's decision met with his approval. He was, at this stage, still leaning heavily on the State Department in such matters.

From Flensburg, the so-called Fuehrer spoke to the disinterested world once more, hopefully suggesting that a place might be found for him and his government in the new scheme of things, whatever they were to be. 'I do not yet know,' he said, 'what I shall be able to do in these hard times. . . . With the occupation of Germany power has passed into the hands of the occupation forces. It depends on them whether I and the Reich Government formed by me will be able to continue in office or not. If it can be of assistance to the Fatherland by continuing in office, it shall continue to do so. . . . If my duty calls me to remain in office, I shall try to help you all I can.' The diplomatic correspondent of the London *Times* said that the exact standing of Doenitz, and his pretensions to speak on behalf of Germany, were being examined. Meanwhile, with no sign of any Allied troops at Flensburg, the Fuehrer and his government held court. Goering was found by the US Seventh Army near Salzburg, with a few *Luftwaffe* officers, and told everyone at hand that he had done his best to persuade Hitler to resign so that peace negotiations could have begun earlier. He found plenty of willing listeners, and as he was dined and wined by his captors at Kitzbuhel he must have thought that his well-known charm was going to win the day for him once more. His champagne days, however, came to a rude halt after an outcry in the American Press, and he was taken to Augsburg prison camp with his two cases of drugs (he was taking a hundred mild paracodeine tablets daily), his leather toilet-case with its assorted face-creams and body powders, his silk underclothing, his three enormous rings of ruby, emerald and diamond, his gold pen, pencil and cigar-case, the unset emerald which he always carried with him, and his four watches—everything, in fact, which was most dear to him. He was entertained liberally at Augsburg in the officers' mess, and drank heavily with the Americans, while still patiently waiting for the summons from Eisenhower that never came. He was taken away to a more hardy captivity on May 21st; a bare cell in which he had to stand naked beside his bed during the frequent inspections.*

In Ireland there had been a series of sudden and unpleasant blows to the conscience of this uncomfortable neutral nation. De Valera's action in sympathizing over the death of Hitler had caused a violent reaction in Dublin the following day, when outraged students of Trinity College raised the flags of the Allies over the main gate of the college, in the heart of the city. They were joined on the roof overlooking the large throng gathering below by members of the staff, and sang 'Rule Britannia'. Townsmen thereupon attempted to force their way into the college to take down the flags, and disorder was

---

* Goering was taken to Nuremberg prison in September. With Keitel, Frank, Jodl, Seyss-Inquart and others he was sentenced to death in October 1946. Two hours before the execution he took poison, probably given him by his American guards. In 1962 Hess, Speer and von Schirach were still in Spandau prison; Doenitz had been released in 1956, and at the time of writing was living in Schleswig-Holstein and drawing on a State pension.

increased rather than diminished when the police made repeated baton charges in attempts to disperse the crowds. It was the most serious riot in Dublin since Independence. The atmosphere was not relaxed when de Valera agreed, in contrast to the other neutral nations, that the Irish Government would look after the German Embassy until an envoy of the new Government should arrive. The Irish Premier's attitude was raised in the House of Commons. Sir Herbert Williams, Conservative, asked the Under-Secretary for Dominion Affairs whether a protest had been made against the action of the Prime Minister of the Irish Free State, one of His Majesty's Dominions, in tendering to the German Minister in Dublin his regret at the death of the chief British enemy, Adolf Hitler. A similar question was asked from the other side of the House. Mr Emrys Evans, replying to both questions, said: 'No, sir. Mr de Valera can safely be left to realize for himself the universal feeling of indignation which his action has aroused in this country and throughout the United Nations.' A few days later the Irish received another jab, when the Buchenwald pictures were issued there for the first time, some weeks after the rest of the world. Nothing till then had been allowed in the Irish newspapers about the concentration camps.

At Dunkirk and the besieged French Atlantic ports still held by the Germans the garrisons, a total of about 50,000 men, surrendered promptly. There was also a quick surrender in Holland, which was, however, marred by German Marines firing from upstairs windows on the large crowds in the streets below. Several people were killed, and there was some panic. The German Marines were sent to one of the concentration camps. In Denmark the first Allied officer to arrive in Copenhagen was a British major who entered from Sweden. He was followed by a parachute battalion and British warships. Over 300,000 German troops surrendered in Norway, and men of the Norwegian Resistance gradually took control from the German troops until the arrival of the British First Airborne Division two days later.

In most of the liberated countries the governments-in-exile resigned on return to their homelands, and made way for Socialist administrations in which ex-Resistance fighters were well represented. In Belgium there was a great deal of bitterness. King Leopold had been found by the Americans near Salzburg. The Socialist Party issued a declaration that it would support any action to obtain the King's abdication, thus incensing the Catholic Party.

After five years of exile, King Haakon of Norway returned to his country and a moving reception; a new government was formed with Trygve Lie as Foreign Minister. In Denmark the population was quickly settling down to the needs of peace; agricultural productive capacity was almost intact, and the larder was full. In Holland the German occupation had created greater difficulties; food supplies were pouring in, but infant mortality had risen to 60 per cent. Queen Wilhelmina had returned to a poor and desolate country before the Allied occupation was even complete.

A long-awaited event was the freeing of the Channel Islands, the only United Kingdom territory occupied by the Germans during the war. A force of twenty-two artillerymen arrived off Guernsey in the destroyer HMS *Bulldog*. The German officer who came to meet them, however, refused to sign an unconditional surrender, and sulkily said he had come to receive Armistice terms. This came as a shock as the twenty-two gunners, without any artillery, were clearly no match for the powerful German garrison of 10,000 men. The German Commander-in-Chief, Major-General Heine, was sent for, and, in full-dress uniform, eventually signed the surrender on an up-ended rum barrel. Although it was already late at night, the artillerymen went ashore. A police inspector and a sergeant, Guernsey men, were the reception party at the dock and both of them, according to the official account, were choking back tears when, speechless, they shook hands. The tiny force formed up on the dockside, fixed bayonets, and marched into the town, to the tumultuous ringing of church bells and the cheers of the inhabitants. The throng hurled themselves on the artillerymen with embraces and handshakes, and they re-formed before the Court House with some difficulty. The Union Jack was unfurled and the crowd sang the National Anthem. Douglas Willis of the BBC reported on the radio: 'The people had been drying blackberry leaves for pipe tobacco, or to use as tea. A packet of cigarettes made with locally-grown tobacco cost £2 8s. Butter, bought on the black market, cost £3 a pound.'

In the ruins of Berlin yet another total surrender, this time for the benefit of the Russians, was signed by von Friedeburg. There appears to have been no practical reason for this ceremony, as the total surrender had already been signed at Rheims, except to impress the Russian people. The Western allies were persuaded to send a party, under Tedder, to witness the signing, and at the vodka 'banquet' which followed many senior officers collapsed and three generals had to be carried from the room. The Western deputation were aghast at the still smoking ruins of the city. Russian troops went wild and raided cellars and shelters in search of women. There was, by all accounts, an orgy of rape, from which neither young children nor elderly women were safe. Looting was also the order of the day, and for a few days the Russian officers, who themselves appeared to British and American observers to be permanently intoxicated, seemed to have lost control of their troops. A few Berliners began to appear from underground and stumbled about over the ruins. There was practically no water. But gradually some order was restored. One of the first places to start functioning again was the famous Adlon Hotel, once well loved by Goering, Goebbels, foreign correspondents and diplomats, but now a shattered ruin apart from one wing, which, sticking up like a monument, had somehow survived the desolation all around. While Russian officers carried up bottles from the cellar, the skeleton staff, which had returned to work for want of anywhere better to go, began preparing rooms from what bedding they could find. The staff were told that the hotel, or what remained of it, no longer belonged to the Adlon family. It would be run by the authorities 'on behalf of the people'. The war was not over a week when their first civilian guest arrived. He was a Count from Saxony who had always visited Berlin at that time of year. Stepping over the rubble, he entered the hallway. The boy who was told to take his bag said: 'It was just as though nothing had happened. I wanted to weep.'*

In London, Parliament was assembled with the lantern behind Big Ben shining forth once more as a signal that the House of Commons was sitting. After lighting the lantern from a switch behind his chair, the Speaker said: 'I pray that, with God's blessing, this light may shine not only as an outward and visible sign that the Parliament of a free people is assembled in free debate, but also as a beacon of fresh hope in a sadly torn and distracted world.' On May 15th the Prime Minister expressed the deep feeling of the whole country towards the King. 'I remember well,' he said, 'how in the first months of this Administration the King would come in from practising with his rifle and tommy-gun in the garden at Buckingham Palace, and if it had come to a last stand in London, a matter which had to be considered at one time, I have no doubt that His Majesty would have [remained in London].'

The BBC, which during the past five years had deservedly won

* The surviving wing of the Adlon still functions as a small guest-house.

universal respect and extraordinary prestige, burst out in a veritable flood of Victory broadcasts. The bands of Geraldo, Albert Sandler and Jack Payne vied with one another in the playing of old wartime tunes like 'Johnny Got a Zero', 'The White Cliffs of Dover', 'Comin' in on a Wing and a Prayer', 'Roll out the Barrel', and, especially, 'When The Lights Go On Again'. The famous Music-While-You-Work programme, that had been relayed for years to countless head-scarfed factory workers, became a little less martial in tone. 'This Week's ENSA Artist' was Frances Day. The Western Brothers and Evelyn Laye were among the stars, supported by Charles Shadwell and the BBC Variety Orchestra, in a 'Victory Music Hall' programme. During the afternoons there were commentaries from the Victory Cricket Match at Lord's between the RAAF and a British Empire XI. The key word, all the time, was Victory. Bebe Daniels, Vera Lynn, Sandy Macpherson—and the Archbishop of Canterbury—all made special Victory broadcasts. So did J. B. Preistley. He said: 'At home here we've done things, often desperate things, our way, and on the whole it's a very good way. We've built machines but never lost ourselves inside them. People have had to be pushed about, and we've all got grievances, but they've been left space enough to be human and individual in, to feel fairly free. The notion that people cannot devote themselves to the community without feeling like ants in an ant-heap has been proved to be false.'

On the night of Thursday, May 10th, there was V-Itma, the victory edition of the country's most irreverant and popular weekly variety show. It was perfectly in keeping with the spirit of the nation, even perfectly apt, that this raucous and sometimes lewd show should have immediately preceded the Victory broadcast of Winston Churchill on the anniversary of his fifth year of office. Repeated on broadcasting networks around the world, this speech had one of the widest audiences in the history of radio. For the occasion Churchill had prepared what was perhaps his most resounding performance. After a long and bitter denunciation of Ireland's neutrality in the war, which surprised everybody by its severity, he spoke about the recent victory. 'For us in Britain,' he later wrote, 'and the British Empire, who had alone been in the struggle from the first day to the last and staked our existence on the result, there was a meaning beyond what even our most powerful and most valiant allies could feel. Weary and worn, impoverished but undaunted, and now triumphant, we had a moment that was sublime.' He said in his broadcast: 'I wish I could tell you tonight that all our trials and troubles were over. Then, indeed, I could end my five years' service happily, and if you thought that you had had enough of me and that I ought to be put out to grass, I would take it with the best of grace. But, on the contrary, I must warn you, as I did when I began this five years' task—and no one knew then that it would last so long—that there is still a lot to do, and that you must be prepared for further efforts of mind and body and further sacrifices to great causes if you are not to fall back into the rut of inertia, the confusion of aim, and the craven fear of being great. You must not weaken in any way in your alert and vigilant frame of mind. . . . There would be little use in punishing the Hitlerites for their crimes if law and justice did not rule, and if totalitarian or police governments were to take the place of the German invaders. We seek nothing for ourselves. But we must make sure that those causes which we fought for find recognition at the peace table in fact as well as words, and above all we must labour to ensure that the World Organization which the United Nations are creating at San Francisco does not become an idle name, does not become a shield for the strong and a mockery for the weak. . . . We must never forget that beyond all lurks Japan, harassed and failing, but still a people of a hundred millions, for whose warriors death has few terrors. . . . [The] Dominions came to our aid in our dark times and we must not leave unfinished any task which concerns their safety and their future. I told you hard things at the beginning of these last five years; you did not shrink, and I should be unworthy of your confidence and generosity if I did not still cry: Forward, unflinching, unswerving, indomitable, till the whole task is done and the whole world is safe and clean.'

5 Widening Chasm

5 WIDENING CHASM

While the victorious and liberated nations were thus basking in the joys of victory, and while the conference of the United Nations at San Francisco, which carried so many of the hopes of ordinary men and women everywhere, assembled, the chasm between East and West, only dimly suspected by the public at large, continued to grow. Each day seemed to make its closure more difficult.

During the collapse of Germany the Polish question in particular had been dragging on, with the Russians stubbornly sticking to their position and the Western allies being powerless to move them. A joint protest from Truman and Churchill met with no success. Eden and Stettinius met in Washington and agreed to press again for the entry of Western observers into Poland. They also agreed that the Soviet Government should be pressed to delay their intended treaty with the Lublin Poles. Before they could do so, news arrived that the treaty had been concluded. The two Foreign Secretaries met Molotov the following day and protested in vain. At length, Churchill decided on a long, detailed, personal and indignant appeal to 'Uncle Joe'. Among other points raised in this very long message was: 'We are all shocked that you should think that we favour a Polish government hostile to the Soviet Union. This is the opposite of our policy. There has grown up throughout the English-speaking world a very warm and deep desire to be friends on equal and honourable terms with the mighty Russian Soviet Republic and to work with you, making allowances for our different systems of thought and government. . . . We have given repeated instructions that your interest in Rumania and Bulgaria is to be recognized as predominant.' He concluded by saying that: 'There is not much comfort in looking into a future where you and the countries you dominate, plus the Communist parties in many other states, are all drawn up on one side, and those who rally to the English-speaking nations and their associates or Dominions are on the other. It is quite obvious that their quarrel would tear the world to pieces and that all of us leading men on either side who had anything to do with that would be shamed before history. Even embarking on a long period of suspicions, of abuse and counter-abuse, and of opposing policies would be a disaster hampering the great developments of world prosperity for the masses which are attainable only by our trinity.' Stalin's reply to this carefully worded appeal was cold and to the point: the Prime Minister's 'attitude excludes the possibility of an agreed solution of the Polish question'. Churchill was bitterly disillusioned by the disappearance of sixteen representatives of the non-Communist Polish resistance, who had gone to Moscow under a safe conduct to negotiate about representation in the Lublin Government.* With all this in mind, Churchill decided that nothing more could be done about Poland except at a meeting of the Big Three. On May 6th he proposed to President Truman that such a meeting should be held as soon as possible.

Meanwhile the Russians were creating obstacles in Vienna, which, like Berlin, was to be controlled, as had already been agreed, by the four major Allies, while Austria was to be split into zones of occupation similar to those in Germany. By the end of the war, however, the Russians had already announced that a Provisional Government had been formed in Vienna, and they were now refusing to let Western missions fly in.

To Churchill's relief and pleasure, Truman needed no prodding to send off a strong protest to the Soviet Government on the Vienna situation. Indeed, in the last weeks of April, and throughout May, the British found an encouraging tightening of American policy towards the Polish and Austrian questions; especially after Harriman,

* They appeared later in the year at a trial in Moscow, at which they all 'admitted' being guilty of espionage and subversion.

over from Moscow for the San Francisco conference, met the new President and warned him that the world was now faced 'with a barbarian invasion of Europe'. The decision to take an uncompromisingly firm line with Russia over the Polish question was made at an important meeting on April 22nd at the White House, attended by Truman's principal advisers, including Harriman. Leahy has written: 'The concensus of opinion among the group Truman had called together was that the time had arrived to take a strong attitude towards the Soviet Union.' This decision, taken under the lead of the new President, can be seen to be a turning point in United States' policy with regard to the USSR. It was, however, only in these two spheres that the British and American policy was at last beginning to harmonize. It other matters the views of the State Department as yet still held sway. This view was, according to Churchill, as follows: 'The United States must be careful not to let herself be drawn into any antagonism with Soviet Russia. This, it was thought, would stimulate British ambition and would make a new gulf in Europe. The right policy should be for the United States to stand between Britain and Russia as a friendly mediator, or even arbiter.' A rather different British view of the State Department's policy was that it was considered there that the efforts of the war had turned Britain into a second-class power, and that the United States therefore thought it would be well advised to 'go it alone' in dealings with Russia and not get encumbered with British attempts to retain world influence.

The most noticeable Anglo-American divergence at this time was over the question of the German occupation zones. The Americans were making it plain that they intended to withdraw from the Elbe to the zone already agreed upon as soon as it was practicable; a withdrawal of some 120 miles. Churchill protested vehemently about this, considering it folly to give away to the Russians an enormous chunk of territory while the occupation of Vienna was still unsettled. He realized that for the first time the Western powers had a bargaining counter that might be of great use. But the Americans, who seemed to have a predilection for going to the conference table unarmed, remained unimpressed by British pleadings. The influence of Eisenhower on Truman over this question seems to have been decisive. In a long cable to the President, the Supreme Commander said he was determined to withdraw as soon as possible as he refused to have the American forces 'badly embarrassed'. He said: 'I do not quite understand why the Prime Minister has been so

determined to intermingle political and military considerations. . . .'
The President was anxious to try to stick to a policy of good faith
with the Russians as far as Germany was concerned. 'The only
practical thing to do was to stick carefully to our agreement,' he
has said.

Churchill was now more anxious than ever for a meeting of the
Big Three, but on pressing for this he was startled to be told by a
special envoy of Truman's, Joseph E. Davies, that the President
would like to meet Stalin first at such a meeting; it would be more
convenient if the British arrived later. Churchill was outraged. His
note to Truman on the subject was the least friendly he ever
personally directed to Washington: 'The Prime Minister declares
that London, the greatest city in the world, and very heavily battered
during the war, is the natural and appropriate place for the Victory
meeting of the three great powers. However, if this is refused, His
Majesty's Government will none the less discuss with the United
States and with Soviet Russia what is the best place to be appointed.
The Prime Minister received with some surprise the suggestion . . .
that a meeting between President Truman and Premier Stalin should
take place at some agreed point, and that the representatives of His
Majesty's Government should be invited to join a few days later. It
must be understood that the representatives of His Majesty's
Government would not be able to attend any meeting except as
equal partners from its opening. . . . It must be remembered that
Britain and the United States are united at this time upon the same
ideologies, namely, freedom, and the principles set out in the
American Constitution and humbly reproduced with modern
variations in the Atlantic Charter. The Soviet Government have a
different philosophy. . . .'*

Concurrently with this move in London, Truman was also probing
in Moscow. He had sent Harry Hopkins, the faithful but sick
emissary whom he had inherited from Roosevelt, to see Stalin on a
number of matters, particularly the Polish question. According to
the verbatim record of one of their meetings as given in Sherwood,
Hopkins and Stalin talked at length on the differences between
Russia and Britain on the Polish question. Stalin laboured his point
that it was not American policy he was suspicious of, but British, and
Hopkins intimated that there was also a rift between the two

---

* Truman has denied he wanted a separate meeting with Stalin at this time, only a
private conversation at the conference. He must have known that such conversations
invariably took place at the Big Three conferences, and would hardly have sent a
personal emissary to raise such a point.

Western allies. Apparently satisfied about American goodwill, if not British, the Russian dictator showed signs that he might shortly agree to break the deadlock over the Lublin Government negotiations.

Churchill was not impressed. There was extremely bad news still coming in from Rumania and Bulgaria, where all opposition to the Communists was being indiscriminately labelled 'Fascist'. The situation in Yugoslavia was not much better, and the Czechs were also under Russian pressure. The position was complicated by the fact that in the Balkan countries it was not entirely a matter of Red Army domination; there was also an increase in the popularity of local Communist Parties, stemming from war-weary peoples who hoped in a wave of idealism to thrust aside for ever the régimes and conflicts of the old order. Europe, it seemed, was coming to the boiling-point. Churchill had already sent out a series of instructions to his Chiefs of Staff. All reduction of Bomber Command was to be stopped. Demobilization in the RAF and in the army was to be slowed up and even halted. In a memorandum of May 27th, Churchill wrote: 'You cannot at this moment throw yourselves heartily into the business of demobilization. I had hoped that this would be so, but I am sure that we had better get some solution in the main field of international relations.' The only classes to whom Churchill permitted instant release were doctors and women. German rifles were not to be destroyed. Not a single German aircraft or spare that fell into British hands was to be destroyed without express Cabinet permission. No matter what illusions were still harboured in Washington as to the honourable settlement of the Polish and other questions with Soviet Russia, the Prime Minister, exactly three months after the end of the Yalta conference, wrote to President Truman on May 12, 1945: 'An iron curtain is drawn down upon [the Russian] front.'

(ii)

As the war ended, there were crises nearly every day, not only between Russia and Britain, and America and Britain, but between many other nations as well. For the collapse of Germany had left parts of Western Europe and the Mediterranean in a dangerous vacuum. Newly liberated countries rushed like greedy old crones to grab a few square miles here and there, and nations that had once been proud allies bickered and snapped at each other as in a nursery. Thus had Eisenhower's 'Crusade', which had at times been bound with ties of almost religious fervour in quest of the common goal, been replaced by the national self-interests that had lain only just beneath the surface for so long.

The Yugoslav forces of Marshal Tito had arrived at the ancient port and trouble-spot of Trieste almost simultaneously with the Second New Zealand Division under General Sir Bernard Freyberg. The fact that the New Zealanders were there at all was due to the ceaseless urgings-on of Alexander by Churchill, who, despite all the various areas of crisis, was well aware of potential dangers to British or Western interests in any corner of the globe. Freyberg took the surrender of the German garrison and occupied the all-important dock area of the city. This quick and determined action by Churchill and Alexander frustrated Tito to the point of making difficulties in every way short of open hostilities. He had hoped to snatch the port and the surrounding area, to which he laid claim as the proper outlet for Yugoslavia on the Mediterranean. However, the Americans, too, were anxious for the port of Trieste; it was the obvious and most convenient entry for supplies for the occupation zone they hoped to have in Austria. The same applied to the British (although Truman gives, without evidence, a baser British motive: control of the Eastern Mediterranean). Reports soon began to reach the Western Press of atrocities and widespread looting in Trieste by the Yugoslavs. There was no doubt a great deal of truth, and of propaganda, in these reports, but it is unlikely that the looting was any more widespread than in Western Germany. The effect of this publicity, however, was to change Tito's standing in the West almost overnight. He had previously been regarded as a romantic leader, who, partly through his own successes and partly through the well-intentioned efforts of a number of left-wing or gullible writers, had become a popular figure in the English-speaking countries. Now he became the ogre of the Balkans who was threatening the peace that had only just been won. Truman was as annoyed at Tito's refusal to return behind his own border, as was Churchill. He felt strongly that here was a case of a country acquiring assets by force; just the kind of thing that the United States had been fighting a war to stop. The new President was, however, extremely apprehensive of the Balkans and was most reluctant to become involved in a controversy in an area which 'had long been a source of trouble and war'. He made it plain that, while he tacitly supported the British stand in Trieste, he could not consider material support. He said he was unable to involve the United States in a war in the Balkans. Although the atmosphere in Trieste had become extremely tense, with both New Zealand and Yugoslav troops fingering their triggers, Churchill replied that there was no question of war with the Yugoslavs, but that immediate action was necessary if the British and Americans were not to be held up before the world as unable to maintain the observance of the principles for which they had just been fighting a European war. With the Russians beginning to exert pressure on behalf of Tito's claims, the situation remained explosive and grave.

In the far eastern end of the Mediterranean, which was becoming increasingly overshadowed by Arab-Jewish suspicions and hatreds in Palestine, the Anglo-Americans were having trouble with their French allies. Worried about the prospects for continued French interest in the traditionally French areas of Syria and the Levant, de Gaulle had sent troops into Syria. Britain had already guaranteed post-war Syrian independence, and was thus placed in a difficult position by her ally. As French troops began landing at Beirut and pouring into the Lebanon and Syria, it was clear that here, like Trieste, was another test of will for Britain and the United States. The world watched to see whether they would let the ally that had been closest to them get away with such a blatant use of force. The San Francisco conference was threatened, as the smaller countries, particularly the Arab nations, believed that if the French escaped with this action the major countries, protected by the veto, would be able to get away with anything. The French, despite protests from Churchill and Truman, proceeded to behave in the same proud and stubborn way as they were to do in territorial matters for more than a decade to come. De Gaulle seemed to cherish the delusion that what Britain had achieved with Egypt in 1936 France could obtain by force with the Levant States in 1945. Riots, demonstrations and disturbances in Syria inevitably became all-out fighting. De Gaulle remained totally insensitive to protestations from the British and American Ambassadors in Paris. It was, he said, a matter of prestige. Fierce street fighting broke out in Damascus between Syrians and French troops. French artillery opened fire, and their troops occupied the Syrian Parliament buildings. There were about 2,000 casualties in the city in forty-eight hours. Clearly this was the most ruthless and cynical form of colonialism. At this point Churchill ordered British troops into Syria in order to restore order. He gave as his reason the theory that the Middle East, being an important link in communications to the Japanese theatre of war, had to be kept free from disturbance. De Gaulle immediately gave way, explained that he had already ordered a cease fire, and that the presence of British troops was unnecessary. A large part of the French force was escorted to the coast by British troops, and the Governments of Syria and Lebanon were guaranteed, by the British, against further French pressure. There was an outcry of hurt French pride in the National Assembly. Speaking in the House of Commons, Churchill said of this sordid episode: 'The less said the better.'

But this was not the only area in which the French leader was causing grave embarrassment to the Western allies. Unbearably humiliated by the débâcle of 1940, and obsessed with the idea of restoring French prestige and influence, he saw the best way of doing so by using his troops, entirely American equipped and supplied, for presenting a *fait accompli* and then daring the British and Americans to do something about it. During the advance into Germany it had fallen to the French army of General de Lattre de Tassigny to move south through the city of Stuttgart. Having reached Stuttgart, however, the French troops stopped, and then showed no signs of moving out. On being ordered to move on, the local French Commander stated that he had been ordered by de Gaulle to remain in the city, and thus was unable to comply with the order from SHAEF. It seemed that de Gaulle was, in fact, determined to force the Allied hand by staking out an occupation zone of his own. Truman was outraged. Discussions about a French zone were already under way, and, as he says, 'land-grabbing was out of order'. Like Roosevelt, Truman was unable to get on any kind of terms at all with de Gaulle. With personal intervention by Eisenhower and then by the President failing to move the French troops, Truman ordered the cutting of their supplies. The French troops moved out.

An even more serious clash with de Gaulle occurred over the Franco-Italian frontier. In the closing days of the war, the French First Army, instead of chasing Germans, went over the border into Italy and occupied a part of the Italian province of Cunio. This area was under Alexander's command, and not Eisenhower's. The latter, therefore, ordered the French to withdraw. This they showed no signs of doing, and within days reports appeared in newspapers of French efforts to take over the area on a permanent basis. French currency was introduced. Italian flags were removed. In less than a week the whole area was bristling with French troops, who seemed even to outnumber the civilians. De Gaulle answered American protests by declaring he was merely arranging 'minor frontier adjustments'. The local French Commander, General Doyen, answered attempts to set up Allied military government in the area with two written threats that any such moves could result in hostilities between French troops and the American troops occupying north-west Italy. On both occasions he made it plain that he was acting under the direct orders of de Gaulle. Churchill, on being shown these messages, was astounded. He wrote to Truman: 'Is it not rather disagreeable for us to be addressed in these terms by General de Gaulle, whom we have reinstated in liberated France at some expense of American and British blood . . . ?' Truman was even more outraged. For de Gaulle had chosen this very moment to suggest that he should be invited to the pending Big Three conference and, as proof of American recognition of France's status as a great power, he asked that French troops should be allowed to join in the final blow to Japan. Their weapons, equipment, supplies and transport were still to be provided by the United States. Infuriated, Truman received the French Foreign Minister, Georges Bidault. He explained that only if French troops were prepared to obey Allied commands, and they plainly were not, could he possibly furnish the planes and other supplies that would be needed to get them to, and to operate in, the Pacific theatre. It was an extremely frigid meeting. As the French still showed no signs of evacuating the area of Italy they had penetrated, the President, after a meeting with the US Chiefs of Staff and the State Department, ordered that issues of ammunition and equipment to the French be stopped. He prepared a statement for the American Press explaining that he had been forced to this decision as there was a threat by the French that they would use such supplies against American soldiers. He asked for Churchill's concurrence, and the Prime Minister agreed. At the last minute Truman decided to hold up the statement to the Press to see what action de Gaulle would take. In a message to de Gaulle he described the French action as 'extremely churlish . . . and in complete contradiction of the principles [for] safeguarding a hardly won peace: namely to abstain from military action for political ends'. He pointed out, in high indignation, that the French action had taken place on the anniversary of the Normandy landings, which had begun the liberation of France. He threatened to tell the

American people of the whole situation unless there was an immediate French withdrawal. Churchill told Truman that 'the publication of your message would have led to the overthrow of de Gaulle', whom he considered 'one of the greatest dangers to European peace'. He said that although no country needed French friendship more than Britain, he was convinced that in the long run no real Anglo-French understanding would ever be achieved under de Gaulle. The French leader, however, reacted immediately on receipt of the American ultimatum, and the statement was never released to the Press. De Gaulle said that there had never been any intention to oppose by force the presence of American troops in the small corner of Italy in question. In a cold and formal reply to the President, he said: 'Our expulsion from this district and what the English are at present doing to us in Syria is a coincidence which is displeasing to French feelings.' Having failed to force the issue, de Gaulle fell back on diplomacy. The squabble with the Italians continued behind the scenes for many months, and on one occasion de Gaulle offered to support the return of Libya to the Italians if they would agree to review the demarcation of the Franco-Italian frontier.

The affair ended in another defeat for de Gaulle's ambitions; but not before suspicions that had been deeply laid on all sides cracked still further the thin veneer of the so-called 'Alliance'.

(iii)

In Germany there was an extraordinary situation. The government of Doenitz continued to put up every appearance of taking itself seriously, as, for a time, did the British and Americans. Both the Western allies were reluctant to dismiss this powerless authority, believing it might be of use in enforcing law and order. In a memorandum to the Foreign Office, Churchill said: 'I neither know nor care about Doenitz. He may be a war criminal . . . the question for us is, has he any power to get the Germans to lay down their arms and hand them over quickly without any more loss of life? We cannot go running round into every German slum and argue with every German that it is his duty to surrender or we will shoot him. . . . I deprecate the raising of these grave constitutional issues at a time when the only question is to avoid sheer chaos. . . . It must of course be remembered that if Doenitz is a useful tool to us that will have to be written off against his war atrocities for being in command of submarines. Do you want to have a handle with which to manipulate this conquered people, or just to have to thrust your hands into an agitated ant-heap?' This tolerance of Doenitz, and also that extended to Goering by the Americans in the south, was regarded with acute suspicion by the Russians. In an attempt to dispel these suspicions two statements were made at SHAEF on May 16th. Lieutenant-General Lucius Clay, the American Deputy Military Governor in Germany, said that both Doenitz and Goering were to be treated as prisoners of war; both men were on the list of war criminals. He said that Doenitz and his government were being used temporarily to carry out duties connected with the feeding, disarmament and administration of the German armed forces. Mr Robert Murphy, Eisenhower's political adviser, said on the same occasion that there would be no more broadcasts from Flensburg in the name of the Doenitz Government, but not before Speer, 'Minister for Reconstruction', had made a somewhat self-pitying broadcast in which he stated that 'never before has a land been laid so waste by the fury of war as has Germany'. A Russian party arrived at Flensburg shortly after the American statements in order to see for themselves that nothing underhand was being done there. It was their arrival which, no doubt, expedited the end of this remarkable episode. Doenitz was placed under arrest on May 23rd, having been summoned to an Allied ship in the harbour. At the same time two battalions of the Cheshire and Herefordshire Regiments, and men of the 15/19th Hussars, moved in on the castle. All officers, officials and troops were captured. Special squads of searchers removed documents and records found there. Extraordinary scenes followed. German Marines were marched away through the ancient courtyard, singing *Wir führen gegen England* as von Friedeburg took the salute. Jodl bade farewell to his staff with stiff formality. The various Ministers, including von Krosigk and Speer, were whisked away in a procession of staff cars, with German troops springing to the salute as they passed.

The three-week régime of the 'Second Fuehrer' had come to an abrupt end.

A skeleton German military framework was kept up for the time being in order to facilitate Allied rule. The German commanders were able to do this well enough without the Doenitz organization, which made Anglo-American excuses for retaining that self-styled 'government' somewhat limp. Even now, however, the senior

German commanders attempted to cause a rift between the Russians and the West. Montgomery has said: 'The German military leaders, having been saved from the Russians, were only too willing to be friends with the British and do whatever was wanted. But in return for this co-operative attitude they expected to be treated as allies of the British against the Russians.' He had to send for Field-Marshal Busch, the German Commander-in-Chief in North-West Europe, and severely reprimand him for maintaining this attitude.

The documents which had been seized at Flensburg were only a small part of the mass of secret information and records about the Reich now being collected by a special staff especially trained for this task. The men had advanced into Germany immediately behind the forward troops, at places already earmarked by Intelligence, and commandeered everything of interest. They were particularly responsible for preventing the destruction or concealment of research work and plants. In one instance the managing director of a company engaged in secret production was actually disturbed while giving instructions on the disposal of research. In this manner an entirely unsuspected infra-red searchlight, for blinding tank crews, was discovered. Other things now discovered, on which the Germans had been working, were non-inflammable synthetic rubber for car tyres, indestructible by bullets; piloted flying bombs; controlled torpedoes which could follow the course of a zig-zagging ship; jet-submarines; half-track tanks with extremely low fuel consumption; and air-to-ground controlled projectiles. Whereas most of the Flensburg documents fell into British hands, those of the Berlin departments that had fled to the south were confiscated by the Americans. Much of the rocket research, and some of the scientists, also came into the hands of the Americans, and both were swiftly transported across the Atlantic, but not before the British had succeeded in firing two German V.2s from Cuxhaven into the North Sea.

Throughout May the Allies wrestled with the problem of restoring normal life to Germany, but the problem was so immense that the result of their efforts was hardly noticeable. The three Allied representatives on the Control Council were named as Zhukov, Eisenhower and Montgomery. These three men had, in effect, absolute rule over their respective areas. Their problems were immense. The total devastation in the cities caused by saturation bombing stretched in many cases for mile after mile. But an official observer, Wing-Commander John Strachey, summed up prevailing opinion about this in a BBC broadcast: 'It would have been an unpardonable crime to withhold a single bomb, the bursting of which on Germany could shorten the Nazi tyranny over Europe by an hour.'

In one of his most vivid dispatches, Alan Moorehead reported: 'All around us are things too monstrous to grasp. Starvation. Fifty great cities in ruins. Ten million people roaming helplessly through the countryside without homes, their relatives lost, and all normal hope gone out of their lives. For the next year the prospects are the starvation of anything up to five million people, the spread of disease. . . . The Third Reich is simply a dead carcass and there is no need for any of our generation to think that we will again be hurt by it in our lifetimes. Hitler has taken his country with him to the grave. . . . I have tramped through twenty towns where the débris of three-year-old bombings has long since returned to its original dust; locomotives and churches and city halls lie tossed aside in the streets. That is the normal background of life here now. You live in the cellars. Gas, running water, electric light, windows? Oh, no, you cannot expect those luxuries any more. And you walk. If it's three blocks or a hundred miles, it's all the same. You walk. The women are ugly. No new clothes; precious few cosmetics. They dress to keep warm. The men are grey-faced and dirty. Speak to them and they run to answer obsequiously.'

The food situation became so serious that the Americans cut by 10 per cent the rations of their own troops and of their prisoners of war. The needs of the homeless masses in Europe were so great that a severe food shortage seemed inevitable over the world. In order to keep up exports the meat ration in Australia was cut by $12\frac{1}{2}$ per cent. Canada also reduced its meat consumption.

By the end of the month the majority of the Allied prisoners-of-war were either home or on their way home—a considerable feat in itself. Work was begun in clearing ways through the ruins of the great cities. German servicemen were being discharged according to their trades and occupations, with priority for farm workers. Displaced persons were passing through camps, on their way home, fairly speedily, although Polish slave labourers and German refugees from the Russian sector were mainly refusing to go. According to Montgomery large areas east of the Elbe had been completely denuded of Germans, so total had been the migration before the advancing Russians. Some experts began to ask what was to become of these people. But everyone else was too busy to care;

fully occupied in moving the hundreds of thousands who were only too willing to go to their homes. The Russian slave labourers moved away to the east with special speed. Of those of all nationalities who could be accounted for, about 5,800,000 persons, nearly 3,300,000 had been sent home by the end of June. In twenty-five days half a million people left Germany. As they passed through camps, each person was sprayed with a new insecticide called DDT. But there were many more who avoided all control and authority and made their own ways, as best they could, across frontiers and through armies. George Orwell, reporting on the problem for the London *Observer*, wrote that 'more and more displaced persons simply escape and take to the roads, often with the idea of walking back to their own countries by the shortest route'. Some of the gangs that these people had formed themselves into before the end of the war continued to run riot through the countryside raping, robbing and murdering.

The Allied commanders frequently broke from their labours during these days in order to pin their country's highest honours on each others' chests. General Bradley pinned the Legion of Honour on Konev's uniform, and then presented him with a brand new jeep. Rokossovsky invited Montgomery to his headquarters, having first gone to great trouble to find out the British leader's tastes in wine and cigars. On being told that the Field-Marshal cared for neither, an envoy discreetly informed the British that in that case a party of beautiful women would be provided for Montgomery's pleasure. It was explained that this would not be necessary. The Russian envoy who had been sent to inquire into these matters is said to have exclaimed at this point: 'What the devil does he do all day?' The meeting with Rokossovsky took place, despite all these disappointments, and one British officer got so drunk that he fired off his revolver in answer to the Russian twenty-one gun salute. The apparently indestructible Montgomery met his own undoing a few days later when he received the freedom of Antwerp. He was offered course after course in an enormous banquet in the Hotel de Ville. The food was, for him, unaccustomedly rich. As Field-Marshal Montgomery was afterwards driven through the streets packed with wildly cheering Belgian crowds, he was prostrate on the floor of his open car being violently sick; he has been one of the most honoured citizens of Antwerp ever since.

At Eisenhower's headquarters, which had now moved from Rheims to the I. G. Farben works at Frankfurt, Montgomery received the Distinguished Service Medal from Eisenhower. Zhukov came to Frankfurt and distributed a large number of Russian medals among American officers there, and presented Eisenhower and Montgomery with the Order of Victory. As the latter remarked, this was not only a great honour—it being the first time the decoration had been accorded to a foreigner—it was also of great intrinsic value, being set with rubies and diamonds. After this presentation the Americans produced a luncheon cabaret for their Russian guests; the most striking feature of this was a dance by girls stripped to the waist.

All this conviviality, however, did not hide the marked differences already appearing between the Allied zones. The lack of any common economic policy was inviting criticism in the Press. In the British sector trade unions were being dissolved: in Berlin trade unions were being proclaimed. The most dramatic difference was in the policy of non-fraternization. Although during these weeks there was a complete shut-down on news from the Russian sector in Germany, and from the Russian-occupied countries—no foreign correspondents or observers being allowed in—Scandinavian visitors brought back enough information to make it clear that the Russians, far from practising non-fraternization with the Germans, were mixing with them and inculcating them with the tenets of Communism. In the western area of Germany, on the other hand, the non-fraternization rule was strictly applied; this was especially the case in the American Zone. All contact was forbidden apart from that absolutely necessary for officers of the military administration. On June 5th the three Allied commanders, with General de Tassigny, met in Berlin to discuss their mutual problems. Zhukov insisted that nothing could be done until the British and Americans had withdrawn to the areas already set out for them. Montgomery, on Churchill's advice, resisted this suggestion; he knew that the Prime Minister was determined that the Anglo-Americans should go to the pending Big Three conference in a position of strength. The Americans were not anxious to stay on the Elbe, and, after some haggling, Montgomery got 'fed-up' and sent word to Churchill that he thought the Anglo-American forces should move back. Churchill did not agree, and the conference broke up after a long declaration had been signed. The basis of this declaration had already been long agreed, first at Casablanca and then at Yalta. A Control Council was to be set up, and the four zones of Germany were delineated (the French one having been largely carved out of that allotted to the

Americans). The area of Greater Berlin was to be occupied by forces of each of the four powers. The first American troops arrived in Berlin on July 3rd, and the first British, the famous Seventh Armoured Division (the 'Desert Rats'), arrived the following day. SHAEF was disbanded on July 14th; Montgomery thought this a major 'nationalistic' error on the part of the Western allies. By that act Eisenhower lost all authority outside the American Zone.

The British and American commanders agreed at this time that their troops were to be allowed to play with and speak to small German children.

On May 24th it was announced that Himmler had been captured wandering about in Bremervoerde on May 21st. He had been disguised with a black patch over his eye, and he had shaved off his moustache. With him had been two of his adjutants. They were not at first recognized by their British captors, but after Himmler revealed his identity he bit open a phial of cyanide, concealed in his mouth, during the final stages of a medical examination at Lüneburg. It took him fifteen minutes to die. Among other leading war criminals arrested was William Joyce (known as 'Lord Haw-Haw'), who had achieved notoriety by broadcasting for the Germans. During capture, near the Danish frontier, he was wounded by a British officer. He was duly remanded at Bow Street on June 25th and committed to trial under the Treason Act of 1351.*

The only other countries in which the Germans had recently capitulated, and in which the Western allies had occupying forces, were Austria and Czechoslovakia. In the latter there had been a rapid and encouraging movement towards some normality, and there were few disturbances. In comparison with the cities in Germany, both Prague and Pilsen were relatively undamaged. Dr Benes arrived in Prague on May 16th and a government under M. Fierlinger was set up. The two most serious difficulties the country had to face in its early days of freedom were the breakdown of discipline among Russian troops and Russian territorial demands. In a hopeful gesture of appeasement, the Czech Government agreed to cede the tip of their country, Ruthenia, to the USSR. The Russian frontier thus passed beyond the Carpathians for the first time in that country's history. There was considerable looting in the small American-occupied area of Czechoslovakia, but this was brought under some control after a week. By the end of the month discipline had been restored in the Soviet Army (but not until the sale of alcohol had

* He was found guilty of treason and executed on January 3rd, 1946.

been banned to Russian troops); little information reached the West from the Russian-occupied area.

In Vienna the horrors of battle had left the once-gay population in misery. The Russian troops there almost excelled those in Berlin for their savagery, and for two weeks the Viennese lived in constant terror. 'Requisitions', especially of machinery and fuel, began to pour eastwards. Agreement about the zones of occupation in Austria was eventually reached. The arguments between the Anglo-Americans and the Russians as to the occupation of Vienna, however, continued, while the Russian-sponsored Government began to impose its will. The Americans were in Upper Austria and the Tyrol, and the British, having first pushed back a force of Tito's partisans (who laid claim to the area), were in Carinthia. It was clear that a clash between East and West was possible.

In the British sector of Austria was the picturesque town of Linz. It was here that Adolf Hitler had planned his grandiloquent new opera house. But Linz in the spring of 1945 was not a place that Hitler would have wanted to visit. A BBC correspondent reported: 'There are in Linz many urgent things to be done. The purification of the water supplies, the restoration of gas supplies, for instance. But the matter which I found the newly elected council debating when I arrived was the rechristening of the Town Square, which had inevitably been called Adolf Hitler Square. In fact the history of Austria was written in this problem. It had originally been called Emperor Franz Josef Square; and then, after the collapse of the Hapsburgs, the Square of the Twelfth November; then the Dolfuss Square; and latterly Adolf Hitler Square. As I left the Town Hall I learnt that the council had decided to take no risks in the future and was calling it simply the Main Square.'

(iv)

In Britain there was still a widespread mood of relaxation, which the constant urgings to further effort in the war against Japan were not able to diminish. The King and Queen visited their newly liberated islands of Jersey and Guernsey, amid scenes of great enthusiasm. On Whit Monday, the first carefree Bank Holiday in Britain since 1939, the King attended Ascot races, accompanied by Princess Elizabeth. The first garden-party at Buckingham Palace since before the war was almost entirely given over to 1,800 British and Dominion repatriated prisoners-of-war. The King took the salute in Hyde Park at a farewell parade of representatives of all the Civil Defence Services. But the ceremony which affected London's heart most was the conferring of the Freedom of the City of London on General Eisenhower. Having already been mobbed in Hyde Park in the morning, when he had gone from the Dorchester Hotel for a quiet stroll in order to compose his speech, he spoke to an admiring and receptive audience of 30,000 outside the Mansion House. The criticisms of the Supreme Commander that had appeared in the British Press only a few months before were all forgotten. It was an occasion of some emotion. After the Prime Minister had praised Eisenhower's undoubted and valuable capacity for making the Allies co-operate—although few in the crowd could have been aware just how close to failure he had sometimes been—Eisenhower said: 'Whether you know it or not, I am now a Londoner myself. I have as much right to be down in the crowd yelling as you have.' From then on 'Ike' Eisenhower, whose open smile and quiet manner had already won over most of the British public, was Britain's favourite American.

For the first time in five years Parliament was able to concern itself chiefly with domestic affairs. There was a great deal of argument about financial matters. Everyone wanted to know when the unbearable burden of taxation could be eased. In his Budget speech Sir John Anderson, one of the most widely respected of the wartime Coalition Ministers, had already held out a definite promise: 'The present level of taxation is unquestionably oppressive to the spirit of enterprise and industry. It is of the first importance that when the compelling incentive of working for victory is no longer present there should be an early alleviation of the existing heavy obstacles to the normal incentive to work.' He had revealed that in the financial year 1944-45 total national expenditure had exceeded £6,000 million. Five and a half years of war had involved an expenditure of £27,400 million, more than 50 per cent of which it had been impossible to meet out of current revenue. Now a little more was revealed about where the money had come from. A great deal had been raised by savings, which had reached extraordinary and unprecedented levels; 'a striking record', as Anderson said, 'of individual sacrifice and effort'. It had, however, been necessary to dispose of the greater part of the country's foreign investments. In some areas, such as in South America, where British investments and holdings had for long predominated, the loss was practically total. Not only that, but heavy liabilities had accumulated overseas. Excluding aid from the United States and Canada, this, it was said, would amount to £4,000 million or more. Less easily defined than these estimates, but perhaps more serious still, was the indirect cost through lack of investment in capital goods that had occurred during the war. The tremendous finances had been channelled into war goods instead of into building houses, making good wear and tear, and adding to factories and machinery. Already there were isolated incidences reported in the newspapers of the hardships caused by the lack of housing, but few people were prepared to face the problem as a whole—what the war had cost and what was going to be done about it. The Chancellor of the Exchequer stated that the purchasing power of the £ had declined by more than 50 per cent since 1939. But *The Economist* declared that the war had been largely paid for already. The influential City column in the *News Chronicle* said: 'The war has not ruined us . . . we can be better off than ever before.'

The public found other revelations more interesting than financial statistics and economic matters. It was revealed that during the European war the Royal Navy had lost 730 ships through enemy action, including five battleships, eight aircraft-carriers, twenty-six cruisers and 128 destroyers. For the first time the population heard of the wartime experiences of Parliament. It was revealed that early in the war plans for the evacuation of the Houses of Parliament to the Shakespeare Memorial Theatre at Stratford-on-Avon had been made. But when the air-raids had reached their pitch there became a growing conviction, indeed wish, shared by Members of Parliament of all parties, that Parliament should meet its fate at Westminster; and, despite the bombing of the House of Commons, there it had remained.

Overriding all other parliamentary factors, however, was the future of the Coalition. This Government, which had successfully steered the nation from the brink of defeat to victory, was beginning to show cracks even before the end of the war. The Government had been completely dominated by Churchill, and the record of Cabinet members, even those from the Labour Party (with the exception, perhaps, of Stafford Cripps), was not good in that respect. Even in the House itself only a very few, and notably Aneurin Bevan, had either felt like criticizing or dared to criticize Churchill in the previous two years or so. Now some of the Labour leaders, especially Herbert Morrison, began to itch for open party strife. Churchill himself, much to his later regret, had sounded the death-knell of the Coalition the previous October when he had virtually promised in the House that an election would follow the defeat of Germany. An election was clearly needed; no one under the age of thirty had ever cast a vote. The last election, in 1935, had been in a dim, distant age which bore no relation to present circumstances. The only question was, which was more important: holding an election, or maintaining the Government to win the war against Japan without any distraction or delay?

Morrison had little difficulty in rallying support to his view. It was obvious that Labour were in a strong position. Results at by-elections had been encouraging, and it seemed more than likely that a wave of 'brave-new-world' thinking, similar to that after the previous war, would be attracted to Socialism. Above all, the Labour Party election machinery was, for the first time, better prepared than that of the Conservatives. The core of the party was in the trade unions, and many of their organizers, through their vital importance to war production, had not been called up for military service. Nearly all the Conservative agents, on the other hand, were in the Services, with their constituencies unattended. Churchill was utterly against holding the election at all, but not for this tactical reason. He had come to think of the Coalition Government as the personification of 'One Nation'; this united aspect of the country at war moved him greatly. He dreaded the return to out-and-out party politics, knowing that it would abolish this national unity and that it would also cause him much personal pain. He also had a natural feeling that his grasp and knowledge of contemporary world affairs, especially in the matters of Soviet ambitions and American suspicions, were indispensable at least till the war against Japan was over. His principal advisers on party matters, although not on governmental, were the two powerful adventurers Lord Beaverbrook and Brendan Bracken, men greatly feared, disliked and distrusted by the Labour politicians, to whom they were known as 'M and B'. They advised him that if Labour insisted on an election, then it was imperative to have it as soon as possible, probably in July, rather than to wait until October, which Morrison was now offering to do; for by October a new electoral roll, which it was thought would benefit the Labour candidates, would be in operation.

The Labour Party Conference was held at Blackpool, and there Morrison manoeuvred with gusto and spirit. Attlee, leader of the party, managed to gather the reins, but not, apparently, without some difficulty. He, like Hugh Dalton and Ernest Bevin, having served in the special atmosphere of the wartime Cabinet, was not altogether anxious to bring it to an end. Bevin had particularly appreciated the historical feel of Churchill's Government; he was even willing to consider a Churchill proposal that the Coalition should continue for two years after the end of the war. Aligned with Morrison was the fiery Bevan, seen by many as a 'real' Socialist, unlike Attlee, and as a future leader of the party who would lead it to the promised land. Bevan, however, went even further than Morrison. He wanted, like some of the Conservatives, to have an election immediately, for he had absolutely no doubt whatever that Labour would win no matter when the election was held. After a half-hearted effort, led by Harold Laski (the new Chairman of the Party Executive) and Ellen Wilkinson, to replace Attlee with Morrison, the party leader came out strongly on the side of an election. This may well have been in an effort to consolidate his own position, as he was not the man to be swayed by arguments from Morrison and Bevan, and he had previously let it be known that he was in favour of continuing the Coalition until the conquest of Japan, as Churchill wished. The whole affair is now clouded under contradictory assertions and denials. Years later Attlee wrote: 'There was never any question of either Bevin or myself being opposed to Labour fighting the election on its own or favouring a post-election Coalition.' Churchill, however, was under the definite impression that Attlee wanted the Coalition to continue for a while. Attlee replied to Churchill's request in unfriendly tones, accusing him 'of departing from the position of a national leader by yielding to the pressure of the Conservative Party', by suggesting an election, if there were to be one, in July rather than October. There is no doubt that Attlee was bitter at the thought of this tactic (using the out-dated electoral role). After this letter there was no future for the Coalition. On May 23rd, being confronted by a complete breach between the two most important parties, Churchill reluctantly tendered his resignation to the King, having first replied to Attlee: 'I have concerned myself solely with trying to create tolerable conditions under which we could work together. It is clear from the tone of your letter and the feelings of your party that these no longer exist, and it is odd that you should accompany so many unjust allegations with an earnest request that we should go on bickering together till the autumn.' Thus ended the Coalition Government, an administration which by any test had deserved the appellation 'great'.

Winston Churchill set about forming another government to take over affairs during the short interim period before the election. The Conservatives held a majority of a hundred over all other parties combined, but Churchill strove to make the basis of the Caretaker Government, as it was known, as broad as possible. A number of people now found themselves in responsible positions for apparently little other reason than that they happened to be un-attached to any of the parties. Ten of the twenty-four Ministers of Cabinet rank were not Conservative Members of Parliament. All those non-party members of the Coalition, such as Sir John Anderson, remained at their posts. Ministers in the Caretaker Government included the redoubtable Lord Beaverbrook, Lord Privy Seal, and Brendan Bracken, First Lord of the Admiralty. Duncan Sandys was Minister of Works and Leslie Hore-Belisha was Minister of National Insurance—much to everyone's surprise as, throughout the war, he had been one of Churchill's few outspoken critics in the House. R. A. Butler, Minister of Labour, Oliver Lyttelton, President of the Board of Trade, and Harold Mac-millan, Secretary for Air, replaced respectively Ernest Bevin, Hugh Dalton and Sir Archibald Sinclair, leader of the Liberal Party.

The Labour Party ended its conference on a challenging note. It endorsed the executive's policy for the post-war period, em-bodied in a pamphlet entitled *Let Us Face the Future*, which had been prepared by Morrison (who was entrusted with running the campaign). The drastic policies contained in this would, it was said, win the peace for the people. The whole economy was to be over-hauled and a large dose of Socialism injected into it. There was to be nationalization of the gas, coal and electricity industries; of air, land, road and canal transport; and of the iron and steel industries. The Bank of England was to be taken over by the State, there was to be public supervision of monopolies and cartels, and general economic and price controls. There was bitter criticism at the con-ference of the rejection of the nationalization of land. The conference rejected a suggestion to combine forces with the Communist Party. There was much class bitterness at the root of many speeches, and those who traditionally voted Conservative had observed the proceedings with deep misgivings and some disbelief. Could it really be, they asked, that Socialists, their own countrymen, were going to turn the whole country upside-down just when it was at its greatest peak?

Churchill held a tea-party for the members of the Coalition at Downing Street on May 28th. Here, for a brief moment, the enmity that had recently crept back into political affairs dispersed for an hour or two, and there was an atmosphere of friendliness and good-will. Men who had served the country in its time of greatest danger, with no feelings of political rivalry, parted with dignity. Many of the Labour ex-Ministers spoke to Churchill personally, expressing their pride at having served in the wartime Government. Standing be-hind the green baize Cabinet table, the Prime Minister addressed the forty or fifty people present. He said that he intended inviting 'my good friend Clem Attlee' to go with him to the Big Three conference so that he would be well briefed in the latest moves if there were a change in government. With tears streaming down his cheeks, he said that they had all come together, at a very difficult time, as a band of friends. If a similar danger ever presented itself to the country, he was sure the same thing would happen again. Their united stand would be recognized by history: 'The light of history will shine on all your helmets.'

Attlee and Sinclair made brief replies, and then everyone went out into the garden to be photographed together; but it began to rain.

The following afternoon the parties faced each other across the House once more as Government and Opposition. To many the traditional arrangement felt uncomfortable and strange; to others it felt refreshing and exciting. Attlee formally accepted the Prime Minister's invitation to accompany him to the Big Three con-ference, an action which was the cause of querulous comment by Harold Laski. Parliament was dissolved on June 15th; it had been the fourth longest in British history, and the longest since 1679. Polling day was to be July 5th, but owing to the vast amount of servicemen's votes that had to be sent home from abroad a further twenty-one days were to elapse before the counting and declaration, fixed for July 26th. When it was learnt that the ballot-boxes would be in the custody of the British Government for three weeks, the opinion was voiced in some countries abroad that there could be little doubt as to the result.

But the renewal of party warfare and the forthcoming General Election were only a part of the kaleidoscope which made up the domestic scene in Britain immediately after the end of the German war. In early June there was an acute shortage of bread, and bread queues were more noticeable than they had been since 1940. Military bakers and Italian prisoners-of-war were called in to ease the shortage of labour in the bakeries. The cooking-fats ration was cut from 2 oz a week to 1 oz, and the weekly bacon ration was reduced from 4 oz to 3 oz. The price of potatoes went up by 3d. per 7 lb. In London there was talk of a bus strike. In Wales, despite every effort, coal production continued to decrease. An ominous note for the future was sounded when the *News Chronicle* reported: 'Many evacuees from the East Coast areas who have been told by the Ministry of Health that they can now return home will find it difficult to qualify for a free voucher—they have no homes to go to. Nowhere is the housing shortage so acute as in the East Coast towns.' There were also many hundreds of child evacuees, trace of whose parents had been lost; they were causing a worrying social problem. Another matter that was interesting many was the future of the 500,000 uniformed women. After their experience, training and responsibilities, could they be expected, it was asked, to go straight back to the kitchen sink or the comparatively humble jobs in which women before the war had mostly been employed? As the London *Evening Standard* said: 'Any day now they will be throwing away their low-heeled shoes, dressing themselves in the best civilian clothes that their £12 10s. grant will buy, and looking about for a job.' It was pointed out that girls who had done such highly specialized work as manning searchlights, coding messages, and important Intelligence duties, were going to be an awkward responsibility on society. Not least important for these women was the question of civilian clothing. High-heeled shoes and silk stockings were virtually unobtainable except on the Black Market. It was stated that: 'The Board of Trade and the Ministry of Supply have this question very much to the fore. These women will not be at a disadvantage with those who have remained in civilian life.' A special allotment of clothing coupons was to be allowed ex-servicewomen. A typical programme on the weekly BBC *Women's Page* consisted of: 'Extracts from *A Bride's Guide to the USA* recently published to help the 20,000 British girls who have married American servicemen; a talk on the new Education Act; and answers to problems sent in by women war-workers.' The Education Act of the previous year, presented in the House of Commons by R. A. Butler, was on everyone's lips; establishing free secondary education for all, most people agreed that it was a brilliant piece of legislation that reflected much credit on the Coalition Government. Typical of the surge of interest in social matters that had been increasing like a great wave since the start of the decade were the books being published in Britain during the late spring and early summer of 1945. They included such titles as *Nutrition and Relief Work*, *Rebuilding Britain*, *Civil Aviation and Peace*, *The American Senate and World Peace*, *How Should We Rebuild London?* and *Making a Better World*. All these books appeared within a few weeks of each other. The top-selling book was *Odd Man Out*, by F. L. Green, a story of the IRA in Belfast which had enjoyed critical success as well as wide popularity. The *Sunday Times* said: 'A fine piece of imaginative writing'; the *Observer*: 'A *tour de force* and a brilliant one'; the *Spectator*: 'Of unusual interest and distinction'. Other popular books were *Green For Danger* by Christianna Brand, *The Island* by Francis Brett Young, *Maquis* by George Millar, *The Next Horizon* by Douglas Reed, and *Left Hand, Right Hand* by Sir Osbert Sitwell.

At the London theatre the most popular shows were Ivor Novello's *Perchance to Dream* at the Hippodrome, Terence Rattigan's *Love in Idleness* at the Lyric, *Sweeter and Lower*—a very successful revue—at the Ambassadors, *Gay Rosalinda* at the Palace, *The Shop at Sly Corner* at the St. Martins, Sid Field in *Strike It Again* at the Prince of Wales, and Tommy Trinder in the patriotic variety-show *Happy and Glorious* at the Palladium.

Among the leading films were Laurence Olivier's *Henry V*, which had been running in the West End for over six months, Noel Coward's *Blithe Spirit*, *A Tree Grows in Brooklyn*, and *The Picture of Dorian Gray*, with Edward G. Robinson and Joan Bennett. The theory that the social history of an age can be best found in its films was amply sustained in *Perfect Strangers*, in which a humdrum married couple (Robert Donat and Deborah Kerr) are jolted out of domesticity by the war. He joins the Navy, she becomes a Wren. With new outlooks on life, both dread going back to their partner; the film dealt in some depth with the post-war readjustments common to many marriages. It was the golden age of British documentary films, and among those on release, the first two with scripts by Dylan Thomas, were *A City Reborn*, *Our Country*, *The True Glory*, and *Western Approaches*.

But the radio remained, as it had during the worst days of the war, the main source of relaxation and entertainment for millions. For the first time since 1940 the nine o'clock news, which had a vast audience, was being read by anonymous news-readers. Among the most popular shows, apart from the beloved ITMA, were *Merry-*

go-Round (an 'entertainment for all in khaki and two shades of blue'), *The Jack Benny Programme*, with Mary Livingstone, Rochester and Phil Harris, and *Here's Wishing You Well Again*, with Bebe Daniels.

There was a brisk market in second-hand cars (there having been no new ones for five years). Many private cars had been laid up since 1939, and now that an increase in the petrol ration seemed likely, many people looked around in search of a vehicle. A 1934 Vauxhall drophead coupé fetched £70, a 1939 Triumph Dolomite £300, a 1938 SS Jaguar £585, a 1939 Rover 12 £900, and a 1938 Lagonda £1,500. Sporting events began to revive, and cricket matches attracted large crowds. At the Queensberry Club in London a young heavyweight boxer called Bruce Woodcock attracted some notice by knocking out a Canadian flight-sergeant in three rounds. At the Royal Academy Exhibition the exhibits which caused most comment were the two drawings of Sir Giles Gilbert Scott's plan for a new Coventry Cathedral. In the personal columns of the newspapers, especially those of *The Times* and *Daily Telegraph*, there were long lists of notices, from which returned prisoners-of-war asked for news of missing relatives. At a session of the Brains Trust the question was asked: Are women drinking more and, if so, how can the trend be stopped? Mr Emanuel Shinwell said he saw no harm in women drinking in moderation, and Commander A. B. Campbell said his only objection was that they helped make whisky and gin shorter than ever.

In Ireland, Eamon de Valera had replied to the bitter comments made by Winston Churchill in his Victory broadcast. He said he was not going to retaliate in a similar tone. 'Allowances can be made for Mr Churchill's statement—however unworthy—in the first exuberance of his victory. No such excuse could be found for me in this quieter atmosphere.' Apologies were made to the British and American representatives in Dublin for the damage done to their offices during the rioting at the announcement of the end of the war. De Valera announced in the Dail that for the remainder of the year clothing and food to the value of £3,000,000 would be sent to Europe; this gesture would mean reductions in the rations of sugar and butter. His announcement did something to soothe sensibilities elsewhere in the Commonwealth, which had been considerably roused, especially in Canada (where there had been a widespread demand to curtail diplomatic relations with Eire). In that Dominion a Federal General Election was held on June 11th, resulting in a victory for Mackenzie King's Liberal Party. Canada, at any rate, was clearly not ready for even the mild form of Socialism advocated by some of the opposition parties. In New Zealand, the Prime Minister, Walter Nash, revealed that the war had cost the Dominion over £500,000,000, of which by far the greater part had been borrowed. On June 2nd an air service between Britain and Australia was inaugurated when a Lancastrian aeroplane converted to civilian use did the journey in eighty hours. The Australian Prime Minister, John Curtin, became ill in June, and his condition deteriorated; he died on July 5th.

In the United States, the atmosphere was vastly different from that in Britain, Europe and the Dominions. The war had not made America as drab as it had Britain, and thus relief and jubilation had been less noticeable and less dramatic. There was nothing in America like the switching on of the lights in Piccadilly Circus; the two main non-war talking points were the extraordinary run on Broadway of *Life With Father*, which had now completed well over 2,000 performances, and the phenomenal best seller, *Forever Amber*. The Japanese war was still, it seemed, a long way from completion. The bloody battle of Okinawa, with an ever-lengthening casualty list, continued amid mounting public criticism. President Truman was now well settled into his office at the White House, and his administration was beginning to function less haphazardly and more smoothly. He was even beginning to see that the Presidential post had its enjoyable side after all. He had sent the Presidential plane, the *Sacred Cow*, to bring his mother to Washington for Mothers' Day. It was her first trip by plane; the elevator, which had been fitted for Roosevelt's use, stuck while letting her down. The President's mother, by all accounts a remarkable and formidable woman, was not amused. The President had also spoken, with some glee, to his old schoolmistress on the telephone to ask her what she thought of her ex-pupil now.

However, as Harry Truman had feared, being President was by no means all fun. He was beset not only by problems in Europe, but also by troubles at home. The organization for rationing and price-control was causing great resentment and criticism in the community, and sugar supplies were so short that consumption had to be cut still further. Chester Bowles, the Administrator of OPA, told the President that his office was so unpopular that it was becoming almost impossible to keep it functioning. Many of his staff wanted to resign; some had already done so. To make matters worse, about 50,000 men were out on strike in various industries throughout the United States; and when the head of the United Mine Workers, John L. Lewis, called a strike, the industrial situation became a matter of the greatest urgency. Truman was angered. 'Here we were,' he later wrote, 'in the midst of one of the gravest conflicts in the history of civilization. Men were dying in battle. Our citizens were tightening their belts and making every sacrifice to help save the world from tyranny. . . . But John L. Lewis, undisturbed by what it would do to the nation, ordered his coalminers to strike.' Truman brought the mines under the direction of the Secretary of the Interior, which meant that the mineworkers were for the time being working for the Government. This bold tactic was subject to much adverse comment. Truman had also done much to reorganize the executive machinery of the Government, and especially that of his own office, which he had found in an unsatisfactory state. The White House organization was reshaped and its channels of communication with the other branches of the Government reviewed. Late in June Stettinius, on being appointed United States representative to the United Nations Security Council, was replaced as Secretary of State by James F. Byrnes, a move that had been widely predicted. The State Department had thus had three Secretaries in less than a year: Cordell Hull, Stettinius and Byrnes.

European problems continued to loom large in the minds of America's policy-makers. Not only were there the constitutional and territorial problems, there was also the worrying matter of food and supplies for weak and crippled nations. What responsibility did the United States bear in such matters? Henry Wallace, Secretary of Commerce, said during a speech in New York: 'The United States has the responsibility of world leadership for the first time. It is much the same kind of leadership as that which England gradually assumed after the Napoleonic Wars. . . . We are the only great nation with industries unbombed and with highways and railways in good working condition. Our economy is ready not only to give our own people a higher standard of living than they have ever had, but also, through a programme of sensible investment in those nations who want to help themselves, to bring about a restoration of world productivity.' A leading article in the *Kansas City Star* noted that 'Europe is hungry and will have to be fed . . . the conclusion is inescapable that staggering responsibilities will fall on the Allied powers with the possibility that the United States will be called upon to shoulder a heavy part of the load.' But these were, on the whole, voices in the wilderness. Most people considered that the United States had done its share in Europe and could not be expected to act as fairy-godmother indefinitely. Truman invited ex-President Herbert Hoover, responsible for food relief after the First World War, to the White House (it was his first visit there since 1932) to discuss the situation. When Leo Crowley, Foreign Economic Administrator, and Joseph C. Grew, Acting Secretary of State, arrived in the President's office one afternoon and asked him to sign a piece of paper diminishing Lend-Lease supplies, Truman signed. It had already been tacitly agreed, during a visit to Washington by Lord Keynes the previous year, that Britain would receive Lend-Lease until the end of the Japanese war; at the time, however, the American negotiators had refused to sign a protocol to that effect. Truman has since said that he very much regrets having signed the cancellation; and he is convinced that if he had read what he was putting his signature to he would never have done so. The result was immediate and dramatic. The 'Anti-Lend-Leasers' had, it seemed, won a notable victory. Ships actually on their way to Europe were turned about in mid-ocean. There was an outburst of surprised indignation from abroad. Truman, shocked by the reaction, said in a radio and Press conference on May 23rd that his intention was not so much a cancellation as a gradual readjustment of supplies following on the defeat of Germany. Supplies would continue; allocations would be completed. Russia, especially, was to receive all shipments already agreed upon. (Truman was always mindful of the Soviet's promise to join the war against Japan.) Five days after his reassurances he received an appeal from Churchill, in the form of a personal telegram. The Prime Minister ended: 'I hope that your people can be told that the principles your predecessor and I agreed on at Quebec will stand, and in particular that the appropriations given your War Department will be enough to provide for our needs as finally worked out between us.' Truman made his position clear in a reply to a letter from five eminent Congressmen. 'I am in full agreement,' he said, 'that the Lend-Lease Act does not authorize aid for purposes of post-war relief, post-war rehabilitation, or post-war reconstruction, and that in the liquidation of any Lend-Lease war supply agreements articles transferred after they are no longer necessary for the prosecution of the war should be disposed of only on terms of payment.' Lend-Lease was at an end for all those countries not actually at war with Japan; but a special grant of $10 million was given to Italy for the prevention of disease and unrest. Some of the President's advisers maintained that Lend-Lease could be continued legally even in Europe. The issue was kept very much alive by the many public figures who feared that the supplies would continue to pour out of the country as freely in time of peace as in war. These suspicions were directed particularly towards Britain. The fact that the Lend-Lease budget submitted to Congress for the year following VE Day included a sum of $935 million for Soviet Russia, if the USSR entered the war against Japan, brought forth little commend.

At the isolated air base of Andover Field, in the desert of Utah, a force of 'Flying Fortresses', known as the 509th Composite Group, were endlessly rehearsing the dropping of a secret weapon. Only their Commanding Officer, Colonel Paul W. Tibbets, had even the sketchiest idea of what the weapon was to be; but he was forbidden to impart even this knowledge to his men, who referred to the weapon as 'The Gimmick'. Their planes had all the turrets and guns stripped from them except for tail guns, and had been modified to carry an outsize device of some kind in the bomb-bays. Exceptionally strict discipline was maintained in the unit, and Colonel Tibbets insisted on instantaneous obedience to all orders. During May the unit, with a number of scientists, began leaving for the air base of Tinian, in the Marianas, within striking distance of Japan.

(v)

While the remaining defenders of Iwo Jima were dying of starvation in their sealed-up caves, their comrades on Okinawa were still putting up a fierce and powerful resistance. Supported by planes from Japan, many of them on suicide missions, they fought literally for every yard of ground. An average of twenty to thirty suicide planes attacked every day, and the Japanese also tried human suicide-torpedoes, but with less success. The Tokyo Government attached great prestige value to the retention of the island. The decisive stage of the struggle, which took place in the last week of May and during June, centred round the height known as 'Sugar-Loaf' or Conical Hill. During the previous seven weeks of fighting an advance of only seven miles had taken place. The defence had not only been determined, it had also been skilful. Despite almost ceaseless bombardment from naval guns, artillery and aircraft, the main line of defence had not been broken. The American infantry found it very difficult to take advantage of their superior fire-power. The Japanese did not hesitate to use cold steel, and were psychologically and emotionally hardened to facing death. At last, after it had changed hands eleven times, Sugar-Loaf Hill was finally secured by the Americans towards the end of May. Shortly afterwards a desperate Japanese air effort met with some success, but a success out of all proportion to the 166 machines shot down. One bomber made a belly-landing on a US airfield and disgorged a number of frenzied Japanese airmen who destroyed some American aircraft with hand-grenades before they committed suicide. To add to their difficulties, the Americans had to concern themselves with the jurisdiction and welfare of the 135,000 civilians crowded into their part of the island. During the first week in June a further serious obstacle to American progress appeared in the presence of deep and glutinous mud, in which all those engaged in the battle became caked; thirteen inches of rain had fallen during May. All supplies had to be carried forward by hand. Nevertheless, the advance continued more rapidly after the capture of the heights, and by the end of the second week in June only sixteen square miles of Okinawa were left to the Japanese. But the defenders continued to fight furiously, and attacks from their supporting aircraft were as desperate as ever. In one day Washington announced the loss of three warships at Okinawa from air attack. On June 17th Lieutentant-General S. B. Buckner, commanding the Tenth US Army, was killed by shell-fire while watching Marines go forward. Two days later Brigadier-General C. M. Easley, commanding the 96th Division, was killed. By June 21st the defence was in its last stage, packed tightly into two small pockets backing on to the shore of the southern coast. Scores of Japanese threw themselves off the cliffs 150 feet high. As was their wont, the Americans announced that day the 'end' of battle before it was over. The final defenders clustered around a series of caves, and fought on with bitterness although there was no hope of success or relief, and despite American leaflets and radio broadcasts pointing out the uselessness of further loss of life. While one of the caves was being stormed, the Commander of the Okinawa naval base cut his throat. With the Americans only a few yards away, the Japanese Commander-in-Chief, General Mitsuru Ushijima, emerged at the mouth of his cave with his Chief of Staff, followed by orderlies and staff. The two Generals were in parade uniform, with medals. They knelt down on white sheets; each thrust a knife into his own abdomen, and was then slashed across the back of the neck by an adjutant. Most of the rest of the garrison died in hopeless charges or by suicide with their own grenades. The remainder, pressed back on the sea, walked out into the water and drowned.

Thus ended the bloody and horrible battle for the island of Okinawa. There were 102,000 Japanese dead, almost total annihilation of their entire force. There were only 8,000 prisoners. The US military casualties were 39,420, a high proportion of the six divisions which took part. Naval casualties were 9,724; thirty US ships had been sunk, mostly by *kamikaze* action. The shock and anger of the American public was so great that Admiral Nimitz felt obliged to defend the campaign in American newspapers.

The Chiefs of Staff were now more than ever convinced that an Allied invasion of the mainland would result in such terrible fighting that the casualties could hardly be perceived.

In Burma, meanwhile, the victorious Fourteenth Army was unable to rest on its laurels. Actions officially described as 'mopping-up', but in reality a lot more than that, continued until July. Between 60,000 and 70,000 Japanese troops, cut off in Burma, remained unconquered. Many of them roamed about in small groups, and to deal with these tactics the British force was split into various columns which were sent off to track down the hostile units in sweltering, soaking monsoon weather. The strongest Japanese force, estimated to be 44,000 strong, was in the east of the country preparing to launch a break-out. Elsewhere, guerrilla activity was combatted successfully by Karens, who had risen against the Japanese conqueror, and by the Burmese National Army. The commander of the latter, Aung San, made it clear to Slim that he was determined to keep his army in existence after hostilities had ceased, indicating just one of the many political difficulties with which the British administration were being presented by those whom they had just released from the Japanese yoke. Many British units were engaged in stiff jungle fighting while elaborate victory celebrations were taking place in Rangoon. The large forces of Japanese in inaccessible areas were proving very difficult to overcome, but the authorities continued to act as if the Burma campaign was over. On May 31st the long-threatened withdrawal of the US Air Force from the area was finally announced. Churchill congratulated Mountbatten 'upon the culminating victory of your Burma campaigns'. In honour of Slim's great advance a special decoration was announced, and the ribbons were flown out to SEAC. No other campaign ribbon of the 1939-45 War is more proudly worn than the Burma Star.

The Japanese policy, despite its lack of success everywhere, was still to try to cling on to all the newly won acquisitions in the East. Pride, recklessness and Allied domination of the seas precluded the wiser course of a concentration on pre-war territory. In Japan itself a tremendous US aerial onslaught, only slightly less than that which had been showered on Germany, was under way. These raids caused great loss of life, as Japanese precautions were rudimentary in comparison with those that had been adopted in Britain and Germany. Discontent over this, and over the loss of Okinawa and the defeat in Burma, brought criticism and pressure to bear on the new Prime Minister—he had been appointed on April 5th— the seventy-seven-year-old Admiral Suzuki. Both the Emperor and Suzuki, speaking in the Diet, referred to the struggle as a holy war, and Suzuki admitted that an invasion of 'the homeland' was to be expected. If such an assault was to occur, the Japanese people, with death-defying courage and the advantages of geography, would bring the war to a successful conclusion. An evacuation of Tokyo by all but 200,000 essential workers was prepared. Behind all this bellicose talk, the new government began considering ways and means of procuring peace. It was decided that efforts might be made through Moscow, a move which it was thought (as the Germans had hoped before) might somehow cause a split between the Allies, and, if territorial concessions were made, might produce a powerful and influential friend for Japan in Soviet Russia. Meanwhile, the capital was being battered from the air. One night 334 US bombers, from Guam, Saipan and Tinian, took part in what was politely known to American commanders and planners as 'area bombing', i.e. the saturation bombing of areas picked for the density of population and regardless of military installations. This force concentrated on the Asakusa area of Tokyo, in which 103,000 persons lived to the square mile. The force met no fighter opposition, and very little flak. Some 30,000 Japanese were killed. On the way home the American tail-gunners reported seeing the glow of the burning city 150 miles away. Two days later a force of 313 B-29s visited the city of Nagoya, causing similar destruction. Kobe, Osaka, Yokohama, Kawasaki . . . all suffered equally from saturation bombing and the resulting fire-storms which, owing to the wood-bamboo-plaster construction of most of the small buildings in tightly packed Japanese urban areas, raged uncontrollably. Conditions were intolerable; not only from the bombing, but also from the shortages caused by the successful Anglo-American blockade, especially the US submarines—omnipotent in the Pacific. Few people were able to find enough food to use up all their ration points. Beef was unobtainable, so was fish. There was widespread eating of dog and horse-meat. Chicken and eggs were reserved for children, expectant mothers and hospital patients. Beer and *sake* were practically impossible to obtain except on the high-priced black market. Typhoid and tuberculosis were both rampant. Malnutrition had become so serious that bottles of vitamin pills were being issued to night-workers, miners and naval personnel. A Home Guard, armed with bamboo spears, was formed. Shipping had practically ceased; only about a sixth of the pre-war merchant fleet remained, and its movement was hopelessly restricted. There had been no import of fuel oil since April.

There seemed little hope of success in any of the remaining outlying areas of the Empire. Even in China, where the Chinese were beset with domestic squabbles, things were going badly for the Japanese. Although, as was not uncommon, there had been several large-scale and inexplicable surrenders of Chinese Nationalist troops during the spring and early summer, the Japanese forces were on the retreat. Although information as to the fighting was obscure and scanty, it was clear that American assistance in arms, supplies, advice and air-power was having an effect. The position, however, was confused by the existence of provincial armies, ostensibly part of the Nationalist forces, but mostly parochial in objectives and operations. There was also the matter of the Communist army in the north, with which military co-operation was intermittent and tenuous. The Communist army was certainly the most effective in China, and it was achieving the most success. The Americans had made efforts to bring about a reconciliation between Chiang Kai-shek's Kuomintang régime, centred at Chungking, and the Communists. These had met with some unpublicized success. The Yenan Government, run by the Communists, had offices in Chungking, and its newspaper was printed there. Some of the Communist officials were drawing their salaries from the Nationalist Government. And it was agreed that the Chinese delegation to the San Francisco conference should include a representative of the Communists. Much of this success was due to the unceasing efforts of Chiang's great admirer, General A. C. Wedemeyer, Stilwell's successor as American adviser and Chief of Staff in China. But already voices could be heard in the United States saying that America was not providing Chiang with enough help in the face of the Communist threat from the north. All this was somewhat off-set by propaganda and harsh attacks on the Kuomintang régime from Russia. Moscow associated itself with the Communist demands for a coalition government, and social reforms in free China; and it accused Chiang Kai-shek of preparing to wage a civil war. The confident and devious Chiang Kai-shek seemed to some American observers to spend more efforts on intrigue, in consolidating his own position, and in keeping the Americans and the Communist Army mutually antagonistic, than he was in freeing China, much of which was still in Japanese hands.

To the south a lonely French army, practically unsupported by the Allies, was fighting a savage war against strong Japanese forces in the interior of Indo-China and near the Chinese border. In the Philippines ferocious last-ditch stands were being conducted on Luzon and the smaller islands. The conquest of the archipelago was a remarkable feat of amphibious warfare. As MacArthur's land commander, General R. L. Eichelberger, said: 'In one forty-one-day period alone these troops conducted fourteen major landings and twenty-one minor ones, thus rolling up a landing every day and a half. . . . There has never been another army just like it.' The Japanese were shooting their own women and children before committing suicide, and hospital patients were being killed rather than let them fall into American hands. On June 28th MacArthur announced that 'the entire island of Luzon is now liberated'. This was not strictly accurate, but congratulatory messages from the world's leaders poured in, and Douglas MacArthur was at the pinnacle of his fame. General Yamashita continued to hold out with a large force in northern Luzon. Also in MacArthur's theatre was the invasion of Borneo, begun by the seizure of the off-shore islands of Labuan and Tarakan by Australian and Dutch troops. The capture of Tarakan, rich in oil, was especially welcome to the Allied forces in the South Pacific. MacArthur waded ashore with the assault troops at Labuan, with the Australian Commander, Lieutenant-General Sir Leslie Morshead,* and came under fire; ignoring protestations, he refused to drop face-down in the water. The Japanese force hastily disappeared into the steaming jungle and rocky gorges of Borneo, some of it hardly explored, where it was obviously going to be excessively difficult to defeat it.

* The heroic commander of the Tobruk garrison in 1941.

There was heavier fighting on Bougainville Island, where the invading Australian Third and Eleventh Divisions were engaged in fearful combat throughout June. Everywhere the ring was closing round the stubborn and fanatical Japanese military hierarchy.

(vi)

While the war was still raging in the Pacific and the East, the attention of the peoples of the world was being held by the efforts at San Francisco to secure a lasting peace. The conference to agree on a charter for the new world organization had dragged on through May as one difficulty after another had been encountered. There were wide diversities of opinion on nearly every subject, and the various nations had splintered off into small groups. In this atmosphere the high hopes and idealism that had typified the start of the conference had gradually deteriorated. But although there was considerable disillusion in some delegations, especially those from small nations, by and large the main representatives were all aware of the opportunity that was now presented to them, and of the importance of a strong world authority for the post-war years. There was much talk of the failure of the League of Nations, especially from the Russians and the Americans. President Truman followed the deliberations closely; Stettinius had to report to him every day. The President studied in great detail Woodrow Wilson's failure after the First World War to get the United States into the League. He was determined that the United Nations organization should be set up, even if it meant compromising on many points, and that America should be part of it. He has written: 'Throughout the long discussions I was always trying to work out a way to keep Russia and Great Britain in harmony.'

The White Russian and Ukrainian Republics were admitted to membership unanimously. But the membership of Poland was not so easily solved. Czechoslovakia, indicating how much that country had come under the sway of the Soviets, proposed that the Lublin Government should be invited to the conference. Eden, however, was adamant that Britain could agree to no Polish representation until the Yalta agreements on Poland had been respected by the Russians. He was supported by Stettinius. On the other hand, the Argentine, to the disgust of many of the Allied nations, was voted into the conference notwithstanding the widely held suspicion that the Argentine had pro-Nazi sympathies. It seems that Truman, on the advice of the State Department and the Under-Secretary of State, Nelson Rockefeller, had insisted on the Argentine's membership for the sake of 'Western hemisphere solidarity'. This decision so annoyed Molotov that he left the conference on May 9th, leaving Gromyko in charge of the Russian delegation. It soon became clear after his departure that the Russians were no longer able to take decisions, and everything was held up for days on end while matters were referred to Molotov in Moscow. For various reasons, which were no doubt strengthened by the Russian tardiness and the consequent inability of the conference to move at anything but the most sluggish speed, many of the other leaders of delegations returned home. One of the most important was the Belgian Foreign Minister, M. Spaak, who had played a significant role in the first days. He was followed by Eden and Attlee, who returned home because of the imminence of the General Election, as did Mackenzie King of Canada. Eden had made a great impression on the conference; many of the delegates from the smaller countries, being mostly statesmen who had emerged during and since the war, had never before met him. His opening speech had been received by a respectful audience. Referring to the conference as 'the world's last chance', he had said that the only alternative to an organization for the peaceful settlement of international disputes was another war, which would mean 'the utter destruction of civilization'. This prophecy had been received in startled silence; no one could quite understand what it meant.

One of the main problems was the fight for special rights by the so-called Middle Powers, led by Canada and Holland. Their delegations felt they could not return to their native countries without gaining some recognition for national prestige. They were supported by Britain in these ambitions, but after much argument all they won was the recognition that in election to non-permanent places on the Security Council their claims should receive special consideration. France, of course, was unable to accept the position of a Middle Power, and eventually achieved recognition as one of the Big Five. Another issue was that of trusteeship. During the deliberations on this Britain came under fire from many quarters, including from her allies and from other colonial powers. It was widely accepted that Britain was the most dangerous of the imperialist nations. The recent intervention on behalf of the Syrians had made little difference to this view. These insinuations were effectively silenced by a brilliant speech by Lord Cranborne* after a long session on June 20th. He said that the general principles of self-determination which the conference was so anxious to recognize were mainly of British conception. He pointed out that if it had not been for the loyalty and support to Britain of the various nations and colonies of the Empire during the period of the war when they had stood alone, and while all the other nations present at the conference were either defeated, disengaged or neutral, it was most unlikely that the present conference would be sitting at all.

The main problem that the San Francisco conference had to face was the voting procedure in the Security Council. Britain, Russia and the United States all came in for a great deal of criticism for upholding the veto principle, which seemed to give the great powers a protection that was not afforded the smaller countries. The Australian delegate, Dr Herbert Evatt, led the condemnation, strongly supported by Peter Fraser of New Zealand. The debate on the subject was world-wide. Speaking in the House of Commons, Sir William Beveridge said that if a small power were deprived of the support of the world organization in a dispute with a great power, it would inevitably seek security in an alliance with or dependence upon one of the other great powers; this would lead to two great blocs and a Third World War. Under pressure the British inclined to a modification of the voting procedure, but the Russians held fast to the original agreement. The Americans took up the intermediate position that was now becoming their almost traditional place. Truman, however, knew that 'our experts, civil and military, favoured it, and without such a veto no arrangement would have passed the Senate'. It was the Senate which had killed Wilson's hopes for the League of Nations. 'I told Stettinius that we would stand by the Yalta formula on voting in the Security Council.' The veto was imperative to the national interests of the great powers, and they intended to stick to it even if it meant wrecking the organization. The only point at issue was what was exactly meant by the veto. Gromyko, acting as Molotov's mouthpiece, insisted that even the discussion of a dispute could be stopped by the veto. The State Department began to suspect, not for the first time in recent months, that Stalin was not fully aware of the stalemate that negotiations had reached. Hopkins, who had been sent to Moscow, put the position fairly before Stalin, whom it was clear had not been kept

* Later the Marquess of Salisbury.

fully informed by Molotov. Stalin at once overruled Molotov, and agreement on the veto was reached. No single power would be able to prevent the hearing of a dispute by the Security Council. This gesture made on behalf of the smaller powers did little to soothe their fears, and Dr Evatt remained an embarrassment to the Big Five until the very end. He found little comfort in the fact that the dangers to small nations could be discussed without any action being taken to protect them.

The final session of the conference was held on June 26th, starting at 6 a.m. The signing of the Charter by about 200 delegates lasted well into the afternoon. The best speech was by the South African delgate, General Jan Christian Smuts. He said: 'Our Charter is not a perfect document. It is full of compromises over a very difficult and tangled plan for peace.' Smuts had written the long-winded preamble to the Charter, blatantly inspired by the American Constitution. President Truman spoke to the conference at the Opera House, and also stressed the element of compromise in the Charter. This view, suggesting that the United Nations Organization was the best that could be expected in the circumstances and that it was a near miracle that it at least appeared to have a chance of making itself a success, typified the view of most people. The President finished: 'Let us not fail to grasp this supreme chance to establish a world-wide rule of reason, and to create an enduring peace under the guidance of God.' The Opera House rang with enthusiastic cheers for many minutes after he had finished.

(vii)

While many fine sentiments were being uttered for public hearing at San Francisco, the yawning rift between the Allies was widening still further behind the scenes. After firm Anglo-American pressure on Moscow, Tito finally agreed to withdraw his troops from Trieste. This was a gratifying victory for Truman and Churchill, and served to show how, when presented with a determined and united front from the West, the Russians were prepared to give way. Unfortunately this lesson was not very well learnt in Washington. Truman, who, when he acted more on his own instincts than on the advice of the State Department, presented a tough and, in this instance, successful approach to Stalin, had by no means entirely shaken off the anti-British and pro-Russian advice and pressure he had inherited from Roosevelt. The Yugoslav forces left Trieste without incident, and with a dignity that surprised British and American observers. The dispute about Tito's régime, however, continued. Twice Churchill wrote to Stalin complaining about the lack of recognition of the fifty-fifty agreement that had been made in connection with that country: 'I must say that the way things have worked out in Yugoslavia certainly does not give me the feeling of a fifty-fifty interest as between our countries.' Stalin complained of the attitude of Field-Marshal Alexander, who was publicly referring to Tito in derogatory terms. Stalin said that the Yugoslavs had played a part in the war against Germany, and their territorial and constitutional wishes should be accepted. Churchill replied: 'We do not see why we should be pushed about everywhere, especially by people we have helped, and helped before you were able to make any contact with them.'* Meanwhile, the Tito régime, encouraged by the Russians, and with but few gestures towards the royalist opposition, consolidated its position with cynical disregard for democratic processes. Of the thirty members of the Tito-Subasic Government which had been formed in March under pressure from Churchill and Stalin, only three were not closely associated with Tito. In Vienna, too, the Russians were maintaining their awkwardness. British and American missions, which had been allowed into the city, were suffering intolerable restrictions. Even the Americans were now beginning to question whether the decision to withhold Patton's advance had been the right one.

Meanwhile, Hopkins' visit to Moscow had ended in a blaze of glory for the sickly but indefatigable American emissary. Not only had Stalin agreed to admit, at long last, some non-Communists into the Lublin Government, he had also confirmed his Yalta agreement to join in on the war against Japan. He left no doubt in Hopkins' mind that Russia intended to attack Japan in August. He also agreed to use his influence to promote unification of China under Chiang Kai-shek. Hopkins cabled Truman: 'He further stated that this leadership should continue after the war because no one else was strong enough. He specifically stated no Communist leader was strong enough to unify China.' What Hopkins did not know was that Stalin, although still the source of ultimate decisions, was no longer in a position of widespread power. Towards the end of the

* The message to Stalin from which this is taken is given in *Triumph and Tragedy*, p. 488, but is not in the Moscow collection of the Churchill–Stalin correspondence. A much milder note is substituted (No. 497). It may be that Churchill's note was, unknown to him, toned down in London before dispatch.

war he had given over much of his time to the conduct of military matters. Now, in a thoroughly exhausted condition, he was slowly becoming less active and more of a figure-head. Molotov was not only in charge of foreign affairs, but was also taking increasing responsibility for domestic matters as well. By the time of Yalta a small group of men, mostly anti-Molotov, had begun to have some influence. One of them was the strangely titled Marshal Bulganin, an unmilitary intellectual who had acquired his high rank without ever having been in command of armed forces. Bulganin advocated a new Soviet policy, differing in some respects from that of Molotov, for the post-war world. Its main object was to prevent the creation of an irresistible world bloc antagonistic to the USSR. Bulganin had said in February: 'As soon as the war is ended the USSR will be subjected to encirclement; the countries in its zone of influence will be torn from it one by one, thanks to the economic and financial superiority of the USA. . . . Thus, despite its dazzling victory, the USSR may very soon find itself in a very menaced position.' Among the measures he recommended to combat this were a divided Germany and immediate Soviet control of all Russian-occupied countries. The fact that this would undoubtedly increase the likelihood of an anti-Soviet bloc, which he said was inevitable anyway, was countered by the fact that without Germany and Eastern Europe such a bloc would be weakened and well-cushioned from Russia. To further weaken the anti-Soviet position it was imperative to prevent the unification of China under Chiang Kai-shek. These general theses had been adopted by the Politburo before Hopkins' arrival in Moscow. Stalin, well aware of all this, was therefore engaging in idle talk with Truman's special emissary. The old dictator, however, was not talking idly when he suggested that the Allies had no need to insist on the unconditional surrender of Japan. A modified surrender should be acceptable, he said, so long as the destruction of Japanese military might was ensured.

With the questions of Poland, China and Russian entry into the Japanese war apparently well on the way to being solved, Hopkins returned to the United States in some triumph. It certainly looked as if he had justified once and for all the American contention that they could get on best with the Russians when left to themselves. Churchill, having concurred with the proposals at the Stalin–Hopkins talks ('for what they were worth'), sent a cable of hearty congratulations to the American—a man whom he personally much admired.

Talks between the Chinese and the Russians now took place.

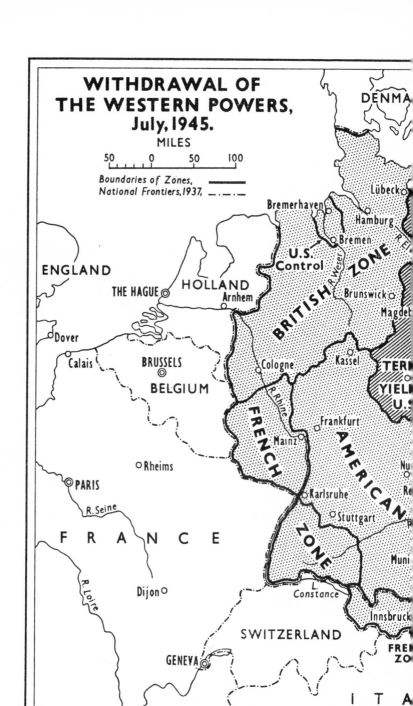

WITHDRAWAL OF
THE WESTERN POWERS,
July, 1945.

MILES

50   0   50   100

Boundaries of Zones, ————
National Frontiers,1937, — .— .—

DENMA

Lübeck

Bremerhaven

Hamburg

Bremen

U.S.
Control

ENGLAND

BRITISH ZONE

THE HAGUE

HOLLAND

Arnhem

Brunswick

Magdel

Dover

Calais

BRUSSELS

BELGIUM

Cologne

Kassel

TER
YIEL
U.S

FRENCH

R.Rhine

Frankfurt

AMERICAN

Rheims

Mainz

PARIS

Karlsruhe

Nu

Re

R.Seine

Stuttgart

F R A N C E

ZONE

Muni

R.Loire

Dijon

L.
Constance

Innsbruck

SWITZERLAND

FRE
ZO

GENEVA

I T A

Chiang Kai-shek, however, did not prove quite as obliging as the Americans had hoped over the concessions to Russia that had been agreed without his approval at Yalta; namely the questions of Port Arthur, Dairen and Outer Mongolia. When the Chinese General-issimo requested American diplomatic help in the matter, Truman curtly told him to 'reach complete understanding' with the Russians forthwith. Stalin had hinted that Russia would be reluctant to enter the Japanese war until the talks had been satisfactorily concluded.

On the departure of Hopkins from Moscow, the Polish talks were renewed with more hope of success than for many weeks. The influential Micolajczyk went to Moscow, and he and others were admitted to the Lublin Government despite the protestations of their erstwhile friends in the London Polish Government.* According to Harriman, they joined owing to their fears of what was happening in Poland while they deliberated; fears so great that they were prepared to accept any compromise in the hope of exerting some influence for freedom of the individual and Polish independence later on. After five months of constant arguing, during which the Russians had fought every inch of the way, a Polish government that bore some pretensions to a broad basis had therefore been formed—although elections were still not in sight. Having achieved this much, Harriman now strongly recommended that the new government should be recognized. Truman, deciding that 'no useful purpose would be served by further delay', informed Churchill that he intended to recognize the Polish Government immediately. Churchill, somewhat taken aback by the speed of events (for better or worse things were moving much more rapidly under Truman than under Roosevelt), asked for a delay in order to warn the Poles in London, who had an army (mostly still in Italy) of 170,000, all of whom would probably demand three months' salary upon disband-ment. The unpleasant news was conveyed to the wretched remains of the once-proud descendants of the 1939 Warsaw Government. On July 5th, recognition was announced in Washington and London of the Polish Provisional Government of National Unity.

The Potsdam conference was now being prepared, and Churchill saw little reason in further international activity before the Big Three met. The military and diplomatic advisers to the President, however, were still pressing Truman to agree to withdrawal of US

---

* Micolajczyk's wife had just arrived in London, a number branded on her hand, after her release from Oswiecim concentration camp; their son was at Harrow.

troops to the occupation zone in Germany before the conference. It seemed to them that the United States ought to go to the conference table with a clean record of having fulfilled all her obligations. In that way the goodwill of the Russians would be procured. Churchill still clung to the opposite view. He felt that Russian actions in Europe since the zones had been drawn up had created an entirely different situation; no action should be taken until matters of difference with the Russians had been straightened out. Truman, however, heeded his own advisers rather than the voluble English statesman. Churchill wrote to the President: 'I view with profound misgivings the retreat of the American Army to our line of occupation in the central sector, thus bringing Soviet power into the heart of Western Europe and the descent of an iron curtain between us and everything to the eastward. I hoped that this retreat, if it has to be made, would be accompanied by the settlement of many great things which would be the true foundation of world peace. Nothing really important has been settled yet, and you and I will have to bear great responsibility for the future.' The British forces in Germany were not as concerned as were the Americans, but they, too, occupied some of the Russian Zone. Churchill was presented with a *fait accompli*. As always in 1945, the British, who found themselves in a totally different position in the world of power politics than that in which they had been before the war, followed the American example. Churchill, in one of his most sombre messages, told Truman: 'Obviously we are obliged to conform to your decision.' He made it plain that he was convinced that a grave error had been made. He has written: 'Thus in the moment of victory was our best, and what might prove to have been our last, chance of durable world peace allowed composedly to fade away.' Churchill's agreement was received with amazement in Washington, where, according to Leahy, it had been entirely unexpected.

The evacuation began on July 1st. American trucks rolled back along the roads up which they had come less than three months previously, watched from the roadside by the great mass of trudging refugees who were on the move westwards once more.

(viii)

In Britain, the General Election got under way during the first week of June, although party politics had been returning to the boil before that. On the whole, in the constituencies, it was a quiet election. There was a widespread feeling that in the Japanese war there was a task still unfinished. Nearly all observers remarked on the thoughtfulness of the electorate, the willingness to listen and the desire to question intelligently at local meetings. Morrison wrote: 'Their silence was remarkable. It was not the silence of lethargy but the quietness of thoughtfulness.' Dalton noted an identical mood: 'There was much evidence of a serious mind among the electors and of a thoughtful interest in many questions; much more thoughtful and intelligent than before the war.' But in the national area it was far from quiet, and characterized by bitterness unusual in Britain even at election time. It came as a surprise to many people to realize that the fount of this bitterness was the speeches of the Prime Minister himself, who had been so anxious to preserve the front of national unity; now he was in the forefront of violent and unpleasant exchanges—although many believed he was acting on the advice of Beaverbrook and Bracken. These two men had great influence over the conduct of the campaign, especially the former, who revelled in a fight. Certainly Churchill was preoccupied with preparations for the conference at Potsdam, and was unable to give full attention to the direction of the Conservative Party's campaign. His lieutenant, Anthony Eden, was ill and was unable to take much part in the election. Churchill was annoyed at the Labour decision to leave the Coalition, which he took as a personal affront; above all, he was tired.

Broadcasting played an important part in the election. The first and last broadcasts in the campaign, on June 4th and June 30th, were made by the Prime Minister. The country listened to the famous voice that had so recently been the unchallenged, authentic voice of Britain, in its renewed partisan role, with some discomfort. It seemed indecent to hear Winston Churchill talk of Labour leaders almost as he had once spoken of the Nazis. The opening broadcast was controversial to a degree. He said that a Socialist policy was inseparably interwoven with totalitarianism; liberty in all its forms was challenged by the fundamental concepts of Socialism. A Socialist state could not afford to suffer opposition; a free parliament was odious to the Socialist doctrinaire. No Socialist system could be established without a political police, and such a system would therefore have to fall back on some form of Gestapo.

The word 'Gestapo' reverberated through the country. It was heard with astonishment. Only the most die-hard and singleminded Conservatives were able to believe Churchill's long list of warnings. For during the war there had been a great leavening of the classes; men from all walks of life had fought side by side. Servicemen listened to Churchill and wondered. They listened to Conservative charges that Harold Laski had advocated achieving Socialism by violence.* They listened, too, to the level tones of Mr Attlee, who spoke quietly and in calculated contrast to Churchill about the Labour Party's policy for the post-war age. Morrison insisted that this policy should be presented with complete honesty; there were to be no bones about it, the Party was offering unadulterated Socialism. He has said: 'My feelings in drafting the programme were inspired by one major factor: the changed nature of the electorate. I knew that victory would go to the party which recognized and served this mature and thoughtful public. . . . The very honesty and simplicity of the campaign helped enormously. We had not been afraid to be frank about our plans.' While the Conservatives, following Churchill's lead, hit hard, the Labour candidates played a more muted note; their programme spoke for itself. Morrison himself was perhaps the hardest-hitting of the Labour Party leaders. In a broadcast he attacked 'private enterprise' as Churchill had done Socialism. He said the election was about whether 'the speculators, the buccaneer barons of Fleet Street, the sluggish leaders of big-business monopolies and cartels, are to sit comfortably—on the backs of the people—for another shameful period of national decline'. Attlee's speeches were calmer, patiently appealing to reason. He refused to be drawn by Churchill's charges, on one occasion going so far as to say that they were not really the Prime Minister's own words at all: 'The voice we heard last night was that of Mr Churchill, but the mind was that of Lord Beaverbrook.' Ernest Bevin, apparently appalled by the whole business, refused to take much notice of what he called 'these libels on our party'. Unable to draw the Labour leaders, Churchill's speeches became more and more far-fetched. Men like Cripps and Morrison, he said, would use a Labour majority to stifle or curtail the right of Parliament. The Labour leaders themselves were not personally concerned about these serious charges; they knew Churchill of old. Morrison, Dalton and others later put down the whole affair to political simulation, which it certainly was, inspired and directed by the Conservative hierarchy. But the country at large was amazed. Similar accusations to those voiced by Churchill were displayed in the popular *Daily*

* Laski lost a libel action about this assertion in November 1946.

Express, while the *Daily Mirror* evolved a clever slogan for the Labour cause from a reader's letter: Vote For Him! This catchphrase undoubtedly influenced a large number of women voters whose husbands were in the Forces overseas. Another Labour slogan was: You Can't Trust the Tories. The Conservative campaign was crude and confident; that of Labour was shrewd and careful.

What few people noticed were the many similarities in both parties' programmes; the prosecution of the war against Japan, close co-operation with the United States and the USSR to further the United Nations Organization, the maintenance of the Commonwealth, Indian self-government, emergency measures for housing needs, the expansion of exports, and the resettlement of servicemen and women—all these figured prominently on the programmes of both the major parties. The main issue was nationalization, and most other things were forgotten. Churchill tried to present his Government as a National one, not as Conservative.* 'I shall stand myself as a Conservative and National candidate,' he said on the radio. There was much talk—by the Liberals—of a 'Liberal Revival'. The Liberal Party, which was backed by a £200,000 fighting fund, was hampered by a lack of active support from the younger generation, it was elbowed out of the contest. The party laid much stress on the plan for social security and full employment, supported by all parties, but which had been elaborated by Sir William Beveridge, who was a leading Liberal. While the two major parties were allotted ten broadcasts each, the Liberals were only allowed four. But however handicapped they were by this fact, they were entirely discounted as being of any influence when their leader, Sir Archibald Sinclair, in a broadcast on June 13th, went to laborious lengths to plead that the election was not just a private fight between Conservatives and Socialists; from then on everyone knew that indeed it was.

In the constituencies the hasily improvised or rejuvenated party organizations fought an election that in many ways was different to any other that had occurred before. Many regulations were still in force. For the first time in history candidates had to be rationed for the paper with which to conduct their campaigns; one ton of paper for each candidate in a constituency of 40,000 voters, with a proportionate increase for electorates over 40,000. One of the chief problems was that a vast migration of population had taken place in the recently past years; there had never been anything like it in Britain,

* i.e. descended from Baldwin's National Government of 1935.

traditionally a country of parochial people, before. Conscription, evacuation from bombed towns and cities, direction of industrial and agricultural labour, and the establishment of munitions factories in new areas—all combined to baffle the political experts and organizers. A total of 1,683 candidates was nominated for the 640 seats; 622 Conservatives and supporters, 603 Labour, 307 Liberal, twenty-three Common Wealth (the party led by Sir Richard Acland), twenty-one Communists, and assorted Welsh, Scottish and Irish Nationalists, and Independents. About one-third were servicemen (or recent ex-servicemen); only eighty-eight were women. The chief surprise was the appearance of an Independent to oppose Mr Churchill at Woodford.

One of the most publicized features of the election was the tour the Prime Minister made from London to Scotland, stopping at many places *en route*, and during which he made over forty speeches. Everywhere he went he was received by rapturous crowds, a fact which caused some dismay to the Labour officials. But it was the progress of a triumphant national hero, one of the most popular and well-loved in British history, not of a party political leader. Through the Midlands, Lancashire and Yorkshire he went, and on into Scotland; everywhere he raised his fingers in his familiar Victory sign, everywhere he was seen to be smoking one of his enormous cigars. The cheering was so great and so continuous that few could hear what he had to say; even fewer cared. A similar tour in London was less rapturous. At an open-air rally at Walthamstow Stadium, attended by nearly 20,000 people, the Prime Minister was subjected to heavy heckling. At Lewisham, where Morrison was standing, his reference to the insinuations of local Conservatives that the Home Office (Morrison had been Home Secretary) had not acted as promptly as it might have done during some of Lewisham's bombing disasters, was greeted with shouting and jeers.* Morrison had deliberately chosen to stand at Lewisham, regarded as one of the country's safest Conservative strongholds, in an extraordinary show of confidence. Churchill himself, who in the past had not been averse to the cut and thrust of political life, was not enjoying the election. He wrote: 'Strenuous motor tours to the greatest cities of England and Scotland, with two or three speeches a day to enormous and, it seemed, enthusiastic crowds, and, above all, four laboriously

---

* This accusation caused a personal rift between Churchill and Morrison; it was satisfactorily healed some months later. Despite the apparent bitterness of the campaign, this was one of the very few instances in which personal relationships were affected.

prepared broadcasts, consumed my time and strength. All the while I felt that much we had fought for in our long struggle in Europe was slipping away and that the hopes of an early and lasting peace were receding. The days were passed amid the clamour of multitudes, and when at night, tired out, I got back to my headquarters' train, where a considerable staff and all the incoming telegrams awaited me, I had to toil for many hours. The incongruity of party excitement and clatter with the sombre background which filled my mind was in itself an affront to reality and proportion.'

The campaign reached its peak over the question of Attlee's authority and responsibility at Potsdam. Harold Laski had raised the point that the Labour Party could not be committed to decisions arrived at by the conference, even if Attlee were present, as the conference would be discussing matters not yet considered by the Labour Party executive (of which he was chairman). This statement of Laski's, made without consultation with Attlee—the two Labour men did not get on well together—seemed to cast some doubt on where power lay in the Labour Party: with the party leader or with Harold Laski. At any rate, the Conservatives, sensing a valuable debating point, immediately began to voice this doubt. Churchill referred to Attlee as the 'titular Socialist leader'. He said that Laski 'has reminded all of us, including Mr Attlee, that the final determination of all questions of foreign policy rests with this dominating Socialist executive'. In his final broadcast he spoke of the 'revelation that the chairman of the national executive committee should have the right to lay down the law to the publicly proclaimed leader of the Labour Party'. Attlee was more annoyed with Laski than with Churchill. He asserted that: 'The chairman has not the power to give me instructions.' The debate continued in the columns of the Press, in the form of a correspondence between Churchill and Attlee. Despite the late arrival of Churchill's letters, Attlee always contrived to get his answer in the same day's newspaper, which even the Conservative newspapers were perforce obliged to print in full. He argued in the restrained and reasoned tones that he had maintained throughout the election. One of the features of the election had been Attlee's touring the country in his own car with his wife driving; this unostentatious method of travel had contrasted brilliantly with the entourage that, of necessity, accompanied Churchill. Attlee noted with satisfaction that his modest travelling arrangements were 'given a great deal of prominence in the Press'.

The election was closely followed in the United States; more so perhaps than any previous British election. The campaigning received a great deal of space in the American Press. The general opinion was that Churchill would win, although many commentators felt that an autumn election would have suited the Conservatives better. The *New York Daily News*, which had been extremely critical of some of the Prime Minister's political statements in the past, said: 'We would say that if he and his party do not win this election there is no gratitude in England. He has steered Great Britain through its most perilous passage since Napoleonic times.' The *Detroit Free Press* said that Churchill had 'placed his countrymen under a greater debt than they have owed to any man since William Pitt the Elder'. The *Cleveland Plain Dealer* said: 'Perhaps at no time since we achieved our independence has a British General Election been as worthy of wide American interest. The British Labour Party [has] presented a platform which, if approved by the British electorate, would make the United Kingdom virtually a Socialist State and leave the United States the lone remaining powerful capitalist democracy in the world. On an international level a Labour Party victory would seem at first to make for close relations between Russia and Britain, which might very well leave the United States politically isolated.' The *St Louis Globe Democrat* gave as its opinion that 'it would be a calamity if the man who rallied the world to fight Hitler is rejected now by his own people'. On the radio William L. Shirer said: 'It is not surprising that Churchill decided to have an election immediately when the Coalition refused to carry on till the end of the Japanese war. But Labour is accusing Churchill of having a rush election similar to the Khaki Election after the last war. . . . I do not see how Churchill can lose this election. . . . We can scarcely criticize Britain for holding it when we held ours in the heat of battle.' One of the few more cautious notes was sounded in the *Wall Street Journal*, which printed the headline: 'Churchill may squeak through in British vote despite trend to Left.'

It was with some relief that Britain went to the Poll on July 5th. Many of the politicians were able to relax for the first time in six years, as the servicemen's votes were collected in the three-week interval before the count and declaration. The country returned to the war effort. The mood of election fever died away. There was nothing to do but work and wait; the country had made its decision, but no one knew how. Winston Churchill, thoroughly exhausted, went to south-west France for a short holiday before going straight to the Potsdam conference.

(ix)

The Potsdam conference lasted from July 17th to August 2nd, with a brief interruption from July 26th–28th while the British delegation returned to London for the result of the General Election. The three delegations were quartered in large mansions in the not inaptly named town of Babelsberg, about twelve miles south-east of Berlin in a wooded area on the way to Potsdam. The President's quarters were No. 2 Kaiser Strasse, which had formerly been the residence of a leading film producer; the producer's wife now served the American party. As all the large houses in Russian-occupied Germany had been stripped of their furnishings, the houses for the delegation, and the palace at Cecilienhof near by where the meetings were to take place, had to be entirely refitted. This had been done, and conditions were an improvement on those at Yalta earlier in the year, although, owing to bad water, all three delegations suffered abominably from diarrhoea. The atmosphere throughout the conference was more strained than it had been on the Crimea or at Tehran in 1943. Truman, although by now full of confidence and in command of his job, was uncomfortable. He did not enjoy all the fuss that went with a President of the United States travelling abroad; as he said: 'I had always been in the habit of making my own travelling arrangements —buying my own railroad tickets—carrying my own bags.' He tried hard to achieve the same cordiality with Stalin and Churchill as his predecessor had done, joking with them and entertaining them on the piano. But Churchill, who was impressed with Truman's 'obvious power of decision', was disillusioned with the Russians, and to a lesser extent the Americans, and was vaguely depressed throughout. He knew Truman's inexperience gave him the chance to snatch leadership of the West for Britain and present the Russians with a tougher line, but he knew, too, that Britain, economically and financially weak, depended on the goodwill and support of America. He, too, tried hard to recapture the conviviality of old, but, somehow, without one of the founder members of what he had always liked to look on as the world's most exclusive club, things were not the same. Stalin, also, missed 'F.D.R.'; he was strangely subdued, in comparison with the previous conferences. He suffered a minor heart attack shortly before the conference was due to begin, and was thus late in arriving. When he did so, he tried to capture a grandeur and style befitting the occasion of a victorious meeting by turning up in an ornate railway carriage that had been used by the Czar and had been kept in a museum ever since. Because of his health he was unable to show off his drinking abilities, and had to confine himself to sips of wine; this made him irritable. General Hollis recalled: 'In the eighteen months since Teheran his hair had gone as white as the tunic he wore.' During the conference sessions, however, he was his usual courteous and unruffled self. The emergence of Bulganin as a policy-maker, and of other members of the Politburo, made it possible for him to leave day-to-day matters in the Soviet delegation to the many hands only too anxious to relieve him. Molotov continued to behave with arrogant independence, and once again the State Department officials were convinced that Stalin was not always being given the full story. Occasionally, when approached direct, Stalin would agree to something that had been blocked by Molotov at Foreign Ministers' meetings. At Potsdam, Molotov, known as 'Molly' to the Western delegates, did a great deal of the talking at the conference table. There was some indication that Molotov, Vyshinski and their advisers were intoxicated by their recent diplomatic successes and their exciting victory over Germany. Their attitude at the conference table, in contrast to that at Yalta, was often openly teasing or hostile. The new Secretary of State, James F. Byrnes, found Vyshinski particularly implacable ('he sits across the table looking at you with his cold, grey, piercing eyes').

Russo-British relations had deteriorated to such an extent that even the old convivial rivalry of Stalin and Churchill was dimmed. American policy was still much the same as it had been under Roosevelt; to steer a middle course, to make the most of the unprecedented conditions to secure the trust of the Soviets, and to build a permanent and satisfactory relationship with them, even if it meant concessions to them and friction with Britain. Byrnes' three chief advisers, Bohlen, Cohen and Matthews, had all enjoyed influence under the Roosevelt régime. Byrnes has stated that the words of Roosevelt's last message to Churchill were still fresh in the minds of the American delegation; he also says that at the time the Soviet Union benefited from a feeling of more goodwill in the United States than any other country probably enjoyed. Truman's influence, however, resulted in a slight hardening towards the Russians.

Truman quickly summed up the two other men. He was impressed with Churchill, perhaps a little overawed by his reputation. He liked to sit and listen to Churchill talk, and the Prime Minister was a man who was always happy to talk. He was also relieved to find that Stalin was quite human. He was surprised at the Marshal's short stature, noticing with some satisfaction that when the two of them stood together to have their photograph taken Stalin took care to stand on one step higher (not much escaped the eyes of the man from Missouri). He found Stalin 'extremely polite'.

At the first private lunch of Churchill and Truman the Prime Minister did a great deal of talking. Churchill always liked plenty of time to develop his theme to his own satisfaction, and Truman, feeling his ground, was at this point willing to accommodate him. Churchill pointed out that Britain, as a result of her effort during the war, was in a dire financial position; a great deal of her foreign investments had been sold; there was an external debt of some thousands of million pounds. Truman, without making any promises about Lend-Lease, said he appreciated the sacrifice Britain had made and would do his best for her.

At a dinner attended only by Stalin, Churchill and the interpreters, Stalin tried to reassure the Prime Minister about Soviet ambitions. He said he was personally against Sovietization of the countries occupied by the Red Army; he insisted that they would all have free elections. He spoke of the continuity of Russian policy; if anything were to happen to him, there would be a good man to step into his shoes. Churchill complained once more about Yugoslavia, referring to the fifty-fifty arrangement that had been made concerning that country. Stalin said that Russia also had not got its 50 per cent; often he did not know what Tito was going to do. They then spoke about Germany. They agreed that the danger from the Germans was that they were like sheep, and Stalin recounted his favourite story, which he had told Churchill before, about the time in Germany in 1907 when he had seen 200 Germans miss a Communist meeting because there was no one at the station barrier to take their railway tickets.

Although there were the usual number of private lunch and dinner parties (on one occasion Truman ate two lunches on the same day; first with Churchill, then with Stalin), to say nothing of the banquets, they played less part in the conference than hitherto. With a new member of the club, it was not so easy to divide up the world with such informality without some awkwardness; besides, Marshal Stalin was no longer the potentate he had once been.

Perhaps the most extraordinary event at any of the banquets was when the formidable Generalissimo jumped to his feet and went round the table collecting autographs on his menu-card, much to the astonishment of all the Western guests.

One such behind-the-scenes meeting, however, was very important. On July 17th the message 'Babies satisfactorily born' had arrived at the American delegation's headquarters; it signified that an atomic bomb had been exploded in New Mexico. The explosion had taken place at 5.30 a.m. on July 16th, about thirty-five miles from the village of Carrizozo, the 1,500 inhabitants of which had been awakened in terror by a sudden intense lighting of the early morning, followed nearly two minutes later by an enormous roar. Observers had been stationed twenty miles from the hundred-foot tower on which the bomb had been mounted, and, half-blinded despite thick goggles, most were convinced they had been far too near. Up till that moment there had been many who had doubted the success of this project, which had cost the United States vast sums of money. About 100,000 persons were employed, under the direction of General Leslie R. Groves, by what was known as the Manhattan Engineer District, with its tentacles at the vast plant at Oak Ridge, in Tennessee, at a disused stadium field in Chicago (where in December 1942 Enrico Fermi, an Italian refugee, had set off the first controlled nuclear reaction in a squash court), at Harford, in Washington, and especially at the enormous plant which stretched across the New Mexican desert at Los Alamos. At the latter, assembled under the direction of a thin young theoretician named J. Robert Oppenheimer, were the finest physicists in the world; men like Fermi, Niels Bohr, Hans Bethe, Otto Frisch, James Chadwick; most of them had (or would shortly have) the Nobel Prize. Never before had there been a gathering comparable to them. They had worked, not in scientific abstract (as some have tried to claim), but on the distinct problem of producing a bomb of incredible destructive power.

More from an enormous relief that the success of the test meant vindication of the administration in spending this fortune than from any other reason, there was considerable excitement and jubilation among the American delegation at Potsdam. It had been agreed by Roosevelt and Churchill years before that neither Britain nor America should use an atom bomb without the consent of the other, and Churchill was immediately informed and the strategic implications discussed. It was at this Anglo-American conference that

Truman, having heard all of the argument for using the bomb but not all of the argument against its use, agreed that it was to be used at an early date against Japan. British consent to use the bomb had already been given on July 4th, and thus the final decision rested with Truman alone. Neither President nor Prime Minister was aware of the exact nature of the bomb, although their scientific advisers had done their best to explain it to them, and neither was able to envisage much more about it except that it was a giant bomb capable of enormous destruction. It was immediately realized that with this new weapon the whole situation in the Japanese war was changed. In the first place, the Americans, and to a lesser extent the British, would very likely be able to avoid the terrible slaughter to their own troops that an invasion of the Japanese mainland implied. The casualties at Okinawa had been very much in Truman's thoughts. Secondly, it was no longer necessary to cajole the Russians to enter the war against Japan, and thus the Russians had at a stroke lost their best bargaining power. The decision lay with the President as whether or not to use the new weapon. It does not seem to have occurred to anyone that the decision could be anything but in the affirmative; after all, the bomb had cost two and a half billion dollars. Churchill has said of this secret meeting at Potsdam: 'The decision . . . was never even an issue. There was unanimous, auto-matic, unquestioned agreement around our table; nor did I ever hear the slightest suggestion that we should do otherwise.'* There had, in fact, been considerable pressure to do otherwise in the United States, but Churchill would not have known of this. Britain, which had played an all-important part in initial research for the atom bomb, had, even before Pearl Harbour, agreed to combine in development of the bomb with the United States—in America. British scientists like Chadwick, John Cockcroft, William Penney and M. L. E. Oliphant had gone to America with their secrets. Since then, to Churchill's extreme chagrin, the United States had been clamping down on information about the bomb to Britain in a rather dubious interpretation of the original Churchill–Roosevelt agreement on the subject. This had been yet another cause of Anglo-American mistrust and bitterness, minor only in the sense that so few people knew about it. Because of this the Anglo-American atomic committee was unworkable, with the British demanding information and the Americans refusing to give it. As early as 1943

* At least two present at the conference, Eisenhower and Leahy, were against using the bomb.

Churchill had complained to Hopkins: 'The War Department is asking us to keep them informed of our experiments while refusing altogether any information about theirs.' Although some information was granted on a 'military-need-to-know basis', there was a complete clamp down on peaceful and post-war applications. To the British, whose scientists had played a more important role than those of any other nation, and who had volunteered to part with their secrets for the common cause on the distinct understanding that there would be full collaboration between the two nations, this attitude was infuriating and dishonourable. At length the main source of British information was through the Canadians, who had been brought into the secret as being the possessors of almost the only available uranium (discovered by a French-Canadian from Haileybury, Ontario, in 1930). After years of this squabbling (the background of which was not known to Truman), Churchill was somewhat disgusted by the whole affair, and had pretty well washed his hands of the whole business.*

The main question at Potsdam was what to do about the Russians. Truman decided to casually inform the Generalissimo that the United States had a bomb of exceptional and unusual power and to leave it at that. It was also decided to convey an ultimatum to the Japanese calling for an immediate unconditional surrender of Japanese armed forces; Churchill and Stalin had suggested forgoing surrender so long as the Allies could obtain this in fact if not in so many words, but the President and the US Chiefs of Staff could not agree to this. The ultimatum was published on July 26th. It contained the pregnant sentence: 'The might that now converges on Japan is immeasurably greater than that which, when applied to the resisting Nazis, necessarily laid waste the lands, the industry and the methods of life of the whole German people.' After one of the plenary sessions, when they were walking out to their cars, Truman mentioned the new weapon to Stalin. Stalin seemed pleased, but asked no more about it, much to the President's relief. Churchill sidled up to the President while they were waiting for their cars and asked how it had gone. 'He never asked a question,' Truman replied. As it happened, Stalin felt he had no need to ask questions, as he knew about the bomb already through the extensive Soviet espionage system in the United States and Canada (including Klaus Fuchs, who was a senior member of the 'Manhattan' group,

---

* Truman later agreed that 'British scientists had initiated the project and were contributing much of the original atomic data'.

Harry Gold and David Greenglass; Nunn May was also active at this time). The expert opinion in the USSR was that the American attempt to produce an atomic weapon would not succeed.

Such was the background to the Potsdam conference.

At the first proper session of the conference, Truman was invited by the other two leaders to take the chair. Almost immediately the lack of agreement that was to characterize the conference began to emerge. The United States wanted Italy to be allowed to join the United Nations, but Churchill protested that Britain, on her own, had fought Italy in a desperate struggle in North Africa, and the British people were not yet ready to forget that. The Russians, moreover, were determined that no favour should be granted to Italy that was not acceded Rumania, Bulgaria and Hungary. The Anglo-Americans, on the other hand, insisted that no agreements could be reached about these countries until Western Press representatives were allowed in, and until some gesture had been made about the large amount of British and American-owned capital in the Rumanian oil-fields which had been confiscated by the Russians. The Americans, however, put forward a plan to set up a Council of the Foreign Ministers of Britain, France, China, the USSR and the United States to draft the peace treaties and settle boundaries. Neither Churchill nor Stalin was happy about this; Churchill preferring to thrash out matters first in the Big Three meetings, and Stalin objecting to the inclusion of China. However, they eventually agreed, and an increasing number of subjects concerning the enemy countries were passed on to the Foreign Ministers. As session succeeded session, very little seemed to be getting settled. Churchill and Stalin argued and bantered for hours on end, not always on points on the agenda, and Truman, with hidden but increasing impatience, tried to speed things up. The President, whose previous experience of such affairs had been restricted to the more mercurial world of domestic American politics, and who was not imbued with the leisurely patience of the patrician as his predecessor had been, became increasingly edgy.

Stalin raised the question of Spain. Franco had recently approached Churchill with the suggestion that their two countries should join forces to promote a Western alliance against Russia; Churchill had sent a frosty reply, a copy of which he had sent to Stalin. The Russians now demanded the outlawing of Spain. The Anglo-Americans, while expressing a distaste for the Franco régime, flatly refused to do anything about it. This appeared to be a defeat for the

Russians, but it was customary at conferences for them to raise matters in which they did not expect to succeed in order to be able to demand concessions on other matters the success of which concerned them much more. When the discussion turned to Yugoslavia, and Churchill and Stalin continued their well-worn arguments, Truman at last exploded. He said that he did not wish to waste time listening to grievances. If they did not get to the main issues he intended packing up and going home. Nothing quite like it had ever happened at a meeting of 'The Club' before. Stalin said that he would like to go home, too.

There were informal discussions between the Americans and British on the question of Palestine. Truman told the British, who had for long recognized Jewish ambitions in that territory, that he favoured as many Jews as possible being allowed to enter it; but he had no desire to send American troops to maintain peace there.

The arguing and squabbling at Babelsberg continued. There seemed to be nothing on which the three powers could agree. What annoyed Truman was Russian intransigence and British volubility. Churchill's policy was to put decisions off till after the election result was known, and then, if he returned, to bring matters to a head and have a show-down with the Russians (in the event, it was the Americans who had to bring matters to a head). In the American camp, even among Byrnes' staff, there seemed to be a growing awareness that the curtain that Churchill had mentioned was indeed falling.

As far as the public were concerned, the main question settled at Potsdam was what to do about Germany, although this had, in fact, been largely agreed on before the conference met. The four zones were formally set up; disarmament and demilitarization of Germany was to be carried out; all Nazi and quasi-Nazi associations were to be abolished 'in such a manner as permanently to prevent the revival or reorganization of German militarism'; all Nazi laws which established discrimination were to be abolished; the judicial and educational systems in Germany were to be remoulded. It was stated that: 'It is the intention of the Allies that the German people be given the opportunity to prepare for the eventual reconstruction of their life on a democratic and peaceful basis. If their own efforts are steadily directed to this end, it will be possible for them in due course to take their place among the free and peaceful peoples of the world.' It was also agreed that Nazi criminals, including leaders, supporters and high officials, were to be brought to judgment; the stage for the Nuremberg trials was thus set, despite the warnings and advice given by Churchill at Yalta, where he had suggested immediate execution without formal trials.

Other points of discussion were Iran, where the Russians demanded an Anglo-American withdrawal (it was agreed that Allied troops should leave Tehran), and Syria and Lebanon. With regard to the latter countries, Churchill said it was impossible to withdraw British troops because that would result in the undoubted massacre of all French civilians in the area; Stalin withdrew his demand. There was also a discussion about Vienna, where the British and Americans were at last installed. Churchill complained that the half-million Viennese in the British zone could not be fed because the feeding grounds of the city lay to the east, and the Russians there were clamping down an unnatural barrier. Stalin promised to look into the matter. There was also the question of the Black Sea Straits. The Russians wanted their own fortifications in that area in order to protect their approach to the Mediterranean. Churchill and Truman protested that they could not agree to such an affront to Turkish sovereignty, but they both supported an internationally guaranteed freedom of the Straits. In this argument, Molotov had blandly referred to Russo-Turkish treaties of 1805 and 1833. Churchill made the point that Britain, though her losses had been terrible, was not expecting any gain out of the war; but the Russian delegation was not interested in British scruples, and asked for, and got, the East Prussian port of Konigsberg (already occupied by the Red Army).

The two main issues of the conference were the questions of reparations and of the Polish boundaries. The former controversy, which had been studied by a three-power committee in Moscow after the Yalta conference with no agreement, dragged on day after day. Russia demanded a great deal, and the American objection was that it was evident that they had already taken a great deal. Churchill was prepared to barter and bargain, but the Russians, it seemed, would never be satisfied. Stalin now demanded one-third of the German merchant and naval fleet. Molotov insisted on the original Yalta demand of 50 per cent of total reparations to go to the USSR, and still stuck to the sum of ten billion dollars in kind. The American delegation was not at all keen on the reparations idea; after the First World War the United States had provided Germany with loans which had been used to buy raw materials which had then been converted into goods offered as reparations—

America was not anxious to repeat the performance. Molotov admitted to Byrnes that a great deal of material, including even domestic household goods, had already been taken away to Russia; but he insisted on a definite figure for more formal and official reparations. Without any prior and definite policy on the matter, the Anglo-Americans hedged and postponed a decision.

Another difficult problem was the Polish frontier; difficult to the Anglo-Americans but not to the Russians, who had presented their allies with a *fait accompli*. It had been agreed at Yalta that Russia should advance her western frontier to the Curzon Line, and it had been recognized that Poland, in turn, should receive as consolation a chunk of Germany. The only question was how much of Germany should Poland receive. The Anglo-Americans had said as far as the Eastern Neisse, but the Russians insisted on the Western Neisse. The Red Army was now in control of the entire area, and the new Polish Government was claiming land up to the Western Neisse. Churchill was particularly disturbed, as he knew that much of this area was inhabited by Germans; he knew they would have to be moved in a mass migration. He also believed that: 'One day the Germans would want their territory back.' Molotov and Stalin, however, were absolutely adamant in claiming that there were no Germans left in the area; they had all fled before the Red Armies. The area was important for feeding the Poles and the Russian troops; there was nobody left to cultivate the land except the Poles, and the Poles had therefore poured in without the Russians being able to stop them. There was nothing Churchill could say, and he tried hard, that would make either Molotov or Stalin deviate from this somewhat unlikely story. Churchill was disinclined to believe it, and Truman's opinion was that the Russians had either killed off all the Germans in the area or had forced them into the western zones. Stalin insisted that 'not a single German remained in the area'. As for the resulting difficulties of the population of West and Central Germany, who had formerly greatly relied on these important agricultural lands, Stalin said he did not mind creating difficulties for the Germans. If the East Germans had to supply the West Germans with farm produce, then the West Germans ought to supply the East Germans with coal from the Ruhr. Churchill said that Britain was acutely short of coal, but was exporting to Holland, Belgium and France. Stalin said that the situation in Russia was even worse than that in Britain. He suggested passing the matter on, as so much else, to the Foreign Ministers, but Churchill would not agree to this, arguing that in the meantime the Poles would be settling themselves in. He asked for the leading figures of the Polish Government to come to the conference at once.

This was arranged, and two days later Churchill met the Polish President, Bierut. In a private talk he gave the Polish leader what amounted to a thorough telling-off. He pointed out that Britain had taken a great interest in Poland, which had cost her much. The British people now expected that there would be free and un-fettered elections in Poland, and that the Poles would not cause a rupture between the Allies by demanding too much territory. Bierut protested that Poland was going to develop along the lines of Western democracy; that the Russian Army was leaving Poland; that there was no attempt to suppress religions; that elections in Poland would be even more democratic than British elections.

The Russian delegation had meanwhile demanded that all the assets and armed forces of the old *emigré* government in London should now be transferred to the new Provisional Polish Government. Churchill agreed that this would be done, but he asked for time. The British Government, he pointed out, was in a delicate situation. The Poles had £20,000,000 in gold frozen in Britain and Canada, and this had not been touched during the war. The British Government had paid for the army, diplomatic service and other expenditure of the exiled government. It had cost Britain about £120,000,000; they had even paid the three months' salary due to the government employees in London.* The Polish Army, of 180,000 men, now in Italy and Germany, was in a highly excited state. They did not like what was happening to their country. If the Polish Government could make their country more attractive, then, Churchill said, he would be better able to persuade these men to return to their own country.

When the news was leaked that Poland had been represented at the Potsdam conference, de Gaulle and the French were by no means pleased.

On July 25th Churchill and Attlee returned to London for the result of the election, and the conference was adjourned. It was confidently expected by most delegates that Churchill would return alone; few people had taken much notice of Attlee in his unusual position of holding a watching-brief at the conference. Stalin told Churchill that all his information, from Communist and other

---

* Churchill's figure was a little high. The Poles agreed to pay £13,000,000 of this sum in instalments; in December 1962 £4,000,000 was still outstanding.

sources, confirmed that the Conservatives would be returned with a majority of about eighty.

(x)

Churchill's wife met him at Northolt Airport, and after a quiet family dinner the Prime Minister went to bed confident that the results which would begin coming in the following morning would keep him in power. He based his view on the assurance of his party advisers. Just before dawn, however, he woke with a sudden start of almost physical pain, convinced that he was beaten. Late in the morning he went to the Map Room, where the staff had prepared a complicated chart to illustrate and analyse the results as they came in. He was with his brother Jack, who had a room at 10 Downing Street, and who had looked after the Prime Minister's personal affairs throughout most of the war. The two men had no sooner sat down than news came in of the defeats of Harold Macmillan and Brendan Bracken. Already there were a surprising number of Labour gains, although some of these had been expected by the Conservative Central Office. By midday the results were flooding in, and nearly every other one seemed to be a Labour gain. The Prime Minister was joined by Lord Beaverbrook, 'who sat with him for much of the day leaning back in his chair with his legs comfortably crossed and betraying no visible sign of surprise or emotion, although the voting was running completely counter to all the predictions of his newspapers'. The result for Woodford came in, and it was learnt with a shock that the completely unknown Independent who had stood there, A. Hancock, who had campaigned for a one-day working week, had polled 10,488, well over a third of the Prime Minister's poll. Labour gains had by now mounted to forty-four; there was one gain for the Conservatives. Mrs Churchill, who had been at Woodford for the declaration, rushed up to London to be with her husband. As she arrived at the Map Room she was told: 'It's a complete débâcle.' The shocks came in one after the other. Lord Beaverbrook made his apologies and departed for lunch with his son, Group Captain Max Aitken, who had been elected with a majority of 925 for Holborn (the previous Conservative majority in the constituency had been 7,329). Bracken had now joined Churchill, who sat in silence staring blankly at the wall in front of him. L. S. Amery—Out; Sir James Grigg—Out; Hore-Belisha—Out; Colonel J. J. Llewellin—Out; Geoffrey Lloyd—Out; Duncan Sandys—Out; Captain Peter Thorneycroft—Out; Lord Dunglass—Out; Miss Horsbrugh—Out. These were less than half of the Ministers and Under-Secretaries who had lost their seats. Churchill got up and began to wander about the room. By six o'clock the Labour Party had a clear majority. Winston Churchill ordered drinks and cigars. He then departed for Buckingham Palace to tender his resignation to the King. Constitutionally he could have waited till Parliament met, but, as he said, 'the verdict of the electors had been so overwhelmingly expressed that I did not wish to remain even for an hour responsible for their affairs'.

A small crowd had gathered at the gates of Buckingham Palace, and the resigning Prime Minister, shocked and immeasurably hurt, gave them his Victory sign, presumably as an unthinking habit. He was with George VI for a quarter of an hour, during which time he recommended that the King should send for Attlee to form a government. As far as he was concerned, the choice of Attlee, the recognized leader of the Labour Party, was a mere formality. Five minutes after Churchill was driven away through St. James's Park, a small black car drove up to the Palace unnoticed by the growing crowd. At the wheel was Mrs Attlee, and beside her was the man who was going to be the next Prime Minister of the United Kingdom. The King conversed with Attlee for some time, while Mrs Attlee sat waiting in the car outside; among other things, he questioned him about his Ministerial appointments. Attlee, who had undergone a hectic day at the Labour Party's headquarters at Transport House—but who, despite everything, had not forgotten to honour a prior engagement to meet his wife for tea at the Great Western Hotel, Paddington—had been putting his mind to this, but had been unable to come to any decision. Clearly he would have to make an immediate choice as to Foreign Secretary, as Stalin and Truman were waiting to resume the Potsdam conference. It was between Dalton and Bevin, and at that moment Dalton seems to have been uppermost in Attlee's mind. The King made it clear that he would much prefer Bevin.

Churchill returned to the Map Room, where he learnt that the election was a landslide comparable only with the great Liberal victory of 1906, when the Conservatives had won only 157 seats. He then called together a few of his ex-Cabinet colleagues and they discussed in bewilderment what had happened. For Churchill himself it was a blow of acute and subtle agony. All around him, in the Cabinet Offices and the Map Room, was the organization for waging war that he had built, an organization that through custom and association over the years he had begun to consider almost his own. He had been acclaimed as one of the greatest and most popular leaders in the history of the country. It had been through him alone that the nation had found a new defiance and vigour when it had been on the brink of almost unthinkable disaster. Now he had not only lost an election, he had been rudely thrown out. There had been nothing like this rebuttal of a victorious leader in modern history. He issued a statement from 10 Downing Street, which, in its dignity, humility and grace, might well serve as a model for all democratically defeated leaders. 'The decision of the British people has been recorded in the votes counted today. I have therefore laid down the charge which was placed upon me in darker times. I regret that I have not been permitted to finish the work against Japan. For this, however, all plans and preparations have been made, and the results may come much quicker than we have hitherto been entitled to expect. Immense responsibilities abroad and at home fall upon the new government, and we must all hope that they will be successful in bearing them. It only remains for me to express to the British people, for whom I have acted in these perilous years, my profound gratitude for the unflinching, unswerving support which they have given me during my task, and for the many expressions of kindness which they have shown towards their servant.'

The last result, which came in by ten o'clock, gave Labour a clear majority over all other parties of 153.* The Government had gained eight seats and lost 199; Labour had lost four and gained 214. The Labour Party had formed governments twice before, in 1924 and 1929, but only with the help of the Liberals. This was the first occasion since Keir Hardie—the first Socialist MP—had taken his seat fifty-three years before that Labour had won a clear mandate from the country to socialize the nation. For the Liberals the election had been humiliating. They were left with only eleven seats in the House of Commons, the smallest representation in the party's history. Among their prominent former MPs who had been defeated were the party leader himself, Sir Archibald Sinclair, Lady Violet Bonham-Carter, Sir William Beveridge, Sir Percy Harris, Dingle Foot and Honor Balfour. The Communists had

* The final overall majority, after thirteen late declarations, was 146. Labour secured 11,992,292 votes against 9,960,809 for the Conservatives and 2,239,668 for the Liberals.

gained one seat (giving them a total of two). Their leader, Harry Pollitt, said that they pledged their full support in assisting the Labour Party in its aims. Perhaps the most remarkable Labour victory had been that of Morrison himself. He had turned the 6,449 Conservative majority at Lewisham into a majority of 15,219 for Labour. Bevin, who had fought his first election (he had previously been unopposed), had won Central Wandsworth by 5,174 from Brigadier J. Smythe, VC. All the other Labour leaders were comfortably returned, although Attlee's majority in Limehouse had been reduced. Among the new members were H. T. N. Gaitskell (a brilliant young economist, who had increased the Socialist majority at South Leeds tenfold although seriously ill with an undiagnosed illness), G. A. Brown and J. H. Wilson. In many ways it was a Parliament quite different from the one it had superseded. More than 300 of the MPs were newcomers to Westminster. There was a significant decrease in the number of trades union MPs among the Labour members; 119 compared to 164 in the old House. About 200 of the new Labour MPs came from the professional classes, or from middle- and upper-class backgrounds.

Back at Transport House, Attlee found himself being lobbied by sundry Socialists anxious for a job in his Government. There was some confusion, and much excitement; there was even talk that Attlee was not to be the Prime Minister at all. After all, it was pointed out, the new Parliamentary Labour Party had not yet met to pick its leader. Once again Laski and others promoted Morrison. Morrison, too, no doubt sensing that there was a real chance for him here (he denies it), insisted, at a hurried meeting at Transport House, that no one could be Prime Minister until the party leader had been elected. Attlee says: 'I recall that he expressed reluctance to serve under me as he thought the party might want him as Prime Minister.' In a crowded room at Transport House, Attlee, who considered himself Prime Minister since the King's summons, held a Press conference. He said: 'We are facing a new era and I believe that the voting at this election has shown that the people of Britain are facing that new era with the same courage as they faced the long years of war. We have no illusions as to the difficult tasks which face this country and the world in the next few years, but I am convinced that we can carry the thing through to success to get into a world in which we shall not again be faced with periodical world wars and periodical world slumps. I believe we are on the eve of a great advance of the human race.' Morrison spoke after Attlee;

he referred to the Conservative campaign at the election. 'Mr Churchill joined in the stunts, cultivated the red herrings, and was as good as anybody in inventing irrelevancies, as was shown by his statement about the Gestapo. He accepted a lot of bad advice from his political advisers . . . a feature of the election was the swing of the middle-class votes to Labour. The Labour Party has held the bulk of the manual workers' votes for many years, but hitherto they have not really had a grip of the middle-class voters.'

The Labour Party held a jubilant rally at the Central Hall, Westminster. Harold Laski, referring to himself as 'the temporary head' of the party, made a triumphant speech: 'At long last we have made possible full friendship with the Soviet Union . . . we shall give no help either to decaying monarchs or obsolete social systems.' Laski, the man who had been most bitterly attacked by Churchill and the Conservatives, in the midst of his excited speech gave tribute to the resigning Prime Minister. 'On the day his rule as Prime Minister draws to a close, I want in the name of the British Labour Party to thank Mr Churchill for the great service he has rendered to this nation.' To the bewilderment of the foreign correspondents present, this brought forth an enormous roar of cheering, easily the greatest of the rally. Attlee spoke more soberly. He began by saying: 'We have great tasks before us.' He was heard with some impatience. Then Ernest Bevin got up. Speaking with laborious and booming care, he said: 'When I saw the results I had a feeling that the British people had put an end to the very conception of personal government in this country. It is a grand thing to have lived to see the day when the British electorate cast their votes for policy, not personality.' Morrison, speaking at another meeting, just outside the hall, said: 'We have lifted aloft the torch of progress —the torch of enlightenment. We will build a fine Great Britain and a prosperous world.'

While these bold and rousing sentiments were being voiced to the happy Socialist and Labour-voting crowds, Winston Churchill was sitting with his daughters Sarah and Mary (who had dressed in their smartest evening dresses in an attempt to please their father) in the drawing-room at 10 Downing Street. His initial shock was now giving way to a wider depression; the realization that his recent intense preoccupation with, and involvement in, world affairs was suddenly cut off as if by a pair of scissors through a cord. His daughters were entertaining two friends, one of whom was Robin Maugham. Churchill told the two young men, 'We must give them a chance—let's see what they can do.' After a long and unpleasant day, he retired to bed.

The following day was one of hectic manoeuvring by Labour politicians. Overwhelmed by events, Attlee, who had not expected a victory (according to Francis Williams), let alone a landslide, sent off a message to Stalin at Potsdam saying that he would not be able to arrive until the following day. 'I . . . should be much obliged if provisional arrangements could be made accordingly, if this would suit your convenience. I greatly regret the inconvenience caused by this postponement.' Potential Ministers searching for Attlee were unable to find him. Even Transport House did not know where he was. He was, in fact, in a room in the Cabinet Offices in Great George Street. During that day, July 27th, 1945, Attlee became the centrepiece in what were to become two controversies that were to rage for many years.

The pro-Morrison group gathered strength during the morning, and by the time Dalton met Bevin at noon Laski had written to Attlee on the matter of the leadership. Attlee had replied with the splendid words: 'Dear Laski, thank you for your letter, contents of which have been noted.' Morrison also was still arguing that Attlee should not accept the King's commission to form a government until the new Parliamentary Party had a chance to elect a leader. He said the decision should be delayed for forty-eight hours. According to Dalton, he also wrote a note to Attlee. Cripps and Maurice Webb had apparently joined Laski and Ellen Wilkinson in this move. Morrison, who admits asking for the delay in order to elect a leader, denies that he wanted the Premiership himself. To complicate matters, the prominent trade unionist, Arthur Deakin, had been canvassing for Bevin as the leader, with Morrison as his deputy. Bevin, however, would hear of none of these suggestions. With some prescience, he had great faith in Attlee as the only man who would be able to weld the Labour leaders into a team. 'We're all bloody *prima donnas*,' he said, with some accuracy. According to Dalton, Bevin said to Deakin, 'How dare you come and talk to me like this?'; and to Morrison, 'If you go on mucking about like this, you won't be in the bloody government at all.' (Morrison has denied that this was said.) There was a meeting at Transport House at 3 p.m. and all went smoothly. Morrison, on this occasion, made no challenge for the leadership, and as the day wore on Attlee—who had never himself been in the slightest doubt as to who was Prime Minister—was secure. It seems more than likely that Morrison's part in this affair (he says he was 'pressed') was, not for the only time in his career, misunderstood by even his closest colleagues. Laski, however, appears to have been under the impression that he possessed more power than he did; there also seems to have been a surprising miscalculation among some people as to the kind of man they were dealing with in Clement Attlee.

While the brave new world was being ushered in, in this somewhat unseemly way, Attlee was still struggling with his Ministerial appointments. He decided to fill only the major posts and to leave the rest until he returned from Potsdam. He saw Dalton and told him that he was 'almost certainly' going to offer him the Foreign Office. He said they would be leaving the following morning, and advised Dalton to get a bag packed. Dalton asked whether he would need evening dress. Attlee said, No, Stalin did not dress, but advised Dalton to take a light-weight suit as it was hot in Berlin. But at four o'clock Attlee rang Dalton up and said he was going to send him to the Treasury after all. He had decided to give Bevin the Foreign Office. Dalton, somewhat confused, was disappointed; he had always wanted the Foreign Office, and Bevin had always wanted the Treasury. This switching of appointments began another controversy that lasted many months. It was alleged that George VI had enjoyed unconstitutional influence. Although he certainly made his preference perfectly clear,* the King was meticulous in his respect for constitutional procedure; moreover, Attlee had made it clear to Dalton that he wanted him for the Foreign Office *after* he had seen the King. Other names mentioned were Sir Alan Lascelles (Private Secretary to the King), Sir Edward Bridges (Permanent Secretary to the Treasury), and Churchill himself. It was strongly rumoured that Attlee had lunched with Churchill that day. Whatever the background to the matter, Attlee was saved from making an unwise decision; for Dalton, a recognized authority on public finance, was not known for either tact or patience, and to have had Bevin and Morrison together on home affairs would have caused difficulties. Attlee has stated that it was his own initiative that prompted him to change his mind; but it would seem likely that there was more to it than that. Whatever the background to the affair, only one man knows the full story, and he has never revealed it (there is no mention of it in Attlee's biography).

The following morning the new Prime Minister's first Cabinet appointments were announced in the Press: Morrison—Lord

* As stated in the official biography by J. W. Wheeler-Bennett.

President of the Council; Bevin—Foreign Secretary; Dalton—Chancellor of the Exchequer; Cripps—President of the Board of Trade; Arthur Greenwood—Lord Privy Seal; Jowitt—Lord Chancellor.

In America the news of Churchill's defeat had been greeted with astonishment; there was a widespread desire to hear more about Clement Attlee, which the American newspapers found it difficult to satisfy. But in Washington there was a feeling, once the shock of Churchill's dramatic departure wore off, that the change might well be advantageous to United States policy. It was not forgotten that Westminster under Churchill had been almost as much of a problem to the State Department as had Moscow. This prevalent mood was summed up by H. V. Kaltenborn, commentator of the National Broadcasting Company, in the following words: 'There is a feeling here, justified or not, that the Churchill Government represented old-time British Imperialism. There is also a feeling, justified or not, that the Labour Party has a more constructive attitude towards the aspirations of the underprivileged people of the world. For those reasons I feel confident that the emergence of Labour as a dominating force in British politics will favour rather than hinder those good relations between Britain and the United States which are so essential to the making of a sound peace.' Democratic Senator Joseph Guffey said: 'I am not surprised. Franklin Roosevelt told me this would happen three years ago.'

On the whole, there was a feeling of strange calm throughout Britain; a widespread sense of the half-bashful revelation of a secret; a sense of a difficult job safely accomplished. There was not a great deal of excitement; people got on with their work. In some quarters there was a natural apprehension as to what Labour's policies would mean personally; the British Medical Association happened to be meeting in London, and there was some consternation when its Secretary, Dr Charles Hill, interrupted business to read out the result. A number of doctors and surgeons spoke to the Press in violent criticism of the proposed National Health Service (although this was not, in fact, a measure peculiar to Labour—it was supported by all parties). There had been a rapid fall in prices on the Stock Exchange; the worst since the fall of France in 1940. But, on examination, this turned out to be not from widespread selling—indeed, there was practically none—but merely a pessimistic precaution of the jobbers in marking down their prices to discourage selling. There was no panic in the Conservative Press. *The Times*, in its top leader, blamed the Conservative failure fairly and squarely on 'the conduct of the election itself. Mr Churchill himself introduced and insisted upon emphasizing the narrower animosities of the party fight. As a result the great national programme was allowed to slip into the background; the Prime Minister's own stature was temporarily diminished; and the voters, who were deeply interested in real, urgent and essentially non-party subjects such as the housing of the people, seem to have visited their disappointment on the side which could be represented, on this showing, as taking but a perfunctory interest in the reconstruction programme, and as relying for success rather upon charges against the probable mis-conduct of their opponents than upon any creative virtues of their own.' Attlee later said: 'I always thought Churchill was led away by Beaverbrook and Brendan Bracken in the election. He had a great opinion of Beaverbrook, who had brought down two governments, and I think he listened to him and Bracken on how to fight the election and they completely misjudged the public mood. . . . Even those who would have liked Churchill weren't prepared to have him if it meant having the Tories too.' Churchill's mistake appears to have been that he did not appreciate that Beaverbrook, a brilliant political manoeuvrer, was only good at bringing down governments, not at setting them up. In the new Conservative Party that was to struggle from this defeat, there was to be little heeding of the advice of 'M. and B.' ever again. But it was typical of British democracy that on the morning that the Conservative Party was seen to have sunk so low in public esteem the very newspaper which had campaigned so vigorously and sensationally against the Labour Party, the *Daily Express*, said in its leader column: 'There will be no captious criticism of the new Government, no attempt to turn the nation's discontents into party capital. The new Govern-ment must be given its chance in this difficult period of the aftermath.'

Mr R. K. Law, who twenty-four hours previously had been Minister of Education and had now lost his seat at Hull, had a more jaundiced reaction. 'The British people,' he said, 'will have a very unpleasant awakening.'

(xi)

On arrival at Potsdam, Attlee took Bevin to be introduced to Truman, Byrnes and other members of the American delegation. Truman, who had spent much of the short recess with Eisenhower at Frankfurt, was longing for home. He was, owing to the late hours favoured by Churchill and Stalin and to his own early rising habit, tired out; an unusual condition for him. Throughout the conference he had been dealing with countless other matters, both domestic and foreign, that had been sent from Washington for his attention. With the return of the British, and of two left-wing men at that, he hoped to be able to finish off the conference in a day or two. Both Byrnes and he, however, immediately gained a very bad impression of Bevin. Here, it seemed, was a man even more stubborn than Churchill had been; what was more, his manner, blunt and blustery, they found rather unpleasant. The conference reassembled on Saturday, July 28th, at 10.15 p.m., only forty-eight hours after Attlee had been elected. The new Prime Minister apologized once again for the inconvenience he had caused through 'domestic occurrences', and the conference then returned to the subject of the recognition of Italy, Rumania, Hungary and Bulgaria. Like Truman, Stalin had tired of the conference; faced now by two Western leaders he did not know, he no longer felt the enjoyment he had experienced at previous 'Big Three' conferences. Molotov became more than ever in evidence; he had been astonished at Churchill's defeat, apparently convinced that the elections would be 'fixed'. Leahy has written that there was 'a noticeable coolness' from the Soviet delegation towards Attlee and Bevin, which surprised the Americans, who had hoped a left-wing British Government would find favour with the Russians. After Byrnes had complained that the United States found it impossible to agree with both the Soviet Union and Great Britain at the same time, the question of recognition was passed over. When the discussion turned to reparations, Bevin immediately began to curtly and brusquely cross-examine Stalin, who was clearly taken aback by this kind of treatment. The Americans and the Russians were surprised by the continuity of the British policy. Attlee and Bevin, whose appearance at the table had been such a dramatic demonstration of the way a democracy changes its government, were carrying on as if they were reinvigorated versions of Churchill and Eden who had returned from London; the effect was the more uncanny as in manner and appearance the two men were about as unlike Churchill and Eden respectively as any two men could be. Byrnes was clearly disappointed. Bevin was now the dominant personality of the conference. He picked up all the threads of the various subjects that had been under discussion, and appreciated the various national attitudes on them, with remarkable speed. He was highly suspicious of all Russian intentions, and did not bother to hide it. Whenever on unsure ground, he relied on the goodwill of the Americans, and supported them.

The following day Truman, on his return from church service, found Molotov and his interpreter waiting for him. Molotov was obviously anxious to do a deal on Poland behind the British backs. Truman called for Byrnes, who said that the United States was definitely prepared to accept Polish influence up to the Eastern Neisse and the Oder, including Danzig, and all of East Prussia. This was a concession, but Molotov stuck out for the Western Neisse. The British were informed of this meeting later in the day.

On the morning of July 31st Byrnes told Molotov that the United States wanted the three outstanding issues—Poland, reparations and the ex-Axis countries' membership of the United Nations—all considered together. He was offering, in fact, a bargaining session over what became known as a 'package deal'. Molotov tried to prevent this, but Byrnes made it plain that the Americans were only prepared to agree on all or none, and intended leaving for home either way. At the plenary session that afternoon, the United States put this proposal forward, despite the protests of Stalin. The three problems were quickly settled. Stalin, persisting in his demand for a definite figure for reparations (the Americans were tired of explaining to him that such figures were virtually meaningless), eventually agreed to accept '10 per cent' outright reparations from the three Western zones, as well as 15 per cent which the Russians were to pay for with food and raw materials. This gave them, as well as anything they wished in their own zone, 25 per cent of all capital goods in West Germany unnecessary for the peace economy of that area. Bevin argued, with some justification, that this gave them more than the overall 50 per cent agreed on at Yalta. This agreement was reached after a long fight by Bevin—reparations would mainly come from the Ruhr, which was in the British Zone. Byrnes then read out the proposal that Polish influence was to extend to the Western Neisse, thus reducing the old German territories of 1937 by a quarter. This was a complete reversal of his view expressed to Molotov the previous day. According to Byrnes' own account, he had only agreed to the reparations figure if the Russians would make no demands on the other two matters; but he was now giving way also on the question of the Polish frontier. He maintains—and so does Truman—that as the conference Protocol declared that 'the final delimitation of the western frontier of Poland should await the peace settlement', and that the intention was merely to establish temporary administration of the area, there was no concession at all. This is a weak argument. The Poles, backed by the Red Army, were already in control of the area; all that they needed was international recognition of their *fait accompli*—this they had now gained. Bevin was taken aback. He said that his instructions were to hold out for the Eastern Neisse. Truman and Byrnes appear to have competed with each other in soothing Bevin's fears, pointing out that no permanent cession of territory was involved. Reluctantly, Bevin concurred. The third part of the deal, the terms of entry to the United Nations, was quickly agreed. Arrangements for peace treaties with Italy and the Balkan countries were to be prepared by the Foreign Ministers in London.

At the final meeting, the Protocol to be issued to the waiting world was examined. To the disgust of the increasingly impatient Truman, the Russians and the British still found points over which to argue. Molotov suggested an amendment to the text concerning the Polish frontier. It was granted. He then suggested another. Instead of the words 'subject to examination by experts', he suggested 'exact line on ground should be established by experts of the USSR and Poland'. At this point Bevin, supported by Attlee, put his foot down. He said this was asking too much altogether, and he would not countenance such a suggestion. This was described by Truman as 'prolonged and petty bickering'. Nevertheless, Molotov withdrew his suggestion.

Truman stated that there was no further business and that the conference was ready to adjourn. He expressed the hope that the next conference would be held in Washington, to which Stalin replied, apparently in English, 'God willing'. He was no doubt thinking of his health and the younger men, greedy for power, who seemed to be rising everywhere around him. Thus ended the second great international conference of the year; a conference which proved once more that it is no good in a world of nationalism to go to the conference table unarmed; but if US politico-strategic thinking had been abreast of the sudden new advance in weapons, the Western allies would have been well armed indeed.

On the way home to the United States, Truman met George VI on board a British battleship at Plymouth; the King held out his hand to him and said: 'Welcome to my country', although in truth the President hardly had time to set foot in it. The Captain of the

USS *Augusta* was ordered by the President to steam his ship as fast as she would go for the United States; the maximum speed possible of 26·5 knots was set for the crossing. A 'homing' cable was sent to Mrs Truman.

Byrnes believed that the Potsdam conference had been a success; Truman inclined to the same belief, but in a nationwide broadcast on his return he admitted that 'nearly every international agreement had in it the element of compromise. The agreement on Poland is no exception.' As few people knew of the sudden and tremendous increase in America's power deriving from a new weapon, few similarly questioned the necessity or reason for such compromises. Attlee and Bevin, however, were not happy about what seemed to them to be a number of unnecessary concessions to the Russians. The general public, who knew no more than what was contained in the Protocol, relaxed under the belief that the three great powers seemed to be settling the post-war world in full accord.

In London, meanwhile, the new House had met briefly for the election of the Speaker. Mr Churchill's appearance had been greeted by prolonged applause, and the Government had risen to its feet *en masse* and sung the Red Flag.

The final structure of the Cabinet was announced after Attlee's return. A. V. Alexander resumed his wartime post of First Lord of the Admiralty; J. J. Lawson was given the War Office; Viscount Stansgate received the Air Ministry; the rebellious 'Nye' Bevan was given the Ministry of Health (the exact position he had wished upon himself)—at forty-seven, he was the youngest member of the Cabinet; George Isaacs, who had been Chairman of the Trades Union Congress General Council, was to be Minister of Labour; Emanuel Shinwell, one of the few outspoken critics of the Coalition, became Minister of Fuel and Power, which was clearly going to be one of the most difficult political tasks; Ellen Wilkinson became the only woman member of the Cabinet as Minister of Education. A proposal from Laski that he should be sent to Washington, presumably as Ambassador, was ignored. It was noticeable that among the junior Ministers there were many peers, and three MPs who were new to the House of Commons. These appointments were announced on August 4th, not long after the preoccupied Attlee had returned from Berlin. On that same day, across the surface of half the globe, at the small Pacific island of Tinian, the crew of the United States B–29 bomber, the *Enola Gay*, were briefed about a secret mission they were to undertake to the Japanese city of Hiroshima.

6 Momentous Decision

6 MOMENTOUS DECISION

While still at Potsdam, Truman had authorized the order to 509th Composite Group to deliver its 'special bomb' on one of the four, somewhat arbitrarily selected targets of Hiroshima, Kokura, Niigata and Nagasaki. This brought to a head many months of soul-searching and argument as to the use of the atomic bomb. Whether any other decision than the one arrived at was possible, bearing in mind the extraordinary cost of the new weapon in which a whole new industry had been built up from nothing on the tax-payers' money without the elected representatives of the people knowing anything about it, is debatable. If thousands of American servicemen had been killed as a result of not using the bomb, the President would (as Groves pointed out) have been 'crucified'; later knowledge shows us that it is unlikely that they would have been.

The atomic-bomb project in the United States had been born in 1939 when Albert Einstein was persuaded to write a warning letter to the President, by other scientists, who were aware that the nature of recent discoveries in nuclear physics made an atomic bomb a possibility. In Britain and in Germany research had already been reaching a crucial stage. It was eventually decided that the United States would launch a research programme, especially as many of the world's leading physicists happened to be in America owing to the war in Europe. On May 6th, 1940, an extraordinarily well-informed report had appeared in the London *Daily Telegraph* describing 'a new substance, and a potential source of vast power.... Already the implications the effect of this discovery might have on the outcome of the war have been discussed.' An article in the *Sunday Dispatch* on January 11th, 1943, was headed, 'One Little Bomb That Would Destroy The Whole Of Berlin'. The article mentioned 'a bomb that would blast a hole twenty-five miles in diameter and wreck every structure within a hundred miles. . . . The explosive in this bomb would be the energy contained in the uranium atom.'

It was the last that the public heard about the new source of power until August 1945. Strict censorship was imposed on both sides of the Atlantic, while British scientists and those now working in America began to co-operate. In 1942 German and Anglo-American progress was about level (Japan was also engaged in similar research), but during the summer of that year Speer made the decision that the German atom-bomb project under Otto Hahn would not get priority; Hitler favoured the V-weapons. German research and production had been hindered by the sabotage of resistance workers and by Allied bombing of their heavy-water plant in Norway. An entirely contrary decision was made by the Allies, and the Manhattan project was founded by Churchill and Roosevelt in the same month as Speer made his fateful decision. It was preferred to such other scientific weapons as bacteriological destruction of the Japanese rice crop, put forward by some of Roosevelt's advisers. By 1944 the American atomic programme had taken on a huge size and vast expense. Many of the scientists engaged in it began to have doubts as to whether the military-politico executive power behind the project was aware of all the implications. Among a section of the scientists involved there were distinct feelings of fear and guilt; this was the section which were not themselves closely involved with the military-politico machine. One of the leaders and spokesmen of this group was James Franck. A Committee on Social and Political Implications was formed by the scientists themselves, and Franck was made its chairman. During the spring of 1945 Franck and others worked on a statement—a document that became known as the Franck Report. At the same time a committee had been set up by Truman to study the use and implications of the bomb. The chairman of this committee was Henry Stimson, the Secretary for War; a man who had taken the closest interest in the Manhattan project since its earliest days; no non-scientist had given the matter more thought, and certainly no one better understood the implications. Stimson's growing concern about the whole project was the result of remarkable and creditable foresight. Many of his juniors and contemporaries, such as Admiral Leahy, had little time for the project. Many others, such as Eisenhower (earlier on) and MacArthur, knew nothing of it. Even the State Department knew nothing about it until the arrival of Byrnes (Stettinius was completely in the dark). In a memorandum to Truman, Stimson stated: 'Within four months we shall in all probability have completed the most terrible weapon ever known in human history . . . various segments of its discovery and production are widely known among many scientists in many countries. . . . It is extremely probable that the future will make it possible for atomic bombs to be constructed by smaller nations . . . the world in its present state of moral advancement, compared with its technical development, would be eventually at the mercy of such a weapon. In other words, modern civilization might be completely destroyed.'

Truman's committee met on May 31st and June 1st in the Pentagon. On it the military-politico men were completely outnumbered by the scientists, who were of a different group from that led by Franck. The two most prominent scientists were Fermi and Oppenheimer, both men who had been involved with and had worked with civil servants, politicians and soldiers for some years. Oppenheimer expressed the opinion that 20,000 people would probably be killed by an atomic bomb. The question was raised whether the first bomb should be used to kill or just as a demonstration. There were a number of drawbacks to a demonstration; the Japanese might fill a given area, if warning were made, with American prisoners-of-war. It was also apparent that there would be long intervals between the completion of each bomb; besides, none of the scientists on the committee was apparently convinced that a demonstration would inevitably be a technical success (they had been warned by Groves to expect a life-time of congressional investigations if it were not). A British scientist, Sir Geoffrey Taylor, has described the betting at Los Alamos among scientists as to whether the bomb would work. The scientist-dominated committee struggled with the question, and eventually voted *for* military use and *against* demonstration. Oppenheimer has since said that the committee knew nothing of other plans to defeat Japan, such as prolonged blockade, but all took it for granted that invasion was the inevitable alternative to the bomb. American strategy had, indeed, developed along those lines, and a two-phase strike at the main Japanese islands was now favoured. But American strategy at the time was not well defined; no doubt because the Secretary for War and others knew so well of the atom bomb. An invasion date of November 1st for the first stage had been fixed, and the Army had asked for nine atom bombs to be dropped in conjunction with the invasion. It had been agreed that British troops would be there, and the Dutch, French and Australian authorities had also been clamouring to take part. General Marshall estimated that a force of 190,000 combatant troops would be necessary, of whom less than 63,000 would be casualties.

Stimson was not entirely happy about the committee's decision; nor was Joseph C. Grew, an Under-Secretary of State, who had once been US Ambassador to Japan, and who was pleading with Truman to modify the doctrine of unconditional surrender. Many other Japanese experts, both in America and Britain, were worried by this same point. If such a surrender meant the death or removal of the Japanese god-emperor Hirohito, which it clearly could, then it was possible that many Japanese, perhaps even the majority, would never give in. In Britain the implications of this fact had been accepted by Churchill, who was more anxious to stop the war on harsh but acceptable terms than to continue until the Japanese were annihilated. The unconditional surrender policy, the pros and cons of which were now openly discussed in American newspapers, was, however, close to American hearts. Truman, supported by Byrnes, was reluctant to climb down, or even to appear to do so, on this point.

Some time early in June the Franck Report was delivered to Stimson's office. It stated that although in the past science had been able to devise protection for new weapons, this could not be expected for the atom bomb. It was suggested that Japan should be given an ultimatum or the chance to evacuate threatened regions. The report was in favour of a clear warning to the Japanese. It doubted whether American public opinion 'would approve of our own country being the first to introduce such an indiscriminate method of wholesale destruction of civilian life'. It was pointed out that the decision to introduce such a weapon into warfare might later be regretted by the United States, which, through its concentrated areas of population, was itself particularly vulnerable to such attack. This warning ran contrary to the advice of Truman's committee which had recommended the use of the bomb, 'without specific warning, as soon as possible, and against such a target as to make clear its devastating strength'.

By this time the 509th Composite Group were well established at

Tinian and making practice runs. Exactly what happened to the Franck Report is not clear; it is doubtful if it ever reached the President. As no action seemed to be coming from the report, one of the 'Manhattan' scientists who had worked on it, Leo Szilard, organized a petition pointing out the dangers of setting a precedent by using the bomb. He collected the support of sixty-seven scientists. The petition was delivered in Washington about the middle of July, and the names on it and its content remained secret. A number of other scientists organized a counter-petition pointing out how American lives would be saved if the war were brought to a sudden end. Another 'Manhattan' scientist, Farrington Daniels, on July 12th conducted a poll of 150 of his colleagues; only 15 per cent said they wanted the weapon initially used for full military effectiveness. But, owing to the extremely ambiguous form of questioning, the scientists on the Truman committee tried to argue that the majority of the poll were in favour of immediate 'military use'. Admiral Leahy, Chief of Staff to the President, had already spoken out strongly against use of the bomb, as he had done of the invasion alternative: 'It was my opinion at the time that a surrender could be arranged with terms acceptable to Japan and that would make fully satisfactory provision for America's defence.' But by the time of the Potsdam conference the President was taking more note of the advice of Stimson and Byrnes than of anyone else. Byrnes, who was not himself happy about using the bomb, felt that it was the lesser of evils and that it would have to be used ruthlessly. Marshall too was for using it. Besides the vacillating Stimson and the dogmatic Leahy, Generals Arnold and Eisenhower (now that they knew of it) were also dubious about using the weapon without a demonstration. In the end Stimson agreed with Byrnes. It was at Potsdam that Truman decided that the bomb was to be used on a Japanese city if there was an unfavourable answer to his ultimatum.

Such is the brief background to the order given to the 509th Composite Group on July 24th.

This order was delivered before the answer to the Potsdam ultimatum; but Truman's supporters claim that it could easily have been rescinded. It was, they say, necessary in order to set the wheels turning. He himself, on inquiry, has insisted that he gave another, final, order after the ultimatum, when on the *Augusta* (but he omitted to mention this order in his memoirs, and there is no record or mention of it elsewhere). His critics claim that the warning contained in the ultimatum was not the kind that Stimson and others had been

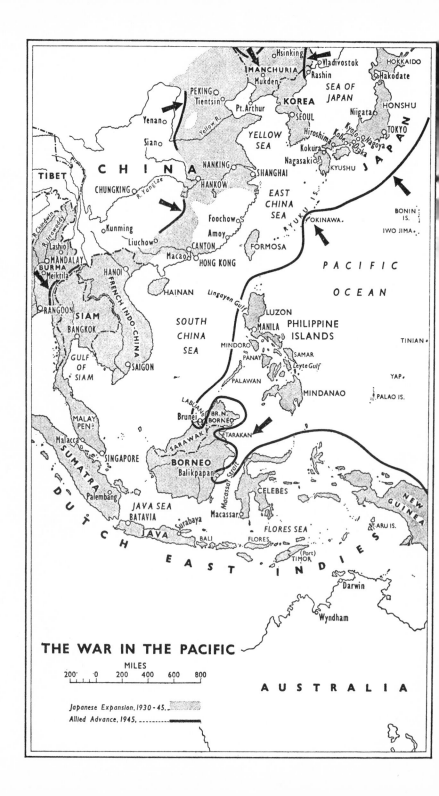

THE WAR IN THE PACIFIC

MILES

200 0 200 400 600 800

Japanese Expansion, 1930-45,
Allied Advance, 1945,

urging, and that it was not in the least specific; that there was no mention of an exceptional weapon. In Leahy's opinion it contained 'no hint' of such a weapon. The order, devised by Groves and senior Pentagon staff, read in part: 'The 509th Composite Group, 20th Air Force, will deliver its first special bomb as soon as weather will permit visual bombing after about August 3, 1945, on one of the targets: Hiroshima, Kokura, Niigata and Nagasaki. . . . Additional bombs will be delivered on the above targets as soon as made ready.' All the order needed was Truman's authorization, and this it got. Thus even the final wording of this fateful message, as so much else regarding the whole Manhattan project, was done not by the half-aware President himself, but by a few of the countless obscure people all of whom were involved and played their part. In effect, the decision had already been made, and not by any human being but by the project itself, which had grown so vast and cost so much that no one seemed to know how to stop it from justifying itself had they even wanted to. A copy was sent to MacArthur and Nimitz 'for their information'; the two commanders were preparing for the invasion of Japan. In a reorganization of the Far East theatre, MacArthur had been given command of all land forces, and Nimitz of all naval; the Air Force was directed from Washington by Arnold, with General Carl Spaatz about to take up local command.

By now Japan was in a hopeless state of split personality; while the military hierarchy were sternly bracing their forces for a long last-ditch stand, the diplomats were involved in a frenzy of desperate peace-making. In Switzerland two Japanese officials contacted the Swedish economist Per Jacobsson, who was in close touch with Allen Dulles. They, and the Japanese Naval Attaché at Berne, attempted to discover whether the Americans would modify the unconditional surrender demand, especially in regard to the position of the Emperor. Dulles dashed hither and thither, reporting to Stimson, but at length it appeared that his cloak-and-dagger efforts were all in vain; the Japanese in Switzerland did not have the backing of the Japanese in Tokyo. Togo, the Foreign Minister, concentrated his efforts to secure a peace through Moscow. While Russia was hastily arranging to declare war before it was too late—in order to get the benefit of the Far East concessions made at Yalta—the Japanese Ambassador in Moscow was anxiously trying to get Molotov to act as go-between with the Americans. On July 28th, the military wing still holding the upper hand in Tokyo, the Japanese Government at last announced the rejection of the American ultimatum from Potsdam, in the form of an informal news item on the radio. Four days later an enormous force of US bombers delivered what was officially described as 'the greatest air attack ever'; five cities were struck, almost entirely with incendiaries. The damage was worse even than anything known in Germany.

By now most of the material for the first atomic raids had arrived at the island of Tinian—not without mishap. Some of the most vital parts had been in a plane which had encountered technical trouble and had been forced to crash-land at Sacramento. Another consignment had been aboard the battleship *Indianapolis*, which had been sunk, with the loss of over 1,000 lives, by an enemy torpedo four days after discharging its cargo on July 26th. If it had been sunk before, the atom bombing might very well have been delayed so long that peace would have come first. The final consignment of U–235 (from uranium) was split into three particles, each in a suitcase carried by a security agent. They travelled from Oak Ridge, via Los Alamos, to San Francisco, accompanied by a guard armed with tommy-guns, shot-guns and carbines. They then flew to Tinian by way of Honolulu. At Honolulu observers were amazed to see the plane of General Spaatz, on his way to Guam to assume command of the new Strategic Air Force, being held up on the runway while the three security men were given priority. Spaatz had the delicate task of shortly having to go to Luzon to explain the Manhattan project to MacArthur, and to tell him that his plan to invade Japan would very likely not be needed. In his pocket Spaatz carried the written order for the use of the atom bomb; he had refused to accept it when given verbally. Meanwhile the planes of the 509th had been out on frequent practice runs over Japan, launching on each mission only a single bomb (to the astonishment of Japanese Service experts and civilians alike). The plane which was to drop the first bomb was the *Enola Gay*. On August 5th the crew found that they could not enter their own plane for routine inspection as it was surrounded all day by security guards. After a briefing which succeeded in bewildering the crew even more than they were already, the *Enola Gay* rumbled down the runway at Tinian and took off at 2.45 a.m., August 6th. Cradled in a steel brace in its bomb-bay was the large, cumbersome-looking bomb, known as the 'Gimmick'. The bomb had been assembled in an airfield hut on August 1st and was about fourteen feet long and five feet in diameter. The plane was followed at two-minute intervals by two other B–29s, which were to observe the bombing.

As the plane gained altitude and thundered through the night sky, its engines breathing out the familiar angry-looking blue and red flames, a Navy scientist, Captain William Parsons, fiddled with the detonating system of the bomb. He had only discovered how to do this satisfactorily the previous day. The intention had been to prepare the bomb ready for delivery before take-off, but Parsons and others were alarmed at the thought of what would happen if the plane crashed on take-off. On his own initiative, Parsons had decided to arm the bomb in flight. An expert on ballistics, he had been the chief scientist on the bomb delivery group at Los Alamos. He now worked alone with 'The Gimmick' as the *Enola Gay* headed across the Pacific towards Japan. By 4 a.m. the first grey light of dawn was beginning to light the interior of the plane. About an hour later Colonel Paul Tibbets, at the controls, informed the other eleven men on the plane (the normal crew plus Parsons) that from then on the intercom conversation was to be recorded. 'This is for history,' he said, 'so watch your language. We're carrying the first atomic bomb.' Most of the crew had never before heard of the atomic bomb, and they were still none the wiser. Down below, through breaks in the clouds, they could see the coastline of Japan. Tibbets' orders were to approach Hiroshima first and, if the weather was bad, to go on to Kokura and Nagasaki in turn (Niigata had been dropped as being too far away from Tinian). Somewhere high along the chain of command it had been decided that visual aiming was more sure than radar, with which the planes were equipped. To help Tibbets in his decision, three weather planes had preceded the *Enola Gay* and reported on conditions at the cities; the report from Hiroshima was that the area was covered in thick cloud but above the city itself there was, strangely, a gap in the clouds about ten miles across.*

The city of Hiroshima was known throughout Japan for its exceptionally beautiful willow trees. While practically every other city in Japan had received devastating attention from US bombers, Hiroshima had been almost unscathed during three and a half years of war. (It is believed that only twelve bombs had hitherto been dropped on the city.) It was a port and manufacturing centre (mainly of light industry), but a place that was not often heard of outside Japan. Its population was over 250,000 but many more people, perhaps 50,000, came into work each day from the surround-

* The pilot of the plane which reported on conditions at Hiroshima was Major Claude Eatherly, often mistakenly thought to have been the pilot of the *Enola Gay*; convinced that there should have been a demonstration, he has been in and out of mental hospitals for some years. Tibbets went on in the Air Force to achieve high command.

ing countryside. The Army had recently established their southern headquarters in an ancient moated castle in the city, and there was a large military garrison. By 7.30 a.m. local time the life of Hiroshima had already begun. Early morning sunlight streamed down on the city and bathed it in gentle warmth. Children were on their way to school from the outskirts of town, and commuter trains were rattling in from the country behind. In the city itself women in nearly every home were cooking breakfast over the customary charcoal burners. All over the town work-parties of old men, women and children were gathering for their day's duty in 'patriotic' tasks; their main occupation that day was to help in making the firebreaks in the city centre which were to combat the incendiary-bomb attacks the authorities were expecting. At 7.9 the air-warning system had sounded, and in the break of the clouds over the city a single plane had been seen crawling along in the sky far above. No one had taken much notice, as lone US planes over the city had become quite frequent in recent weeks, and eventually the plane had disappeared and the all-clear had sounded at 7.31. At 8.06 a look-out station in the hills east of the city reported sighting two planes, and three minutes later reported another. A few minutes after that the same report was made by a searchlight unit, and then by an anti-aircraft battery. No warning was sounded, and people, bathed in bright sunlight in the streets, gazed up and could plainly see and hear the three planes high in the blue sky.

In the *Enola Gay* Tibbets was staring down at the city laid out below. Only a few wispy clouds hindered the expansive view, and these marked the city with scattered dark patches of shadow. There were no fighters to be seen and no flak. Tibbets asked Parsons, who had completed his task and was now standing at his shoulder, whether he agreed that it was Hiroshima. Parsons said he agreed. Tibbets ordered everyone to put on the goggles with which they had been issued (even these had been especially designed and made under the giant Manhattan project), and he then gave over control of the plane to Major Thomas W. Ferebee, a veteran of European bombing missions who had been personally selected by Tibbets months before to be the bomb-aimer.* For a few moments the glistening plane above and the basking city below hung suspended in time as their now-inevitable destinies reached out the one for the other. The aiming point, the centre of a bridge, moved towards the cross-hairs of Ferebee's bombsight, just as he had seen it in countless

* Ferebee also rose to high command in the Air Force.

examinations of aerial photographs. At 8.15 plus seventeen seconds the *Enola Gay's* bomb-doors sprang open and the uranium bomb tumbled out broadside, its guiding parachute opened, and it plummeted for the earth nose first.

The *Enola Gay* and the two accompanying planes broke off sharply and veered away in sixty-degree turns.

The bomb exploded exactly on target, 1,000 feet above the ground; it turned into a ball of white-hot fire 1,800 feet across with a temperature at its centre of about one hundred million degrees. It was precisely 8.16 a.m. on Monday, August 6, 1945, and the world had entered into a new age.

(ii)

Those few who survived and could remember anything of the first instant of explosion, speak only of a blinding light. But most people within a mile of the explosion did not even see that; they were burnt to nothing in a flash. A few of them left testimony to their deaths in the form of shadows burnt into the roads and on walls, but most just disappeared. In the city trams blackened corpses sat on the frames of what had been benches a split second before. Everywhere, in houses and out, black bodies lay where they had fallen. Those who had survived the explosion started in horror and were then released from their agony of burning flesh by the hurtling of millions of pieces of shattered glass, wood, material and metal that shredded their bodies into many pieces; for the centre of Hiroshima had literally disintegrated. Tiny fragments of every conceivable object flew outwards with enormous force. Workers in the fields outside the town were peppered with grass and straw. Buildings lay in a heap of smouldering rubble; only a few concrete walls of buildings especially constructed to withstand earthquakes were left standing. For two miles across the centre Hiroshima had become a pile of débris. Survivors looked around in their pain and found themselves, mostly naked or in tattered clothes, in unrecognizable surroundings; the black skins of women were covered in accurate detail with the patterns of the kimonos they had been wearing. Those who had been farther off found themselves cruelly and terribly marked by burns; the marks of braces, which had afforded some protection, were visible on men's chests; men who had been wearing caps were disfigured up to a neat line on the forehead; people who had been sitting at windows were mutilated and burnt on one side only. Some lost their faces, with the rest of their bodies intact, others their hands.

Dr Hachiya had been resting on the floor of his home after a night on duty at the hospital. His first knowledge of the bomb was the sudden disappearance of shadows from the garden through the window. Next he found himself naked in the garden, with a piece of wood protruding from his thigh and his cheek torn away. Running towards the street, he tripped over a man's severed head. A group of soldiers who had been wearing caps had their hair neatly parted and undisturbed, but had lost their faces; eyes, mouths and noses had been burned away. The doctor was able to do nothing for them but pray. Thousands of maimed and dying commuters lay in the main station, screaming for succour and water. Within a few minutes a rain of black ash began to fall on the ruined city, gently descending on survivors and rubble. A few people started to collect together, dazed and bewildered, in small groups. Those on the outskirts of town began running out towards the fields and the hills. What had happened? Just as the remaining inhabitants of what had once been a city called Hiroshima were beginning to ask themselves this question, they were struck by a further disaster; a huge gust of hot air blew back towards the centre. Most of those who had jumped into the seven delta rivers of the town in an attempt to soothe their bodies were drowned in giant waves; others were killed by yet more hurtling débris. As nature, outraged by the injury that had been done to her, gradually subsided, the survivors of the atomic explosion and its immediate after-effects at Hiroshima fled the city. Within a half-hour the whole place was ablaze; the fire continued until the evening, and when it went out Hiroshima as a city for human habitation had ceased to exist.

About 90,000 men, women and children were killed outright or shortly afterwards; about 25,000 of them were babies or boys and girls under the age of eighteen.* The figure was thus more than four times as much as Oppenheimer's estimate. There were half as many permanently injured and disfigured. These figures are little more reliable than a Japanese fatality figure of 150,000. (By 1962 survivors were still dying at the rate of two a week from causes directly attributable to the explosion.)

* These are the generally accepted, approximate figures, although the US Atomic Energy Commission downgrades the fatality to 68,000. The first official figure, issued on February 3rd, 1946, was 78,150.

The crew of the *Enola Gay* knew nothing of what was happening far below. The whole area was hidden by an enormous but tidy cloud that presently began to take on a familiar and homely shape. There was excited comment over the intercom as the crew realized that the cloud looked like an elongated mushroom. As it was clearly impossible to make a report on the effect of the bomb, there being nothing apart from the cloud to see, the three planes headed for base —carefully keeping a good distance from the mysterious cloud as they circled. The somewhat self-conscious comments of the crew were all faithfully recorded: 'Holy Moses, what a mess. . . . My God, what have we done? . . . The war's over! . . . Don't fly so close to that mushroom. . . .' Someone expressed the opinion that Ferebee had missed the city altogether, as it was nowhere to be seen. Another said the reason they could not see the city was because it did not exist any more. During the homeward run the crew philosophized. Tibbets sent off a message to Tinian saying that the mission had been successful. From Tinian the news was flashed to Groves in Washington, who received it shortly before midnight local time. He decided not to disturb Marshall and Stimson at that late hour, and the two men did not receive the news from Groves until more than seven hours later. An hour or so after that a message was sent to the President aboard the *Augusta;* he was bored and homesick and spending most of his time playing poker and swapping stories over bourbon with the Press. Truman, in fact, received news of this momentous event, for which he has taken entire responsibility, over twelve hours after its occurrence; jubilant and excited, he went around the messes on the ship announcing the explosion of an atomic weapon to an uncomprehending crew. 'We won the gamble!' he told them, with evident relief. A statement from Truman had already been prepared, and orders were now given for its release.

By this time the *Enola Gay* had arrived back at base, roared down the runway more than 10,000 lb lighter than it had left, and taxied to a standstill. As the last propeller turned slowly to a halt, a crowd of emotion-charged men crowded round the plane; admirals and generals jostled with clerks, scientists and mechanics. As Tibbets, unshaven and tired-eyed, climbed down, General Spaatz stepped forward and pinned the Distinguished Service Cross on his overalls.* In the interrogation hut the crew were given an oversize measure of whisky each. There was a great deal of joking and natural relief at the successful termination of an important mission.

* Every other serviceman who had participated in the mission was later decorated.

(iii)

In Tokyo, shortly after the explosion, the control operator of the Japanese Broadcasting Corporation noticed that his telephone line to the radio station at Hiroshima had gone dead. He tried to re-establish a connection, but without success. Twenty minutes later the railways signals centre at Tokyo realized that the main telegraph line to Hiroshima had stopped functioning. There was a certain amount of confusion as the previous day the US Air Force had launched a mass raid, of 820 bombers, on various cities, including Kobe; reports of a great deal of damage from incendiaries and heavy demolition bombs were pouring in, and there were a number of uncontrollable fires. Shortly afterwards news came in, from villages north of Hiroshima, that some kind of huge explosion had taken place in the city. About three-quarters of an hour after the bomb had dropped, army head-quarters in Tokyo received news of a mysterious disaster at Hiroshima; it was unable to contact southern command headquarters. It was not until well after midday that a message was received from the army shipping depot on the waterfront at Hiroshima. It stated simply that the city had been annihilated by one bomb. Similar information was beginning to arrive at the newspaper offices, and in mid-afternoon the editors of the five big Tokyo newspapers and the manager of the Domei news agency were called to the Information and Intelligence Office and told that the bomb dropped on Hiroshima was different in conception to an ordinary one, but that until more information had become available the story was not to be treated in any way as exceptional. Tokyo Rose, the famous propaganda broadcaster, mentioned, without referring to the bomb, that train services to Hiroshima had been temporarily discontinued. The authorities were, in fact, almost certain that this had been the first atomic bomb; their own scientists had examined the possibility of such a bomb, and their extremely competent naval Intelligence service had reported US work on such a bomb in 1944. As the news began to filter through government departments, those politicians and diplomats, backed by the Emperor, still free of the military wing knew that at last the crisis they had feared and put off so long had come; there were only two alternatives—a complete show-down with the military, or national suicide.

In Hiroshima those survivors who had been unable to leave the centre of the city had crawled and staggered to one of the few ruined buildings of which parts of the walls were still left standing; that of a newspaper. They lay about, screaming for help; the empty shell, stripped of furniture and windows, acted as a vast sounding-box, and the noise that the five hundred suffering people who gathered there put up was clearly heard on the outskirts, for three days, like a mourning wail over the gutted city. The remnants of the southern army headquarters had fled their shattered castle and, in rags, were attempting to reorganize from a hill-side cave. After twelve hours a few soldiers could be seen doing their best to relieve the dying. Trucks pounded over the débris, collecting corpses, which were thrown into pits; there were no discernible roads in the centre of the city.

The first people to arrive at Hiroshima from the outside world were a Major Hirano and a team of official investigators who flew from Tokyo in a light plane. The officer who came out to meet them as their plane landed presented a horrifying spectacle; his face was sharply and neatly divided straight down the middle, one side smooth and unhurt, the other black and a mass of blisters.

(iv)

In the United States there had been fine and enjoyable weather throughout the nation. There was wide interest as to the way the war was going, but few people expected an invasion of Japan before the autumn. To most people it had been a working Monday just like any other. The musical *Oklahoma!*, which had been a tremendous success, was about to set up a milestone when its touring company earned the show's millionth dollar at its performance that night in Philadelphia. In Los Angeles there had been a slight sensation in the morning when a popular crooner, Frank Sinatra, had dived into the harbour to save a three-year-old boy from drowning. In New York there had been scenes almost reminiscent of pre-war days when the *Queen Mary* had sailed with nine hundred passengers of whom some were actually civilians, with trunks, boxes and flowers instead of kit-bags and rifles. On loan to the United States, she was returning to Europe to pick up more American troops being sent home from Germany. As people began to drift home or to the cinema, they glanced at the afternoon newspapers. There were a number of good new films including *Anchors Aweigh*, and Danny Kaye in *Wonder*

Man. In automobiles radios were switched on and the popular tunes of the moment were played by the popular bands, like those of Tommy Dorsey and Les Brown; tunes like 'Don't Fence Me In', 'The Trolly Song', 'Sentimental Journey', and 'June is Bustin' Out All Over'. And then, suddenly, on the front pages of the newspapers and on news flashes on the radio, there was an unexpected and electrifying announcement: 'Sixteen hours ago an American plane dropped one bomb on Hiroshima, an important Japanese army base. That bomb has more power than 20,000 tons of TNT. It had more than 2,000 times the blast power of the British Grand Slam, which was the largest bomb yet used in the history of warfare. . . . It is a harnessing of the basic power of the Universe.' The announcement bore every sign of having been carefully prepared from a propaganda and justification point of view; although issued in Truman's name, and authorized by him before he had left Potsdam, it was not written by him. The mention of the horrific Grand Slam, not an American weapon, seemed on the face of it to be somewhat beside the point; there were also careful mentions of Pearl Harbour and of the German V-rockets. The statement was not entirely honest; it was said that the Germans had been working 'feverishly' to build such a bomb, although American Intelligence knew that this was not so; it was also said that the ultimatum from Potsdam had been a clear warning to the Japanese people to save them 'from utter destruction'. If they did not accept the ultimatum now they could expect 'a rain of ruin from the air the like of which has never been seen on this earth'. Finally, it stated that 'under present circumstances' it had been decided, 'contrary to the habit of scientists of this country or the policy of this Government', to withhold the secret of the bomb's manufacture. At Oak Ridge, Tennessee, an enterprising newsdealer sold 1,600 copies of a local newspaper at one dollar each in half an hour to the amazed workers who had helped produce the bomb without knowing it. The following afternoon the *Augusta* entered Chesapeake Bay after a record run from Europe, and late in the evening the President was considerably gratified to be back in the White House once more, after having been away for a month. There he waited anxiously, like millions of others throughout the world, to hear what had happened to Hiroshima.

In Britain the news had been announced late on Monday, but was not widely known until the morning papers of August 7th were read. It had been the traditional August Bank Holiday, the first in peacetime for six years. In some ways it had been the happiest day for all that time; even more satisfying than VE Day itself. For there had been a prevailing mood of 'back to normal' about the day to which many people had contributed and many enjoyed. There had been racing at Ascot, where the King and Queen had arrived in time to see the King's horse win the fourth race. Apart from a brief thunderstorm in mid-afternoon, it had been a fine summer's day with blue skies over which occasional white clouds leisurely passed. Attendances at sporting events had seldom, if ever, been surpassed. At Lord's cricket ground, in London, the fourth Victory Test between England and Australia had drawn a crowd of 34,000, a record for the ground; a young Australian Air Force officer, K. R. Miller, had scored a scintillating 107 not out. The gates had been closed soon after the start of play. At the White City Stadium there had been what *The Times* described as 'the most important athletics meeting held there for many years'. In the mile Arne Anderson, of Sweden, had come in first, in 4 min 8.8 sec, with Corporal Sidney Wooderson second. The two miles had been won by the great Swedish runner Gundar Haegg. The stadium was closed by the time the meeting had begun, with an attendance of 52,000, the largest crowd ever assembled until that time for an athletics meeting in Britain; throughout most of the day over 50,000 more waited patiently, in well-ordered queues, outside, although there was no hope of getting in—some people said that, after the regimentation of the war, queues had become such a habit to the British that they could not resist joining them whenever they were sighted. Long queues at Odeon cinemas throughout the country waited to see one of the most popular British films ever made, *The Way to the Stars*, with leading film stars like John Mills, Trevor Howard and Michael Redgrave, and a haunting theme tune. It was the age of the cinema; other popular films on general release were *A Song to Remember*, *Meet Me in St Louis*, *Wilson*, and *The Constant Nymph* with Charles Boyer and Joan Fontaine, and *National Velvet* with Elizabeth Taylor, a twelve-year-old discovery. In the world of variety and music-hall a flood of popular new personalities were emerging from the disbanded concert-parties of the Services. Boats and bathers had appeared on the Thames; and the seaside resorts, still littered with rusty barbed wire and ugly concrete blocks, were crowded with sunbathers and visitors, most of whom arrived by train, there still being comparatively few cars on the roads. The 51st season of the Promenade Concerts was to begin the following day at the Albert Hall.

It was late on that Bank Holiday night that the new Prime Minister made his announcement; he took a very easy way out of a difficult problem, and after a brief introduction he frankly issued the statement that had been prepared by and for Churchill some weeks previously. Many of the words were obviously Churchill's. Typically, Churchill kept all sign of the Anglo-American breach over the bomb from public view: 'The smoothness with which the arrangements for co-operation which were made in 1943 have been carried into effect is a happy augury for our future relations.' These words were, as he has since revealed, almost the exact opposite to what he was thinking. He explained why British work on the project had been transferred to America: 'Great Britain at this period was fully extended in war production, and we could not afford such grave interference with the current munitions programmes on which our warlike operations depended. Moreover, Great Britain was within easy range of German bombers. . . . The decision was therefore taken to build the full-scale production plants in America.' Churchill ended in characteristic vein: 'This revelation of the secrets of nature, long mercifully withheld from man, should arouse the most solemn reflections in the mind and conscience of every human being capable of comprehension. We must indeed pray that these awful agencies will be made to conduce to peace among the nations, and that instead of wrecking measureless havoc upon the entire globe they may become a perennial fountain of world prosperity.' Churchill at this time did not have grave doubts as to the use of the bomb, but Attlee, who had acquiesced in the decision at Potsdam, was more concerned than his issuing of Churchill's statement would indicate. On August 8th he sent a personal telegram to Truman in which he noted: 'When we were at Potsdam the potentiality of the atomic bomb had not become actuality and the pressure of immediate problems was too heavy to give us the opportunity of discussing the implications. . . . There is widespread anxiety.' He urged careful consideration on the problems of control of atomic weapons.

Among those who heard the Attlee–Churchill statement with great interest were the group of German nuclear physicists, headed by Otto Hahn, who had been engaged on the similar German project, but without material encouragement from the Nazis. They were now interned at an English country house. Hahn was so depressed at the thought that the Allies had succeeded in making the bomb, when he was convinced that he, too, could have done so, that his colleagues had to sit with him till he fell asleep in case he took his own life.

There was also an announcement in Canada in which the important contribution of Canada as the supplier of the raw material, and the provider of research facilities at Montreal and elsewhere, was stressed. It was not made clear whether Canada, in its strong position as virtually the only practical supplier of uranium ore, had been consulted over the dropping of the bomb.

While the world waited to hear what the Japanese reaction to the atomic bomb was to be, newspapers and authorities of all kinds gave their views as day after day went by and no Japanese surrender was announced. In Britain, which had suffered so heavily itself from the destruction of war, the news was received sombrely and with cold appraisal; one of the major reactions was a desire to know precisely how much Britain had been responsible for the scientific achievement; there were conflicting reports about this. The London *Times* wrote of 'a revolution in earthly affairs', and its Scientific Correspondent, in an article 'Atomic Bombs Explained', warned that such bombs could lead 'to wars which, in twenty years' time, can only have one end, the total extinction of civilization'. Niels Bohr, writing in the same newspaper, reflected on 'the present crisis of humanity'. Dean Inge, in an article in the *Sunday Dispatch*, was in particularly pessimistic vein. He wrote: 'It may well be that we have come to the parting of the ways. The spectacle of a possible suicide of civilization, to be followed by a long Dark Age, is now before our eyes.' In his column in the same newspaper, the popular philosopher, C. E. M. Joad, had a more encouraging prediction: 'There is the hope that fear and horror may do what wisdom and decency have always failed to do—stop war.' He also said: 'Will nobody stop these damned scientists, put them in a bag and tie them up?' A few days later Sir Arthur Harris, of Bomber Command, said: 'The atomic bomb has put invasions out of date. Coupled with the scientific direction of missiles, the possibilities do not bear contemplation. We are at the end of a thousand-year phase of stability in weapons. Clearly the next war, if it occurs, will be the atomic war. No country will be able to remain outside it. All that is required now is range.'

In America, on the other hand, there was a feeling of shock and uncertainty throughout the country; the reaction to the news surprised the administration. It seemed that the Franck Report, in warning that the American public would not be pleased to know that it had been the United States which had introduced this weapon to war, was proving to be correct. A critical statement was issued on behalf of the Federal Council of Churches by a leading Republican and lawyer, John Foster Dulles: 'If we, a professedly Christian nation, feel morally free to. use atomic energy in this way, men elsewhere will accept the verdict . . . the stage will be set for the sudden and final destruction of mankind.' The *New York Times* said: 'In the bewilderment that such a stupendous announcement must bring one consequence stands clear: civilization and humanity can now survive only if there is a revolution in mankind's political thinking.' The paper's military specialist said: 'We have been the first to introduce a new weapon of unknowable effects which may bring us the victory quickly but which will sow the seeds of hate more widely than ever; we may yet reap the whirlwind.' The *Herald Tribune* said that, in comparison with the 'unlocking of the atom', defeat and victory in the war were merely tiny ripples on the surface of history. The *Baltimore Sun* revealed that there had been a secret committee which had reported unfavourably on the use of the bomb; why the authorities had decided to go against the advice of the committee was 'a matter of conjecture'.

During the week Japanese broadcasts began admitting the extent of the damage at Hiroshima, and the fact that the United States possessed a new, powerful weapon. One broadcast said that the damage was so great that the authorities had been unable to ascertain its full extent. This was the first news the world—by now acutely inquisitive as to what had happened at the city—had received of the damage. It was not until Thursday that the United States announced the results of a reconnaissance flight; 4·1 square miles of the city had been obliterated. Japanese broadcasts became more indignant; one said that the employment of the bomb was 'sufficient to brand the enemy for ages to come as the destroyer of mankind and as the public enemy of social justice'. The horrified world learnt from another, which was widely reported, that 'the impact of the bomb was so terrific that practically all living things were literally seared to death by the tremendous heat and pressure engendered by the blast'. It was stated at Strategic Air Force headquarters on Guam that dead and wounded might exceed 100,000. Millions of people, the world over, read and pondered.

The Swedish newspapers were second only to the Japanese in denouncing the use of the bomb. The important Stockholm evening paper *Aftonbladet* said in a leading article: 'Although Germany began bomb warfare against open towns and civilian populations, all records in this field have been beaten by the Anglo-Saxons. The so-called rules of war which were hailed in 1939 must brand the bombing of Hiroshima as a first-class war crime. It is all very well if atom raids can shorten the war, but this experiment with the population of an entire city as guinea-pigs reflects no martial glory on its authors.' The Vatican newspaper *Osservatore Romano* said that 'this incredibly destructive instrument remains a temptation for posterity'.

Still the world waited anxiously for the announcement of a Japanese surrender.

The Anglo-American allies displayed their confidence by revealing, shortly after the release of the Smyth Report, which gave some non-secret data about the atomic bombs, yet another of the great secrets of the war: radar. The whole story of this technique and its secret use in the war was described in long articles in the newspapers and magazines. In America, it was an American achievement; *Time* magazine attributed it to two US Navy scientists, Albert Taylor and Leo C. Young. Officially it was said that radar had been pioneered in the United States in the 1920s and 1930s. In Britain, it was a British achievement, attributed to Sir Robert Watson-Watt. As with most scientific discoveries, it was difficult to prove any one person's contribution as the decisive one, but it was certainly Watson-Watt who had produced the first practical proposals for locating aircraft by radio beams. The facts were that, while the United States, Britain and Germany had all been working on the principles of radar in the 1930s, the British were the first to evolve the high-powered magnetron that made it a workable proposition; the design was brought to America in great secrecy in the autumn of 1940 by a British engineer who delivered a small black bag, containing design and model, to an official of the Bell Telephone Company. By that time Britain was completely covered by radar defence; the first radar station (the first in the world) had been set up as long before as 1935, and in Easter 1939 a twenty-four-hour radar watch along the whole British coast from Scapa Flow to Portsmouth had been instituted. The radar defence system had been the winning card in the Battle of Britain; without it there is grave doubt as to whether the battle could have been won. The rather cross British attitude was summed up by Sir Stafford Cripps, the new President of the Board of Trade, in a Press conference on August 14th: 'The Americans will be announcing the great part they had played,' he said. 'There is no competition for glory between the two countries, for they have worked hand in hand.' He then went on to give a long and exhaustive history of the work of Watson-Watt and other British scientists.

(v)

The Russian leaders, sensing it would soon be too late, had hurried their country into a war with Japan two days after Hiroshima, although it had been thought this action would not be possible until mid-August, and although the Russo-Chinese talks were still not completed. Harriman saw Molotov and Stalin, and the Marshal mentioned casually to him that he had heard of the Hiroshima bombing with great interest, and that Soviet scientists had been working on the same problem but had been unable to solve it. Harriman promptly reported this interesting piece of information direct to Truman. The American administration had now got what it had been angling for, despite the advice of Eisenhower, Leahy and others, for so long, and for which it had made so many concessions: Russian participation in the Japanese war. But now, far from being a blessing, it was an embarrassment. A statement by Molotov explained the declaration of war as follows: 'Taking into consideration Japan's refusal to capitulate, the Allies have addressed to the Soviet Government a proposal to join in the war against Japanese aggression, thereby shortening the duration of the war, reducing the numbers of victims, and assisting in the speediest restoration of general peace. True to its duty to the Allies, the Soviet Government has accepted the proposal of the Allies and has associated itself with the Allied declaration of July 26th.' The implication was plain; only by Russia entering the war, albeit somewhat reluctantly, would the Allies be able to end it quickly. The suggestion that the Allies had asked Russia to join in the war only *after* the rejection of the ultimatum was incorrect. There had been no such request since Potsdam; and, since the successful atom explosion test, no need for one. Within hours Red Army mechanized units were pouring into Japanese-held Manchuria in four main thrusts, and were also threatening to move southwards down the island of Sakhalin. Within forty-eight hours, meeting only spasmodic opposition, they had already covered about sixty miles on all fronts. (Japanese Intelligence had—correctly—forecast an American invasion at Hangchow Bay planned for the autumn, and had built up a force in that area at the expense of their forces on the Russian border.)

During all this time US Air Force units kept up a daily battering of cities and towns in Japan, concentrating on the ports of the main islands of Kyushu and Honshu. On the day after Hiroshima, 130 planes had bombed Japan; the following day 420 took part in day and night attacks. Admiral Halsey's Third Fleet had reached Japanese home waters and was steaming up and down the coast bombarding the shore with almost complete impunity. As early as July 11th the Secretary of the Navy had stated that the Allies had complete control of all Pacific waters right up to the Japanese coast. There was little opposition from any quarter. The planes received scant attention from the defenders, and the ships, although attacked by an occasional *kamikaze* (by now there were few airworthy planes left in Japan), suffered no serious losses after the sinking of the *Indianapolis*.

The plan to launch the second atom bomb, the plutonium one known affectionately by its makers as 'Fat Man', had been brought forward from August 11th to August 9th, it being believed that a swift one-two ploy would have the best psychological effect on the Japanese, and that bad weather expected shortly might delay the bombing. Spaatz's command also requested permission to use a third bomb, shortly to be available, on Tokyo. It was desired to use the bomb on the capital at night-time, but Washington was unable to come to a decision on this point. The campaign requesting the citizens of the big cities to leave them immediately was stepped up; many thousands of leaflets had already been dropped, but not, unfortunately, on Hiroshima. Truman and Marshall both took an interest in this matter. New leaflets were now dropped, including one with a picture of the cloud over Hiroshima taken by one of the crew of the *Enola Gay*. It read in part: 'You should take steps now to cease military resistance. Otherwise we shall resolutely employ this bomb and all our other superior weapons to promptly and force-fully end the war. Evacuate your cities now!' Some millions of these were printed, and a few hundred thousands found their way to Japan. It was agreed that they should be dropped on the city of Nagasaki.

'Fat Man' left Tinian at 3.49 a.m. on August 9th. Unlike 'Little Boy', it was not possible to arm it in flight and, fearful of a crash on take-off, fire-fighting and fire-engines, perhaps a little puny in the circumstances, had lined the runway as the B–29 roared off into the night. On board one of the two observation planes were two British observers, Group Captain Leonard Cheshire, VC, late of 617 Squadron RAF, and a scientist, William Penney. They had been at Tinian for a month, and with some difficulty London had persuaded

Washington to let them go as official British observers. A reporter from the *New York Times*, William L. Laurence, also went along. Kokura was found to be completely covered by cloud. After three passes over the city innocently going about its morning business below, the planes reluctantly went on to Nagasaki. It, too, lay hidden beneath a layer of cloud. Countermanding Washington's orders, the bomb run was begun on radar; the captain being somewhat anxious about shortage of fuel. It has always been insisted that at the last minute a hole was found in the clouds and that the bomb was aimed through this. The bomb exploded three miles off target, near one of the best hospitals in the Far East; although a greater explosion even than that of the uranium bomb, it caused less damage, but it was still the second greatest man-made catastrophe the world had known.* As at Hiroshima, no one really knows the exact figures of casualties and fatalities, or anything like them, but it is probable that about 40,000 people were killed outright or died shortly after, and about 25,000 permanently blinded, afflicted or crippled; it seems that there were more immediate deaths from burning and less from flying débris than at Hiroshima. Among those who died were British and Dutch prisoners-of-war in the prison camp at the city; it was the presence of this camp that had made the inhabitants of Nagasaki confident that they would not suffer a fate similar to that of Hiroshima. Also killed were 40 per cent of the city's Christian community, which had always been the largest in Japan. About one-third of the city was obliterated, including six hospitals, a prison, two schools, a home for the blind and dumb, and two war plants. Laurence, watching from the plane above, described the cloud that rose above the town as 'a living totem pole, carved with many grotesque masks grimacing at the earth'. As Nagasaki groaned and suffered in its agony, it had a further visitation from the Strategic Air Force; this time the planes dropped thousands of fluttering leaflets urging the population to evacuate their ruined city—it was possible, said the leaflets, that Nagasaki would be attacked by a new and devastating bomb.†

Leonard Cheshire was soon flying on his way to Attlee to report what he had seen.

---

* The largest unnatural explosion before Hiroshima was when the *Mont Blanc*, carrying TNT and 2,300 tons of lyddite, blew up at Halifax, NS, in 1917.

† Both cities have recovered from the devastation; Hiroshima's main occupation is a macabre tourist industry, one of the biggest in the world (2,000,000 visitors a year). Survivors carry green cards authorizing them free medical attention anywhere in Japan; there are deformed births and cases of leukaemia.

It was a few hours after the bombing when President Truman went on the air to say: 'I urge Japanese civilians to leave the industrial cities immediately and save themselves from destruction.' He said that atom bombs would be dropped on Japan one after the other until she surrendered, apparently unaware that it would be many months before the bombs could be manufactured at more than a tiny trickle. After the bomb expected to arrive shortly at Tinian, only the fourth to be made, there was no telling how long it would take before another would be available. One of the most striking features of the whole episode is the clear indication that the left hand of the US administration was strangely out of contact with the right hand. It is almost as if the bombs, guided by some evil force, had thrust off human control altogether. It is clear that final control, and thus responsibility, was not being placed on any single person. Neither Spaatz, Groves, Arnold, Marshall, nor even Stimson was holding firm control over events; because of the unique nature of the weapon, and the circumstances, they were all looking elsewhere, mainly towards the President, who in turn failed to grasp the reins and stared back at them once the order of July 24th had been authorized by him. That order can be seen now to have been far from satisfactory, permitting as it did the use of four bombs when the effects on a city of one had not been seen; circumstances after the first bomb were certainly going to be different from those existing before it.

Intense political and diplomatic activity took place in Tokyo after Hiroshima. Togo, the Foreign Minister, had made desperate efforts to get the Russians to mediate; but with no success. At least one of the leading Tokyo newspapers was writing openly of the advisability of surrender. For the first time some of the militarists began admitting that Japan faced defeat, but they still insisted that the country would find glory and honour in fighting till the last despite the atom bombs. They were prepared to negotiate for peace, but were too proud to accept unconditional surrender. Togo, with the backing of the depressed and dispirited Prime Minister, Suzuki, called on Hirohito and explained the atom bomb to him; he said he believed the only possible course was surrender. The Emperor agreed. He had been prepared to sue for peace for some time (according to one source since February 1944), and had formally proposed it at an Imperial conference on June 22nd. The only question had been how much of the conquered territory could be retained for Japan's crowded and seething millions. He now ordered that all time-wasting negotiating for advantageous conditions should stop, and the war should be ended immediately. This, however, was easier said than done because the militarists were still powerful, although they were now without the support of the Emperor. When the Supreme War Council met on August 9th, word had just been received of the disaster at Nagasaki. Coupled with the news the previous day that Russia had entered the war, it was now clear to even the most fervent patriots that Japan was finished. The Council argued all day, with only short breaks for refreshments. The War Minister held his bloc together, and Togo his; the voting was even. Suzuki was reluctant to break the stalemate by casting a vote himself, but solved the situation honourably for all, and avoided taking the ultimate responsibility on himself, by a brilliant manoeuvre; in the early hours of the morning he proposed that the decision should be left to the Emperor himself. The War Minister and his colleagues agreed. Hirohito, who had been in touch with the deliberations through his Lord Privy Seal, himself went to the Council chamber and said that the surrender was to be accepted. Acceptance of the Potsdam terms, on condition that the Emperor was to be retained, was announced on the radio later that day, and was picked up on short-wave radio by a San Francisco engineer. But the Allies refused to accept this as official, and hostilities did not cease, especially in outlying theatres (such as New Guinea, where the Australians were still advancing) and in Manchuria (where the Russians were collecting as much territory as possible in the time available). Nimitz ordered: 'Offensive action shall be continued.' In China there were reports that the Communist armies were approaching Peking.

While approaches were made through Switzerland and Sweden (for great nations at war do not correspond directly, even when they want the war to end), the world waited.* Press comment on the news of Nagasaki had become a little hysterical. The London *Times* said: 'It is believed that a large part of Nagasaki, a city of 250,000 people, no longer exists.' There were few people in the world who wanted any more atomic bombs. But Japan's answer, in diplomatic code, took a long time to creak through the uncertain radio channels between Tokyo and Berne. Everyone knew the war was over, but nobody could quite believe it until the President said it was really true. In London, street celebrations on the night

* The war imposed a heavy strain on the Swiss diplomatic service; a staff of sixty was required in London to look after German interests. The Swiss had been unable to relieve their Legation in Tokyo since 1942.

of the 10th fizzled out in the early evening; but London, with its mass of American and British troops on leave from Europe, had been a celebrating city for over three months. For weeks it had been practically impossible to get a taxi, which were all packed with American troops sightseeing in the city. On nearly all West End streets, and at all the famous meeting places, vendors with Allied flags and rosettes had long been doing a brisk and apparently inexhaustible trade. A statement was issued from Downing Street, saying: 'No official confirmation has yet been received of the many rumours at present circulating. . . . It is in the national interest that work should continue.'

In America there was a great surge of excitement and relief. Truman held a meeting to discuss the offer. The difficult question of the Emperor had been discussed many times before, but no decision had ever been reached; public opinion regarded Hirohito as a war criminal, but the British and some of Truman's own advisers and experts considered him essential for maintaining law and order in Japan. Many considered that Japan would have surrendered already if his safety had been made plain in the Potsdam declaration. Stimson and Leahy felt that the Japanese should be allowed to keep their Emperor. Forrestal thought that a carefully worded reply should be made, accepting in practice, but insisting on a rigid interpretation of the Potsdam ultimatum in theory. Byrnes favoured total unconditional surrender. Truman asked Byrnes to prepare a reply along the lines suggested by Forrestal. This, in turn, had to be shown to the other allies: Britain, China and Russia. It was agreed by all, except by the British, who suggested that Hirohito should not himself be made to sign the surrender, only to authorize it. Truman agreed to this, despite Chinese pressure. Molotov insisted that the peace communiqué should include an announcement implying joint Allied occupation of Japan, but Harriman protested vehemently, and after Stalin intervened Molotov retracted.

For four days the world waited in an agony of half-suppressed joy and excitement.

In Japan there was near-chaos; the military attempted a *coup d'état*, and there was some fighting. Another huge bomber raid was launched on the morning of August 14th; over four hundred bombers took part in the assault, one of the main targets of which were the railway yards near Hiroshima. Rebels raided the Imperial Palace, but somehow, after three days, a reply to the American note was delivered in Washington by the Swiss *Chargé d'Affaires*. Like the Allied statement, it neither indicated whether the Emperor would remain or whether he would go.

On the evening of August 14th the White House correspondents were assembled and briefly told that the war was over, and the world started to hear very soon afterwards; as soon as he had told the correspondents, the President did not forget to telephone the good tidings to his mother. New York had already accepted a news broadcast earlier in the day as being authoritative (it had been based on a false report from Berne), and was celebrating hard. As on VE Day, the first spectacular celebrations had occurred on the subway. In the packed trains office workers and young people shouted, sang, waved flags and streamers, and blew whistles. The holiday mood had increased during the day, and by early evening the jostling, cheering crowd was estimated by the police to be 100,000 strong. Truman, for ever cautious, announced to the correspondents that an official VJ Day would not be held until the surrender document was actually signed. There was evidence that Americans were not prepared to heed this further delay. Dancing, singing and every kind of noise continued in many streets throughout the night. The correspondent of the *Daily Telegraph* wired to London: 'It is difficult to imagine to what heights this celebration will reach. It promises to be the wildest New York has experienced.' It was the same story of riotous crowds in all other major cities.

In London it was late at night when the news came through. A great melody of wailing rose from ships' sirens on the Thames. In many parts of the country bonfires blazed as far as the eye could see. The Prime Minister made a broadcast at midnight. His attitude was different from that of the President. He said: 'Here at home you have earned a short rest from the unceasing exertions which you have all borne without flinching or complaint for so many years. I have no doubt that throughout industry generally the Government's lead in the matter of victory holidays will be followed, and that tomorrow and Thursday will everywhere be treated as holidays.' That was enough, and two more days of boisterous and uninhibited celebration were ushered in with official blessing. By the time it was over most people were to be well sated with Union Jacks, 'Land of Hope and Glory', rattles, beer and paper-hats on which were written 'Kiss Me Quick'; but it was with such ritual that the greatest war the world had ever known ended in many a city and town in Britain, the United States and the Dominions.

By coincidence the following day, August 16th, had previously been arranged as the occasion of the opening of the first new Parliament for ten years. The drive of the King and Queen from Buckingham Palace to Westminster, in the Royal coach, had over-night become a victory procession watched and cheered by a vast crowd that assembled with gaiety, singing and fireworks during the night and morning. During the drive, as was only to be expected, it began to rain. The Queen, in a light blue costume and delicate hat, sat bolt upright, soaking wet, and acknowledged the madly cheering and waving crowds with a happy and glowing smile. In Parliament, George VI read out his speech, which, as tradition demanded, was s declaration of the new Government's policy; never before had a British sovereign formally uttered measures of such strong Social-ism. There had been some talk of how long the monarchy could last in the new era being brought in, and the Prime Minister obliquely referred to this. 'We have had a General Election which has brought great alteration in the composition of this House. (Cheers.) We have had a change of government, but in the midst of change there are things which remain unaltered. Among them is the loyalty and devotion of the House to His Majesty. It is the glory of our demo-cratic constitution that the will of the people operates, and the changes which in other countries are brought about only through civil strife and bloodshed, here in these islands proceed through the peaceful method of the ballot-box. The institution of monarchy in this country, worked out through long years of constitutional development, works free from many of those evils which we have seen arise in other countries. The peaceful transfer of power from one political party to another works very smoothly, and its acceptance has been a demonstration to the world of the workings of a real democracy.' This was followed by a moving tribute to the King from William Gallacher, Communist. The King returned to Buckingham Palace, having heard that the monarchy was as safe as it had ever been, something which he had himself never for a moment doubted. That it was, in his own modest person, perhaps more popular than ever before in its long history was amply demonstrated throughout the next two days when huge crowds assembled outside Buckingham Palace and repeatedly called for and cheered King George VI. That same night the King broadcasted to his people throughout the world, and the speech, spoken in the familiar, soft, struggling, slightly slurred tones that were so strangely hypnotic, was relayed to a crowd of nearly a quarter of a million in St James's

Park (probably the largest gathering in British history). He finished with these words: 'In many anxious times in our long history the unconquerable spirit of our peoples has served us well, bringing us to safety out of great peril. Yet I doubt if anything in all that has gone before has matched the enduring courage and the quiet determination which you have shown during these last six years. . . . The world has come to look for certain things, for certain qualities, from the peoples of the Commonwealth and Empire. We have our part to play in restoring the shattered fabric of civilization. It is a proud and difficult part, and if you carry on in the years to come as you have done so splendidly in the war, you and your children can look forward to the future not with fear, but with high hopes of a surer happiness for all. It is to this great task that I call you now, and I know that I shall not call in vain. In the meantime, from the bottom of my heart I thank my peoples for all that they have done, not only for themselves but for mankind.'

In Whitehall the great throng chanted outside the Ministry of Health building, as it had just over three months before, for Winston Churchill. But Churchill was not there, and a new leader came out on the balcony to speak to the crowd. But Clement Attlee was not this time the man the crowd wanted, and his speech, in comparison to the tremendous and breathless silence in which the VE crowd had listened to Churchill, was half lost in explosions, rattles, laughter and songs. The crowds in London and the provinces on VJ night were, if anything, a little larger than those of VE night, but the abandon was, if anything, a little less; some observers noticed a prevailing feeling of guilt due to the atom bombings.

In Australia there were scenes described as the wildest in the Dominion's history. There were celebrations of varying intensity in all Allied capitals, and there was some rather half-hearted rejoicing in Germany.

In New York and other American cities the day was a little quieter than the preceding one, many people still recovering from too little sleep and too much drink. Most of the population of the country took the day off, although the President had specifically announced that there was to be no holiday yet except for government employees. The centres of many cities resembled minor battlefields. In San Francisco street-cars were wrecked, shop windows broken, and liquor stores looted; five people had been killed and three hundred injured. In Chicago paper and confetti was ankle deep; many people had been injured by trampling. New Orleans had 'gone wild', and public transport in Detroit had come to a standstill as thousands of workers had flocked from war plants on hearing of Truman's announcement in the White House. The scene at Pearl Harbour was described as 'bedlam', every ship in the harbour firing off guns and signals despite urgent commands to stop from Naval HQ; the somewhat alcoholic celebration 'continued for three or four days'. On Okinawa there was a similar outburst, with as many guns going off as in the height of battle; six men were killed and thirty wounded. During August 15th it was announced in Washington that the Army's munitions programme was being cut back immediately by 94 per cent; that seven million men would be demobilized during the next year; that petrol rationing would cease immediately.

In the East, spasmodic fighting continued for a few days in Bougainville, in New Guinea (where the 14,000 starving troops had received no supplies from Japan since April 1944) and in Burma, where local Japanese commanders were loathe to believe the Allied leaflets announcing the surrender. In Malaya an invasion of the peninsula, that had been planned, anyway, for September 9th, took place peacefully. In Japan, Hirohito dismissed the Suzuki Government, and crowds lay prostrate outside the Imperial Palace. The expected mass suicides did not occur, but there were a number of individuals who took their own lives, including the War Minister, the Chief of Staff and his wife, and the Commander of the *kamikaze*, who left a message saying: 'You have died as human bullets, convinced of final victory which did not come true. I wish my death to express my regret and sorrow to you and to your loved ones left behind.' The Emperor had made his first broadcast, in which he said: ' . . . What is worse, the enemy, who has recently made use of an inhuman bomb, is incessantly subjecting innocent people to grievous wounds and massacre. The devastation is taking on incalculable proportions. To continue the war under these conditions would lead to the annihilation of our nation.' His subjects listened to the Imperial voice, many of them on their knees, with wonder but little understanding—as the Emperor spoke in court Japanese.

MacArthur, who had been appointed Supreme Allied Commander for Japan, and Mountbatten organized the urgent problem of occupying and relieving such Japanese-held territories as the Dutch East Indies, Borneo, Indo-China, Hong Kong (where sniping continued till September 2nd), Luzon (where Yamashita offered to surrender on August 25th in a message written in immaculate and formal English), and the remaining occupied islands of the Philippine Archipelago and the Pacific. A British officer reached Hong Kong on August 30th, more than two weeks after the capitulation, to the extreme annoyance of Chiang Kai-shek who had been hoping his own troops would reach the colony first in order to accept the Japanese surrender. British warships arrived off Singapore on September 3rd and a force landed from HMS *Sussex* on September 5th; the take-over took place peacefully. The Union Jack with which Lieutenant-General A. E. Percival had gone to surrender to the Japanese three and a half years before, and which had been hidden by prisoners-of-war in Changi Jail, was raised over the city. The released prisoners at Singapore, as elsewhere, presented a horrifying spectacle. Slim wrote of them: 'All emaciated, many walking skeletons, numbers covered with supurating sores, and most naked but for the ragged shorts they had worn for years or loin cloths of sacking.' Relief teams were parachuted into these foul camps, but it was many days before all were relieved.

The war was over. What people wanted to know was: How had it been won? Churchill later wrote: 'It would be a mistake to suppose that the fate of Japan was settled by the atomic bomb. Her defeat was certain before the first bomb fell, and was brought about by overwhelming maritime power.' The debate has lasted ever since, and is not likely to be ever finalized. Truman will always be open to criticism for failing to insist on a real warning of revolutionary weapons in the Potsdam ultimatum; a warning which many advisers had urged him to make and to which he had agreed. The bombs were used, and some Americans' lives were saved by shortening the war; about 130,000 died in order to accomplish that. How much was the war shortened? The evidence now would suggest by two or three weeks; not only were Hirohito and Togo gaining ascendancy over the militarists, a process which would have been, anyway, increased when Russia declared war, but Japan was physically unable to continue effective operations much longer due especially to shortage of fuel, food and raw materials for which she relied to a great extent on overseas supplies; as J. F. C. Fuller has pointed out, Japan's 'strategical centre of gravity lay in her Navy and Merchant Service', and she was unable to use either. United States submarines played the major role in the defeat of Japan. But instead of hastening this process by bombing docks and shipping, the Air Force acted independently of the main strategic theme and concentrated, as in Europe, on industrial and terror bombing that succeeded in completely burning out more than 100 square miles in the five major cities (General Arnold's own figure), the main effect of which, again as in Europe, was to make the first years of peace in Japan almost as difficult and expensive for the United States as the war had been. In the end this air-minded strategy, seemingly so much easier and simpler than the original strategy of isolation or the Army project of invasion, won the day in the use of the atom bombs. American Intelligence, so busy in Europe, was, in the East, either inefficient or unheard.* Japan had been probing for peace since early June. It has been said that the atom bombs were really aimed at Russia and not at Japan, in an attempt to warn Russia of American might. There is no evidence at all to support this view; United States policy at the time was still to try to live with Russia as an ally. Finally, there is no firm evidence that the Nagasaki bomb had any effect on the course of the war whatever. Truman's Chief of Staff, Leahy, has said: 'It is my opinion that the use of this barbarous weapon was of no material assistance in our war against Japan.' One of the strongest critics of area bombing and of the atomic bombing of August 1945 has been the *US Strategic Bombing Survey* itself, in which the categoric opinion is given—'supported by the testimony of the surviving Japanese leaders involved'—that Japan would have surrendered (with the proviso about the Emperor which was eventually granted) not long after August 14th, without invasion, even if the bombs had not been dropped and Russia had not entered the war; the militarists in Tokyo had lost confidence, face and power. This has been confirmed by Suzuki.

The cost of the war had been inestimable; Britain, Russia and Germany had suffered most. From the fifty-seven belligerent nations, about thirty million people had died as a result of the war. Britain had lost 397,762 servicemen killed, to say nothing of civilians; half a million homes had been destroyed, the merchant fleet had declined by nearly one-third, the national and foreign debt had grown to colossal proportions. France had lost 210,671 of her armed forces killed (the number of homes ruined was about equal to that in Britain). The United States suffered 293,986 deaths. The US National Debt had increased by over two hundred billion dollars. Russian losses, even taking account of their unreliable figures, were enormous; 6,115,000 military deaths and over ten million civilians killed. More Russians had died in the defence of Stalingrad than had

---

* Although Wedemeyer states that his own Intelligence reports early in 1945 'proved that the end in East Asia was a matter of weeks'.

Americans in the entire war. Japan had 1,506,000 military losses (including missing); Italy 144,496; Germany 2,850,000.

On August 19th a sixteen-man Japanese delegation arrived at MacArthur's headquarters, in Manila, to receive his orders for the transfer of power. They returned to Tokyo the following day, and on August 28th the first American troops landed at an airfield in Japan. Two days later the main occupation force arrived, 4,200 troops being landed by nightfall. The operation continued for many days. On August 30th, MacArthur himself arrived with the first main body of troops, and was driven into Tokyo, stern-faced and glaring, with thirty thousand immaculate and motionless Japanese soldiers lining the route. MacArthur was, of course, well acquainted with the Oriental mind.

The surrender ceremony took place on September 2nd; a dull, overcast day. It was six years and one day since the start of the Second World War, when German panzer divisions had burst across the Polish frontier and a German battleship, on a 'goodwill' visit to Danzig, had begun bombarding the town. After strong and angry representations by the Navy, the ceremony was held, not on land, but aboard the USS *Missouri*. The Japanese emissaries, formally dressed in silk top hats, frock-coats and striped trousers, were brought alongside in a launch. The new Foreign Minister had a wooden leg, and only managed to clamber up the ladder to the battleship with extreme difficulty. The delegation were not met on deck, and stood waiting in humiliation for about a quarter of an hour before being sent for. The Japanese authorities had brought the war on themselves, and many of their countrymen had fought it with extreme cruelty. The actual ceremony took about twenty minutes. The setting was dramatic and sombre; grey British and American battleships clustered around in the dim light, their guns pointing towards the shore. As MacArthur signed he called for Generals J. M. Wainwright and A. E. Percival, of the stands at Bataan and Singapore respectively, both just released from captivity, to stand at his shoulders. He then pronounced the following carefully composed statement: 'We are gathered here, representatives of the major warring powers, to conclude a solemn agreement whereby peace may be restored. The issues, involving divergent ideals and ideologies, have been determined on the battlefields of the world and hence are not for our discussion or debate. Nor is it for us here to meet, representing as we do a majority of the people of the earth, in a spirit of distrust, malice or hatred. . . . Let us pray that peace be now restored to the world, and that God will preserve it always. 'These proceedings are closed.'

But were they? Not for the countless relatives and loved-ones of those Allied servicemen who had been killed in the war. Not, certainly, for those still struggling for life at Hiroshima and Nagasaki; who picked their ways through the miles of débris, looking for a familiar sign or object to tell them they were at their homes; who lay in the corridors, toilets and offices of the patched-up hospital; who found comfort in the rumour, which they refused to disbelieve, that Japan had also possessed the secret weapon and had dropped one on Los Angeles before the war had ended; who were still dying in thousands more than two weeks after the explosions. They had just been joined by the first detachments of the International Red Cross, journalists and newsreel cameramen to arrive on the scene. One of the Red Cross workers described his arrival: 'Everything had disappeared. It was a stony waste littered with débris and twisted girders. We got out of the car and made our way slowly through the ruins into the centre of the dead city. Absolute silence reigned in the whole necropolis. . . . In what remained of the station façade the hands of the clock had been stopped at 8.15. It was perhaps the first time in the history of humanity that the birth of a new era was recorded on the face of a clock.'

7 Uneasy Peace

7 UNEASY PEACE

Whatever may be said, from a strategic or moral point of view, of the means the United States employed to end the Japanese war, one thing is certain: the war was brought to an end with almost complete confusion and ineptness. It is equally certain that the United States began the peace in the Far East with complete confidence, brilliance and accuracy. The lessons of Europe had been learnt, and the American commander on the spot was of a vastly different temperament —one more suitable for the task—from the commander in Europe. The leaders of the United States slowly began to appreciate that at the start of the new age their country was in a position of tremendous and absolute power; the only pity, from a Western point of view, is that they did not realize it earlier. On August 20th *Time* magazine summed up the situation with its customary succinctness: 'The new political era that began at Hiroshima will break into two parts: (1) the years when the bomb remains the exclusive possession of three close allies, the US, Britain and Canada; (2) the years after other nations develop it. . . . This was a new room, rich with hope, terrible with strange dangers. The door that slammed behind man at Hiroshima had locked. There was no choice but to grope ahead into the Atomic Age.'

The occupation of Japan, carried out in masterful fashion by Douglas MacArthur, was beset with diplomatic snares, all of them unsuccessful and all of them set in Moscow. The Soviets still claimed a part in the occupation of Japan. Other countries had agreed to American handling of the occupation, although Australia and New Zealand demanded roles more decisive than the United States were willing to grant. MacArthur's own representations to the Russians about a quarter of a million Japanese prisoners taken in the brief campaign in Manchuria met with no success. There was also the question of Korea, where the 38th parallel had been fixed as a dividing line for the purposes of accepting the Japanese surrender. The Russians were attempting to make this a permanent, and closed, frontier.

In Japan itself, Hirohito expressed in the Diet his desire that a new national policy would 'win the confidence of the world'. Members of the Diet left the Chamber openly weeping. Addressing both Houses, the new Premier said that Japan had given up against an overwhelming coalition when it was impossible to carry on; the situation was hopeless even before the atomic-bomb attacks. The country had been defeated 'by May or June'. MacArthur was well aware that by using existing institutions in Japan he would be avoiding the difficulties being encountered in Germany. But Hirohito's plea was not helped by the release, on September 5th, of a State Department document on Japanese atrocities; filled with details of bestial and inhuman treatment of American prisoners, it made sickening reading, and there was a wave of disgust directed against Japan and the Japanese that was felt in all Allied countries. The release of emaciated Allied prisoners from camps received priority from the occupying forces. Eighty per cent were suffering from severe malnutrition. Within three weeks most of those who were not seriously ill— veterans of Wake, Bataan and Malaya—were on their way home.

MacArthur's first act on arrival at his new headquarters in Tokyo was to order the unfurling of the Stars and Stripes that had flown over the White House on the day of Pearl Harbour; it had already flown in Rome and Berlin. As the days went on the country began to be properly garrisoned with American soldiers, much to the relief of the first to arrive, who had been outnumbered by armed Japanese troops about a hundred to one; of this MacArthur said: 'There probably was no greater gamble taken in history than the initial landings.' By the end of September there were 232,379 US troops in Japan.* Although the Japanese demobilization went ahead with extraordinary speed, and although MacArthur soon had an executive organization functioning in Tokyo, there were no dramatic scenes of national humiliation and the American public was uneasy and

* At the end of the war there were 2,576,085 Japanese troops on the home islands.

disappointed. Criticism of MacArthur, and his 'soft handling' of the Japanese, began to appear in the American Press, to which he felt it necessary to reply at length on several occasions. Nevertheless it was true that the friendly disposition of US troops and MacArthur's use of the existing government, and his recognition of the Emperor, did much to reassure the nervous Japanese and alienate the American public; but although Hirohito continued to reign, it was MacArthur who ruled. His greatest problems were the recovery and maintenance of essential services, the repatriation of nearly four and a half million Japanese troops overseas, the establishment of civil reforms, and the purging of militarists from Japanese society. For the time being he decided to concentrate on the former two. The surprising absence of rancour in Japan in the early days of the occupation, and the good American–Japanese relations, were commented on by several observers. But Truman, uneasy at MacArthur's apparently growing and uncontrolled authority, suggested he should go home for a short visit. MacArthur refused to accept both this and a stronger note urging a brief trip to the United States. In October the Japanese Government was forced to resign when MacArthur demanded the dismissal of the Home Minister. A new Prime Minister, Shidehara, was appointed. It was announced that nearly seven million Japanese troops would be disarmed and demobilized within two months.

On September 9th the final indignity took place with the formal surrender of a million Japanese troops to the Chinese in Nanking; the eight years' war in the Far East was over. Conversations took place at Chungking between representatives of the Communists and the Kuomintang, but they made no headway; the Communists refused to surrender control of their army. China remained in a chaotic condition, with American and European missions in Peking attempting to send home the prisoners-of-war sent to camps in that area by the Japanese, and relying on Japanese troops to maintain law and order. Washington, which had long striven to prevent civil war, began to support more openly the Kuomintang régime's efforts to gain control over the country (although continuing to deplore as imperialism similar British, Dutch and French efforts elsewhere). The Russo-Chinese treaty was at last signed—after the resignation of T. V. Soong, the Chinese Foreign Minister. Its most surprising feature was that the Russians appeared to have come out in favour of the Kuomintang Government and abandoned the Yenan Communists. As well as promising moral and material help to Chiang Kai-shek, Russia agreed to evacuate Manchuria, into which the Red

Army had so recently burst, and recognize it as Chinese. In return China concurred to most of the Soviet Eastern rights agreed to by Roosevelt at Yalta. Chiang Kai-shek had thus, it seemed, some reason to congratulate himself and his negotiators for having salvaged a great deal when it had looked as if they were being sold down the river by the United States.

Meanwhile two colonial powers were having some difficulty in enforcing their claims to their former territories. In Indo-China the French found themselves in the somewhat ridiculous situation of having to agree to a Chinese column accepting the Japanese surrender at Hanoi, as their own small force had been chased away by the Japanese into the wilderness; the local French commander refused to attend the ceremony as the place reserved for him was 'unacceptable'. The southern part of Indo-China was occupied for France by troops of the British Fourteenth Army, flown in after disorder and anti-French disturbances. British troops had to intervene in fierce fighting between Annamese and French in Saigon. The situation was not calculated to please General de Gaulle, and after some diplomatic activity the Chinese assured him that they would respect French rights in the area. In the Netherlands East Indies the Dutch were in an even more embarrassing position. About a quarter of a million Japanese were estimated to be in the islands, and the Dutch only had a force of about 6,000 men available to go there. The most prominent local leader was Dr Soekarno, who had expressed his loyalty to the Dutch Government at the outbreak of war, had befriended the Japanese during the occupation, and was now making advances to the British and Americans in the hope of receiving aid from them in the cause of independence for the islands. While the Japanese on Java awaited the arrival of Allied troops, who showed no signs of arriving, they equipped and trained a local Indonesian army. Liberated Dutch prisoners were murdered by this undisciplined force, who soon appeared to have broken free from Soekarno's control. On September 29th a British force, a battalion of the Seaforth Highlanders, landed on Java. It was stated by the officer commanding these and other British troops shortly to arrive that their only purpose was to rescue prisoners-of-war and disarm the Japanese: 'We have no interest in internal politics; British and Indian troops will not become involved.' The Viceroy of India, Earl Wavell, said: 'Our troops are not there to suppress the Indonesians; they went there on an errand of duty and mercy—to dismiss the Japanese and rescue Allied prisoners.' No one quite knew what to think, for the British commander, Lieutenant-General Sir Philip Christison, then said he intended to bring Indonesian leaders and Dutch officials together at a conference, and that 'something must happen at once'. The situation deteriorated rapidly. Christison came in for heavy criticism for apparently supporting Indonesian desires. Outbreaks of fighting became frequent, and the thousand Scottish troops, and the 5th Indian Division which joined them, found themselves in a thankless and bewildering situation—incurring the wrath of Indonesians, Japanese and Dutch alike.

In India the advent of the Labour Government had met with general approval, as the constitutional reform for which politicians and agitators had pressed so long, and about which they had received so many promises, seemed more likely to take place with a Socialist Government at Westminster. The demand for self-government, already promised, was becoming irresistible. The Viceroy did his best to bring all conflicting interests together; it was clear, however, that he was gradually sinking in the morass of endless talk, religious bitterness and indecision that bedevilled Indian affairs. Although he accepted his task of preparing for the end of the British Raj as inevitable, his heart was not in it; he was pessimistic about the outcome. Wavell, a man of outstanding character and great talents, had experienced a long and disappointing war, and had been given many thankless tasks to perform. He was essentially a tired man. In September he visited London to meet the new Government. Ministers and friends found him dispirited and depressed. He had been in London only a few months before for discussions with Churchill, but had been kept hanging around and had accomplished little, as everyone had been busy with the election. Wavell pondered on his guiding hero Allenby, who had faced the problem of complete independence in Egypt after the First World War and had encouraged the Government to hasten its plans; now he found himself in a similar predicament. Attlee was uneasy about Wavell's ability to handle the situation: 'I did not think that he and the Indians could really understand each other.' As it turned out, he was wrong; many Indians have written that they understood Wavell well enough and that he understood them only too well—which no doubt accounted for his depression. But Attlee's instinct was right, as it was so often to be, if not his reasoning. On his return to India, Wavell put forward a new plan giving Indians complete autonomy in Foreign Affairs, Police and Finance, with final power resting in a predominantly Indian Viceroy's Council. But Jinnah would not agree.

While Wavell continued to labour ceaselessly with Jinnah, Ghandi and others to bring an end to the bickering and procrastination of the factions in India, Attlee was discussing in London the future of India with such experts as Stafford Cripps and Lord Pethick-Lawrence. There were riots in Calcutta, and the Governor of Bengal, the Australian R. G. Casey, alerted the Army to be ready to intervene. Casey wrote in his diary: 'It was difficult to discover what it was all about.' But India was not the only problem in the disturbed and troubled British Empire. The end of the war also acted as a spur to discontent and agitation in Ceylon and Burma. At the year's end the brave but despairing Wavell appealed to all these peoples to avoid violence and strife when they stood 'at the gate of political and economic opportunity'.

(ii)

Immediately after the war's end de Gaulle visited President Truman in Washington. In the course of a number of conversations the Frenchman attempted to exert his influence, but with no success. At the opening meeting Truman insisted on confining the discussion to the French fuel situation. This did not please the General at all. The President promised to see that all French requests for mining machinery would receive absolute priority, although it is not clear whether the French had asked for any. In a later meeting de Gaulle managed to bring the discussions round to Germany. He said that the unity of Germany would be dangerous; it would lead to a new Reich which would end by allying itself to the Slav bloc that had been brought into being by the decisions made at Yalta and Potsdam to which he had not been party. He would like to see the internationalization of the Ruhr. The President remarked that the Russian representatives to the Potsdam conference had also urged this course.

On the question of boundaries, de Gaulle denied that France had ever wished to annexe the Val D'Aosta. All that France insisted upon was that 'the frontier should be slightly adjusted'. But France did not support the Italian-frontier claims of other powers, such as Yugoslavia. The General regretted the fact that the United States had given moral support to 'the deplorable British intervention' in the Levant. Truman admitted that the United States had been over-influenced by Britain.

The London *Times* reported: 'Politically and militarily the talks were not as broad or as thorough as the highest French hopes.' This was a fine example of British understatement. Somewhat frigid, and not a little irritated by the apparent American unwillingness to treat his views—coming as they did from the liberator and leader of France—with the respect that they deserved, de Gaulle went off to New York. There, somewhat to his and everyone else's surprise, he received a tumultuous reception.

(iii)

The Council of Foreign Ministers to draw up peace treaties with Italy and the Nazi satellite states, in response to the decision made at Potsdam, met at Lancaster House, in London, from September 11th. The Foreign Ministers were those of the 'Big Three' countries and France and China. The first treaty to be discussed was that with Italy, and right away the conference was faced with numerous and seemingly insurmountable difficulties. The conference had no sooner opened than the British Dominions, led by the Australians (whose External Affairs Minister, Dr Evatt, was in London), demanded to be heard; it was pointed out that many Australian and New Zealand troops had fought and died in Italy. As they had earlier in the year, the Dominions seemed to be questioning whether the Big Three had the right to settle the world's affairs on their own. As a concession to these demands, the Dominions, and Italy and Yugoslavia, were invited to the conference to give their views on the Yugoslav–Italian frontier. Eventually it was agreed that Trieste should become a free port in one form or another, but Molotov insisted that it should be under Yugoslav sovereignty. He refused to alter this opinion. On most other Italian problems, such as the future of her former colonies and reparations to be demanded from her, Molotov found himself in a four-to-one minority. He claimed that Russia should have a trusteeship over Tripolitania; a claim which Bevin rejected with some heat. The conference dragged on with no agreement being reached. While Byrnes (supported by John Foster Dulles, now a Republican spokesman on foreign affairs) and Bevin tried to keep the discussions to Italy, the French tried to bring in the question of Germany, and the Russians tried to open up a reappraisal of the occupation of Japan.

It seemed that the Russians were not prepared to make concessions with regard to their excessive demands about Italy until the Anglo-Americans were prepared to recognize the existing puppet governments in Rumania and Bulgaria. This neither Byrnes nor Bevin was prepared to do—not, an any rate, until there had been free elections in those countries. They said that the United States and Britain could not contemplate making peace treaties with governments which they considered undemocratic. Molotov retorted that at Yalta and Potsdam the Anglo-Americans had insisted that they wanted to see governments friendly to the Soviet Union in the Balkans. Byrnes said that this was so, but they had to be democratic, too. This simple argument continued for some days; Molotov always charging that the United States was anxious to see governments hostile to Russia in all countries adjoining Soviet territory, and Byrnes denying it absolutely. As for Soviet troops, Molotov insisted that these were essential in the area in order to protect Russian lines of communication to the occupying forces in Austria. Byrnes said that the American objective was a government in Bulgaria and Rumania that was both democratic and friendly to the Soviets. Molotov, who was proving to be more difficult than ever before, said he did not believe it. He said that electoral or governmental disturbances in Rumania might lead to civil war. Byrnes was to some extent sympathetic to Russian fears, but neither he nor Bevin wilted in the face of constant and bitter pressure from the Soviet delegation. Bevin's attitude towards the Russians was much harder than that of the Secretary of State. Molotov was apparently bewildered at their obstinacy, for he could not understand how they could profess to want pro-Soviet governments while demanding elections which were out of the question as such elections might return anti-Soviet governments. The only certain way to ensure Russian security, he said privately, was for Russia to nominate her own governments in these countries. At length Molotov, imprisoned, as always, in his own suspicions, realized that the Americans and British were not going to give way on this point, and the Russians, convinced that any further discussion was a waste of time, decided to end the conference with a cynicism that was to become familiar in later years, but which on this occasion deeply shocked the world. On September 22nd Molotov told Byrnes that he could no longer agree to the inclusion of France and China in all conference sessions; in future they should only be admitted when matters were being discussed which closely affected them. This was, he said, the correct interpretation of the ruling which had been agreed upon at Potsdam, but which had been abused during the conference so far. China should be excluded from all European treaties and France from all but German and Italian treaties. When this was discussed at a later meeting, Bevin, angry and disappointed, compared Molotov's action to the 'Hitler theory'. Molotov got up and walked out; although he came back, the conference was over. No compromise could be reached, as the Americans and the British were not prepared to cynically abandon their partners in front of a watching world.

As a last attempt to save the conference, the two Western Foreign Ministers decided to approach Attlee and Truman to discuss with Stalin what had actually been agreed on at Potsdam in the hope that the old Generalissimo would, as so often before, overrule his Foreign Minister. Attlee's message to Stalin on this matter was, in fact, the only one he sent during the year, apart from mere formalities—which well illustrates how Britain, since the fall of Churchill, had lost much of such little initiative in international matters as she had possessed, and how her foreign affairs were once more being conducted in the traditional way, at Foreign Secretary level. Truman's message was actually written by Byrnes and sent by Leahy, in the President's absence from the White House, thus illustrating how much American foreign affairs, since the decline of Roosevelt, were also being carried out below the highest level. Both messages received a cold reply from Stalin, backing Molotov's stand.

The conference broke up on October 2nd. At a Press conference Byrnes denied that it had ever been thought possible to draft the peace treaties at the meeting; there were bound to be further conferences. In the House of Commons, Ernest Bevin said: 'We should have had to say in effect to the representatives of France and China: Now you must leave the room while we are discussing these matters. And when we came to the Finnish treaty we should have had to invite the United States to withdraw as well. Such a request by some of the powers to their partners would obviously have created international difficulties which the United States and British delegations did not feel they should be called upon to face.' By far the strongest public statement given about the background to the ending of the conference was given by John Foster Dulles. He said that the reason for public dismay was that for more than four years all conferences between the great powers had been followed by statements giving the impression that complete harmony had been achieved. He described this as 'a diet of soothing syrup'. The differences which had in fact always existed were now coming to light. The Russians at the conference had tried to get the United States to agree to peace treaties with governments which were not democratic by threatening to break off the conference altogether with unreasonable demands. 'They also knew that we were anxious quickly to conclude peace with Italy. They wanted to find out how much of our principle we would sacrifice to attain these goals. They found out that the United States was not willing to sacrifice its principles or its historic friendship with China and France. In every important negotiation there comes a moment when the negotiators test one another out. It was inevitable that the time would come when the Soviet Union would want to test us out. . . . We are at the beginning of long and difficult negotiations which will involve the structure of the post-war world. We are emerging from six years of war during which morality and principle have increasingly been put aside in favour of military expediency. The war has now ended and, with that ending, principle and morality must be re-established in the world. The United States ought to take the lead.'

Very few people indeed outside the United States, and not all that many in it, had ever heard of John Foster Dulles before. Certainly not since before the war had they heard such strong words directed against Soviet Russia, which most people looked upon as a noble if difficult ally which was led by the gruff but kindly 'Uncle Joe'. It was a far cry from the kind of thing another American adviser of foreign affairs, Harry Hopkins, had been saying earlier in the year. Even now, in notes for a book he intended to write, Hopkins was saying: 'The Russians trust the United States more than they trust any power in the world. I believe they . . . are determined to take their place in world affairs in an international organization.' In an impassioned speech in the House of Commons, Bevin denied vehemently the creation of an anti-Soviet pact, which he took to be the reason for the fear and suspicions that might have been behind the Russian action in bringing the conference to an end.

The London conference marked the end of the Grand Diplomacy of the war. The once-ceaseless flow of messages between the three heads of state had practically dried up. Two of Truman's five messages to Stalin for the remainder of the year concerned a signed photograph that the Generalissimo had sent him ('I shall always treasure the picture as a happy reminder of very pleasant associations') and a vain attempt to get him to sit for his portrait. Contact between heads of state was fading away. Churchill's most-exclusive-club was no more; Attlee was disinterested and submerged in domestic problems, Truman was disillusioned, and Stalin was tired, pestered by ambitious sycophants and unimpressed with the new leaders in the West. Dulles' words marked the beginning of the end of all pretensions to Allied unity. Informed people began to speak of the post-war world as being a confrontation between two great blocs—the Soviet and the American. In London, J. L. Garvin asked the question: Does Russia want war? He came to the conclusion that it did not. The war was over; but there was a strangely cold nip in the air of peace.

(iv)

While the conference had dragged on, life in London, and in Britain generally, had not noticeably changed with the sudden arrival of peace and a Socialist Government. Things were much as they had been for six years. Everyone, rich and poor, was shabbily or plainly dressed. The appearance of the country, compounded from its cities, villages and people, was distinctly dowdy. Food was meagre and unattractive. There were no sudden increases or abolition of rationing; on the contrary, matters were becoming steadily worse. It was announced that only one 'domestic pack of dried egg' would be allowed per person every two months. The marmalade ration was reduced to 1 lb for a four-week period. It was warned that the milk ration might have to be reduced to two pints a week. The new Food Minister, Sir Ben Smith, said that he could hold out no prospect of any immediate improvement in rations. He asked the public to be patient. He made a similar pronouncement every few weeks, and he was not the only Labour Minister who found himself issuing pleas to the public rather than ushering in the promised land of Socialism. Every day the Ministry of War Transport was besieged by between seventy-five and a hundred people begging and shouting for car permits, without which it was impossible to purchase one of the new cars, a few of which were beginning to role off production lines hastily converted from wartime use. Many thousands of postal applications arrived each day; they were treated 'strictly on a basis of priority'—a phrase which had been voiced so often in the years recently passed that many people believed it meant absolutely nothing. The advent of a Labour Government did not seem to have noticeably improved labour relations. There was a dock strike in October which infuriated the public; many food-ships had to wait days before they could be unloaded. Troops were called in to unload ships; the dockers were eventually granted a minimum wage of 19s a day. The railways were in dire circumstances, suffering from acute need of capital investment and overloading during the war; one of the very first pay increases after the war was awarded to the railwaymen, who received an extra 7s a week, bringing their basic wage to 87s in the London area and 85s in the provinces. The state of the railways could be judged by two bad crashes before the end of the year: at Bourne End, where thirty-nine passengers lost their lives, and at Northwood, where three died; on January 2nd, 1946, fifteen more died in a rail accident at Lichfield. There was trouble in the mines, where production showed no signs of improving now that nationalization was about to take place. The Minister of Fuel, Emanuel Shinwell, seemed to spend a great deal of his time issuing appeals to the coal-miners. He said: 'We can see in the immediate future the realization of our long-sustained demand for the national ownership of the coal-mining industry; let us now make our best contribution to the short-term problem.' The problem was that British coal stocks for the coming winter looked like being the lowest for any winter even during the war. The situation was critical. The colliery owners issued the following important statement: 'The colliery owners believe that private enterprise is the right basis for the efficient conduct of the coal-mining industry in the national interest. But in view of the fact that legislation for the transfer of the industry from private enterprise to public ownership is to be proceeded with, and having regard to the statement made on behalf of the Government that the industry would be fairly treated so far as compensation is concerned, the colliery owners, through the Mining Association, place themselves at the disposal of the Government in connection both with the working out of the necessary organizations to be created on the basis of public ownership and with the arrangements that will be necessary to facilitate the transfer. . . . In the interim period it is of vital national importance that the output of coal should be increased, and the colliery owners will co-operate with the Government in the fullest possible manner.' The Mineworkers' Union mounted an intensive propaganda campaign in every coalfield in conjunction with Labour MPs representing mining constituencies. Speeches, posters and pamphlets bombarded the miners. But they were not the only section of the public to be urged on to 'greater efforts' for the sake of the nation. Posters everywhere begged people to save for peace, just as only recently they had been begging them to save for war. The London Thanksgiving Week Savings Campaign raised £125,000,000 for the nation in one week. The Chancellor of the Exchequer made a strong plea for the continuance of saving. He explained: 'If a large number of people all try to spend their money at the same time while supplies are so short, the only result would be to drive up prices or, where these are subject to price control, to encourage large-scale black-market operations.' The King appealed for more savings. The Queen appealed for more savings. The Prime Minister appealed for more savings. There was a great deal of talk about Britain having to 'export to live'. Few people took much notice of Sir Patrick Hannon, President of the National Union of Manufacturers, when he said: 'The strength and efficiency of our export trade depends entirely on a sound and flourishing home market. It is not economic to manufacture for export only. If the Government insist upon us doing this, we will be pushed off all the markets by the US.'

There was much agitation for an increase in the rate of demobilization which, because of the truculence of Britain's allies, had been secretly slowed down by Churchill earlier in the year, and which seemed to most servicemen to be scandalously slow. There was a great and widespread longing to throw off battle-dress and uniforms and return to homes, families, local communities and the jobs of what seemed a distant past. To men who had dreamed for years of walking down the High Street on a Saturday morning, and going to a football match (Charlton were top of the League) in the afternoon, as free men once more, any further delay was unbearable. But although men were being 'demobbed' at a fair speed, the new Government found itself faced with many undreamed-of responsibilities throughout the world; in Indo-China, in Java, in Germany and elsewhere there seemed no escape for British troops. At Aldershot there was rioting and mutiny among Canadian troops waiting to go home. The worried Prime Minister personally wrote to Truman asking for the return of the *Queen Elizabeth*, *Queen Mary* and *Aquitania*, which had been loaned to the United States during the war for troop transportation. These ships were now being used for the return of American soldiers to the United States. There was some angry correspondence on this matter. Attlee called Truman's attention to the fact that many British soldiers had been on active service and away from their homes for over five years; owing to the sudden termination of the Japanese war, the conditions in which they had been loaned no longer existed. The US Chiefs of Staff, however, refused to let them go, owing to 'the necessity to return US forces from Europe as expeditiously as possible'. Not only that, but they were, as Attlee then suggested, unable to provide equivalent American transport facilities. Attlee persisted: 'I must ask you most earnestly to provide us in the immediate future with an equivalent lift for these three ships.' In the end Truman, who had seen Attlee's point all along, directed the Chiefs of Staff to provide the British with equivalent shipping, although nothing could be as convenient and speedy as the two Queens themselves. The two great liners had already transported over 1,000,000 American servicemen home. MPs received thousands of letters of protest about demobilization from indignant servicemen and their families. The TUC, flexing its muscles with a Labour Government in power, demanded acceleration in demobilization. The Minister of Labour, George Isaacs, had the unenviable task of standing up to constant harassing and pestering from all quarters.

The men who found themselves in the longed-for 'civvy' life once more, found the High Street at home a very different place from the one they had left six years before. Not only was it grubbier and grimier, but whole chunks of it had been cut away as if by a giant with some huge knife. Through the rubble of bomb-sites, weeds and tufts of grass were already sprouting; on bared and lonely walls tattered wallpaper flapped idly in the breeze like the flags of defeat more than of victory. The people in the High Street were faced with problems different from those of 1939. The BBC had initiated a weekly series of trans-Atlantic broadcasts, *Here Comes the Bride*, the object of which was to enable English brides of GIs to talk to their in-laws. A distinct crime-wave, especially among young people, was apparent; to combat it Scotland Yard introduced a fleet of 200 cars equipped with radio telephones, directed from a 'plotting table similar to that used by the RAF', which would, it was hoped, make it 'almost impossible for smash-grab raiders and car thieves to operate successfully'. The problems of marriage, many of which had suffered from the stresses and demands of war, seemed to be disturbingly touched on in the new film *Brief Encounter*, the story of a married woman's love for a man she meets on a murky wartime railway station. Another new film, *Caesar and Cleopatra*, gave further evidence that the British film industry had reached a peak that could not at the time be rivalled anywhere in the world. Further cause for national satisfaction was found during November in the new world air-speed record established by the Gloster Meteor jet, which attained a speed of 606 mph. As they settled into civilian life with all its problems, men contemplated that even war, like all human existence, was not entirely bad. They remembered with gentle nostalgia the comradesip of service life; the dusty roads of Burma; bathing in the warm, blue waters of the Mediterranean with the rolling desert stretching away behind; the Sunday bells of great cathedrals in France. And to remind them of the places they had been to and the things they had seen, souvenirs and relics like old cartridges, Japanese swords and Nazi daggers were set up at home in places of honour.

In Parliament party politics were quickly returning to their pre-war intensity, with the dramatically outnumbered Conservatives sitting uncomfortably on the Opposition benches. The first day's ordinary business was intense and highly charged. One of a group of brilliant young men who were all new Labour MPs had been chosen by the party to make the first speech. In the dark green uniform of a major in the Rifle Brigade, John Freeman, who had been awarded the MBE in 1943, and who had taken the surrender of Hamburg, wearing a number of decorations, erect and dramatically handsome, spoke in his maiden speech in clear and pleasant tones of the spirit of 'high adventure' that illumined his party and of 'the magnificent venture of rebuilding our civilization'. It was a stirring and exciting speech which seemed to sum up the fine hopes and ideals of all the young socialists he represented. It remained to be seen whether practicalities would be kind, whether politics would corrupt ideals, and whether disillusion would set in. He ended: 'Today we go into action. Today may rightly be regarded as D-Day in the Battle of the New Britain.' Attlee later took Freeman to Churchill in the Smoke Room. Meeting this upstanding young man, who might well have been expected to be Conservative by background and inclination, and who seemed to have just spoken on behalf of his generation, Churchill broke down and wept. Attlee himself made a fine tribute to Churchill in the House: 'A General Election has resulted in Mr Churchill being on the Opposition benches at a time when the fruits of his long leadership of the nation in war are being garnered. However we may be divided politically, I believe I shall be expressing the views of the whole House in making acknowledgement here of the transcendant services rendered by Mr Churchill to this country, to the Commonwealth and Empire, and to the world during his tenure of office. There is a true leadership which means the expression by one man of the soul of a nation, and its translation of the common will into action. In the darkest and most dangerous hours of our history this nation found in him the man who expressed supremely the courage and determination never to yield which animated all the men and women of this country.' It was a speech unusual not only in the generosity of its terms to someone sitting across the House, but also in that it was delivered by a man not given to emotion and high-sounding phrases. In a short speech, Churchill said he had faith in the new Parliament, and promised to help make it work. He pointed out that many of the measures put forward in the King's Speech would also have been taken by the Conservatives had they been returned to power. He spoke of the atom bombings, and defended the decision to use them, which he said was that of 'President Truman and myself at Potsdam'. (In his war memoirs he acknowledges that the final decision was Truman's alone.) He was surprised that worthy people, who had no intention of proceeding to the Japanese front themselves, should argue that rather than use the bomb 1,000,000 American and 250,000 British lives should have been sacrificed in the desperate battles of an invasion of Japan.

On moving out of Downing Street, Churchill had moved into Claridges Hotel, and later into the flat of his son-in-law, Duncan Sandys. After a few weeks he entered into negotiations for buying a house in Hyde Park Gate. Everywhere he went he was received with unconstrained applause, more so even than during the war; this, contrasting with his rebuff at the election, genuinely puzzled him. At a performance of Noel Coward's *Private Lives* the entire audience rose and applauded him for some minutes immediately he entered the theatre. At the end of the play John Clements made a speech about him, and once more the cheering continued for several minutes. It was the same on every occasion he appeared in public. He became increasingly active as Leader of the Opposition, attacking the Government with venom on tardy demobilization (notwithstanding that this was largely due to his own measures) and on plans to nationalize industry. Rumours were heard from time to time that Attlee was about to see, or had seen, the ex-Prime Minister; they no doubt originated among those people who doubted whether the country could survive at all without him. When he went for a holiday to Cap d'Antibes in the South of

France, reports even appeared in the newspapers that Attlee was preparing to visit him to seek his advice on the many problems facing the new and inexperienced Government.

Attlee had, in fact, settled down very quickly, although the same could not be said for all of his Ministers. He was a firm believer in the value of the committee, and the kind of governing with which he was later to become identified was already in evidence; valuable and argumentative Cabinet meetings at which he himself said little; and a tendency to concentrate most of his energies on keeping his more ebullient Ministers on the rails, to act as a co-ordinator rather than as a leader. Already he seemed to be encouraging an inner circle of senior Cabinet Ministers to act as Co-ordinating Ministers, or 'Overlords'; some sceptics began saying that he would finish up with nothing to do himself, but they underrated the task of making a team out of a group of volatile, brilliant, touchy and mutually suspicious men. For the first time for some years the Foreign Secretary enjoyed great freedom. Attlee has said: 'Except for a couple of occasions, I was content to leave foreign affairs in the competent hands of my Foreign Secretary.'

Plans were already under way for loosening the links of Empire, not only with India but elsewhere, and as Britain had apparently no intention of seeking instead a close relationship with Europe, and sought complete independence from the United States, her future as a great power was becoming arguable. As for nationalization, an order of priority had been adopted. It was clear that the coal industry was in more urgent need of Socialist attention than was that of iron and steel. National Insurance was already in an advanced state of preparation; a national health service was not. But most Ministers found urgent immediate problems facing them, which were inclined to use all the energies of themselves and their Ministries and left little opportunity for planning and preparing utopias. That there were no widespread second thoughts on the part of the public was confirmed by the first two by-elections of the Parliament, at Smethwick and Ashton-under-Lyne, both of which were comfortably held by Labour. One who worried about the new Government more than Attlee did was King George VI. This was not because of its left-wing nature, but because of its inexperience. The King's biographer has written: 'He himself was a progressive in political thought and a reformer in social conscience, but he was distrustful of undue haste and of political extremism in any form.' Lord Mountbatten, one of his closest personal advisers, had told the King that the senior Labour Ministers might well look to him for advice and guidance. To some extent this turned out to be true, and George VI now played a more active role in affairs, although always discreetly, than had been the case with the monarchy since the time of Queen Victoria. This was partly due to the increasing discussions and difficulties over India in which, being the so-called Emperor, he naturally took a close interest. The early meetings at the Palace between the King and Attlee were awkward and un-comfortable, both being essentially reserved men, but soon a good relationship developed between them. Early in the Parliament the King urged Attlee to take drastic action to increase housing, and to do something about making new clothing more readily available ('my family are down to their lowest level').* He got on very well indeed with Bevin, whom he had, of course, strongly suggested for the Foreign Office. There is little doubt that at this time the King was worrying increasingly, and often unnecessarily, about public affairs. There are frequent mentions in his diary as to his worries. His official biographer has written: 'The mantle of elder statesman lay heavily upon the King's shoulders. In his talks with Ministers he was not infrequently successful in presenting arguments which caused them to reconsider decisions at which they had already arrived. But he was exhausted physically and mentally. "I feel burned out" was his frequent remark.'

(v)

With many convulsions and difficulties, the United States, too, was taking the first uncertain steps to returning to peacetime conditions. VJ Day, in America, when it was at last announced on September 2nd, had been something of an anti-climax; everyone had known a week and more before that the war was over, and there were few celebrations. In some ways the rich and varied mozaic of American life seemed already to be back to normal. In California an escaped convict took to the highway, thumbed a ride, and was arrested by the driver: the prison warden. In Toledo, Mrs Margaret Cook's car blew a tyre at a railroad crossing, careered down the tracks and

* Churchill had earlier made strenuous but apparently unavailing efforts to ease the clothing shortage, which in a memo to the Board of Trade he had described as 'intoler-able'.

struck a signal switch that stopped an approaching train. In Cedar Rapids, Iowa, James F. Williams, sixty-one, got his thirteenth divorce and promptly married for the fourteenth time.

Travel in the United States was becoming increasingly difficult. Never before had train, plane and hotel reservations been harder to get. Most hotels refused to accommodate people for more than a week, and lines of people waited every evening at reception desks. It seemed that this was to do with the flurry in civilian activity accompanying demobilization and reconversion from war production. There was a critical shortage of housing owing to a sharp decrease in building during the war. In October 320,000 government housing units and 35,000 trailers were sold at cost.

On September 6th Truman had sent the twenty-one points of his intended domestic legislation to Congress. Sixteen thousand words long, it was the longest Presidential platform sent to Congress since Theodore Roosevelt's in 1901. The programme in it was of careful but progressive liberalism. It was the beginning of what came to be known as the Fair Deal. As servicemen began returning to the nation's labour force, unrest became evident in many industries. Workers who had not been in the Services were faced with redeployment, reductions in overtime pay, and competition for jobs; they demanded assurances that their earnings would be maintained now that war contracts were ending. Demobilized servicemen naturally demanded and expected their old jobs back; they were not so worried about hours and pay. Feelings ran high. By the end of September railway workers were seeking a thirty-six-hour week at the same rates of pay they had been paid for a forty-eight-hour week. Steel workers were asking for an increase in the basic wage of twenty-five cents an hour. In the automobile industry, where the end of the war had suddenly made 300,000 people idle, workers were asking for an increase of 30 per cent in wages. To add to the administration's problems, there were dangerous inflationary trends; by the end of the year it was clear that the decontrol of prices was not practicable, and an unpopular decision faced the Democratic Government.

As demobilization was speeded up and the labour force rapidly expanded, the situation deteriorated. Nevertheless, as in Britain and the Dominions, the demobilization programme was not going nearly quickly enough for the public's liking. Many troops would still be needed for a while, especially for the occupation of Japan (that of Germany was not expected to last long), and a points system was established to determine the order in which troops should be released. On the whole the organization of this complicated scheme was too much for the administration, and as the protests grew and the releases became more and more numerous the operation of the scheme became more and more haphazard. It was hoped to return 5,500,000 men from the Army to civilian life by July 1st, 1946; the Navy intended demobilizing at the rate of 260,000 a month. Within a month of the Japanese surrender soldiers were being sent home at the rate of 15,200 a day. Truman has said that despite 'the dangerous speed' with which the programme was being carried out, pressure on him and the heads of the Services to speed it still further became intense. Organizations pleaded for the release of various professions and groups; Members of Congress, overwhelmed by telegrams and letters from constituents, spoke on behalf of individuals; in patient statements the President and the Services did their best to explain the difficulties. At a Press conference on November 29th Truman said that 3,500,000 men and women had been demobilized, and that the amazing figure of 93 per cent of Government war plant had been reconverted from wartime to peacetime production. Unemployment was not as serious as had been expected, and had recovered from the slump after VJ Day. Reconversion had been brutally enforced by the Government, for within a week of the Japanese surrender 30,000 telegrams had gone out cancelling nearly all war contracts. Industry had thus had to set up peacetime assembly lines and sometimes obtain different raw materials at breakneck speed; fortunately it had been long preparing for such a crisis. The Goodyear Tyre & Rubber Co had begun producing tyres and plastics for civilian use immediately. The Bendix Corporation was producing civilian radio sets almost from the first day. General Motors had their Pontiac assembly lines mapped out. Westinghouse Electric Corporation had prepared two new post-war products—a home deep-freeze unit and a dishwashing machine. Du Pont were able to switch to civilian nylon stocking production on receipt of the cancellation telegram. Towards the end of the war American businesses, which had often grown to gross proportions during the war, had not neglected to prepare for peace.

The war was over; the stations and bus terminals were jammed with happy, smiling GIs going back to the dream world that had existed in their minds for so long. In New York the bars had seldom done such business as parties of comrades-in-arms, returned in the boats from Europe, had their farewell parties with many a promise to write and keep in touch.

All over the world the mass homecoming was taking place; a migration of amateur soldiers, sailors and airmen. For many it ended with the happiest days of their lives; but for many there was a hangover that was not easily or quickly eased.

The world was hungry. The UNRRA organization, which had been set up especially to cope with the immediate post-war task of providing liberated areas that were unable to pay in foreign exchange, was unable to cope with the task. Only in Greece was it able to mount operations on the necessary scale. Although it poured in shiploads of medical supplies, food, wool, raw cotton, agricultural machinery, animals, seeds and fertilizers, it still was not nearly enough. The Director-General, Herbert Lehman, said that although he had knocked on every door, the supplies were nothing like enough. 'These peoples who fought in the underground armies,' he said, 'who struggled under the Axis yoke, do not ask us that we create for them a Utopia of ease and comfort. They ask only that we give a small part of our own substance so that they may live to start their own lives anew. If the contributing countries fail to implement their promise rapidly, efficiently and generously, the name of the United Nations will be a mockery in Europe this winter.' But it was already clear that such nations were not willing, and in some cases not able, to support UNRRA on the necessary scale. It was also clear that there would be widespread famine unless something on a much grander scale was launched; and only one nation in the world was in a position to undertake such a task: the United States. The only question that remained was whether the United States would accept this terrible but inevitable responsibility.

The answer that was to come so clearly and so generously was not at first easily discernible. Truman has said: 'The threat of famine became almost global during the winter. More people faced starvation and even death for want of food during the year following the war than during all the war years combined. America enjoyed a near-record production of food and a record crop of wheat.' By the end of the year Attlee was pleading with the President for his 'personal and active interest' in the crisis, which he said threatened widespread famine in Europe and Asia.

Lend-Lease had finally ended on August 21st. It had ended absolutely, and no room was left for any Allied illusions. The statement had declared that all outstanding contracts were cancelled, and could only be completed if the governments concerned were prepared to pay for them. The abruptness of the statement caused some dismay in several capitals, although it had already been made plain that such a move was inevitable with the ending of the war. Few Americans were able to find fault with the decision. In the House of Commons both Attlee and Churchill spoke of the announcement in the gravest words. It was immediately announced that Lord Keynes, the Government's economics adviser, was leaving with a team of experts to discuss the matter in Washington. Lend-Lease had already accounted for forty-six billion dollars of the American taxpayers' money. Britain, however, had already returned four billion dollars of her share. Russia had received 25 per cent of the Lend-Lease total, and the United States had supplied that country with complete rolling-mills, petroleum refineries, electric power-plants, chemical factories, vehicles and locomotives, and tyre plants, among many other items. In his report to Congress on Lend-Lease aid, President Truman urged the United States to write off the whole sum as a part of the price of victory. He had not forgotten Churchill's long warning at Potsdam on the seriousness of the British post-war financial position. Truman was here brilliantly served by his economic advisers, if not always by his foreign affairs advisers. The report stated: 'If so huge a debt were added to the enormous financial obligations already incurred by foreign governments, it would have a disastrous effect on our trade with the United Nations, and hence on employment and production at home. Any attempt to enforce the payment of the debt would repeat the mistakes of the last peace, would result in desperate international financial rivalry, and help to sow the seeds of a third world war.' Britain had received by far the largest share of Lend-Lease (69 per cent), but it was pointed out that Britain's part in the war, by bearing the brunt in the early years, had greatly benefited the United States, and that such aid could not be measured in monetary terms. An eloquent chart accompanied the report showing how Britain had spent a far greater percentage of her national income to pay for the war than any other Allied country. Attention was also drawn by the President to inventions which had been passed on to the United States by Britain, such as Pluto, the oil pipe-line under the sea, and Fido, the fog-dispersal technique. 'The sole purpose of Lend-Lease has been to make the most effective use against the enemy of the combined resources of all the

United Nations, regardless of the origin of the supplies or which of us used them.'

From the beginning the United States–United Kingdom economic negotiations became enmeshed in considerable disagreement. Whereas the American negotiators agreed that a loan to Britain was essential for international stability, they could not agree with the British negotiators, headed by Lord Keynes and Halifax, on what form it should take. Keynes had decided not to dwell on the dangers of Communist Russia running riot across an impoverished Europe in the absence of a strong Britain. His biographer, R. F. Harrod, has pointed out: 'The American people did not regard Russia at that time as a potential threat to the Western democracies.' The atmosphere was totally different from that in 1947, when General Marshall propounded his European Recovery Programme. Keynes argued that the loan would help world prosperity by renewing and expanding British trade. Britain could not trade with the world if she were bankrupt. The Britons argued that it would be to the benefit of the United States and the world in general, as well as to the United Kingdom, if the loan was generous in its terms. The Americans did not agree with this; while agreeing with the necessity for a loan, they saw no reason why it should not be on the best possible terms for the United States. The Americans were in far the strongest position, for, no matter what terms they asked, the British would still have to accept. There was also disagreement on the seriousness of the British position. Towards the end of September Keynes said that his country needed six billion dollars but would accept five. The American delegation disagreed among themselves, but eventually it was stated that they had decided on three and a half billion dollars, with four billion as a maximum. Truman took the initiative at this stage and personally decided on three and three-quarters billion dollars. This was a disappointment to the British, but they nevertheless accepted it with alacrity when it became apparent that the United States was prepared to go no higher. There were a number of strings attached to the loan, especially on how the money was to be spent. The British requested that two billion should be interest-free, but this was turned down and a rate of interest of 2 per cent per annum was fixed. In return for the loan, the United States demanded that Britain relinquish many of the Commonwealth trade agreements by which the United States had been placed at a disadvantage in the sterling-bloc area. Altogether the negotiations had been unsuccessful for Keynes and

Halifax; the Americans had driven a much harder bargain than they had been prepared for, and there was nothing much they could do about it. The British Government was bitterly attacked in Parliament for not having fought harder for easier terms. The Opposition said it had been presented to the country as a *fait accompli* (Keynes himself admitted as much). Mr Robert Boothby described the loan as 'one of the most formidable obligations ever undertaken in the country's history'. In the Lords, the Opposition challenge was led by Lord Beaverbrook, making one of his rare appearances; his son, Max Aitken, spoke against the loan in the Commons. There were also misgivings, and some dismay, among Labour MPs. Hugh Dalton parried critics by a short speech in which he posed a question not easy to answer: 'What is the alternative?' On his return from America, Keynes went straight to the House of Lords and made a brilliant speech defending the loan which did much to soothe fears that the Government was putting the country into everlasting debt.

By the time Clement Attlee went to Washington in November, primarily to discuss the problems arising from the splitting of the atom, there was little or nothing that could be done to improve the British position.* Attlee, calling for the meeting, had written to Truman that: 'We have, in the light of this revolutionary development, to make a fresh review of world policy and a new valuation of what are called national interests.'

The responsibility of being the sole possessors of the atomic bomb weighed heavily on the United States. The percipient Stimson, before retiring on September 21st, had pressed for an immediate agreement with Russia about the future use of atomic weapons. He believed that such an approach would be more successful than a general international scheme; it would seek to stop improvement in, and manufacture of, atom bombs; existing bombs could never be used unless all three governments agreed to such use. Dean Acheson, Under-Secretary of State, agreed with much of this. It was realized that, in order to get the Russians to agree to such a treaty, some information would have to be given them about secret American techniques; it was hoped that these could be restricted to peaceful uses of atomic power. The British Minister in charge of atomic matters, Sir John Anderson, prompted by Niels Bohr, had suggested a similar scheme of Russian co-operation as early as the summer of 1944; he had received a sharp rebuff from

* The British Loan Bill became US law on July 15th, 1946.

Churchill. Byrnes also seemed to be in favour of a direct agreement with Russia on atomic policy, although he seemed to some to be working more and more on his own, and it was often difficult to discover precisely what he did think. Others insisted that the United States could initiate an agreement on atomic control with the Soviet Union without actually giving away any secrets; and that the opportunity should be grasped immediately. The Joint Chiefs of Staff, on the other hand, recommended that any pact in which information had to be given to the Russians should not be contemplated. Another holding this view was Fred M. Vinson, Secretary of the Treasury. While the discussions continued, the existing atomic plants started to slow down, and leading scientists began leaving for other employment. This worried Truman, who was urging Congress to enact legislation to set up an Atomic Energy Commission and to retain existing plants. By the time Attlee arrived with the Canadian Prime Minister, Mackenzie King, the arguments were in full sway. Truman himself was inclined to doubt the wisdom of the Stimson suggestion, as his suspicions of the Russian leaders and their motives were thoroughly aroused, despite reassurances from the remaining Roosevelt clique at the State Department and the warnings of Byrnes about being over-suspicious. To his disappointment, Attlee's main preoccupation was not how much should be told the Russians, and what, if anything should be done about international control, but how much should be told to the British. If anything, Attlee felt even more outraged at the way the result of British discoveries were being kept from Britain than Churchill had done.

It was eventually agreed that the wartime atomic collaboration between the three countries should be continued; this was no comfort to the British, who had discovered that such collaboration was almost entirely in one direction. Attlee decided shortly afterwards that Britain would have to cut its losses and go ahead alone in production of the bomb. As for what to do about Russia, it was agreed that there should be no revealing of secret information and that the whole problem of international control should be passed to the United Nations. The three statesmen said: 'We are of the opinion that at the earliest practicable date a Commission should be set up under the United Nations Organization to prepare recommendations for submission to the Organization.' Thus was passed over what may have been one of mankind's greatest opportunities for peace; for already Soviet agents and scientists were working furiously to make up for the sudden weakening of the might of the Red Army which had recently been all-powerful.*

Stalin, all of whose calculations had suddenly gone awry, had been shocked by the success of the Hiroshima and Nagasaki bombs. He had set up a Committee of Atomic Research, with himself as President, and Russian and German nuclear scientists were given priority over all other research. Stalin's ill health and lassitude continued, causing some concern to Soviet theorists, who had built up a kind of deification of the Generalissimo. Extraordinary measures were taken to protect his life. In September he had retired to Sochi for the remainder of the year, having been advised to avoid the Muscovite winter. Meanwhile, Malenkov, Beria and Khruschev, as well as Bulganin, were all jostling for power and attempting to unseat Molotov in a vicious and bitter struggle. A new era was beginning in Russia.

(vi)

In Europe a cold and harsh winter was setting in. On October 27th Bevin said in the House of Commons that there were between twenty and twenty-five million homeless people on the move in Europe. In every country there was a severe shortage of coal; all food supplies were at the bare minimum. The most satisfactory situation, apart perhaps from that in Denmark, was in Belgium, which had suffered comparatively little from bombing and bombardment during the war, and where economic problems had been tackled with energy and success. There was, however, still considerable political unease. King Leopold had refused to give up his throne, but had decided, on the advice of the Government, not to return to his country. In France the policies of General de Gaulle were arousing much discussion, not always favourable; the Communist Party was strong and threatening. But elections on October 21st gave overwhelming support to de Gaulle and his new constitution. De Gaulle asked for a vote of confidence in the National Assembly on November 6th, and was elected unanimously as President of the Provisional Government on November 13th. Four days later, in one of the emotional broadcasts that were becoming a

---

* The first Russian atomic explosion took place in September 1949, by which time the United States had conducted five peacetime nuclear tests.

feature of French life, he threatened to resign. The Communists had demanded from him either the Foreign Office, the War Office or the Home Office. This he was unprepared to grant, as it would ruin his policy 'of maintaining the balance between two very great powers, a policy which I believe to be essential to the interests of France and even to those of peace'. He managed to form a government without the support of the Communists. Among its members were Vincent Auriol, Maurice Thorez, Pierre-Henri Teitgen, Georges Bidault (still Minister of Foreign Affairs), René Pleven, Jules Moch, Jacques Soustelle and André Malraux. The disagreements with Britain continued, and grew worse during December. An Anglo-French agreement on the Levant was reached in London on December 13th, by which French and British troops would withdraw from Syria together, but de Gaulle revoked it when he learnt that British troops intended to stay in the Lebanon until the French left there also ('a result which the English have always worked towards'). At the end of the year the forces of both countries found themselves in an extremely delicate situation; there was considerable animosity.

The trial of Marshal Pétain had ended at the time of the Japanese surrender. Efforts had been made to try French war criminals in a civilized way, in contrast to the scenes of sidewalk justice after the liberation the previous year, when women who had committed the heinous crime of fraternizing with German soldiers had been shorn and marched through the streets, carrying placards, to be spat upon by their countryfolk. Pétain had been found guilty on all the charges brought against him, including treason. His defence, summed up in the sentence, 'I became heir to a catastrophe of which I was not the author', had not been accepted. Admiral Leahy, who had been US Ambassador to Vichy, sent a letter saying that he knew the Marshal had taken action 'favourable to the Allied cause' whenever possible and whenever such action would not result in further oppression of Frenchmen. There was no doubt that Pétain had struggled to maintain autonomy for the Vichy Government, on one occasion even dismissing Laval. Throughout the trial he had treated the court with contempt. He had been sentenced to death, but many Frenchmen believed that the execution of a vain and weak old man, ninety years old, who had once been the hero of Verdun, would bring little credit on the new régime; de Gaulle commuted the sentence to life imprisonment. There had been some criticism, especially in the foreign Press, of the conduct of the trial, but this was forgotten when the trial of Pierre Laval followed shortly afterwards. The shameful handling of Laval's trial shocked the world; some people began to wonder whether France's reputation as the home of justice and modern democracy was not a myth. Neither the prosecution nor the defence had received sufficient time to acquaint themselves with all the evidence. Public revulsion against Laval was widespread, and few people dared to suggest that he had seen his duty to France as one of compromise rather than resistance. Only his wife (like Mme Petain, under arrest) said that her husband believed his policies were best for France, and that she believed her husband. There had been nothing quite like the scandalous scenes in court since the French Revolution, and it was clear from the start that there was no intention of depriving the thirsty public of its blood. The trial has been described thus: 'The conduct of the hearings was outrageous and the courtroom was frequently in a state of uproar which the President was unable to control. The jury was openly biased.' Laval was conducting his own defence, but in protest against the farcical proceedings he and his lawyers refused to attend after the third day. On October 9th, after hearing only six witnesses, some of whom said practically nothing, Laval was sentenced to death. Some leaders of French opinion, such as Léon Blum, were by then even more disgusted with the trial than they had been with Laval; a request for a retrial was made to de Gaulle, who icily turned it down. There was much talk of Laval's death being necessary for France's 'soul', which, no doubt under the influence of de Gaulle's speeches and broadcasts, apparently took precedence over the impartiality of individual justice. Laval's execution, on October 15th, was as sordid as his trial had been; he had taken cyanide and was revived just long enough to be shot dead. The trial, in Oslo, of Vidkun Quisling, who was executed on October 24th, was a striking contrast; it was fair, exhaustive and dignified. The protracted trials, in London, of William Joyce and John Amery, son of L. S. Amery, former Secretary of State for India, were also dignified. Amery was sentenced to death on December 19th and hanged at Wandsworth Prison. The leading American suspect-traitor was the poet Ezra Pound; with him the authorities took an easy way out, and on December 21st Pound was pronounced insane.

In Holland post-war difficulties were immense. Crippled transport, grave shortage of machinery, wrecked factories and flooded agricultural land made the task of recovery long and painful.

Throughout the autumn feverish activity succeeded in closing most of the gaps in the important dykes. Because the Netherlands had suffered 'exceptional loss and damage', a strong claim was made by the Government for German reparations, and it was suggested that the annexation of some neighbouring German territory would be agreeable.* By far the most important matter was the return to normal activity of the Rotterdam docks, which, as the outlet of the Rhine and one of the main inlets for Western Germany and Continental Europe, were the basis of the Dutch economy and essential to the recovery of Europe. Many of the quays had been blown up by German troops at the end of the war, and dozens of ships had been sunk in the channels. A *Times* report said: 'Where quays were still intact, it was discovered that there was no coal available to supply power for cranes and elevators, and when that was forthcoming it was clear that the half-starved dock workers lacked the necessary strength to get the vital cargoes of food and fuel ashore. The British authorities then set up special canteens in the dock area where the workers could be sure of getting one good hot meal a day, and within a short time the workers, revitalized, were answering all the demands made of them.' An Anglo-Dutch monetary agreement was signed to help Dutch sterling payments, and despite the troubles in the East Indies the two countries, which had for long been close by temperament and sentiment, were clearly destined for a further long period of mutual trust and understanding. Anglo-Dutch discussions on Indonesia took place in London in an atmosphere of mutual goodwill, in sharp contrast to Anglo-Dutch relations on the scene itself.

In Germany the occupation was continuing to progress along different lines in the four zones. Political parties, including the Communists, were sanctioned in the British Zone, and civilians were allowed to make applications to publish newspapers, books and plays. Free movement between the Western zones was permitted, but the frontier of the Russian Zone was closely guarded by all occupying powers; nevertheless, large numbers of refugees and displaced persons continued to cross in both directions. Forty thousand refugees infiltrated into the British Zone every week. The Russians had allowed a road, rail and air route for the Western allies to reach their sectors in Berlin, but no deviation was permitted.

* This was granted; but in February 1963 the Netherlands Parliament agreed to sell the territory back to West Germany for £25 million. The area, and population of 10,000, were returned to Germany at midnight on July 31st, 1963.

Reports coming from the Russian Zone indicated that the whole territory had been stripped bare in reparations. It was thought that up to 5,000,000 Germans removed from the lands given to Poland were wandering aimlessly around in the Russian Zone in great distress.

In August Montgomery had narrowly escaped death when his plane had crashed; the plane had been written off, but the wiry Field-Marshal had escaped with two broken lumbar vertebrae. His deputy, General Sir Ronald Weeks, had been replaced by General Sir Brian Robertson during the summer, and both men were constantly involved in inter-zone troubles, as much with the French as with the Russians. The Control Council machinery came up against deadlock through French insistence on vetoing the creation of any central German administrations. Every time one of the other allies suggested inter-zonal co-operation on any subject, the French fought against it. While the French clamoured for international control of the Ruhr, it was announced in London that Britain was taking over the Ruhr mines and that the German owners would be dispossessed and receive no compensation. Russian–American relations in Germany were comparatively good. But the Russian political suspicions of Britain, which had grown steadily through the year, had percolated down to the military. The Soviet command accused Britain of retaining in its zone a large *Wehrmacht* army in open custody. The charge was true. Seven hundred thousand German soldiers were still in camps awaiting disbandment, and this caused acute Russian suspicion. Some of these German troops, nearly 250,000, had been earmarked by the British Government as possible reparation labour, and Montgomery—anxious to retain his excellent relations with Zhukov—asked for the release of all these men. He disbanded them all before receiving authorization. Relations between himself and the Labour Government were not entirely satisfactory; Montgomery's speed in allowing political and trade union growth in the British Zone was considered to be unnecessarily slow by many Labour critics. By the end of the year 62,000 pro-Nazis had been removed from public and business posts in the British Zone, but this process had been pursued with even more fervour in the American and French zones. Eisenhower took a keen personal interest in this matter himself. When General Patton made an unguarded statement about Nazis being politicians in the same way as were Republicans and Democrats in the United States, he was summoned to Eisenhower's headquarters and given a less important command. (Patton died on December 21st, 1945.) In November General Eisenhower, after triumphant visits to most European Allied capitals, including Moscow, was recalled to Washington as Chief of Staff, US Army.

A number of military courts were set up, and Germans were executed for various war crimes. One of the most sensational was that of forty-five men and women, including the notorious Irma Grese, charged with running the Belsen and Auschwitz concentration camps. The court martial, convened at Lüneburg Town Hall by Montgomery, moved slowly because of language difficulties and the frequent breakdowns of key but sick witnesses. The evidence called by the prosecution was widely reported and increased the sense of blackness and disillusion that had swept the world since the camps had been revealed early in the year. Harold le Druillenac, a British subject from Jersey, described how prisoners at Belsen had been reduced to eating flesh from black and rotting corpses. During the last five days before his rescue he had kept himself alive by eating grass. One in every ten of the corpses at Belsen was discovered to have been partly eaten. Agreement had been reached at a conference in London on the trial of the major German war criminals at Nuremberg, despite the doubts of some legal experts, and the proceedings began on November 21st with the American prosecution presented by Justice Jackson. It was soon clear that the trial was going to be a long affair. Everything had to be read in four languages. The case for the prosecution, which amounted to a detailed history of the German part in the war, went back as far as Munich and the events of 1939, and considered such questions as what would have happened if Germany had won the war. But evidence, including film, of the concentration camps, and the question of responsibility for them, was high in the prosecution's case. Many people found the trial, with its pictures of Goering, von Ribbentrop, von Papen, Doenitz and others sitting in the dock, strangely unreal. Among the British lawyers taking part were Sir Hartley Shawcross, Sir David Maxwell Fyfe and Sir Frank Soskice. Lord Justice Lawrence and Sir Norman Birkett represented Britain on the Tribunal. Of the twenty-three defendants, one, Robert Ley, committed suicide before the trial began, and another, Krupp von Bohlen und Halbach, head of the steel and armaments works, was declared too ill to attend. By the end of the year the prosecution was still presenting its case.

In Japan MacArthur ordered the arrest of eleven war leaders, on November 19th, to stand trial for war crimes. Two of them immediately committed suicide, but Tojo, the former Premier and leader of the militarists, succeeded only in shooting himself through the chest (he and six others were executed more than three years later). The trial of Yamashita opened on October 29th, in Manila. The General, considered by some to be the most brilliant of the war, insisted that he knew nothing of atrocities, and had issued no orders that could have resulted in them. If the defence was weak, the prosecution was weaker; but it was not till years later that the trial was to become controversial. The sentence was announced on the anniversary of Pearl Harbour, and the death sentence was not a surprising verdict.

There was every sign that the Germans, despite efforts by the Allies, were in for a long period of disinterest and despair. In Hamburg twenty-one people died from methylated alcohol poisoning during the last six weeks of the year. Stockholm's *Tidningen* newspaper reported a suicide wave in Germany; three hundred people had taken their own lives in Cologne, and many more in Berlin. On October 17th Eisenhower said that venereal disease constituted 'the most extreme hazard to troops in the US Zone'. Prostitution was blatant and rampant, and the night-life, particularly in the cellars of Berlin, abandoned. Nevertheless, under the effect of Allied energy and money, Western Germany at least was being injected with the seeds of normalcy. An almost lone voice in the wide pessimism was that of a report in December by the Institute of International Affairs. It said that Germany's 'agriculture was in an exceptionally healthy condition at the time of her collapse, and her present position is largely due to transport breakdown, political partition, and the withdrawal of foreign labour; it is therefore capable of relatively swift recovery if she can be kept going until next harvest'. Earlier in the year Eisenhower had noted that, 'From the day we entered Germany the willingness of the ordinary citizen to work from dawn to dark for a meagre living was noticeable. Even before we crossed the Rhine I had seen German women and their children in the fields, under sporadic gunfire, spading the ground and planting seed.' Meanwhile the black market, oblivious of military and political zones, reigned supreme.

In Austria progress had been more satisfactory, but there, too, movement between the Russian and Western zones was restricted. In Czechoslovakia an agreement had been reached between Truman and Stalin to withdraw troops by December 1st. The Americans were anxious to go, but the Russians seemed in less of a hurry, and at the end of the year Soviet forces were still present. In Rumania King Michael still clung to his throne despite a Communist Government. In December he appealed to the three great powers to instigate free elections. In Poland the Provisional Government, Communist-dominated, was well established and ambassadors with the United Kingdom and the United States had been exchanged. In Yugoslavia the Tito Government was also well established after one-party elections which King Peter described as a 'farce' but which the London *Times* considered to be fair and well conducted. There was no doubt as to Tito's popularity. King Peter had given up his hopeless quest to influence events there. Appeals to Truman had proved fruitless. The American President had replied: 'You are no doubt aware that it has consistently been the policy of the Government of the United States not to favour one faction in the political life of Yugoslavia.' The King had dismissed the three Regents, who were meant to be guarding the monarchy's interests in Belgrade, but from whom he had not heard since they left London some months before. He gave up all attempt to continue the co-operation with Tito that Churchill had always urged on him, and pinned his hopes instead on the band of hunted royalists led by Mihailovic.* Tito declared a republic.

Throughout the remainder of Europe, apart from the countries which had been happily neutral during the war, the end of the war had produced turbulence and problems the end and result of which no one could foretell. In Greece recovery was endangered by the disastrous financial morass, which Truman was not anxious to enter, and by feuds between Left and Right. In Italy there was much Communist activity, but no one could be sure of the strength of the party until elections were held. There were serious outbreaks of rioting, and armed bands broke into prisons to free or murder political prisoners; groups of bandits armed themselves with the weapons that littered the countryside. Two coalition governments failed to solve the many domestic problems during the year, and a third was formed under De Gasperi in December. Already De Gasperi showed signs of being much the ablest politician on the scene. Victor Emmanuel III sat uneasily and insecurely on his throne. In the Argentine the late arrival of the country into the war had done nothing to liberalize the régime there. The Vice-President, War Minister and Secretary of Labour and Welfare, Colonel Peron, seemed to be increasing his power and gaining wide support among

* Mihailovic was captured, and executed on July 26th, 1946.

both rural and city workers. During October Buenos Aires was in a state of turmoil. The US Assistant Secretary of State, Nelson Rockefeller, bitterly attacked the Argentine Government for failing to keep its promises on entry to the United Nations. Rockefeller had been one of the most persistent advocates for the friendly attitude towards the Argentine, and now resigned. In China two massive armies, the one disciplined and dedicated, the other disintegrating and corrupt, faced each other and manoeuvred for position like clumsy wrestlers, while Chiang Kai-shek visited as much of his country as he safely could, including Peking and Nanking, receiving polite ovations from his inscrutable people.

During the latter half of the year a large number of British visitors had gone to Dublin, where steaks and smartly dressed women were to be seen in profusion; to them it seemed incredibly gay and relaxed, a reminder of what life had once been like. There was some doubt as to Ireland's theoretical position relative to Britain and the monarchy, although the actual position had been made clear enough during the war. Mr Dillon finally asked in the Dail: 'Are we or are we not a republic, that is what I want to know?' To which Mr de Valera replied: 'Eire is a republic, if that is all the deputy wants to know.' Like the other neutral countries, Ireland remained comparatively and blissfully free of major upheaval, although financial difficulties prompted an economic mission to London.

(vii)

The final diplomatic activity of 1945 took place, appropriately enough, in the city from which the diplomatic stage had been set throughout the year: Moscow. Byrnes had 'suddenly recalled', while meditating on Thanksgiving Day, that it had been agreed at Yalta that the Foreign Ministers should meet every three months. He promptly suggested a meeting of the Foreign Ministers in Moscow. He did so against considerable advice, it being expected that little else could be gained from the Russians for the time being. Byrnes offered an important concession regarding the drafting of the peace treaties; after the full peace conference had considered the draft treaties and made recommendations, he said, the final drafts would be prepared and signed only by the states primarily concerned. Apart from the fact that France and China would still be admitted to the discussions, this seemed to be a complete reversal of the Anglo-American stand against the Russian demand at London. This new position had been agreed by Stalin and Harriman in the interval between conferences, but now Molotov refused to accept even this American withdrawal. Byrnes, unabashed, continued his efforts in other spheres, while Bevin, increasingly dubious about the worth of the conference, took less and less part in the proceedings. Eventually Molotov, apparently after pressure from Stalin, agreed to the American proposal and it was decided that the next peace conference should be held in Paris not later than May 1st. Byrnes cabled Bidault, but there was no indication from Paris as to whether the French would support such a set-back to their prestige and claims. The Bulgarian and Rumanian argument received another round of fruitless discussion. Molotov refused to hear doubts as to democratic institutions in Bulgaria, blandly and repeatedly referring to the elections which had been held there; in any case, he said, the Soviet Union would never countenance anything but friendly nations in that area again. There was also the question of Iran, which the Russians were beginning to describe as a hostile nation. The large number of Russian troops in the country still showed no sign of withdrawing. Iran had become one of Truman's major worries. He suspected a thrust into Iran concerted with a Communist *coup* in Greece which would develop into a giant pincers movement against the Middle East oilfields. But Truman was not in touch with Byrnes during the conference, and no progress was made on this or other issues. Byrnes, on his own initiative, raised the question of atomic energy, although Truman had already decided, in conjunction with Attlee and Mackenzie King, against an approach to the Soviet Union. Byrnes asked the Russians to sponsor the resolution of the United States, Canada and Britain regarding giving the United Nations Organization authority over atomic energy. It was agreed that the three Foreign Ministers would take up in stages the question of international control of atomic power, and this was revealed in a communiqué issued after the conference.

This discussion of atomic affairs with the Russians horrified many of Truman's advisers, and on Byrnes' return to the United States on December 28th he received a peremptory summons to the President's office. There he received a wigging perhaps unique from President to Secretary of State. Truman was infuriated at Byrnes' complete independence of action during the Moscow conference. 'A Secretary of State should never have the illusion that he is President of the

United States.' Like many of his advisers, he had recently become most apprehensive of the consequences of the Soviet Union gaining access to the secrets of the atomic bomb. He said he would not support the agreement made about atomic power in Moscow, and considered it 'shocking' that such a communiqué should have been issued without his knowledge. 'I said that I would not tolerate a repetition of such conduct.' Truman was particularly incensed over Byrnes' failure in the Iran question. It seems that he expected the Secretary of State to resign, but at this time Byrnes showed no inclination to do so. There was an unfortunate clash of personalities between Truman and Byrnes that had not been evident in the early days of the administration, but that had now come to a head. By appointing Byrnes, Truman had originally made a brilliant but purely political move to strengthen his position. But now that he felt strong enough to stand on his own feet, Byrnes was clearly dispensable. Byrnes was not the only Roosevelt man to feel the cold wind of Truman's growing confidence, and a number of resignations took place the following year. Truman's anger was not entirely fair, because Byrnes had at least returned from Moscow with agreement on representation at the peace treaties,* and would presumably have kept in closer touch with the President if Truman had stressed this before rather than after the conference. There was also some agreement on the control of Japan, the future of Korea, and the continued need to support Chiang Kai-shek in China at the expense of the Communists (something which the Russians were still more than willing to do; they had already benefited territorially from Chiang's weak Government). There was also agreement at last on Bulgaria and Rumania, the governments of which were to include two non-Communist members before Anglo-American recognition. Not only Byrnes, but Bevin also, was well satisfied with the meeting. But Truman was no longer impressed with promises. He wrote in a memo to Byrnes: 'Only one thing do they understand—"how many divisions have you?"' Thus had American presidential policy turned almost a complete somersault in twelve months; from a position of refusing to suspect the worst to a position of refusing to suspect anything but the worst. On the other hand, Byrnes seems to have made the foolish mistake of drastically underestimating Truman. The division between these two men on their attitude towards the

* Peace treaties with Italy, Bulgaria, Rumania, Hungary and Finland were finally signed in Paris on February 10th, 1947. Each had to pay large reparations and all except Bulgaria suffered territorial loss. The treaty with Austria was signed on May 5th, 1955; that with Japan (the USSR abstaining) on April 28th, 1952.

Soviet Union can be plainly traced in American public life down to today: the one always on guard and not frightened to take a tough and determined line; the other always trying to understand the Russian viewpoint, and anxious to reach some agreement rather than none at all.

(viii)

As the year drew inevitably to its close there were many signs of a return to normality and conditions of peace. In Britain things were, perhaps, particularly deceptive. For most families Christmas had been the first happy, united one for many years. The Prime Minister himself was surely not alone when years later he recalled: 'Of many happy Christmasses which I can remember, perhaps the best was that of 1945. The war was over. My eldest daughter was demobbed. The family was reunited. My wife and I, with four children, spent Christmas at Chequers, a delightful house. . . . On Boxing Day we had a large party with lots of boys and girls, the children of colleagues and civil servants. A secret stair in the old house provided for a surprise appearance of Father Christmas. . . . No red boxes arrived. The cold war had hardly begun. All was peace.' Great hope was placed in the first meeting of the General Assembly of the United Nations, which was to open in London in the first week of the New Year.

On December 31st the Lord Mayor of Bristol, wearing his red civic robes, officially welcomed at Avonmouth docks the arrival of the first banana boat to the United Kingdom since December 1940. Sale was to be restricted to those under eighteen years old. Many children had never seen a banana; others could not remember what one looked like. On the same day the Home Guard, which had prepared to meet the German invasion with pitchforks and scythes in 1940, was disbanded. There was no parade on this occasion; no ceremony of any kind. For nearly six years over a million men had served in this army without pay. The War Office said: 'They pass out of existence. It's just cheerio and thanks, Home Guard.'

In the United States two recent announcements had done little to offset the general feeling of relief and constrained joy at the ending of the war; there was a great urge to accelerate with ever-increasing rapidity to full peacetime conditions. Few people took much notice when the President announced a greatly strengthened National Guard and reserve because of new national responsibilities in the world; and in the last week of the year the War Powers Act, by which price controls were maintained, was extended for six months by Congress to combat growing inflation.

In Jerusalem at Christmas-time a number of 'outrages' had taken place; as the year closed British troops attempted to maintain law and order to a background punctuated by the spatter of rifle fire and the explosions of home-made bombs. At Hiroshima parties of American servicemen on local furlough, the first tourists, were carefully picking their steps over the rubble and taking photographs to send home. In London, New Year's Eve was cold and foggy; celebrations were subdued, but here and there in the West End small groups of merrymakers emerged for a few moments from the swirling fog only to be swallowed up again shortly after. As usual, the occasion of New Year's Eve prompted a number of the world's statesmen to voice their thoughts, both important and trivial, on the year that was passing; a year that had seen more glory, more horror and more lost opportunity than most that had gone before it. Some used the occasion to make political announcements. A New Year's Message from Hirohito denied that he was divine; one from Chiang Kai-shek agreed to a coalition with the Communists and a cease-fire. In South Africa Jan Christian Smuts, calling for renewed faith in idealism, said: 'The international community has at last come to life. That is the thought I would like us to carry forward into 1946.' Once more Winston Churchill issued his annual message to the Primrose League. 'We shall only win the peace, as we have won the war, by character and hard work. Confident in the rightness of our point of view, let us devote ourselves in the coming year to the service of our country, and let us make ourselves effective advocates and defenders of our free and progressive civilization.' His words were redolent of the emerging spirit of the time. For in many other nations the people were being asked, by governments locked in their commitments and suspicions, to be vigilant and to be prepared to defend their ways of life. The very suspicions of the Russian hierarchy, since Yalta and before, of the emergence of a post-war distinct anti-Soviet bloc was helping to rapidly create it—just as Roosevelt had feared. Stalin, no doubt, believed he was no more responsible for the break-up of the alliance, so essential for stability and peace, than the British, and especially Churchill, thought they were. The State Department and the surviving Roosevelt men like Byrnes no doubt felt they had been on the right path all along in trying to preserve the alliance by taking a central position between Russia and Britain. Churchill no doubt considered he had acted in the only possible way in attempting to get the United States to line up against Russia, in the cause of individual freedom, before a rigid Iron Curtain settled across Europe.

But now the curtain was down. Across it the USSR and the United States faced each other, not as allies but as rivals, and everyone had a different view as to why and exactly when it had happened. No one could tell, although some professed to know, whether or not the next act would be the final one in the world's tragedy. Certainly the forces of history seemed to be moving with ever-increasing and apparently uncontrollable rapidity. How would mankind fare in its ancient quest—seemingly unattainable, but now totally imperative—of directing those forces along the channels of peace? Some believed that while the Anglo-American alliance lived, and despite all the stresses and strains of the past year it had indeed survived, there would be hope for the world. Other statesmen prepared to face the new age on the assumption that Britain was no longer a great power; that the world had entered the Second World War with six great powers but had emerged from it with only two. They believed that the question now was how the United States would react to a thankless and unrewarding responsibility: as well or worse than Britain, which had formerly carried out the same task? Others believed that all depended on what occurred in the Kremlin; they waited with anxiety and fear for the removal or death of Stalin.

Already nations were kicking and struggling to free themselves from the tangled net that their interlocking and interplaying ambitions and suspicions had weaved around them. Could they disentangle themselves before it was too late and *rigor mortis* had set in? Would a period of calmness and cool common sense slowly free them at last?

There was hope perhaps in the undoubted fact that no one believed, as so many had done in 1918, that the end of the war had heralded in a millennium of peace; that it had been a 'war to end all wars'. At the time of the Hiroshima bomb many commentators and public figures had spoken with pessimism of the possibility and effects on civilization of a third world war. As the chimes of Big Ben—which to millions of people in Europe had in the past six years become the clarion call of individual dignity and liberty—reverberated over Westminster and the dimly-seen Thames, all kinds of ordinary men who had, it seemed, little or no control over human destiny found a strange comfort in the very fear that swelled in their hearts. The last chime died away; there was peace, but there was no complacency. It was the Age of Anxiety.

SOURCES AND NOTES

A list of all the source books that refer to the events of 1945 would fill a small book in itself, and I make no claim to have read them all. Some aspects and events of the year have been very much more written-up than others; mentioned below are the principal sources used in compiling this book. Considerable use has been made of newspaper reports, but some care has been taken to avoid the snares of propaganda; even in the final year of the war the propaganda experts were glossing over or exaggerating the facts, as much for the sake of domestic consumption as for confusing the enemy. This was particularly the case in the Pacific and in Asia, where rather than admit to the depressing facts of months of inconclusive and unimportant fighting in remote areas, communiqués frequently referred to islands as having been 'conquered', much to the surprise and ire of the men still fighting there. Newspapers have been useful from another point of view: the events in everyday life for the ordinary person. For, as well as attempting to give a serious account of the manoeuvres of great nations during the year, and to describe the problems and characteristics of the world's great leaders, I have tried, too, to recapture something of what it was like to be alive in 1945, especially in Britain and the United States.

Owing to a lack of reliable information, the events from a Soviet point of view have been only lightly painted in; observations of Western diplomats and official communiqués and messages published at the time being preferred to the great deal of conjecture written ever since around Russian motives and behind-the-scenes activities at the end of the war. Unfortunately the ways of international Communism and the writing of frank autobiographies by its leaders are not compatible. The version of the story as told by Stalin, and (perhaps even more fascinating) by Molotov, will never be fully known. Apart from this, three major works have been particularly missed. The relevant volumes of Anthony Eden's autobiography, and of Professor Alan Bullock's biography of Bevin, were unpublished at the time of writing. And the memoirs of Franklin Roosevelt, which he did not have the opportunity to write, would no doubt have thrown much powerful and revealing light on corners still shrouded in darkness or at the best in dim light; for there are some questions on the Grand Disalliance of 1945 to which only he knew the answer.

There are many quotations in this book. I hope I have acknowledged each one in turn in the Sources and Notes that follow, but if I should have inadvertently omitted any owner of copyright I apologize now in advance.

For permission to quote longer extracts I am particularly indebted to the following:

The Controller of Her Majesty's Stationery Office for extracts from official documents, especially those written by Sir Winston Churchill, which are Crown Copyright; Cassell & Co Ltd for extracts from *Defeat Into Victory* by Sir William Slim, *The Testament of Adolf Hitler*, and *The Second World War* by Sir Winston Churchill; Wm Collins Sons & Co for extracts from *Triumph in the West* by Sir Arthur Bryant; Macdonald Hastings for an extract from an article on VE Day; A. M. Heath & Co Ltd for extracts from *The White House Papers* by Robert E. Sherwood, published by Eyre & Spottiswoode Ltd; Hodder & Stoughton Ltd and Emery Reves for extracts from *Year of Decisions* by Harry S. Truman; Hutchinson & Co Ltd for an extract from *My Yesterday, Your Tomorrow* by Lord Boothby; Lawrence & Wishart Ltd for extracts from the published letters and telegrams of Stalin; Frank Owen for an extract from a broadcast talk on Burma; Laurence Pollinger Ltd for extracts from *Eclipse* by Alan Moorehead, published by Hamish Hamilton Ltd; The Roosevelt Trust for extracts from the letters and telegrams of Franklin D. Roosevelt; Secker & Warburg Ltd for extracts from *Defeat in the West* by Milton Shulman; and the proprietors of the *Daily Express, Daily Mail* (for extracts from the *News Chronicle*), the *Daily Telegraph* and *The Times*, for extracts from reports and articles.

I am also indebted to the Imperial War Museum for all the illustrations in this book, except those of the soldier returning home and the VE Day celebrations in Piccadilly Circus, which appear by permission of Fox Photos Ltd and the Radio Times Hulton Picture Library respectively.

Books and publications acknowledged as having been quoted are also in general those that have been used as sources. Authors, publishers and dates of publication are mentioned only in the first instance. Other acknowledgements are made in the text itself.

I

(i) Churchill's New Year Message to the Primrose League, of which he was Grand Master, from the *Daily Telegraph*, December 31, 1945; expectations from *The Second World War: Vol VI, Triumph and Tragedy* by Winston S. Churchill (Cassell, 1954), Appendix C, in a memorandum to General Ismay and Sir Edward Bridges, January 14, 1945. This work is elsewhere referred to as *Triumph and Tragedy*. Hitler's broadcast from the *Daily Telegraph*, January 2, 1945. Sir Robert Bruce Lockhart's comment on Stalin from a Foreword to *The Private Life of Josif Stalin* by J. Fishman and B. Hutton (W. H. Allen, 1962). Material for the short resumé of the war situation from *Encyclopaedia Britannica* and from newspapers of January 1945.

SOURCES AND NOTES

(ii) Quotation from *Battle: The Story of the Bulge* by John Toland (USA 1959, Muller, 1960). De Guingand's remark from *Operation Victory* by Major-General Sir Francis de Guingand (Hodder & Stoughton, 1947). There is an extract from *Soldier* by General Matthew B. Ridgway (Harper, 1956). Some information from *The Battle of the Ardennes* by Robert E. Merriam (USA, and Souvenir Press, 1958). *Defeat in the West* by Milton Shulman (Secker & Warburg, 1947) was also most helpful. Churchill's message to Stalin, 'You yourself know . . .', from *Stalin's Correspondence with Churchill, Attlee, Roosevelt and Truman* (Ministry of Foreign Affairs, Moscow, 1957, and Lawrence & Wishart, 1958)— elsewhere referred to as *Stalin's Correspondence*. Correspondence between Alan Brooke and Montgomery about Eisenhower from *Triumph in the West* by Sir Arthur Bryant (Collins, 1959), based on Field-Marshal Lord Alanbrooke's diaries. Eisenhower's remark about Rundstedt's rushing out of fixed defences is from an Order of the Day, December 22, 1944, quoted by Chester Wilmot in his essential work *The Struggle for Europe* (Collins, 1952). Montgomery's Press conference on January 7th is also quoted in Wilmot. Bradley's views on his staff and on Montgomery from *A Soldier's Story* (Holt, 1951, and Eyre & Spottiswoode). Eisenhower's opinion of Montgomery's Press conference from *Crusade in Europe* by Dwight D. Eisenhower (Doubleday, 1948, and Heinemann, 1948), perhaps the most literate and thoughtful of all the generals' memoirs of the Second World War, in contrast to Eisenhower's memoranda, etc, at the time. Montgomery's view from his *Memoirs* (Collins, 1958). Hitler's speech to the generals from *The Struggle for Europe*. Churchill's speech in the House of Commons from *Triumph and Tragedy*. Also used: *Report by the Supreme Commander to the Combined Chiefs of Staff on the Operations in Europe of the Allied Expeditionary Force June 6, 1944, to May 8, 1945* (HMSO, 1946).

(iii) Churchill's remark about the 'Hitler monster' from a memo to the Foreign Office, April 8, 1945, printed in *Triumph and Tragedy*. The Goebbels remark is quoted in *The Real Stalin* by Yves Delbars (Paris, and Allen & Unwin, 1953). The quotations from Hitler's conference on January 27th are from *The Fuehrer Conferences* quoted in Wilmot (*op cit*). Churchill's agreement with Stalin in Moscow, October 1944, is from *Triumph and Tragedy*. Stalin's observation to Eden is from *The Real Stalin*. The correspondence over Poland between Stalin, Roosevelt and Churchill in December and January is from *Stalin's Correspondence* and *Triumph and Tragedy*. Sherwood's words are from *The White House Papers of Harry L. Hopkins* by Robert E. Sherwood (Harper, 1948, and Eyre & Spottiswoode, 1949). Roosevelt's words to his son are from *As He Saw It* by Elliott Roosevelt (New York, 1946); his words to Stettinius from *Roosevelt and the Russians* by Edward R. Stettinius (USA, and Cape, 1950). Eisenhower's words from *Crusade in Europe*. All the correspondence between Churchill and Stalin over Yugoslavia is from *Stalin's Corres-*

pondence (pages 296–302). King Peter's words from *A King's Heritage* by King Peter II (Cassell, 1955). Sherwood's description of American distrust of British motives in Europe is from *The White House Papers*, as are Hopkins' own words. The exchange between Roosevelt and Churchill regarding a meeting at Malta is from *Triumph and Tragedy*, as is Churchill's message describing his pessimistic view of the forthcoming conference at Yalta. Roosevelt's being 'brutally frank' from *The Second World War: Vol IV, The Hinge of Fate* by Winston S. Churchill (Cassell, 1951).

(iv) Admiral Halsey's words are from *The Great Sea War* by E. B. Potter and Chester W. Nimitz (Prentice-Hall, 1960, and Harrap, 1961). The story about General Kenney and MacArthur is from *MacArthur 1941–1951* by C. A. Willoughby and J. Chamberlain (USA, and Heinemann, 1956). Also used: *The War: A Concise History* by Louis L. Snyder (USA, 1960, and Robert Hale, 1962).

(v) London's casualty statistics from *Triumph and Tragedy*. Duncan Sandys' words are from *Rocket* by Air Chief Marshal Sir Philip Joubert (Hutchinson, 1957). Details of V.2 disasters from reports in the *Daily Telegraph* and *The Times*. Admiral Ingram's words are from the *Daily Telegraph*. Lord Beaverbrook's letter is from *The White House Papers*. Also used: *V.2* by W. Dornberger (Germany, 1952, and Hurst & Blackett, 1954).

(vi) *Panzer Leader* by Heinz Guderian (Germany, and Michael Joseph, 1952); official communiqués and newspaper reports, especially the *Daily Telegraph;* the relevant entry in *Encyclopaedia Britannica* by B. H. Liddell Hart; *The Struggle for Europe*. Stalin's conference is from Delbars (*op cit*).

(vii) Churchill's views on the Italian Front are from *Triumph and Tragedy*. Byrnes' recollections about Roosevelt on the journey to Malta from *Speaking Frankly* by James F. Byrnes (Harper, and the James F. Byrnes Foundation, 1947). Also used: *Crusade in Europe; The Struggle for Europe; Triumph in the West.*

2

The account of Yalta has been pieced together from the various first-hand accounts, and other works, mentioned below.

All Churchill's memories of and sayings at the Yalta conference are from *Triumph and Tragedy*, as is Stalin's speech at the Yusupov dinner. Byrnes' recollections are from *Speaking Frankly*. Some of the details of arrangements at Yalta are from *War at the Top* by James Leasor and General Sir Leslie Hollis (Michael Joseph, 1959). There are a number of small contradictions between the various accounts of Yalta, and Sherwood's *The White House Papers* (for Hopkins' note to F.D.R., Hopkins' views on the success of the conference, and the congratulatory telegrams) particularly has slightly different versions of conversations and facts to the others, and there is some disagreement between Sherwood, Churchill and Byrnes, who took copious short-hand notes, on detail. Parts of the picture are far from clear. The best account is perhaps that in *I Was There* by Admiral William D. Leahy (Curtis, 1950, and Gollancz, 1950). There are important accounts in *Roosevelt and the Russians*, and in *The Real Stalin*, from which Stalin's confidences to Roosevelt about Molotov are quoted, and from which the likelihood that Stalin was under some supervision from the Politburo committee.

Other accounts are in: *Triumph in the West; Memoirs* by General Lord Ismay (Heinemann, 1960), from which Lord Ismay's remark; *Eight Years Overseas* by Field-Marshal Lord Wilson (Hutchinson, 1948); *Stalin: A Political Biography* by I. Deutscher (Oxford, 1949); *Churchill, Roosevelt, Stalin: the War They Waged and the Peace They Fought* by Herbert Feis (Princeton, 1957, and Oxford, 1957); *The Conferences at Malta and Yalta* (US Dept of State, Foreign Relations of the US, Diplomatic Papers, No 6199, 1955). *The Yalta Betrayal; Data on the Decline and Fall of F. D. Roosevelt* by F. Wittmer (Idaho, 1954) is a somewhat one-sided version. General Anders' view is from the *Daily Telegraph*, February 1945. Churchill's and Roosevelt's speeches on returning home from *The Times*, February 1945. Other publications quoted: *Time Magazine, The Christian Science Monitor*, the *Herald Tribune*—all February 1945.

3

(i) Eisenhower's remark on the Siegfried Line from *Crusade in Europe;* Patton's from *War As I Knew It* (Houghton, Mifflin, 1947, and W. H. Allen, 1948). Sgt Drabik's memory from *The War: A Concise History.* For start of the offensive in the West: *Triumph and Tragedy, The Struggle for Europe, Triumph in the West*, Montgomery's *Memoirs*, and *The Battle for the Rhineland* by R. W. Thompson (Hutchinson, 1958). *Daily Telegraph* (quoted). There is an extract from *Eclipse* by Alan Moorehead (Hamish Mamilton, 1945).

(ii) *Defeat in the West;* and *Hitler: A Study in Tyranny* by Alan Bullock (Odhams, 1952). The eye-witness account of refugees in Poland is from the *Daily Telegraph*, February 7, 1945. German News Agency reports from *The Times* and *Daily Telegraph*. Churchill's doubts about saturation bombing, and the AP report, from *The History of the Second World War: The Strategic Air Offensive Against Germany 1939-45*, Vol III, by Sir Charles Webster and Noble Frankland (HMSO, 1961). *The First and the Last* by Adolf Galland (Methuen, 1955) for the effects of saturation bombing. Hitler's activity and life in the Bunker from the magnificent reconstruction given in *The Last Days of Hitler* by H. R. Trevor-Roper (Macmillan, 1947), and revised edition (Pan Books, 1962). Information about Doenitz and the German Navy from Wilmot (*op cit*) and *Swastika at Sea* by C. D. Bekker (Germany, 1953, and Kimber, 1953). Hitler's words from *The Testament of Adolf Hitler*, with an Introduction by H. R. Trevor-Roper (Librarie Artheme Fayard, 1959, and Cassell, 1961), the Hitler-Bormann documents deposited in a bank at Bad Gastein at the end of the war by Bormann's bearer.

(iii) The quotation from Robert Sherrod on the Iwo Jima beach-head is from *On To Westward* quoted in *History of US Naval Operations in World War II*, Vol XIV, by S. A. Morison (Little, Brown and Oxford, 1960). Much else of the information from Morison. The simile about the advance of troops from *The United States Marines and Amphibious War* by J. A. Isely and P. A. Crowl (Princeton, 1951). Kuribayaski's final messages from Morison. Casualties from Morison, and from *The Great Sea War* by Potter and Nimitz (qv above).

(iv) Patton's statement on crossing the Rhine from Wilmot (*op cit*). Churchill as a student of military history from *Triumph and Tragedy*. Churchill and the 'red coats' from *Eclipse*. The story about the washing on the Siegfried Line from a report in the *Daily Telegraph*, March 1945. Simpson's warning to Churchill under shell-fire from *Triumph in the West*. Lord Montgomery's *Memoirs*, *The Struggle for Europe*, and *Crusade in Europe*. For the Eisenhower-Stalin contact seeming to derive from Tedder's visit to Moscow see *Three Years with Eisenhower* by Capt Harry C. Butcher (USA, and Heinemann, 1946), page 639. Butcher was Eisenhower's naval aide; his book, although dedicated to the Supreme Commander, caused Eisenhower perhaps more embarrassment than any other (when it was serialized in the *Saturday Evening Post* he hastily sent off placatary letters to Churchill, Montgomery and others). *The Private Papers of Hore-Belisha* by R. J. Minney (Collins, 1960). The Churchill-Eisenhower correspondence from *Triumph and Tragedy*, as also Churchill's politic message to Roosevelt and his views on the US Chiefs of Staff. Fuller's view from his *The Second World War* (Eyre & Spottiswoode, 1948). Ralph Ingersoll's from his *Top Secret* (Partridge, 1946).

(v) The CO of 41 *Volkssturm*, and General Blumentritt, from Milton Shulman's definitive work (*op cit*); he interviewed them both. *The Struggle for Europe*. Churchill's views on bombing from *Triumph and Tragedy*.

(vi) The definitive work on the Burma Campaign is *Defeat into Victory* by Field-Marshal Sir William Slim (Cassell, 1956). It is one of the military classics of the war, and is twice quoted here. Also newspapers for Fourteenth Army campaign. The British correspondent on the road to Meiktila reported in the *Daily Telegraph*, February 1945. Frank Owen's broadcast was on the BBC Home Service, December 12, 1944; the conditions it described apply equally to those existing a few weeks later, although by then the air supply was perhaps as important as the railway. MacArthur's speech and quotation from Willoughby and Chamberlain (*op cit*). Also used: *The Great Sea War*, Morison (*op cit*), *The Magnificent*

Mitscher by Theodore Taylor (W. W. Norton, 1954), and *The Army in World War II: Okinawa, The Last Battle,* by Appleman, Burns, Gugeler and Stevens (Washington, 1948).

(vii) The fact that Roosevelt wanted to delay announcing the veto voting agreement in UNO until a favourable moment, from *The White House Papers.* Churchill's, Roosevelt's and Stalin's correspondence on Poland and the peace moves in Switzerland from *Stalin's Correspondence* and *Triumph and Tragedy.* Also used: *The Struggle for Europe.*

4

(i) Truman gives a fascinating and detailed account of his taking over the office of President in *Memoirs, Vol I, Year of Decisions* (Doubleday, and Hodder & Stoughton, 1955). Also used: *Speaking Frankly, Crusade in Europe, Triumph and Tragedy* (for the messages from Washington), and especially *When F.D.R. Died* by B. Asbell (USA, and Cape, 1961), an extremely detailed montage of all the events around Roosevelt's death. *Daily Express* quoted, December 31, 1962. Other newspapers quoted: *New York Times, Kansas City Star* (both April 1945), and the *Observer,* April 15, 1945.

(ii) *Report by the Supreme Commander* quoted (*op cit*). Bradley's astonishment about the Redoubt from *A Soldier's Story.* Eisenhower's remark to his naval aide from *My Three Years With Eisenhower.* Lord Montgomery's phrases from his *Memoirs.* Alan Moorehead's description of looting from *Eclipse,* as also the relief of Fallingbostel camp. Hitler's orders about Belsen from the *Fall of the Curtain* by Count Folke Bernadotte (Cassell, 1945). The testimony about Dachau is that of Dr Franz Blaha as given in *The Trial of German Major War Criminals: Proceedings of the International Military Tribunal at Nuremberg* (HMSO, 1946). Cadman's report from his *Drive: A Chronicle of Patton's Army* (Little, Brown, 1957). Edward Murrow's broadcast was heard in the United States and on the BBC Home Service, April 1945. Also used: *The Struggle for Europe, Triumph and Tragedy,* and *Crusade in Europe.*

(iii) *Triumph and Tragedy* (Churchill's message to Alexander quoted) for the later Italian campaign; also *The War Memoirs* of Field-Marshal Earl Alexander (Cassell, 1962), and *Calculated Risk* by General Mark Clark (New York, and Harrap, 1951). For the last days of Mussolini I am greatly indebted to *The Brutal Friendship: Mussolini, Hitler and the Fall of Italian Fascism* by F. W. Deakin (Weidenfeld & Nicolson, 1962), and to *Mussolini: An Intimate Life* by Paolo Monelli (Italy, and Thames & Hudson, 1953), which contain magnificent reconstructions of Mussolini's last hours. Also used: *Benito Mussolini* by Christopher Hibbert (Longmans, 1962), which also has a detailed account of the execution, and *Mussolini* by Laura Fermi (Chicago, 1961). A *Times* reporter was present at the garage scenes in Milan. Alexander's communiqué from *The Times*, April 1945.

(iv) Fall of Berlin from the official reports published in *The Times; Flight in the Winter* by J. Thorwald (Hutchinson, 1953); *Follow My Leader* by L. Hagen (Germany, and Wingate, 1951). *The Schellenberg Memoirs* (Germany, and Deutsch, 1956) and *The Fall of the Curtain* for Himmler's peace overtures. More background on this and the end of the war in Germany from *The Kersten Memoirs* by Felix Kersten (Hutchinson, 1956); Kersten was Himmler's doctor. *Swastika At Sea* for the earlier evacuation of East Prussia. The death of Hitler from H. R. Trevor-Roper's indispensable account (*op cit*). *Hitler: A Study in Tyranny* and *Defeat in the West* for background information. The Churchill-Truman recorded telephone conversation is reprinted at length in *Year of Decisions*.

(v) In the following sections considerable use is made of the reports of British war correspondents. No excuse is offered for this; the war reporting of the Second World War reached the peak of the reporter's task—in contrast to that of the First World War. Some of the correspondents, such as Moorehead, Wilmot (both Australians), Leonard Mosley and Ian Colvin, who with their colleagues reported the war with grace, accuracy, bravery and sense of history, later became documentary historians in their own right. Buckley was killed in Korea.

Doenitz's broadcast is from *The Times*, May 2, 1945; that to the *Wehrmacht* from *Defeat in the West*. His later explanation, and for much of the general background, including his show-down with Himmler, from his *Memoirs* (Germany, 1958, and Weidenfeld & Nicolson, 1959). British tank officer from *History of the Argyll and Sutherland Highlanders, 5th Battalion, 1939-45* by Desmond Flower (Nelson, 1950). Churchill's message to Eden from *Triumph and Tragedy*. The report from the banks of the Elbe was from James Wellard in the *Daily Express*, May 8, 1945. Stanley Baron's report for the *News Chronicle* of May 7, 1945. Moorehead's report from Hamburg for the *Daily Express*, May 4, 1945. Christopher Buckley's to the *Daily Telegraph* of May 5, 1945, and the correspondent with the Dorset Regt was Paul Holt in the *Daily Express*, May 7, 1945. Communiqués and statements from Flensburg from *The Times*. Also used: *Hermann Goering* by Roger Manvell and Heinrich Fraenkel (Heinemann, 1962), Lord Montgomery's *Memoirs*, and *Crusade in Europe*. There is an extract from page 252 of *The Big Show* by Pierre Clostermann, DFC (Paris, 1950, and Chatto & Windus, 1951); the second part of the extract is from a slightly later entry in his diary. Alan Brooke's remark on the end of the war from *Triumph in the West*.

(vi) Official statements from Flensburg from *The Times* and *Daily Telegraph*, May 1945. Doenitz's *Memoirs*, Lord Montgomery's *Memoirs*, *Crusade in Europe*, *A Soldier's Story*, and *My Three Years With Eisenhower*.

(vii) Official statements on the end of the war from Flensburg, London,

Tokyo, Moscow and Washington from *The Times* and *The Listener*, May 1945. Churchill's telephone conversation with Leahy from *I Was There*. Alan Moorehead's reflections while driving on the autobahn from *Eclipse*. The report from Utrecht was by Ronald Walker to the *News Chronicle*, May 8, 1945. Excerpt from editorial in *The Times*, May 8, 1945. Churchill's and George VI's speeches on VE Day from *The Times*, May 9, 1945. The report by Macdonald Hastings, quoted at length, was in *Picture Post*, May 19, 1945. Newspapers used as sources for reconstruction of VE Day in Britain: *Daily Express, Daily Telegraph, The Times, Daily Sketch, Evening Standard*.

(viii) The Churchill-Truman correspondence over Prague from *Triumph and Tragedy* and *Year of Decisions*. Doenitz's broadcast from *The Times*, May 9, 1945. The contemporary newspapers consulted for the early post-war scene in Europe and elsewhere were: *Daily Express, News Chronicle, The Times, Daily Telegraph, Sunday Express, Daily Sketch*. The 'official account' referred to in the Channel Islands surrender was a release from the Ministry of Information. Douglas Willis's report from *The Listener*, May 17, 1945. The drunken generals at Berlin from *My Three Years With Eisenhower*. The rape and destruction of Berlin from *Follow My Leader* and *Soviet Staff Officer* by I. Krylov (Moscow, and Falcon, 1951). The story about the Adlon Hotel from interviews with two of the old hotel staff, in Berlin. Information about the BBC programmes, from the *Radio Times*, May 10, 1945. J.B. Priestley's broadcast from *The Listener*, May 17, 1945. Churchill's victory broadcast on May 10 from *Triumph and Tragedy*.

5

(i) Churchill's messages to Truman and Stalin from *Triumph and Tragedy*, as are his views of US diplomacy. Leahy's assertion about Truman's important conference from *I Was There*. Eisenhower's message to Truman, and Truman's view on the withdrawal from the Elbe, from *Year of Decisions*. See *The White House Papers* for a record of the Stalin-Hopkins discussions. *Triumph and Tragedy*, Appendix C, for Churchill's memo to the Chiefs of Staff on demobilization. Also used: Lord Montgomery's *Memoirs*, and *Crusade in Europe*.

(ii) Churchill's sayings about the various spheres of Mediterranean immediate post-war squabbling from *Triumph and Tragedy*, except those about Truman's unpublished statement and about de Gaulle, which are from *Year of Decisions*, as are the Truman quotes in this section. The President's ultimatum to de Gaulle, and de Gaulle's reply, from *War Memoirs: Salvation 1944-46; Documents* by General de Gaulle (Paris, 1959, and Weidenfeld & Nicholson, 1960). *The Times* for background and details of the Trieste and Levant affairs. A number of first-hand reports in the *Daily Telegraph*, especially one of May 14, 1945, from the Franco-Italian frontier.

(iii) Churchill's memo, of May 14th, to the Foreign Office on the Doenitz 'Government' from *Triumph and Tragedy*, Appendix C. Speer's broadcast from the *Daily Telegraph*, May 5, 1945. The capture of the Doenitz 'Government' from a *Reuter's* report. Montgomery's words, and the story about his being entertained, from his *Memoirs*. John Strachey's view of the bombing of Germany from a broadcast on the BBC Home Service, May 9, 1945, and reproduced in *Voices For Britain*, ed H. Krabbe (Allen & Unwin, 1947). Moorehead's vivid dispatch was to the *Daily Express*, May 7, 1945. The BBC correspondent at Linz was Patrick Smith; his report was printed in *The Listener*, May 17, 1945. The *Observer* (quoted). Occupation problems and inter-allied entertaining, etc, from *The Times*, and *A Record of the War: The 24th Quarter* by Philip Graves (Hutchinson, 1947).

(iv) Eisenhower's words at the Mansion House from Butcher (*op cit*). Sir John Anderson's statements from *The Times* (and much of the post-European war picture and statistics from that newspaper). The *Economist*. The *News Chronicle* (quoted, May 8, 1945). *Triumph and Tragedy* (from which Churchill's letter to Attlee quoted). *As It Happened* by C. R. Attlee (Heinemann, 1954) (from which Attlee's letter to Churchill quoted). *The Fateful Years* by Hugh Dalton (Muller, 1957), and Lord Morrison's *An Autobiography* (Odhams, 1960) for background to the election controversies and the Labour Party Conference. Dalton for the Prime Minister's tea party. Attlee's denial of a preference for the Coalition from the *Observer*, October 21, 1962, in a review of *Aneurin Bevan*, Vol I, by Michael Foot (MacGibbon & Kee, 1962) in which it is said that Attlee and Bevin had to be 'hauled out by the scruff of their necks' from the Coalition. Many British newspapers. Those quoted: *News Chronicle* (May 7, 1945), *Evening Standard* (May 8, 1945), *Radio Times* (May 10, 1945). Book reviews from: *Sunday Times, Observer, Spectator. Film Review* by F. Maurice Speed (Macdonald, 1945). De Valera's broadcast from *The Times*. Truman's view of John L. Lewis's strike from *Year of Decisions*, as also the telegram from Churchill, and the answer to the five Congressmen. Henry Wallace's speech from a *Reuter's* report. *Kansas City Star* (quoted). *The Life of J. M. Keynes* by R. F. Harrod (Macmillan, 1951).

(v) *The Magnificent Mitscher* for suicide attacks at Okinawa. Also *The US Army in World War II: Okinawa, The Last Battle*. Description of Ushijima's suicide from *The War: 1939–45* (Cassell, 1960), ed Desmond Flower and James Reeves. *Defeat Into Victory*. Churchill's quoted message to Mountbatten on the end of the Burma campaign from *The Times*. The note on conditions in Japan from a description given by a neutral visitor quoted in *Time* magazine, August 20, 1945. MacArthur's announcement of the end of fighting in Luzon from Willoughby and Chamberlain (*op cit*). The comment about amphibious warfare in the

Philippines from *Jungle Road to Tokyo* by Lieutenant-General Robert L. Eichelberger (Viking, and Odhams, 1951). *The Times* and *Daily Telegraph* for the smaller campaigns.

(vi) Truman's comments on, and words at, the San Francisco conference from *Year of Decisions*. The quoted speeches of Eden and Smuts from *The Times. Speaking Frankly*.

(vii) Churchill's messages to Stalin on Yugoslavia from *Triumph and Tragedy. A King's Heritage* was also most useful. Hopkins' cable to Truman from *Year of Decisions*. Bulganin's thesis from *Revue Bolchevique* quoted in *The Real Stalin*. Churchill's views on the withdrawal in Germany from *Triumph and Tragedy. Speaking Frankly*.

(viii) All personal reflections, etc, in this section from the previously mentioned works of Churchill, Morrison, Dalton and Attlee. Public statements from *The Times*, *Daily Telegraph* and *News Chronicle. Daily Express* and *Daily Mirror* are quoted. Quotes from American newspapers: *New York Daily News*, *Detroit Free Press*, *Cleveland Plain Dealer*, *St Louis Globe Democrat*, *Wall Street Journal*. William Shirer's broadcast from the *Daily Telegraph*, May 25, 1945. *Harold Laski* by Kingsley Martin (Gollancz, 1953). *The British General Election of 1945* by R. B. McCallum and A. Readman (Oxford, 1947).

(ix) There is an excellent account of the Potsdam conference in *Year of Decisions;* also *Triumph and Tragedy*, *Speaking Frankly*, and *As It Happened*. The various quotations are from Churchill, Truman, *The White House Papers*, and, for the formal communiqués, etc, *The Times*. General Hollis's recollection from *War at the Top*. The Russian and Stalin background mainly from *The Real Stalin* and *Stalin: A Political Biography*. The Conference has been more carefully written-up than Yalta, and there is a detailed reappraisal in *Between War and Peace: The Potsdam Conference* by Herbert Feis (Princeton, and Oxford, 1960); in this a different view as to Stalin's health and vigour at the conference is given. For the background to the atom bomb: *Atomic Energy For Military Purposes: US Official Report* by H. de W. Smyth (1945), and the authoritative *No High Ground* by Fletcher Knebel and Charles Bailey (USA, and Weidenfeld & Nicolson, 1960).

(x) The description of Lord Beaverbrook in the Map Room is from *The War and Colonel Warden* by Gerald Pawle (Harrap, 1963), which gives a detailed account of Churchill's day of defeat. Churchill's view of the verdict from *Triumph and Tragedy;* his statement from *The Times*, July 27, 1945. Attlee's recollection from *A Prime Minister Remembers* by Francis Williams (Heinemann, 1961); a book which fills in many but not all of the important gaps in Attlee's autobiography, *As It Happened*, which was also useful. The Press conference at Transport House, and the speeches at Caxton Hall, from *The Times* and *Daily Telegraph*, July 27, 1945. Attlee's message to Stalin from *Stalin's Correspondence*. Bevin's words from Dalton's *The Fateful Years*. Kaltenborn's view from the *Daily Telegraph*,

July 27, 1945, and also R. K. Law's. Also *Daily Express*, July 27, 1945 (quoted), *The British General Election of 1945*, and *George VI* by J. W. Wheeler-Bennett (Macmillan, 1958), and *Aneurin Bevan*. *The Times* view quoted from the issue of July 27, 1945.

(xi) Words from the Potsdam Protocol from *The Times*. Truman's phrases from *Year of Decisions*, which with Byrnes' *Speaking Frankly* was again most helpful; both men make plain their discomfort with Bevin. *As It Happened; Between War and Peace; The Potsdam Conference; I Was There;* and *Stalin's Correspondence*.

6

The fact that the US Army intended using atom bombs in the invasion of Japan from an authoritative statement in *US News & World Report*, November 2, 1959 (quoted in Feis, see below). Extracts from the Franck Report, and the report of the Truman committee into atomic energy, and other information, from the excellent *No High Ground*. Truman's order of July 24 from *Year of Decisions*. Sir Geoffrey Taylor's reminiscence was in a broadcast in August 1945, printed in *Voices From Britain*. Leahy's opinions from *I Was There*. Recorded inter-com talk on the Hiroshima plane from *No High Ground*. Attlee's message to Truman on August 8 from *A Prime Minister Remembers*. Japanese broadcasts from *Time* magazine, *The Times* and the *Daily Telegraph*. Dulles's statement from *Time* magazine, August 20, 1945; Sir Arthur Harris's from the *Daily Sketch*, August 28, 1945. All other speeches, official announcements and statements on the atom bomb, radar and the end of the war were widely reported in the newspapers at the time. The testament of the commander of the suicide pilots from *Bridge to the Sun* by Gwen Terasaki (University of North Carolina Press, and Michael Joseph, 1958). Field-Marshal Slim's words from *Defeat Into Victory*. Churchill's opinion from *Triumph and Tragedy;* J. F. C. Fuller's from *The Second World War*. MacArthur's speech from Willoughby and Chamberlain (*op cit*), which is also the source of Hirohito's peace moves starting as early as 1944. There is a good account of the surrender on the *Missouri* in *The War in Malaya* by Lieutenant-General A. E. Percival (Eyre & Spottiswoode, 1949). The aftermath at Hiroshima, and the clock at the station, from *Warrior Without Weapons* by Marcel Junod (Paris, and Cape, 1951).

Other sources consulted and used for this chapter: *British Official History: Grand Strategy*, Vol VI, by John Ehrman (HMSO, 1956); *Atomic Energy For Military Purposes: US Official Report; The Army Air Forces in World War II, The Pacific, June 1944–August 1945* by W. F. Craven and J. L. Cate (USAF, 1953); *Japan Subdued* by Herbert Feis (Princeton, and Oxford, 1961); *Japan's Decision to Surrender* by R. J. C. Butow (USA, and Oxford, 1945); *On Active Service in Peace and War* by

Henry L. Stimson and McG. Bundy (USA, and Hutchinson, 1949); *Air Bombardment* by Air Marshal Sir Robert Saundby (Chatto & Windus, 1961), which supports the unpopular view that air bombardment was the major factor in Japan's defeat; *Hiroshima Diary* by M. Hachiya (Gollancz, 1955); *The Great Decision* by Michael Amrine (Putnam, NY, 1959, and Heinemann, 1960); *Here To Stay* by John Hersey (USA, and Hamish Hamilton, 1962); *Burning Conscience* letters of C. Eatherly (USA, and Weidenfeld & Nicolson, 1961); *Formula For Death* by Fernand Gigon, translated by Constantine Fitz Gibbon (Paris, and Wingate, 1958); *The Sun Goes Down*, ed J. Larteguy (Kimber, 1956); *The Wedemeyer Reports* (Holt, 1958); *We Of Nagasaki* by T. Nagai (Gollancz, 1951)—although there are many accounts of Hiroshima, strangely little has been written of Nagasaki. The entry in the *Encyclopaedia Britannica* by Robert Ross Smith on the smaller campaigns in the Pacific. The various national war casualty figures from *The War: A Concise History*, and *Encyclopaedia Britannica*. *The Face of Victory* by Leonard Cheshire VC (Hutchinson, 1961). Many contemporary newspapers; those quoted and not mentioned above being—*Sunday Dispatch*, *New York Times*, *Herald Tribune*, *Baltimore Sun*; and *Aftonbladet* and *Osservatore Romano*, both of which were quoted in American newspapers.

7

(i) MacArthur's words in this section from Willoughby and Chamberlain (*op cit*); General Christison's as reported by *Reuter's;* Wavell's from *The Times*, December 1945; Casey's from *Personal Experience 1939–46* by Lord Casey (Constable, 1962); Attlee's from *As It Happened. Life of Mahatma Ghandi* by Louis Fischer gives a delicate and well-drawn portrait of Wavell at this time. Philip Graves (*op cit*). Newspapers, especially the *Daily Telegraph* and *The Times*.
(ii) Report from *The Times*, August 31, 1945. *War Memoirs: Salvation 1944–46*; *Documents*.
(iii) *Speaking Frankly; Year of Decisions;* the statements of Bevin and Dulles were reported in the newspapers. Truman's message to Stalin from *Stalin's Correspondence*. Hopkins' notes for a book he was writing late in 1945, apparently at the instigation of Lord Beaverbrook, from *The White House Papers*. Harry Hopkins died in January 1946.
(iv) Compiled mainly from newspapers, September–December 1945. The speeches and statements of Shinwell, the colliery owners, Dalton and Sir Patrick Hannon were reported in the main newspapers. *Year of Decisions* for Attlee's and the US Chiefs of Staff words about the 'Queens'. The police statement from the *Daily Telegraph*, August 30, 1945. John Freeman's speech and the story about Churchill from Dalton (*op cit*). *The Times* for the other speeches in the House of Commons. The abridged

version of *The Second World War* by Sir Winston Churchill (Cassell, 1959) contains an Epilogue of material continuing from the General Election with which *Triumph and Tragedy* ends. Lord Attlee's words on his Foreign Secretary from a speech in the House of Lords, February 2, 1962. The King's political views from *George VI*, the official biography (quoted). *The War and Colonel Warden, As It Happened,* and Lord Morrison's *An Autobiography. A Record of the War: The 24th Quarter.*

(v) *Year of Decisions* (quoted). Herbert Lehman's statement from *The Times,* August 9, 1945. Keynes' attitude in the economic negotiations from *The Life of J. M. Keynes* by R. F. Harrod (Macmillan). The debate on the US loan, and Sir Robert Boothby's speech, from the relevant report in *The Times. Time* magazine for the post-war scene in the United States, and the situation in various firms. Attlee's words from *A Prime Minister Remembers.* Also used: *John Anderson* by J. W. Wheeler-Bennett (Macmillan, 1962); *The Real Stalin; Stalin: A Political Biography.*

(vi) De Gaulle's words from *War Memoirs: Salvation 1944–46; Documents.* Description of Laval's trial from *The Decline and Fall of Pierre Laval* by Geoffrey Warner (*History Today,* December 1961 quoted), and *Two Frenchmen: Laval and de Gaulle* by David Thomson (Cresset Press, 1951). Montgomery's *Memoirs. Peace and War* by Lieutenant-General Sir Frederick Morgan (Hodder & Stoughton, 1961) for relief work in Germany. *The Nuremberg Trial* by R. W. Cooper (Penguin, 1947). *Tidningen* (Stockholm), quoted in *Time* magazine. Eisenhower on the hazards facing US troops from *The Times,* October 1945. Report of Institute of International Affairs, *The World Today,* Vol II, No 1. Eisenhower's observations on German industriousness from *Crusade in Europe.* Extract from Truman's message to King Peter from *A King's Heritage. A Record of the War: The 24th Quarter,* from which the exchange in the Dail, and much other information.

(vii) *Speaking Frankly.* Truman's view on the power of the Secretary of State, and other remarks, from *Year of Decisions.* Official statements, and background reporting (by now much freer than during the war), from the newspapers.

(viii) Attlee's reminiscence from the *Sunday Times,* December 23, 1962. The arrival of the banana boat at Avonmouth from the *Bournemouth Daily Echo,* December 31, 1945. The War Office statement on the Home Guard from the *Sunday Chronicle,* December 30, 1945; there had been a stand-down parade the previous autumn. New Year statements of Smuts and Churchill from *The Times,* January 1, 1946, as for the New Year's Eve scene in London and elsewhere.

INDEX

Acheson, Dean, Under-Secretary of State, 298
Acland, Sir Richard, 211
Adlon Hotel, Berlin, 159
Admiral Scheer, 133
Aftonbladet, quoted 258
Agno River, Luzon, 30
Agriculture, in Germany, 306
Air raids: on Berlin, 2, 73–4; V.2 rockets and flying bombs on S.E. England, 31–4; flying bombs on Antwerp and Liège, 31; V.2 rockets on Antwerp and Brussels, 33; on German rocket sites, 33; saturation bombing of Germany, 74–5; tonnage of bombs in one week on Germany, 75; saturation bombing of Japan, 83, 107, 195–6, 246, 252, 260–1, 265, 270–1; on the Ruhr, 95; casualties in raids on London, 116–17; on heavy-water plant in Norway, 240
Air-speed record, 289
Air-to-ground controlled projectiles, 174
Airey, General T., 104
Aitken, Group Captain Max, 225, 298
Aldershot, 287
Alexander, A. V., First Lord of the Admiralty, 237
Alexander, Field-Marshal Sir Harold, Commander-in-Chief in Italy, 3, 11, 47, 125, 128; his order of the day on German surrender, 129; sends troops to Trieste, 168; and Tito, 202
Alexandria, 62
Algeria, 11
Algiers, 63
Allenby, Field-Marshal Viscount, 279
Allied Army: Sixth Army Group in

N.W. Europe, 7, 9; Fifteenth Army Group in Italy, 125; Twenty-first Army Group in N.W. Europe, 39, 69
Allied Control Council. *See* Control Council
Amery, John, 302
Amery, L. S., 226, 302
Anders, General, 66
Anderson, Arne, 255
Anderson, Sir John, 180, 184; suggests co-operation with USSR over atomic power, 298
Andover Field, Utah, atom bomb airbase, 192
Antonov, General, Russian Chief of Staff, 48
Antwerp: flying bombs on, 31; V.2 rockets on, 33; honours Montgomery, 176
Aquitania, 287
Arab-Jewish tensions, 169
Area bombing, in Japan, 195
Ardennes, Battle of the Bulge at, 69, 89; coldness of weather, 4; Hitler's offensive, and initial German success, 4–5, 76; the weather improves, 5; air activity, 5–6; confusion in the American lines, 6; danger of a static front, 7; strained Anglo-American military relations, 9–15; Eisenhower's masterly assault, 10–11; German withdrawal, 13–14; casualties, 14
Argentina, 53; admitted to UN, 198–9; rise of Peron, and differences with USA, 307–8
Armies. *See* Allied Army; British Army; Red Army; *and under countries*

INDEX

Churchill, Mrs, 225
Churchill, Winston, 34, 59, 78, 79, 107, 119, 188, 234, 279, 296; predicts date for end of war- 1–2; reprimands Chief of Air Staff, 6; presses Stalin to resume offensive, 7; sends another 250,000 men to the front, 7; desires one overall field commander for thrust into Germany, 13; anxiety over Russian advance into Eastern Europe, 15; confers with Stalin on the Balkans (1944), 16–18; and the Polish problem, 18–19, 102–4, 163–4, 206; US suspicions of his reactionary policies, 20–1; offers USA help in Pacific, 21; and Yugoslavia, 22–3, 168–9, 201, 202, 216, 307; wishes Combined Staffs and Foreign Secretaries to meet, 25–6; pessimistic note to Roosevelt, 27; meets Rioosevelt at Malta, 38–41; at Yalta, 43ff.; visits Athens, 61; at Middle East conference, 61–3; on terror bombing, 75; witnesses Rhine crossing, 86–7; and Eisenhower's strategy, 88–91; criticizes American strategy, 91, 93; on the ruin of Germany, 95; and Russian action in Rumania, 102; presses Roosevelt to act over Polish question, 102–4; and Stalin's anger over alleged separate peace treaty, 105; and Roosevelt's death, 112, 114, 117; and pilotless bombers, 116; on Truman, 117; and the Italian campaign, 125–6; and Mussolini's death, 128; and Himmler's peace overtures, 135; and the end of war in Europe, 149; VE Day broadcast, 152–3, 268; public acclaim of, 154; wishes Americans to capture Prague, 155; tribute to George VI, 159; his Victory broadcast, 160–1; view of the State Department vis-à-vis USSR, 165; angry with Truman over rebuff on Big Three meeting, 166; delays demobilization, 167, 287, 290; and the 'Iron Curtain'. 167, 313; sends NZ troops to Trieste, 168–9; orders British troops to Syria, 169–70; and Truman's ultimatum to de Gaulle, 172; on Doenitz, 172–3; and the zone difficulty in Germany, 177; promises General Election after German defeat, 182; and Attlee, 183–4; forms Caretaker Government, 184; entertains Coalition colleagues, 185; appeals for continuation of Lend-Lease, 191; congratulates Mountbatten, 194; congratulates Hopkins, 203; agrees to US troops in Germany withdrawing to their own zone, 207; his General Election speeches, 208–10; Election tour, 211–12; and Laski, 212; US comment on his election prospects, 213; at Potsdam, 214ff.; agreement with Roosevelt on atom bomb, 217, 218, 240; agrees to use atom bomb, 218; on American secrecy over atomic research, 218–19; and terms for Japan's surrender, 219, 242; defeated in General Election, 225–7, 229–30; Laski's tribute to, 229; Attlee on his electioneering, 233; prepares Hiroshima bomb announcement, 256; considers Japan defeated before atomic bomb, 270; Attlee's tribute to, 289–90; defends atom bombings, 290; as Leader of the Opposition, 290–1; and the clothing shortage, 292n; and the end of Lend-Lease, 296; rebukes Anderson, 298–9; message to Primrose League, 312

Cinema. See Films
Civilian life, the return to, 288–9, 292–5, 311
Claridges Hotel, 290
Clark, General Mark, Commander of Fifteenth Army Group, 125
Clay, Lieut.-General Lucius, American Deputy Military Governor in Germany 173
Clemenceau, Georges, 53n
Clements, John, 290
Cleveland Plain Dealer, quoted, 213
Clothing shortage, in UK, 186, 292

Demobilization: delayed by Churchill, 167, 290; in USA, 269, 293; in Japan, 276, 277; agitation in UK for increase of, 287–8, 290
Democratic Party (USA), 109
Dempsey, General M. C., Commander of British Second Army, 84
Denmark, 14, 78, 119, 133, 134, 141, 300; liberation of, 157, 158
de Tassigny, General, 177
Detroit, 269
Detroit Free Press, quoted 213
de Valera, Eamon: and Hitler's death, 138–9, 156, 157, 188; declares Eire a republic, 308
Dewey, Thomas E., 117
Dillon, Mr, 308
Displaced Persons, 121, 175–6, 300, 304
Doenitz, Grand Admiral Karl, 14, 135, 305; in favour with Hitler, 77–8; appointed to command in the north, 131; informed of and announces Hitler's death, 137–9; tries to keep war going for diplomatic manoeuvring, 139; sets up his government in Flensburg, 140; refuses Himmler office, 141–2; decides to surrender, 143, 144, 147; on American strategic and political aims, 146–7; attempts to woo Allies, 155–6; released from prison, 156n; end of his government, 172–3
Dominions, 293; seek influence in world affairs, 281
Dornberger, Colonel, 32
Downing Street, No. 10, 225, 226–7, 229, 265, 290
Doyen, General, 171
Drabik, Sergeant Alexander, 71
Dresden, air raid on, 74
Dublin, disorders in, 156–7
Duisburg, 70
Dulles, Allen, 104, 245
Dulles, John Foster: on the atomic bomb, 258; at London Council of Foreign Ministers, 281; on Allied disunity, 283–4, 285
Dumbarton Oaks conference, 52

Dunglass, Lord (late Lord Home), 66 226
Dunkirk, 121, 145; German garrison surrenders, 157
Du Pont firm, 294
Dusseldorf, 70
Dutch East Indies, 21, 269, 278

Early, Steve, Presidential Press Secretary, 110
Easley, Brig.-General G. M., 193
East Chinese and Manchurian railroads, 58
East Indian Islands, 27
East Prussia, 78, 235; Russian advance in, 35; Germans cut off in, 72, 133; evacuation of Germans, 133–4
Eastern Front, 76, 78; the great Russian advance, 15, 34–8; reasons for halt of previous autumn, 34–5; Russians nearing Berlin, 72–4; Germans pushed back from Oder, and Berlin attacked, 129–30; disintegration of the German line, 133; the evacuation from East Prussia, 133–4
Economist, The, 181
Ecuador, 53
Eden, Anthony, 22, 25, 26, 40, 62, 103, 117, 208, 234; meets Stalin (1944), 16, 17–18; at Yalta, 45, 54, 59, 61; on Truman, 117; and the Polish problem, 163; at San Francisco conference, 198, 199
Education Act (1944), 186
Egypt, 52–3, 61
Eichelberger, General R. L., MacArthur's land commander, quoted 197
Einstein, Albert, 239
Eire, 156–7, 160, 188; becomes a republic, 308
Eisenhower, General Dwight D., Supreme Commander of Allied Forces in Europe, 135, 141, 144, 146, 148, 156, 168, 170, 234, 241, 260; presses for resumption of Russian offensive, 7; orders Sixth Army Group to Ardennes, and then revokes order, 7, 9; Montgomery and

INDEX

Lüneburg Heath, 143–5; the surrender at Rheims, 146–7; disbanded in British Zone, 304. *Units of:* SS Army Group, 76; Model's Army Group, 94; Sixth Panzer Army, 37; Ninth Army, 131, 132
German High Command, 73, 93, 135
German Intelligence service, discovers Allied dissensions, 15
German Navy: comparative success of, 77; its remnants evacuate East Prussia, 133
German News Agency, quoted 74
Germany, 41, 125, 287, 293; research on rocket bombs, 32; interior lines of communication, 37; her future discussed at Yalta, 49–51; condition of the people, 71–2; military situation in April, 93–5; peace overtures by, 131, 134, 135; the evacuation from East Prussia, 133–4; the end of Hitler, 135–7; Doenitz the new Fuehrer, 138–43; migration of Germans from advancing Russians, 140–1, 175; the surrender on Lüneburg Heath, 143–4; the surrender at Rheims, 146–7; the end of the Third Reich, 147–8; reaction of population to end of war, 150; Anglo-American differences on zones of occupation, 165–6; end of the Doenitz government, 172–3; German military framework used by Allied government, 173–4; Allied rule tries to restore normal life in, 174–7; lack of common economic policy among Allies, 177; Control Council set up, and four zones delineated, 177–8; American forces withdraw to their own zone, 206–7; discussed at Potsdam conference, 221–3; research on atom bomb in, 239, 240; research on radar, 259; VJ Day rejoicing in, 268; cost of war to, 271, 272; discussed by Truman and de Gaulle, 280; zonal government of, 303–5; suicides, alcoholics and prostitutes in, 306
GI brides, 186, 288

Glasgow, 153
Goebbels, Frau, 76, 136, 137
Goebbels, Joseph, 15, 131, 132, 139, 140, 159; on Germany being deserted, 74; in Hitler's bunker, 76; and the *Volkssturm*, 94; campaign against the Communists, 94; and Roosevelt's death, 112; poisons his children, 136, 137; peace overture to Russians, 137; orders SS orderly to shoot him, 137
Goering, Reichsmarschall Hermann, 135, 159, 173, 305; on the Russian advance, 16; discredited, 76, 131; attempts to negotiate with Americans, 131, 141; captured, 156; poisons himself, 156*n*
Gold, Harry, 220
Goodyear Tyre & Rubber Co., 294
Grand Slam bomb, 254
Graziani, Marshal, Italian Minister of War, 126
Great Britain. *See* United Kingdom
Great Bitter Lake, 61
Greece, 17, 24, 25, 309; civil war in, 3; Churchill–Stalin agreement on, 17, 18; UNRRA aid for, 295; financial straits, and Left-Right feud, 307
Greenglass, David, 220
Greenwood, Arthur, Lord Privy Seal, 232
Grese, Irma, 305
Grew, Joseph C., Acting Secretary of State, 191, 242
Grigg, Sir James, 226
Gromyko, Mr, 117; at San Francisco conference, 199, 200
Groves, General Leslie R., director of atom bomb project, 217, 239, 241, 245, 251, 263
Guam, 246, 258
Guderian, General Heinz, 38, 46, 73
Guernsey, 158, 179
Guffey, Joseph, Democratic Senator, 232

Haakon, King of Norway, 158
Hachiya, Dr, 250
Haegg, Gundar, 255

339

Milan, 128, 129; American forces advance towards, 125; Cardinal Archbishop of, 125, 126; Mussolini's puppet government in, 126
Military courts, set up in Germany, 305
Military Government, Allied, its first proclamations, 120. *See also* Germany
Miller, K. R., 255
Mineworkers' Union, 286
Minsk, 38
Moch, Jules, 301
Model, Field-Marshal Walter, 6, 94, 95
Moelln, 140
Molotov, V. M., Russian Foreign Minister, 104, 114; at Yalta, 43, 44, 48, 55, 57; and Rumania, 102; and Poland, 102, 163; and Roosevelt's death, 112; leaves San Francisco conference, 199; increase of his power, 203; at Potsdam, 215, 222, 223, 234–6; and the Russian declaration of war on Japan, 260; and the Japanese surrender, 265; at London Foreign Ministers' meeting, 281–3; attempt to oust him from power, 300
Montgomery, Field-Marshal Bernard Law, 77, 148; criticizes Eisenhower, 9–10; letter to Eisenhower, 10; brilliant manoeuvre in Ardennes battle, 11; differences with American generals, 11–13, 39, 84, 88; desires a powerful narrow front, 13, 91; his Twenty-First Army Group, 69; prepares to cross the Rhine, 84; crosses the Rhine, 85–6; orders a drive for the Elbe, 87; fear of careless planning, 119; races for Lübeck, 119; receives German surrender on Lüneburg Heath, 143–4; refuses to give up surrender document, 147; on German desire to be treated as allies, 174; British representative on Allied Control Council, 174; entertained and honoured, 176–7; advises Churchill that Anglo-American forces move back, 177; on the

disbandment of SHAEF, 178; in plane crash, 304; disbands German troops, 304
Moorehead, Alan, quoted 71–2, 84, 120, 143, 175
Morell, Professor Theodor, Hitler's physician, 77
Morgenthau, Henry, Secretary of the Treasury, 115–16
Morrison, Herbert: and the General Election, 181–4, 208, 209; wins at Lewisham, 211, 228; and the Labour leadership issue, 228, 230–1; on the election victory, 228–9; appointed Lord President of the Council, 231–2
Morshead, Lieut.-General Sir Leslie, Australian Commander at Labuan, 197
Moscow, 45, 46, 89; end of war in Europe announced in, 149; three-power committee in, 222; Foreign Ministers conference in, 308–11
Mountbatten, Admiral Lord Louis, Supreme Commander in S.E. Asia, 95, 97–9, 194, 291; organizes occupation of Japan, 269
Munich, 305; German Army revolt in, 146
Murphy, Robert, Eisenhower's political adviser, 173
Murrow, Edward, 124
Music-While-You-Work programme, 160
Musso, Mussolini in, 127
Mussolini, Benito: his puppet government in Milan, 126, 129; leaves for Como, 126–7; captured and executed by partisans, 127–8
Musy, former President of Switzerland, 134

Nagasaki, 75n, 239, 245, 247, 264, 271, 273, 300; atomic bomb on, 261–2
Nagoya, air raid on, 195
Nanking, 308
Nash, Walter, Prime Minister of New Zealand, 189
National Assembly, French, 300

National Guard, US, 312
National Health Service, 232, 291
National Redoubt, of the Nazis, 118, 119, 131
Nationalization, 210, 291
Nazi Party: administration and leaders retire to National Redoubt, 118; Allied Military Government proclamations regarding, 120; eradication of, and punishment of criminals, discussed at Potsdam, 221–2; members of, removed from public and business positions, 303, 304
Negro combat units, 7
Neisse, River, 56, 223, 235, 236
Netherlands, 21, 143, 144, 223; V.2 rockets fired from, 33; likelihood of famine in, 84; Germans cut off in, 87, 141; penetrated by Canadians, 120; VE Day celebrations in, 150–1; liberation of, 157, 158; post-war difficulties, 302–3
New Guinea, 264, 269
New Orleans, 268
New Year's Eve, 312
New York, 111; excitement in, at end of war in Europe, 148–9; the social scene, near end of Japanese war, 253–4; VJ celebrations in, 266, 268; de Gaulle in, 281; the busy bars in, 294–5
New York Daily News, quoted 213
New York Times, 262, quoted 114–15, 258
New Zealand: war death rate in, 32; war expenditure, 189
New Zealand Army: in Italy, 125; the Second Division in Trieste, 168
News Chronicle, 141, 181; quoted 186
Niigata, 239, 245, 247
Nimitz, Admiral Chester W., Commander-in-Chief Central Pacific: and the proposed invasion of Iwo Jima and Honshu, 80; prepares to invade Japan, 245; continues offensive after unofficial news of Japanese surrender, 264
Normandy, 11
North Sea, 39, 120

Northolt Airport, 225
Northwood, 286
Norway, 14, 78, 133, 141, 142, 145; liberation of, 157, 158; heavy-water plant in, 240
Nottingham 153
Nuremberg Prison, Nazi leaders in, 156*n*
Nuremberg Tribunal, 123, 222, 305

Oak Ridge, Tennessee, 217, 246, 254
Onersalzber, Nazi emergency 'capital', 131, 141
Observer, 115, 176, quoted 187
Occupation zones, of Germany: discussed at Yalta, 49–50; Kesselring secures lay-out of, 76; Anglo-American differences on, 165–6. *See also under* Germany
Oder, River, 37, 56, 234; German defence line on, 38, 72; Russian bridge-heads over, 46; reached by Russian tank vanguards, 73; Russians held up at, 119
Odessa, 155
Okinawa, 112, 189, 195, 218; strategic importance of, 79–80; Japanese preparations for American invasion, 99–100; the naval action, 100–1; the struggle for Sugar-Loaf Hill, 192–3; the end, and the casualties, 193–4; VJ rejoicings in, 269
Oldendorf, Admiral Jesse, 29
Oliphant, M. L. E., 218
Oliver, Sarah Churchill, 38, 44, 62, 229
Oppenheimer, J. Robert, 217, 241, 250
Orwell, George, quoted 176
Osaka, air raid on, 195
Oslo, 150, 302
Osmena, President, of the Philippines, 117
Osservatore Romano, quoted 259
Oumansky, Soviet Ambassador to Washington, 61
Outer Mongolia, 59
Owen, Captain Frank, quoted 96

Palestine, 62, 169; discussed at Potsdam, 221

INDEX

artillery, 32; Minister of Works, 184
Saturation bombing, 28, 74, 195-6
Savings campaign, in UK, 287
Schellenberg, Walter, Head of
German Intelligence, 134
Schirach, Baldur von, 156n
Schleswig-Holstein, Doenitz in,
140-2
Schreier, Lieutenant H. G., 82
Schwerin von Krosigk, Count: appointed Foreign Minister by Doenitz, 142; arrested, 173
Scotland Yard, 288
Scott, Sir Giles Gilbert, 188
Scottish Nationalists, 211
SEAC, 194
Seaforth Highlanders, land in Java, 278
Sebastopol, 46
Secret Service, British, 77
Security Council. See United Nations
Seyss-Inquart, Artur von, Nazi Commissar for the Netherlands, 120, 141; named by Hitler as Foreign Minister, 142; sentenced to death, 156n
Sforza, Count Carlo, 24
SHAEF, 170, 173, 178
Shawcross, Sir Hartley, 305
Sherrod, Robert, quoted, 81-2
Sherwood, Robert E., 166, quoted 20, 23, 44
Shidehara, Japanese Prime Minister, 277
Shinwell, Emanuel, 188; Minister of Fuel and Power, 237; appeals to coal miners, 286
Shirer, William L., 63; quoted 213
Shoumatoff, Madame, 107
Sicily, 129
Siegfried Line, 70, 83
Silesia, 35; the coal-field captured by Russians, 73
Simmons, Bill, Roosevelt's receptionist, 110
Simpson, General, Commander of US Ninth Army, 84, 87
Sinatra, Frank, 253
Sinclair, Sir Archibald, 184, 210, 227

Singapore, 272; relief of, 270
Skyros, 61
Slave-labourers, 121, 140, 175
Slim, Lieut.-General Sir William, Commander of the Fourteenth Army, 4, 96, 97, 194; on the prisoners-of-war released at Singapore, 270
Smethwick, 291
Smith, Sir Ben, Minister of Food, 285
Smith, Lieut.-General Holland, quoted 83
Smuts, General Jan Christian, 201, 312
Smyth Report, on atomic bomb, 259
Smythe, Brigadier J., 228
Sechi, 300
Socialist Party, Belgian, 157
Soekarno, Dr, 278
Soong, T. V., Chinese Foreign Minister, 277
Soskice, Sir Frank, 305
Soustelle, Jacques, 301
South Africa, 312
South America, British investments in, 180-1
Spaak, M., Belgian Foreign Minister, 199
Spaatz, General Carl, 245, 246, 251, 261, 263
Spain, discussed at Potsdam, 220
Spandau, 132
Spandau Prison, Nazi leaders in, 156n
Spectator, The, quoted, 187
Speer, Albert, Minister of Armaments and War Production, 94, 131, 156n, 173, 240
Spilsbury, Sir Bernard, 123
Spitfire fighter planes, 93
Spree, River, 138
SS (Schutz Staffel), 132, 140, 141
Stalin, Josef V., 7, 25-6, 59, 78, 102, 119, 226, 230, 231, 283, 313; ignores niceties of diplomacy, 2-3; Western view of, 3; jockeys for positions in Europe, 15; confers with Churchill and Eden on the Balkans (1944), 16-18; and Poland, 18-20, 104, 163-4, 202; and Yugoslavia, 22, 23,

White Russian Republic, 4, 55; admitted to UN, 198
Wilhelm, Crown Prince, 146
Wilhelmina, Queen of the Netherlands, 21, 158
Wilhelmshaven, 143
Wilkinson, Ellen, 183, 230; Minister of Education, 237
Williams, Francis, 230
Williams, Sir Herbert, 157
Willis, Douglas, quoted 158
Wilson, J. H., 228
Wilson, Woodrow, 198, 200
Wilson, Mrs Woodrow, 117
Winant, Lieutenant John, 121
Winan, John G., 24
Women: British Government compels servicewomen to go abroad, 7; problem of ex-servicewomen, 186; problems of GI brides, 186, 288
Woodcock, Bruce, 188
Wooderson, Corporal Sidney, 255
Woodford, Churchill's constituency, 225
Woolworth's, New Cross, 33
World Instrument for Peace (UN, *q.v.*), discussed at Yalta, 51–3, 55–6; Security Council proposed for, 103

Yalta conference, 25, 38, 101, 109, 118, 167, 177, 206, 222, 223, 245, 278, 280, 282, 308, 312; the delegations, and their accommodation, 43–7; Roosevelt presides, 47; end of conference speeches and hospitality, 56–9, 60–1; the communiqué, and reactions to, 63–7. *Subjects discussed:* military affairs, 48; future of Germany, 49–51; reparations, 50–1; World Instrument for Peace (UN), 51–3, 55–6; Poland, 53–9, 60, 64–6
Yamashita, General Tomoyuki, Commander of Japanese Army on Luzon, 28–30, 197, 269–70; tried and executed, 306
Yenan Communist Government, 196, 277
Yokohama, air raid on, 195
Young, Leo C., 259
Yugoslavia, 14, 47, 49, 167; partisan activity in, 3, 155; Churchill–Stalin agreement on, 17, 18; Tito–Subasic agreement, 22–3; discussed at Potsdam, 221; question of her frontiers, 281; Tito Government established, and republic declared, 307. *See also* Trieste
Yusupov Palace, Yalta, 44, 56

Zagreb, 141
Zhukov, Marshal, 35, 37, 44, 73, 130, 132, 137, 304; Russian representative on Allied Control Council, 174; distributes medals to American officers, 177; insists on British and Americans moving back to their zones, 177
Zuider Zee, 120
Zürich, 73, 104